AF784515

SAFEGUARD MEASURES IN WORLD TRADE

ELGAR INTERNATIONAL TRADE LAW AND PRACTICE

The Elgar International Trade Law and Practice series is a library of works by leading practitioners and scholars covering key issues of substance and procedure in the field of International Trade Law. Each title is analytical in approach, highlighting and unpicking the complex legal issues that are most critical and relevant to practice. Designed to be detailed, focused reference works, the books in this series offer an authoritative analysis of the law and practice in the most significant areas within the field.

For a full list of Edward Elgar published titles, including the titles in this series, visit our website at www.e-elgar.com.

SAFEGUARD MEASURES IN WORLD TRADE

4th Edition

YONG-SHIK LEE

West Virginia University, USA
Director and Professorial Fellow, The Law and Development Institute, USA

ELGAR INTERNATIONAL TRADE LAW AND PRACTICE

Edward Elgar
PUBLISHING

Cheltenham, UK • Northampton, MA, USA

© Yong-Shik Lee 2025

All rights reserved. No part of this publication may be reproduced, stored in a retrieval system or transmitted in any form or by any means, electronic, mechanical or photocopying, recording, or otherwise without the prior permission of the publisher.

Published by
Edward Elgar Publishing Limited
The Lypiatts
15 Lansdown Road
Cheltenham
Glos GL50 2JA
UK

Edward Elgar Publishing, Inc.
William Pratt House
9 Dewey Court
Northampton
Massachusetts 01060
USA

Authorised representative in the EU for GPSR queries only: Easy Access System Europe – Mustamäe tee 50, 10621 Tallinn, Estonia, gpsr.requests@easproject.com

A catalogue record for this book
is available from the British Library

Library of Congress Control Number: 2025931091

This book is available electronically in the **Elgar**online
Law subject collection
https://doi.org/10.4337/9781800887503

MIX
Paper | Supporting responsible forestry
FSC® C013604

ISBN 978 1 80088 749 7 (cased)
ISBN 978 1 80088 750 3 (eBook)
ISBN 978 1 0353 8208 8 (ePub)

Printed and bound by CPI Group (UK) Ltd, Croydon, CR0 4YY

For all those dedicated to scholarship

CONTENTS

PART IV SAFEGUARD REGIME: PRESENT AND FUTURE

EXTENDED CONTENTS

ABOUT THE AUTHOR

Prof. Yong-Shik Lee is an academician, lawyer (USA and UK), and former government counsel. An expert in international trade law, he has counselled and represented governments, law firms, consulting firms, as well as private individuals in the matters of international trade and investment.

Lee studied economics at the University of California at Berkeley (A.B.) and law at the University of Cambridge (BA, MA, PhD). He began his professional career as Legal Counsel for the Ministry of Foreign Affairs and Trade of Korea and later entered academia. He has taught at leading universities around the world, including University of Sydney, University of Manchester, Tulane University, Emory University, Cornell University, and New York University. Lee handled the first WTO panel case on safeguards and appeared at the hearings of the WTO panel and the Appellate Body. He has also participated in multilateral and bilateral negotiations relating to international trade and investment, including the negotiations at the United Nations Commission on International Trade Law (UNCITRAL) and the bilateral investment treaty (BIT) negotiations between South Korea and Japan.

Lee has authored and co-authored several volumes of books including *Reclaiming Development in the World Trading System* (Cambridge University Press, 2006, 2009, 2016), *Law and Development Perspective on International Trade Law* (Cambridge University Press, 2011), *Microtrade: A New System of International Trade with Volunteerism towards Poverty Elimination* (Routledge, 2013), and *Law and Development: Theory and Practice* (Routledge, 2019, 2022). He is considered one of the foremost authorities on safeguard measures. He has frequently been invited to speak on the issues of safeguard measures as well as on other issues of international trade law at some of the most prominent academic forums such as Harvard University Kennedy School of Government and Johns Hopkins University School of Advanced International Studies. His numerous articles have appeared in various leading journals, including *Journal of World Trade*, *Journal of International Economic Law*, *World Trade Review*, *Cornell International Law Journal*, *Minnesota Journal of International Law*, *Northwestern Journal of International Law and Business*, *University of*

Pennsylvania East Asia Law Review, *Arizona Journal of International and Comparative Law*, and the *Law and Development Review*. Lee is currently the editor-in-chief of the *Law and Development Review* and an associate editor of the *Journal of World Trade*.

PREFACE TO THE FOURTH EDITION

For a decade since the third edition of *Safeguard Measures in World Trade*, fundamental shifts have taken place in the international trading system. The failure of the Doha Round has raised uncertainty about the future of the multilateral trading system. The continuing proliferation of regional trade agreements has created complexities in the rule-based international trading system. The incapacitation of the WTO Appellate Body, caused by a US block of all appointments of its members, substantially undermined the WTO's ability to resolve international trade disputes. Increasing unilateralism in international trade by the largest traders, such as the United States and China, in recent years, under the questionable call for the protection of national security, have also encroached the confidence in the multilateral system. New cases have emerged and addressed these issues. This edition examines new developments in the legal disciplines for safeguards as well as their applications and interpretations under this changing environment.

As I complete this edition, the international trading system is facing an unprecedented crisis. In April 2025, U.S. President Donald Trump imposed a 10% universal tariff on nearly all imports under a self-declared national economic emergency. In addition, higher "reciprocal" country-specific tariffs and product-specific tariffs have been applied based on alleged trade imbalances and national security concerns. The WTO compatibility of these measures has been widely debated, and the largest trading powers, such as China and the European Union, retaliated or announced plans to retaliate with their own tariffs. This dramatic case vividly illustrates the critical danger of unilateral trade action taken outside the WTO framework and underscores the vital importance of multilateral cooperation in international trade, including adherence to established rules, such as those governing safeguard measures.

Y.S. Lee

April 2025

Atlanta, Georgia

ACKNOWLEDGMENTS

This book would have not been possible without the valuable assistance of many individuals. Foremost, I would like to thank my family for their understanding and sacrifice during my work for this edition.

It was more than two decades ago, but I remain grateful to the trade ministry of South Korea for giving me valuable first-hand experience on safeguard cases when I was a young lawyer, which provided an important basis for this book. I would also like to thank distinguished scholars and professionals with whom I have had a privilege to be acquainted, such as Professor Petros Mavroidis and Professor Mitsuo Matsushita, leading scholars in international trade law, for valuable advice and excellent reviews over the years. I am also thankful to Edward Elgar Publishing for its decision to publish this edition and to its excellent staff for all the hard work that has brought this book into the light of day.

I also note with appreciation the effort of my student assistants, Monica Vu, Rachel Pearce, Jordan Cohen, Oliver Flint, Kedric Ross, Alex Kim, Melissa Zindel, and Turner Jensen, as well as my wife, Dr. Hye Seong Mun. I am grateful to all the other individuals whose names could not be listed in this limited space but whose support has been, nevertheless, essential in completing this book. I remember them in my heart with a great deal of appreciation.

TABLE OF CASES

GATT DOCUMENTS

WORLD TRADE ORGANIZATIONS DISPUTES

Panel Reports

Appellate Reports

WTO Committee

US JUDICIAL REPORTS

USITC INVESTIGATION REPORTS

TABLE OF LEGISLATION

WTO AGREEMENTS

REGIONAL TRADE AGREEMENTS

US LEGISLATION

US PROCLAMANTIONS

EU LEGISLATION

PART I

DEVELOPMENT OF INTERNATIONAL RULES ON SAFEGUARDS

1

POLITICS AND ECONOMICS OF SAFEGUARD MEASURES

1.1 INTRODUCTION: GENERAL BACKGROUND AND CURRENT STATUS[1]

1.01 *General Background.* It is the fundamental principle of the international trading system under the General Agreement on Tariffs and Trade (GATT) and the

1 The materials included in this book are generally current as of April 2024. Throughout this book, extensive references are made to the author's previous works on safeguards, including: "Emergency Safeguard Measures under Article X in GATS: Applicability of the Concepts in the WTO Agreement on Safeguards" (1999) 33(4) *Journal of World Trade* 47–59; "Review of the First WTO Panel Case on the Agreement on Safeguards: Korea – Definitive Safeguard Measure on Imports of Certain Dairy Products" (1999) 33(6) *Journal of World Trade* 27–46; "Critical Issues in the Application of the WTO Rules on Safeguards – In the Light of the Recent Panel Reports and the Appellate Body Decisions" (2000) 34(2) *Journal of World Trade* 131–147; "Destabilization of the Discipline on Safeguards? Inherent Problems with the Continuing Applicability of Article XIX after the Settlement of the Agreement on Safeguards" (2001) 35 *Journal of World Trade* 1235–1246; "Revival of Gray-Area Measures? The US–Canada Softwood Lumber Agreement: Conflict with the WTO Agreement on Safeguards" (2002) 36 *Journal of World Trade* 155–166; "Safeguard Measures: Why Are They Not Applied Consistently With the Rules? Lessons for Competent National Authorities and Proposal for the Modification of the Rules on Safeguards" (2002) 36 *Journal of World Trade* 641–673; "Continuing Controversy on 'Unforeseen Developments' – Reviewer's Note" (2003) 37 *Journal of World Trade* 1153–1157; "Reflections on U.S. International Trade Law and Practice – Compatibility with the WTO Rules and Call for Modification" (2003) 13(2) *Currents: International Trade Law Journal* 31–43; "Test of Multilateralism in International Trade: U.S. Steel Safeguards" (2004) 25 *Northwestern Journal of International Law and Business* 69–98; "The Agreement on Safeguards," *in* Patrick McRory and Arthur Appleton (eds.), *The World Trade Organization: Legal, Economic and Political Analysis* (Springer, 2005), pp. 749–798; "Toward a More Open Trading System: Should Safeguards Replace Antidumping Measures?" (2005) 1(2) *21st Century Law Review* 3–14; "Not Without a Clue: Commentary on 'The Persistent Puzzles of Safeguards'" (2006) 40 *Journal of World Trade* 385–404; "Bilateralism under the World Trade Organization" (2006) 26 *Northwestern Journal of International Law and Business* 357–372; "First WTO Case on Transitional Product-Safeguard Measure under Section 16 of the Protocol of China's Accession to the WTO: Affirming Discriminatory Safeguard Measure by WTO?" (2012) 44 *Journal of World Trade* 913–936; *Reclaiming*

World Trade Organization (WTO) that the member countries (hereinafter, "Members"[2]) are bound by their negotiated concessions for imports unless those concessions are duly modified in accordance with the existing rules.[3] This principle is essential for the stabilization of the international trading system and for further promotion of trade. There are limited exceptions to this principle, and the term "safeguard" or "safeguard measure"[4] has been used to denote certain restrictions on imports of an emergency nature, irrespective of the importing Member's obligation under its concessions. Safeguard measures are distinguished from some other forms of import restrictions such as anti-dumping actions and countervailing duties that are applied on the basis of "unfair" trade practices by exporters.[5] Safeguards are applicable as a temporary measure where increased imports cause or threaten to cause serious injury to the domestic industry that produces like or directly competitive products,[6] regardless of the existence of any unfair trade practice on the part of exporters.

Certain provisions in various GATT Articles and the WTO Agreements allow Members to depart from their negotiated concessions and restrict imports irrespective of the existence of unfair trade practices. They include GATT Articles XIX, XII, and XVIII; the Agreement on Safeguards; the Understanding on Balance of Payments of the GATT 1994; the Agreement on Agriculture; **1.02**

Development in the World Trading System (Cambridge: Cambridge University Press, 2nd ed., 2016); "Safeguards," *in* Krista Nadakavukaren Schefer and Thomas Cottier (eds.), *Encyclopedia of International Economic Law* (Edward Elgar Publishing, December 2017), pp. 263–266; "Are Retaliatory Trade Measures Justified under the Agreement on Safeguards?" (2019) 22(3) *Journal of International Economic Law* 439–458; "The Steel and Aluminum Quota Agreements: A Question of Compatibility with WTO Disciplines and Their Impact on the World Trading System" (2019) 53(5) *Journal of World Trade* 811–832; and "Safeguards," "Identifying WTO Safeguards," and "Safeguards in Developing Countries," *in* Krista Nadakavukaren Schefer and Thomas Cottier (eds.), *Encyclopedia of International Economic Law* (Edward Elgar Publishing, 2024).

2 The member states of the GATT are also referred to as "contracting parties."

3 GATT 1994, Article XXVIII provides for the modification of schedules.

4 The terms "measure" and "action" are used interchangeably without distinction throughout this book unless indicated otherwise.

5 Those import restrictions such as anti-dumping actions and countervailing duties are applied to offset the "unfair" advantages gained by exporters from price undercuts and subsidies, respectively. The Appellate Body in *United States – Definitive Safeguard Measures on Imports of Steel Wire Rod and Circular Welded Carbon Quality Line Pipe* also observed: "[S]afeguard measures are extraordinary remedies to be taken only in emergency situations. Furthermore, they are remedies that are imposed in the form of import restrictions in the absence of any allegation of an unfair trade practice. In this, safeguard measures differ from, for example, anti-dumping duties and countervailing duties to counter subsidies, which are both measures taken in response to unfair trade practices. If the conditions for their imposition are fulfilled, safeguard measures may thus be imposed on the 'fair trade' of other WTO Members and, by restricting their imports, will prevent those WTO Members from enjoying the full benefit of trade concessions under the *WTO Agreement*." *United States – Line Pipe, infra* note 70, para. 80.

6 Article 2 of the Agreement on Safeguards lays out the general conditions for the application of a safeguard measure. *See* Chapter 4 *infra* for the detailed discussion. For a general discussion of safeguards, *see also* Akhil Raina, "What Is a Safeguard Measure under WTO Law?" (2019) 10(2) *Trade, Law and Development* 463–481.

and Article XII of the General Agreement on Trade in Services (GATS). The Protocol on the Accession of the People's Republic of China provided transitional product-specific safeguard measures only applicable to the exports from China for 12 years after the date of accession, which was December 11, 2001; this provision was terminated on December 11, 2013.[7] These provisions are invoked under different circumstances, and some of those measures are gaining a growing importance in world trade. The general safeguard measures provided under GATT Article XIX and the WTO Agreement on Safeguards (hereinafter, "Safeguards Agreement" or "SA"[8]) bear a particular significance in world trade today since they constitute a major exception to the above-mentioned principle of binding concessions.[9] Safeguard measures provide temporary restrictions on imports that cause or threaten to cause serious injury to a domestic industry. Those general safeguard measures (SGs) are the focus of this book.[10] Some other provisions that also allow similar restrictions on imports are introduced in Chapter 11.[11]

1.03 In relation to the other provisions of the WTO, safeguard measures stand as an exception to Article II of the GATT that requires compliance with tariff bindings, as well as to Article XI that prohibits quantitative trade restrictions. Safeguards also operate as a separate and specific exception as opposed to the generally categorized exceptions under GATT Article XX.[12] Safeguards stand parallel to the other import restraints applicable for "unfair trade practices" such as anti-dumping measures and countervailing measures. Article XIX contained the original GATT disciplines on safeguards. The Agreement on

---

7 WTO doc. WT/L/432 (November 23, 2001), para. 16. The transitional product-specific safeguard measures were available for a limited duration until 12 years after the date of China's accession into the WTO (para. 16:9), which was December 11, 2013.

8 The terms "Agreement on Safeguards," "Safeguards Agreement," and "SA" are used interchangeably throughout this book.

9 As explained below, the significance of safeguard measures is also apparent as the Agreement on Safeguards expressly prohibits "gray-area measures" (Article 11): that is, agreements made between the exporting and the importing countries to limit trade. Those measures were prevalently used in the 1980s to protect domestic producers.

10 The term "safeguard" or "safeguard measure" refers to the general safeguard measure provided in Article XIX and the SA throughout this book unless indicated otherwise specifically or by context.

11 The general safeguard measures are applicable to all products whereas the other safeguard-type measures are only applicable to a limited range of products or do not intend to remedy or prevent serious injury to a specific domestic industry. For instance, "special safeguard measures" under Article 5 of the WTO Agreement on Agriculture and "special safeguard mechanism" being negotiated are only applicable to agricultural products. The "transitional safeguards" under Article 6 of the WTO Agreement on Textiles and Clothing, which was terminated on January 1, 2005, were also applicable to textile products only. The measures for balance-of-payment purposes are not applied to prevent or remedy serious injury to a specific domestic industry.

12 GATT Article XX allows the adoption of trade measures to protect ten categories of public interest, including public morals and human, animal, or plant life or health.

Safeguards expands on the provisions of Article XIX and modifies the rules contained therein.

Historically, safeguard measures originated in the "escape clause" of the United States Reciprocal Trade Agreement of 1942 with Mexico.[13] This clause was also adopted in subsequent international trade agreements including GATT. The escape clause authorized a contracting party to suspend its trade concessions where increases in imports, as a result of the trade concessions, cause serious injury or threat thereof to a domestic industry. The escape clause was subject to criticism,[14] and the new Agreement on Safeguards was negotiated during the Uruguay Round.[15] **1.04**

The justification for safeguard measures is somewhat controversial, particularly in the economic rationale. As noted above, the WTO system requires Members to commit themselves to their previously agreed import concessions and does not, in principle, allow them to withdraw or modify their concessions unilaterally without re-negotiation. Nevertheless, certain exceptions to this principle are found in the WTO rules,[16] the most notable being those restrictions on imports often characterized as "administered protection." Administered protection includes anti-dumping measures, countervailing duties, and safeguard measures. The justification for anti-dumping measures and countervailing duties is that exporters who sell at prices below "normal value"[17] or receive certain trade-related subsidies from their governments enjoy unfair competitive advantages, and therefore, the importing countries should **1.05**

13 The relevant clause provides: "If, as a result of unforeseen development and of the concession granted on any article enumerated and described in the Schedules annexed to this Agreement, such article is being imported in such increased quantities and under such conditions as to cause or threaten serious injury to domestic producers of like or similar articles, the Government of either country shall be free to withdraw the concession, in whole or in part, or to modify it to the extent and for such time as may be necessary to prevent such injury." Agreement on Reciprocal Trade, December 23, 1942, US–Mexico, Article XI, 57 Stat. 833, 845–866. The use of the term "escape clause," referring to a provision for safeguard measures, seems justifiable since the provision allows parties to the trade agreement to "escape" from their commitments made in their import concessions.

14 Refer to the relevant discussion in Chapter 2.3 *infra*.

15 *See* Chapter 2.4 *infra* for a discussion of the negotiation process in the Uruguay Round.

16 "The WTO rules" or "WTO rules" refer to the provisions of the General Agreement on Tariffs and Trade as adopted under Annex 1 of the Marrakesh Agreement Establishing the World Trade Organization, the new agreements negotiated in the Uruguay Round, and other binding instruments agreed by Members.

17 The WTO Agreement on Implementation of Article VI of the General Agreement on Tariffs and Trade 1994 sets out the concept of "dumping": Article 2.1 of the Agreement provides that "a product is to be considered as being dumped, i.e., introduced into the commerce of another country at less than its normal value, if the export price of the product exported from one country to another is less than the comparable price, in the ordinary course of trade, for the like product when destined for consumption in the exporting country."

be allowed to apply counter-measures to offset those unfair advantages.[18] The same justification cannot apply to safeguard measures since they are invoked in the absence of any unfair practice on the part of the exporter. How then is a safeguard measure justified in the absence of any unfair trade practice?

1.06 Safeguard measures are applied to remedy or prevent serious injury to a domestic industry that is caused by an increase in imports.[19] Should such injury be the reason for allowing import restrictions? After all, one can readily expect that any import concession made in multilateral trade negotiations would potentially lead to an increase in imports. The increase in imports may adversely affect the position of a competing domestic industry at a speed or to an extent greater than originally anticipated by the importing country when it made the import concessions. Although the position of the competing domestic industry may deteriorate, the overall economic welfare of the importing country would improve because resources being used in the less competitive domestic industries would then transfer to the more competitive ones.[20] This is the economic rationale in support of international trade and should, therefore, be the reason to participate in multilateral trade negotiations in the first place. What, then, is the justification for a safeguard measure? Does the existence of safeguard measures contradict what Members try to achieve economically through international trade? The remainder of this chapter examines the current status of safeguard measures as well as economic and political rationales for safeguard measures.

1.07 *Current Status.* For the period from January 1, 1995 to December 31, 2023, a total of 424 safeguard investigations were initiated and 213 safeguard meas-

---

18 However, it should be noted that this justification has also faced criticism. Many economists argue that the determination of "dumping" is ambiguous and that anti-dumping actions are often attempts to protect domestic industries at the expense of consumers. For a discussion of anti-dumping law, *see* Jorge Miranda, "Should Antidumping Laws Be Dumped?" (1996) 28 *Law and Policy in International Business* 255–288; Richard Posner, *The Robinson-Patman Act: Federal Regulation of Price Differences* (Washington, DC: American Enterprise Institute, 1976); Thomas W. Ross, "Winners and Losers under the Robinson-Patman Act" (1984) 27 *Journal of Law and Economics* 243; Edwin Vermulst, *The WTO Anti-Dumping Agreement: A Commentary* (Oxford University Press, 2011); Michael Moore, "Rules or Politics?: An Empirical Analysis of ITC Anti-Dumping Decisions" (2007) 30 *Economic Inquiry* 449–466; Thomas Prusa, "On the Spread and Impact of Anti-Dumping" (2001) 34 *Canadian Journal of Economics/Revue Canadienne D'économique* 591–611. The author's work *Reclaiming Development in the World Trading System* also analyzes the current WTO provisions on anti-dumping measures and discusses the needs for major reforms. Lee, *Reclaiming Development in the World Trading System*, *supra* note 1, Chapter 4.2.

19 Agreement on Safeguards, Article 2.

20 Ricardo's classical theory of comparative advantage sets out that international trade always promotes economic efficiency through optimal redistribution of domestic resources. David Ricardo, *Principles of Political Economy and Taxation* (1817).

ures were applied.[21] Most active users of safeguard measures have been India, Indonesia, and Turkey for the cited period, applying 24, 28, and 20 measures, respectively.[22] The United States applied eight and the EU four.[23] In fact, the vast majority of safeguard measures, over three-quarters of the measures, have been applied by developing countries and transition economies of Eastern Europe,[24] showing vulnerability of their domestic industries, particularly at times of economic difficulties.[25] As of October 2023, 45 definite measures and three provisional measures were in effect,[26] and there were six investigations outstanding.[27]

A number of products in a variety of sectors have been subject to safeguard measures: products of the chemical or allied industries (37 measures, 17.4 percent); base metals and articles of base metal (56 measures, 26.3 percent); textiles and textile articles (17 measures, 7.9 percent); and prepared foodstuffs; beverages, spirits and vinegar; and tobacco and manufactured tobacco substitutes (17 measures, 7.9 percent) are the sectors that have been most frequently subject to safeguards.[28] **1.08**

1.2 CONTROVERSY OVER ECONOMIC JUSTIFICATION[29]

Trade concessions often result in increases in imports. A rapid increase in imports may cause a significant strain on the competing domestic industry of the importing country, leading to acute economic problems such as unemploy- **1.09**

---

21 WTO, *Safeguard Measures by Reporting Member*, text available at: https:// www .wto .org/ english/ tratop _e/ safeg_e/ sg_measuresbyrepmember .pdf [https://perma.cc/ 4AF5 -QVDR]; WTO, *Safeguard Initiations by Reporting Member*, text available at: https:// www .wto .org/ english/ tratop _e/ safeg _e/ SG _In itiationsB yRepMember.pdf [https://perma.cc/PCM7-R3HJ].

22 *Id.*

23 *Id.*

24 *Id.*

25 For example, the application of safeguard measures increased by 67% from 2008 to 2009, after the period of recession after the financial crisis of 2008, and the measures were applied by developing countries and the transition economies. *Id.*

26 WTO, *Report (2023) of the Committee on Safeguards*, G/L/1503 (October 26, 2023), Annex 3.

27 *Id.*

28 WTO, *Safeguard Measures by Sector*, text available at: https:// www .wto .org/ english/ tratop _e/ safeg _e/ SG _MeasuresBySector.pdf [https://perma.cc/6YEK-TJ3M]. With respect to the applicable sectors, a commentator opined that the application of a safeguard measure in the solar photovoltaics (PV) sector may impede much-needed efforts to mitigate climate change. Mandy Meng Fang, "Old Wine in a New Bottle? Green Industrial Policy and the Use of Safeguards in the Solar Sector" (2021) 55(4) *Journal of World Trade* 573–596. *See also* Henok Asmelash, "The Turn to Safeguard Measures in the Solar Trade War" (2022) 56(5) *Journal of World Trade* 803–830.

29 The author is grateful to Professor Jai S. Mah of Ewha Woman's University and Dr. Ha-Joon Chang of Cambridge University for their insightful comments and suggestions on the economic analysis of safeguards provided in this chapter.

ment. The subsequent deterioration of a domestic industry may also invoke a series of adverse chain effects on other industries relating to that particular industry, which would magnify the problem. Economic difficulties are often transformed into social and political turmoil. The resulting social and political instabilities, in turn, may create adverse impacts on the economy.

1.10 From the economic perspective, the classical theories of trade by master economists such as Ricardo and Hecksher-Olin conclude that trade settles an economy at an optimal level through redistribution of resources from the inefficient domestic industries to the more efficient ones. Any restriction on trade would interfere with this transition and, therefore, result in a net loss to the economy.[30] Despite this theory, proponents of safeguard measures point out that the redistribution of resources does not take place instantaneously. They conclude that, in reality, the transfer of resources may take a considerable amount of time. For instance, the labor force employed in the declining domestic industries has to be re-educated and re-trained before it can be employed in other industries.[31] This argument supports the use of safeguard measures in that the temporary protection of domestic industry would facilitate this economic adjustment by providing the government and domestic industry with necessary time to deal with the changing economic environment.[32]

1.11 On the other hand, it is not always certain that this protection would induce the domestic industry to make necessary adjustments. While protection is being offered, the domestic industry is not under immediate pressure to make any changes. For instance, it has been pointed out that the continuing

---

30 According to the study of welfare economics, the welfare loss to consumers caused by trade restraints is necessarily greater than the welfare gain by domestic producers, resulting in a net loss to the society. Dominick Salvatore, *International Economics* (John Wiley and Sons, Inc., 11th ed., 2013), pp. 221–228, 257–260. With the proposed steel quota legislation in 1999, it was estimated that the annual cost to American households per steel job saved would have exceeded $800,000. Gary Clyde Hufbauer and Erika Wada, *Steel Quotas: A Rigged Lottery* (Washington, DC: Institute for International Economics, 1999). *See also* Alan Sykes, *The WTO Agreement on Safeguards* (Oxford University Press, 2006), pp. 35–46; Sheela Rai, *Recognition and Regulation of Safeguard Measures under WTO* (Abingdon: Routledge, 2011), pp. 1–14; Fernando Piérola, *The Challenge of Safeguards in the WTO* (Cambridge University Press, 2014), pp. 83–97.

31 In line with this point, the WTO reported that in the presence of labor market imperfection, a tariff may act as an instrument to reduce the costs of adjustment associated with the transfer of workers from a declining industry into an expanding export sector. WTO, *World Trade Report 2009: Trade Policy Commitments and Contingency Measures* (Geneva, 2009), pp. 47–48.

32 The negotiators of the Safeguards Agreement considered this objective important. It is reflected in the Safeguards Agreement. Its Preamble states in relevant part, "Members … Recognizing the importance of structural adjustment and the need to enhance rather than limit competition in international markets … Hereby agree as follows." WTO, *The Results of the Uruguay Round of Multilateral Trade Negotiations: The Legal Text* (Cambridge University Press, reprint 2012), p. 275. The texts of WTO Agreements are also available online at the WTO website, http://www.wto.org/english/docs._e/legal_e/legal_e.htm [https://perma.cc/HDN6-L49M].

protection for the US steel industry has deterred it from making necessary structural changes.[33] Members are required to liberalize safeguard measures that apply for more than one year.[34] However, the current rules on safeguards do not prescribe the pace of the liberalization, and there is no guarantee that the liberalization would be sufficient to induce the domestic industry to make adjustments.

Regardless of the liberalization requirement, prudent producers should plan adjustments because protection by a safeguard measure is only temporary and cannot be repeated until a certain period of time has passed.[35] The existence of future uncertainty, however, may allow producers not to embark on the potentially painful economic adjustment. The maximum stretch of safeguard measures under the WTO Agreement on Safeguards is eight years, including a single extension.[36] This eight-year period is fairly long, and after those eight years the situation may have changed in such a way that the domestic producers are no longer threatened by the imports.[37] Therefore, it is also possible that domestic producers could rather adopt a wait-and-see attitude during the protection period and choose not to go through the adjustment process.[38] **1.12**

The question of economic efficiency has also been raised. Detractors of safeguard measures argue that it would be economically more efficient to use non-trade measures, such as government subsidies for re-education and re-training of the labor force in order to ease the transition.[39] Government subsidies take various forms, ranging from direct grants to tax cuts, and the government will be able to devise specific subsidy plans appropriate to the case **1.13**

---

33 William H. Barringer and Kenneth J. Pierce, *Paying the Price for Big Steel* (American Institute for International Steel, 2000) and Dan Ikenson, *Steel Trap: How Subsides and Protectionism Weaken the U.S. Steel Industry*, Trade Briefing Paper, Center for Trade Policy Studies (March 1, 2002), text available at: http://www.cato.org/sites/cato.org/files/pubs/pdf/tbp-014.pdf [https://perma.cc/CY9D-YGEE].

34 Agreement on Safeguards, Article 7.4.

35 A safeguard measures may be applied for the maximum period of 4 years and extended once for the same period on evidence of adjustment by the domestic industry. Agreement on Safeguards, Article 7.2. According to Dr. Ha-Joon Chang, the adjustment is better achieved if there is a sound state industrial policy. The success of industrial adjustments in Japan from the late 1970s to the early 1980s would be an example. *See also* Ronald Dore, *Flexible Rigidities: Industrial Policy and Structural Adjustment in the Japanese Economy, 1970–80* (Stanford University Press, 1986).

36 Agreement on Safeguards, Articles 7.1 and 7.2.

37 For instance, the loss of a major export market as the result of a safeguard measure, even temporary, may render foreign producers unable to continue production due to the loss of major revenue and, therefore, force them to close their business entirely. Even if foreign producers remain in operation, they may determine that the recovery of their business in the foreign market after the expiration of the safeguard is too costly and, therefore, may decide not to re-enter the foreign market.

38 Therefore, Article 7.2 of the SA requires evidence of industrial adjustment for the extension of a safeguard measure.

39 Sykes, *supra* note 30, p. 58.

at hand. However, it is not conclusive that a government subsidy is always more efficient than trade measures.[40] In addition, the government may simply not have adequate financial resources to provide a subsidy, or the government may have political difficulties in providing a subsidy, in which case trade measures are the only viable option.[41]

1.14 Another economic rationale for safeguard measures is that the protection not only provides the time necessary for transition (e.g., moving resources from one industry to another) but also helps the affected domestic industry improve its competitiveness. Proponents of this argument believe that the temporary protection, in conjunction with an effective liberalization plan, would induce the domestic industry to improve its efficiency. The improvement of the US automobile industry in the late 1980s and the early 1990s is a good example of this point. The US automobile industry suffered critically in the 1980s due to the sharp increase of automobile imports from Japan. Japanese automobiles became popular in the United States because they were reliable, had good fuel consumption, and were priced competitively. While the US government made an agreement with Japan to limit the Japanese export of automobiles into the US market,[42] the US automobile industry made considerable efforts to rationalize their operation and improve their products.

1.15 As a result, the US automobile industry did not vanish, but instead improved significantly in the 1990s. The proponents of this argument contend that had there been no protection, the revenue base for the US automobile producers would have been eradicated by the imports from Japan, and the recovery of the US automobile industry would have been much more difficult.[43] The short-

---

40 A subsidy, for example, may entail sufficiently higher administrative costs. Also, under the WTO Agreement on Subsidies and Countervailing Measures ("the SCM Agreement"), certain trade-related government subsidies are subject to countervailing actions and may be also prohibited. For a discussion of the government subsidies under the SCM Agreement, *see* Lee, *Reclaiming Development in the World Trading System, supra* note 1, Chapter 3.3.

41 The limited taxation capacity of developing countries may contribute to the lack of financial resources for government subsidy. Even when the government has money for subsidy, there may well be political difficulties in persuading the rest of the population that the affected group is entitled to a subsidy.

42 A 1981 automobile agreement between the United States and Japan limited Japanese car makers to exporting 1.68 million cars to the United States in the one-year period beginning in April 1, 1981 and 1.68 million cars plus 16.5 percent of whatever growth occurred in the US market in the year that followed. An annual ceiling on car exports to the United States continued until March 1994. Stephen D. Cohen, *The Route to Japan's Voluntary Export Restraints on Automobiles* (1998), https://nsarchive2.gwu.edu/japan/scohenwp.htm [https://perma.cc/NA2B-832M]. This arrangement was made in the form of "voluntary export restraints." The consistency of this measure with the requirements of the GATT was in doubt. For more discussions, *see* Chapters 2 and 9 *infra*.

43 D. Nelson, "Making Sense of the 1981 Automobile VER: Economics, Politics, and the Political Economy of Protection," *in* A. Krueger (ed.), *The Political Economy of Trade Protection* (University of Chicago Press, 1996), pp. 35–42. The author observed that the VER resulted in a substantial increase in industry profits

coming of this argument is that not all industries can be made competitive against imports by way of protection. It is also possible that a domestic industry that competes with imports is already operating efficiently on a domestic scale and could not be made more competitive against imports. If so, the application of a safeguard would not help the domestic industry.

In this case, the US automobile industry had the technical resources to improve the quality of its products and the managerial expertise to rationalize their operation to become internationally competitive. It also had access to the largest capital market in the world and enjoyed the benefit of a flexible US labor market. Not all industries competing with imports enjoy these favorable conditions, and many of them may never become internationally competitive even if temporary protection were to be provided. **1.16**

Critics of the temporary protection measures also point out that if the capital market was well functioning, an industry with long-term potential would always have access to industry-specific resources.[44] According to this belief, the US capital market should have been able to recognize the long-term potential of the US automobile industry and render assistance to it. The restrictions on the Japanese exports were, therefore, improper. Consequently, it has also been argued that if the problem lies with imperfections of the capital market, then the appropriate action would be to correct these capital market imperfections, not to restrict imports.[45] **1.17**

A plausible economic ground for safeguards may be found in situations where imports increase temporarily because of extraneous factors such as a sudden and radical change in the foreign exchange rate. For instance, a financial crisis in an exporting country may lead to a temporary, yet sharp devaluation of its currency. The price of its exports in terms of the importing country's currency then drops accordingly, giving those exported products a competitive edge. The lower price in the international market would increase the importation of those products, possibly causing injury to the domestic industries of the importing Members. In this case, a safeguard measure can be a proper remedy. **1.18**

International trade promotes economic welfare for all trading nations through optimal redistributions of world resources. However, the temporary increase **1.19**

---

once the US economy recovered from recession and demand for automobiles increased although those profits clearly appeared to reflect primarily increased rent extraction from US consumers. *Id.*, p. 39.

44 Sykes, *supra* note 30, p. 52.

45 J.W. Freebain, "Pros and Cons of Temporary Industry Assistance" (1978) 22 *Australian Journal of Agricultural Economics* 194–205.

in imports resulting from extraneous factors, such as financial disruption, does not reflect an optimal distribution of resources to be achieved by trade. As illustrated by an example below, the financial disruption may distort world trade. The importing countries would then have a legitimate economic ground to apply a safeguard measure to prevent or remedy such a distortion.

1.20 In 1997, a series of financial crises struck many Asian countries, which led to a sharp devaluation of their currencies.[46] In the case of South Korea, for example, its currency, the won, devalued more than 40 percent as a result. Such devaluation reduced Korean export prices accordingly in terms of foreign currencies, giving Korean exporters a significant competitive advantage.[47] Many domestic industries of Korea's trading partners that had been competing with Korea's exports, ranging from the US steel industry to the Israeli plywood industry, suffered injury or threat of injury from the increased imports from Korea.

1.21 Safeguard measures would have been a proper remedy to redress injury or threat to those industries, although Korea's trading partners refrained from doing so in an effort to assist with Korea's economic recovery. The increase in imports from Korea was mainly due to the temporary devaluation of the Korean currency. The cause of the devaluation was short-term financial disruption, and the value of the Korean currency was bound to appreciate as capital flowed back into the country, which actually took place in the months following the outbreak of the crisis. If the affected Members had chosen to apply safeguard measures, they would have been able to protect their domestic industries against the surge of imports from Korea.

1.22 One may wonder how the crisis-stricken countries could get out of the crisis if their exports were to be blocked by such measures – the only thing in their

---

46 For the causes and developments of financial crisis in certain Asian countries, *see* Andrew Berg, "The Asia Crisis – Causes, Policy Responses and Outcomes," International Monetary Fund Working Paper, WP/99/138 (October 1, 1999) and Hider A. Khan, *Global Markets and Financial Crises in Asia* (Palgrave Macmillan, 2004).

47 There is another observation on the nature of the increase in exports from Korea. According to Professor Jai S. Mah, Korea's export had been suppressed before the breakout of the financial crisis due to the unrealistically high value of the won, which was arbitrarily maintained by the government through market intervention. The exchange rate soared during the financial crisis between November 1997 and February 1998 and subsequently returned to the market equilibrium, which was still substantially higher than the pre-crisis exchange rate. According to Mah, Korea's level of export was higher than it should have been only during a few months in which the exchange rate was higher than the equilibrium. This observation is sensible. On the other hand, from the perspective of the importing countries, the fact that Korea's export had been lower than it should have been due to the arbitrarily high value of won was irrelevant. As far as their domestic industries were concerned, the imports from Korea increased substantially, causing injury or threat to their domestic industries, which could have been a legitimate basis for the application of a safeguard measure.

favor is the collapse in their currency value, which makes exports easier. In fact, the collapse of a country's economy due to financial crisis would have triggered a chain effect to the other countries as well, because they would lose their own export market. Therefore, for economic, diplomatic, and political reasons, trading partners of the countries in financial crisis decided to assist with their recovery by refraining from applying safeguard measures against their exports.[48]

Nevertheless, this policy choice does not refute the point that safeguard measures would still be a proper remedy against the temporary increase in imports, caused by some extraneous factors that do not reflect the long-term competitiveness of the imports. Without protection, the domestic industry would be forced to adjust to the new environment caused by this temporary financial factor. Even if the importing Members decide to apply a safeguard measure, they will still be able to control the extent of the measure, which would offer minimally needed protection to the domestic industry and at the same time offer help to those countries in financial difficulties by allowing some increase in imports from them. **1.23**

The argument cited above is not immune from the criticism that the capital market should be able to assist industries with temporary problems and therefore the trade measure is not required. According to this argument, there is no reason to believe that the capital market is unable to detect the temporary nature of the problem and to assist the affected domestic industries.[49] This opinion concludes that it would be better to leave it to the market than to apply a safeguard measure since import restrictions will distort trade and disadvantage domestic consumers. Again, a question remains as to whether the capital market would function perfectly and render the required assistance to affected domestic industries in time. **1.24**

As seen above, economic justifications for safeguard measures are controversial.[50] The arguments in support of safeguard measures have faced the criticism **1.25**

---

48 Nonetheless, less restrictive measures such as anti-dumping measures were applied to imports from South Korea during the financial crisis. *See United States – Anti-dumping Measures on Stainless Steel Plate in Coils and Stainless Steel Sheet and Strip from Korea*, Report of the Panel, WT/DS179/R (December 22, 2000).

49 *See also* Sykes, *supra* note 30, p. 52.

50 Rather negative on the economic case for safeguards, Sykes opined, "the standard economic case for open trade also makes a case against the use of safeguard measures. Such measures will often harm importing and exporting countries alike (focusing on aggregate consumer and producer surplus in each), and in the few instances where they may benefit importing nations, the benefits are only coincidentally related to the legal prerequisites for safeguards and will come at the expense of trading partners. Only if trade compensation were routinely coupled with safeguard measures would there be any basis for optimism that their net (efficiency) impact is potentially benign, but compensation has been the exception rather than the rule in practice." Sykes, *supra* note 30, p. 50.

that non-trade measures such as direct subsidies are more efficient and that the capital market should be the recourse for assistance. With respect to direct government subsidy, problems such as a lack of financial resources and possible political disagreement about the financial commitment may make the subsidy an unfeasible option. The conformity of such subsidies with the WTO subsidy rules could also be an issue if they affect trade.[51] As far as resorting to the capital market, the imperfection of the market is an issue. Curing the imperfection in the capital market is a difficult task and may not be feasible in many countries with limited capital resources. That is not to argue that the decisions by national authorities can always replace the decisions of the market, but in those countries where a well-functioning capital market does not exist, the national authorities' decision may be the only alternative to the economic, social, and political turmoil that can be caused by radical increases in imports. Even in developed countries, we have seen that the market does not always move rationally,[52] and that the government may need to step in when the market refuses to assist a domestic industry that faces a short-term difficulty.

1.3 POLITICAL NECESSITIES FOR SAFEGUARD MEASURES

1.26 The political necessity for safeguard measures seems more straightforward than the controversial economic justifications. Even if international trade improves overall economic welfare, some domestic industries may lose out to foreign counterparts. It is foreseeable that governments would be under pressure from those adversely affected domestic industries to restrict imports. The pressure would be greater where injury or its threat to the domestic industry becomes serious. The pressure may compel the government to take protective measures for the affected industry. The government may find trade measures such as safeguards easier to apply than non-trade measures such as subsidies, since they would not burden the government's budget and they do not involve complicated political negotiations. For this reason, safeguard measures provide the government with a means to relieve itself of the political pressure to "do something" about rapid increases in imports.

51 *Supra* note 40.

52 The financial crisis of 2008, which began in the United States and quickly spread to the rest of the world, is a testament of the imperfect market in developed countries. *See* Stephany Griffith-Jones, José Antonio Ocampo, and Joseph E. Stiglitz (eds.), *Time for a Visible Hand: Lessons from the 2008 World Financial Crisis* (Oxford University Press, 2012) and Gary B. Gorton, *Misunderstanding Financial Crises: Why We Don't See Them Coming* (Oxford University Press, 2012). *See also* Victoria Ivashina and David Scharfstein, "Bank Lending during the Financial Crisis of 2008" (2010) 97(3) *Journal of Financial Economics* 319–338.

This does not mean that the government would not mind abusing safeguard measures to satisfy their political needs where they do not have any legitimate ground to invoke them. The government is concerned about their compliance with the WTO rules. Nevertheless, political considerations still seem to be a key factor in the application of safeguards.[53] As mentioned above, the maximum duration of a safeguard measure, including an extension, is eight years. The government may consider the period of eight years long enough to provide themselves with a sufficient political cushion, regardless of what happens after that eight-year period.[54] **1.27**

Nevertheless, it is not always the case that the competent national authorities apply a safeguard measure when the legal and economic conditions for the application of the measure are met. In applying a safeguard measure, national authorities should, and in fact do, consider the competing interests of the interested parties, including domestic producers and consumers, exporters and importers, and may not apply the measure where the sacrifice of the larger public interest substantially outweighs the need for protection.[55] They may also consider the international political ramifications of the safeguard measure and the possibility of damage to their own exporting industries should the exporting Members decide to apply retaliatory measures against their products.[56] **1.28**

A negative decision against the application or the extension of a safeguard measure may face strong resistance and challenges by the affected domestic industry. For instance, a group of farmers in Korea filed for a judicial review of the government's decision not to initiate an investigation to extend its safeguard measure on the imports of garlic.[57] Even when a positive injury determination is made, domestic producers are likely to resist any attempt to lessen the protection. In the case of the widely publicized US safeguard measures on the imports of steel products ("US steel safeguard measures"),[58] domestic steel producers and unions strongly criticized the decision by the US government **1.29**

---

53 *See* Chapter 14 *infra* for a discussion of political circumstances leading to the application of controversial US steel safeguards in 2002.

54 It is interesting to note that the maximum duration of many democratically elected administrations does not exceed eight years. Therefore, the current administration applying a safeguard measure may avoid possible consequences of the measure after its expiration.

55 The Agreement on Safeguards, Article 3.1 requires national authorities to provide the interested parties with an opportunity to present views as to whether or not the application of a safeguard measure would be in the public interest.

56 The Agreement on Safeguards authorizes the exporting Members to apply retaliatory measures under certain conditions. *See* the relevant discussions in Chapter 8.3 *infra.*

57 "Farmers Bring a Lawsuit to Invalidate the Decision by the Korean Trade Commission," *Hankook Ilbo* (newspaper, US version distributed in Chicago), September 7, 2002, p. 9.

58 A detailed account of the US steel safeguard measures is provided in Chapter 14 *infra.*

to exempt certain products from its safeguard measures in an effort to avoid a major trade conflict with the affected exporting Members.[59]

1.30 Another political utility of safeguard measures is that safeguards may provide a government with the financial resources necessary to prevent or remedy injury to the domestic industry without having to burden its budget. For instance, if a safeguard measure is applied in the form of additional tariffs on imports,[60] the government may use the revenue from the increased tariffs as a financial source for its subsidy to support and re-train the labor force in the affected domestic industry for employment elsewhere.[61] The use of additional customs revenue resulting from safeguards is less likely to force governments to make difficult political compromises and to engage in negotiations in order to secure necessary resources from elsewhere.

1.31 A safeguard measure may also be used as a political instrument to affect those domestic industries protected by the measure. This would be possible through the government's control of the measure itself. Suppose that a domestic industry has been selling product A at a 20 percent mark-up before inexpensive imports were brought into the domestic market. Assume that due to the competitive imports, the domestic industry would now have to sell at 10 percent below their cost to compete with those imports if there was to be no protection. If the government decides to offer protection, the price of the domestic product would depend on the rate of increased tariffs or the amount of the quota set by the government. Therefore, the government can affect the price chargeable by the domestic industry through its control of the measure.

1.32 Article 5.1 of the Agreement on Safeguards provides that a Member shall apply safeguard measures only to the extent necessary to prevent or remedy serious injury and to facilitate adjustment. However, the provision does not specify the precise amount of the quota[62] or the tariff rate; therefore, the adequate level of protection would be subject to the determination of the government. The lower the level of the protection, the more adjustment the domestic industry would have to make. The government would enjoy the position of being able to affect the profitability of domestic industries and to affect their behavior

---

59 "Bush Scales Back Tariffs on Steel" *New York Times*, August 23, 2002, p. A1.

60 Both quantitative restrictions and tariffs are permissible forms of safeguard measures under the Agreement on Safeguards.

61 As discussed above, this government subsidy may be subject to the WTO subsidy rules to the extent that it affects trade. *Supra* note 40.

62 Nonetheless, Article 5.1 of the SA sets the minimum quota level. Refer to the relevant discussion in Chapter 7 *infra*.

through its control of safeguard measures. It would give the government a political bargaining chip to deal with the domestic industries, which is considered another political reason that the government should favor the existence of safeguard measures.

Lastly, safeguard measures may also enable governments to lower barriers to imports generally. Despite the benefit from the liberalization of trade, adversely affected domestic industries tend to resist opening of the domestic market, and such resistance has proven to be a major barrier to the liberalization of trade. The existence of safeguard measures can be perceived as a safety net for the survival of domestic industries, albeit temporary.[63] With safeguard measures in place, governments would be better able to persuade their domestic constituencies to accept further liberalization of trade.[64] This will be particularly relevant in the discussion on the liberalization of service trade. Detailed discussions on this subject are provided in Chapter 10 of this book. **1.33**

1.4 CONCLUSION

There has been a considerable amount of discussion about the justifications for trade restrictions.[65] On balance, there are clearly identifiable political interests in favor of safeguard measures, while the economic justifications are more controversial. A particular concern was raised that political motivations create ample room for the abuse of safeguard measures. This concern was an important reason for the negotiation of the WTO Agreement on Safeguards,[66] which provides detailed requirements for the application of a safeguard measure to minimize the possibility of such abuse. **1.34**

---

63 *See also* Kenneth W. Dam, *The GATT, Law and International Economic Organization* (University of Chicago Press, 1970), p. 106 for this "safety-valve theory."

64 Sykes has considered that the facilitation of trade liberalization is the most plausible political economy accounts of safeguards. Sykes, *supra* note 30, p. 59. He explains that "[i]f each [party] knows that they can revoke burdensome concessions as long as revocation imposes only modest costs on trading partners (it is 'efficient'), both will be better off than they would be if concessions were irrevocable. Likewise, to the extent that some pairs of reciprocal concessions would be unattractive under a rule of irrevocability because they would have negative expected value to negotiating officials, a safeguard mechanism can tip the balance and give the concessions positive expected value" (explanation added). *Id.*, p. 71.

65 *See* Freebain, *supra* note 45. *See also* J.N. Bhagwati, *Protectionism* (Cambridge, Mass.: MIT Press, 1988); W.M. Corden, *Trade Policy and Economic Welfare* (London: Oxford University Press, 1974); G.H. Hufbauer, D.T. Berliner, and K.A. Elliott, *Trade Protection in the United States: 31 Cases* (Washington, DC: Institute for International Economics, 1986).

66 *See* Chapter 2.3 *infra* for the need for the Agreement on Safeguards, which included the lack of procedural transparency in the application of a safeguard measure under Article XIX.

1.35 The process of liberalization of trade involves complicated political compromises that require careful balancing of different and often conflicting interests among various interest groups. The transitional problems, such as unemployment, that can be caused by opening up their domestic market to competitive foreign exports are a significant concern for many governments. Therefore, the governments, as well as affected domestic industries facing radical increases in imports causing serious injury or its threat, may have a legitimate interest in maintaining the *status quo* through temporary protection so that they may reduce the immediate shock from a sudden downfall of those domestic industries and then embark on the needed adjustment.

1.36 Again, there is no guarantee that the protection would facilitate the intended economic adjustment. Even if it does, there is no assurance that the protection would be the best way to facilitate adjustment. The critics of safeguard measures have argued that government interference with international trade is unwarranted.[67] Nevertheless, a safeguard measure, at the minimum, provides

67 Sykes concluded that the suggestion that safeguard measures are useful for restoring the competitiveness of falling industries is not persuasive because the industry under protection may not become competitive at all, direct loans or subsidies may be economically more efficient, and resort to private capital market is more preferable. He also opined that the argument that safeguard measures can effectively alleviate unemployment in the presence of labor market distortions is also problematic, or at least incomplete because direct labor market intervention, such as an employment subsidy, is more effective, safeguards may exacerbate the wage stickiness, the temporary protection by safeguards would only postpone the dislocation to a future point, trade intervention will shift the terms of trade through its effect on exchange rates causing the domestic exports to fall, and safeguards may cause difficulties to exporting countries. He argues that redistributive argument for safeguard measures also has limited persuasive force because limited evidence suggests that workers displaced by import competition do not necessarily spend a longer period of time unemployed or suffer a greater reduction in their incomes than do workers displaced by other causes, skilled workers may have already been compensated through higher wages, and other policy instruments such as retraining programs and public employment agencies, may be preferable to trade protection. Sykes, *supra* note 30, pp. 50–59. This is a plausible observation. However, as discussed above, non-trade intervention, such as subsidy, may not be available, particularly for developing countries with limited financial resources, and there are also inherent political difficulties associated with granting a subsidy to a particular group of constituencies. A well-functioning capital market may not be readily available, again, particularly in developing countries. Even in developed countries, the capital market does not always function optimally, as demonstrated by the 2008 financial crisis, and it may not necessarily detect the long-term potential of the industry and provide assistance in time. As Sykes has noted, safeguards may indeed "transfer" the problems of the domestic industries under protection to the export industries of another country, and some consideration should be given to this issue, particularly for developing countries whose economy may depend on export to developed country markets. Suggestions are made in Chapter 15.1 *infra* to remedy this problem.

opportunity for adjustment without disrupting political and economic stability and also allows government to pursue further liberalization of trade with a political cushion. Despite the criticisms of safeguard measures, the compelling political necessities would likely keep safeguard measures as a lasting part of the world trading system. Many of those who are not convinced of the economic case for safeguards consider that safeguards seem an inevitable political price to be paid for the promotion of trade.[68] Irrespective of whether safeguard measures merely bestow emotional comfort on those who worry about their domestic industry or they indeed facilitate desirable economic adjustment, it would be imperative to apply safeguards properly in compliance with the rules, since the abuse of safeguards would certainly cause a grave disruption in world trade.[69]

An adequate understanding and appreciation of the rules on safeguards would be a prerequisite to the proper application of safeguards. Although the Agreement on Safeguards provides much more detailed rules on the application of safeguard measures than its predecessor, GATT Article XIX, some of those rules are inherently ambiguous and controversial, as shown in recent WTO panel and Appellate Body reports. The following chapters discuss the **1.37**

68 This justification does not seem to apply to another type of major trade measure: anti-dumping measures. *See* Chapter 15 *infra* for the relevant discussion.

69 Safeguard measures may be applied in fear of trade diversion if a major importing country applies a safeguard measure, creating further restrictions on trade globally. *See* Chapter 14.2 *infra* for the discussion of EU's safeguard measure in response to the US steel safeguard measure in 2002. An empirical study has shown an interesting observation that a safeguard measure may cause a decrease, rather than an increase, in the export of the product subject to the safeguard measure to third countries. According to the study, a US safeguard measure has caused Japanese exports to third countries fall by somewhere between 55 percent and 70 percent. Chad A. Bown and Meredith A. Crowley, "Trade Deflection and Trade Depression" (2007) 72 *Journal of International Economics* 176–201.

evolution of the rules on safeguards and examine those rules with an analysis of the various issues raised in WTO dispute settlement cases.[70,71]

---

70 As of April 2024, 17 DSB panels, composed under Article 6 of the Understanding on Rules and Procedures Governing the Settlement of Disputes ("DSU"), have reviewed disputes concerning the applications of safeguard measures under the Agreement on Safeguards and GATT Article XIX and issued reports. Those cases are: *Korea – Definitive Safeguard Measure on the Imports of Certain Dairy Products* ("*Korea – Dairy Products*"), Report of the Panel, WT/DS98/R (June 21, 1999); *Argentina – Safeguard Measure on the Imports of Footwear* ("*Argentina – Footwear*"), Report of the Panel, WT/DS121/R (June 25, 1999); *United States – Definitive Safeguard Measures on Imports of Wheat Gluten From the European Communities* ("*United States – Wheat Gluten*"), Report of the Panel, WT/DS166/R (June 25, 1999); *United States – Safeguard Measures on Imports of Fresh, Chilled or Frozen Lamb Meat from New Zealand and Australia* ("*United States – Lamb Meat*"), Report of the Panel, WT/DS177/R, WT/DS178/R (December 21, 2000); *United States – Definitive Safeguard Measures on Imports of Steel Wire Rod and Circular Welded Carbon Quality Line Pipe* ("*United States – Line Pipe*"), Report of the Panel, WT/DS202/R (October 29, 2001); *Chile – Price Band System and Safeguard Measures relating to Certain Agricultural Products* ("*Chile – Agricultural Products*"), Report of the Panel, WT/DS207/R (May 3, 2002); *Argentina – Definitive Safeguard Measure on Imports of Preserved Peaches* ("*Argentina – Preserved Peaches*"), Report of the Panel, WT/DS238/R (February 14, 2003); *United States – Definitive Safeguard Measures on Imports of Certain Steel Products* ("*United States – Steel Products*"), Report of the Panel, WT/DS248~DS259/R (July 11, 2003); *Dominican Republic – Safeguard Measures on Imports of Polypropylene Bags and Tubular Fabric* ("*Dominican Republic – Polypropylene Bags and Tubular Fabric*"), Report of the Panel, WT/DS415~DS418/R (January 31, 2012); *Argentina – Measures Affecting the Importation of Goods* ("*Argentina – Import Measures*"), Report of the Panel, WT/DS438/R, WT/DS444/R, WT/DS445/R (August 22, 2014); *Ukraine – Definitive Safeguard Measures on Certain Passenger Cars* ("*Ukraine – Passenger Cars*"), Report of the Panel, WT/DS468/R (June 26, 2015); *Indonesia – Safeguard on Certain Iron or Steel Products* ("*Indonesia – Iron or Steel Products*"), Report of the Panel, WT/DS490/R, WT/DS496/R (August 18, 2017); *India – Certain Measures on Imports of Iron or Steel Products* ("*India – Iron or Steel Products*"), Report of the Panel, WT/DS518/R (November 6, 2018); *United States – Safeguard Measure on Imports of Crystalline Silicon Photovoltaic Products* ("*United States – Photovoltaic Products*"), Report of the Panel, WT/DS545/R, WT/DS562/R (September 20, 2021); *United States – Safeguard Measures on Imports of Large Residential Washers* ("*United States – Washers*"), WT/DS546/R (February 8, 2022); *European Union – Safeguard Measures on Certain Steel Products* ("*European Union – Steel Products*"), Report of the Panel, WT/DS595/R (April 29, 2022); *United States – Certain Measures on Steel and Aluminum Products* ("*United States – Steel and Aluminum Products*"), Report of the Panel, WT/DS544/R, WT/DS552/R, WT/DS556/R, WT/DS564/R (December 9, 2022). The Panel did not make recommendations concerning safeguard measures in *Chile – Agricultural Products* as the measure had been withdrawn. Nevertheless, the Panel made substantive findings on the issues raised in the dispute. The Panels in *Indonesia – Iron or Steel Products* and *United States – Steel and Aluminum Products* determined that the measures at issue did not constitute safeguard measures under Article XIX and the SA. In *Argentina – Import Measures*, the complainants invoked Article 14 of the SA, but the Panel did not address this issue.

71 In 12 of the 17 cases, panel recommendations were appealed to the Appellate Body. The Appellate Body issued 9 reports before it lost a quorum and became dysfunctional in December 2019: *Korea – Dairy Products*, Report of the Appellate Body, WT/DS98/AB/R (December 14, 1999); *Argentina – Footwear*, Report of the Appellate Body, WT/DS121/AB/R (December 14, 1999); *United States – Wheat Gluten*, Report of the Appellate Body, WT/DS166/AB/R (December 22, 2000); *United States – Lamb Meat*, Report of the Appellate Body, WT/DS177/AB/R, WT/DS178/AB/R (May 1, 2001); *United States – Line Pipe*, Report of the Appellate Body, WT/DS202/AB/R (February 15, 2002); *Chile – Agricultural Products*, Report of the Appellate Body, WT/DS207/AB/R (September 23, 2002); *United States – Steel Products*, Report of the Appellate Body, WT/DS248~DS259/AB/R (November 10, 2003); *Argentina – Measures Affecting the Importation of Goods*, Report of the Appellate Body, WT/DS438/R, WT/DS444/R, WT/DS445/R (January 15, 2015); *Indonesia – Safeguard on Certain Iron or Steel Products*, Report of the Appellate Body, WT/DS490/AB/R, WT/DS496/AB/R (August 15, 2018).

2

GATT ARTICLE XIX AND NEGOTIATION OF THE AGREEMENT ON SAFEGUARDS

2.1 GENERAL BACKGROUND

GATT Article XIX is the first safeguard provision in the international trading system. Article XIX was brought to the world as a child of a US proposal in 1946. The United States submitted a working proposal for the Charter of the International Trade Organization (ITO) that included an escape clause.[72] It was very similarly worded to the escape clause in the previous US–Mexico Agreement.[73] Although the ITO never came into existence, the escape clause was adopted as part of the GATT provisions. **2.01**

The escape clause of the US–Mexico Agreement set out three conditions for the application of a safeguard measure: an increase in imports; serious injury or threat thereof to domestic producers of like or similar articles; and the causal relationship between increased imports and injury.[74] The notion of safeguard measures as emergency action to prevent or remedy serious injury to **2.02**

72 *United States Suggested Charter*, Department of State Publication No. 2598 (1946), Article 29, p. 22. In February 1947, in the midst of the ITO and GATT negotiations, US President Truman issued an Executive order that required the inclusion of an escape clause in every US trade agreement negotiated under the authority of the 1934 trade act. Exec. Order No. 9832, 3 C.F.R. §§ 624, 625 (February 25, 1947). Therefore, the inclusion of the escape clause was the US priority.

73 *See supra* note 13.

74 The clause also stated that the increase should be "as the result of unforeseen development and of concession granted on any article enumerated and described in the Schedules annexed to this Agreement." The clause that included "unforeseen development" is also adopted in Article XIX. As discussed in detail below, it is doubtful that this phrase should be considered to be a legal condition for the application of a safeguard measure.

domestic industry was also adopted in Article XIX as well as in the Agreement on Safeguards ("SA") five decades later. Both Article XIX and the SA have adopted those three conditions as the general requirements for the application of a safeguard measure.

2.03 Composed of merely five paragraphs, Article XIX is noted for its brevity and lacks detailed substantive and procedural requirements for the application of a safeguard measure. Paragraph 1(a) of the Article provides the general conditions for the application of a safeguard measure. The other provisions include: regulation of the protection of the existing trade preference (paragraph 1(b)); prior notice and consultations (paragraph 2); and compensation and retaliation (paragraph 3).

2.04 The lack of specific and detailed regulations in Article XIX turned out to be a major problem in the discipline of safeguards, since the provisions of Article XIX did not provide sufficient guidelines for a series of important and practical issues in the application of a safeguard measure, such as assessment of serious injury to a domestic industry, specific duration of a safeguard, and investigation process. This lack of detailed procedural and substantive provisions also made it difficult for exporting countries to challenge safeguard measures that were considered to be applied arbitrarily, without clear evidence of serious injury or of the causal link between increased imports and injury. The emergence of "gray-area measures" also raised significant concern.[75] The necessity of more detailed and clear rules on safeguards was evident, and this need eventually led to the conclusion of the Agreement on Safeguards in 1994.[76]

2.05 Although Article XIX lacked detailed provisions for the application of a safeguard measure, the concepts and conditions included in the Article provided the foundation for the Agreement on Safeguards. The significance of Article XIX has been highlighted by decisions of the panels and the standing Appellate Body (hereinafter, "the Appellate Body"), established by the Dispute Settlement Body (DSB) of the WTO.[77] The new Agreement on Safeguards was acclaimed as a substantial achievement of the Uruguay Round negotiations, "a heroic statement of principle."[78] Many considered that this more complete Agreement effectively replaced the old provisions of Article XIX.

---

75 *See infra* Chapters 2.3 and 9.1 for discussions of gray-area measures.

76 More discussions of the need for the SA are provided later in this chapter.

77 DSU, Articles 6 and 17.

78 John H. Jackson, *The World Trading System* (Cambridge, Mass.: The MIT Press, 1997), p. 270.

The Panels[79] and the Appellate Body in *Korea – Dairy Products* and *Argentina – Footwear*,[80] however, ruled that it did not. They found that both Article XIX and the SA and not the latter alone constitute the disciplines on safeguards.[81] As discussed below, there is a controversy about the continuing applicability of GATT Article XIX after the implementation of the SA. Nevertheless, as those Appellate Body decisions stand unchanged, it is necessary to review the provisions of Article XIX and identify those provisions subsequently modified or repealed by the SA and those still applicable. The remainder of this chapter introduces the provisions of Article XIX and also provides a brief account of the negotiation history of the Agreement on Safeguards. The applicability of Article XIX is further discussed in the next chapter, particularly in the context of the controversial application of Article XIX:1(a), the "unforeseen developments" clause.

2.2 PROVISIONS OF ARTICLE XIX

General Conditions. Paragraph 1(a) of Article XIX provides: **2.06**

> If, as a result of unforeseen development and of the effect of the obligations incurred by a contracting party under this Agreement, including tariff concessions, any product is being imported into the territory of that contracting party in such increased quantities and under such conditions as to cause or threaten serious injury to domestic producers in that territory of like or directly competitive products, the contracting party shall be free, in respect of such product, and to the extent and for such time as may be necessary to prevent or remedy such injury, to suspend the obligation in whole or in part or to withdraw or modify the concession.

The leading GATT decision on the application of Article XIX, *Report on Withdrawal by the United States of a Tariff Concession under Article XIX of the General Agreement ("Hatter's Fur Case")*,[82] provided a summary of the essential elements for the application of a safeguard measure. The Report notes in relevant part, "In attempting to appraise whether the requirements of Article XIX had been fulfilled, the Working Party examined separately each of the conditions which qualify the exercise of the right to suspend an obligation or to **2.07**

79 Throughout this book, "Panel" with capitalization refers to a specific panel on a specific dispute and "panel" without capitalization to a WTO panel generally. This distinction is only generally made and not strictly precise.

80 *Korea – Dairy Products*; *Argentina – Footwear*, *supra* notes 70, 71.

81 *Korea – Dairy Products*, *supra* note 70, paras. 7.38–7.39 and *supra* note 71, paras. 74–77. *Argentina – Footwear*, *supra* note 70, paras. 8.52–8.56 and *supra* note 71, paras. 78–84.

82 GATT doc. GATT/CP/106 (adopted by the Contracting Parties on October 22, 1951).

withdraw or modify a concession under that Article."[83] The Report prescribed the following conditions for the application of a safeguard measure under Article XIX:

(a) There should be an abnormal development in the imports of the product in question in the sense that:
  (i) the product in question must be imported in increased quantities;
  (ii) the increased imports must be the result of unforeseen developments and of the effect of the tariff concession; and
  (iii) the imports must enter in such increased quantities and under such conditions as to cause or threaten serious injury to domestic producers of like or directly competitive products.

(b) The suspension of an obligation or the withdrawal or modification of a concession must be limited to the extent and the time necessary to prevent or remedy the injury caused or threatened.

(c) The contracting party taking action under Article XIX must give notice in writing to the CONTRACTING PARTIES before taking action. It must also give an opportunity to contracting parties substantially interested and to the CONTRACTING PARTIES to consult with it. As a rule, consultation should take place before the action is taken, but in critical circumstances consultation may take place immediately after the measure is taken provisionally.[84]

2.08 *Increased Imports.* According to these guidelines, the first element under paragraph 1(a) is increased imports. The remedy of safeguard measures is predicated on the injury to a domestic industry caused by *increased imports.* No safeguard measure can be taken without first identifying the requisite increase in imports. An increase in imports would be easily found where there is an increase in absolute terms. The question is whether an increase only *relative* to domestic production would qualify for the requisite increase in imports. For instance, suppose that the amount of imports of product X from country A decreases from 10,000 tons to 7,000 tons. At the same time, the amount of the domestic production of product X also falls from 10,000 tons to 6,000 tons. Although there is an absolute decrease in the amount of imports of product X, the imports increase *relatively* to the domestic production as the domestic production decreases more than the imports do. In this case, could a safeguard measure be applied to the imported product X?

2.09 The Working Party on "Modifications to the General Agreement" established shortly after the Havana Conference in 1948 found, "It was also the understanding of the Working Party that the phrase 'being imported ... in such increased quantities' in paragraph 1(a) of Article XIX was intended to cover

83 *Id.*
84 *Id.*

cases where imports may have increased relatively…."[85] There is no GATT case which addressed the issue of a relative increase in imports. Some observe that the application of a safeguard measure in cases of "relative increase" poses certain problems. An eminent scholar noted, "This concept of 'relative increase' seems inappropriate in an escape clause that is based on a policy of allocating the burdens of market readjustment… Here no actual increase in imports has occurred, so it seems very difficult to justify placing the burden on the foreign products. It appears that the 'relative' increase concept is a protective device. It is a device that may have little relevance in a general period of increasing economic wealth, but it is a potentially dangerous device if general world economic conditions tend to decline. In that sense protective sentiments will be much more powerful anyway, and this outlet for that sentiment could accelerate a decline in trade and thus accelerate a general economic decline, as such nation tries to shift the burden of declining markets to foreign goods, evoking retaliation and a spiraling downward trade trend."[86]

On the other hand, others believe that safeguard measures should apply to relative increases in imports because domestic producers tend to consider the fact that imports are accounting for a bigger proportion in the domestic market more relevant than the decrease in the absolute amount of imports in recessionary or depressionary economic conditions.[87] Since the need for a safeguard measure is to ensure a minimum safety net for the domestic producers, the authorization of a safeguard measure based on "relative increase" could accommodate the domestic producers' concern about their declining market share. **2.10**

However, it should also be noted that, although a relative increase in imports may qualify for the increase in imports for the application of a safeguard measure, it might be difficult to prove the causal link between a relative increase in imports and the injury to the domestic industry. This is true because where both domestic production and imports fall, it is the general decline of consumer demand, rather than increased imports, that is more likely to be found as the cause for the injury.[88] **2.11**

---

85 WTO, *Analytical Index: Guide to GATT Law and Practice* (Geneva: WTO, 6th ed. 1995), p. 518.

86 John H. Jackson, *World Trade and the Law of GATT* (Indianapolis: Bobbs-Merrill, 1969), p. 555.

87 Raj Bhala and Kevin Kennedy, *World Trade Law* (Charlottesville, Virginia: Lexis Law Publishing, 1998), p. 910.

88 In times of recession, the general effect of recession often outweighs the impact of imports causing injury to a domestic industry. In a US safeguard case, *Certain Motor Vehicles and Certain Chassis and Bodies Therefore,* the US International Trade Commission (USITC) made a negative injury determination after finding that the impact of a recession outweighed that of imports causing the injury. USITC Pub. No. 1110, Inv. No. TA-201-44 (1980). This decision caused a public outcry, and the Congress modified the US safeguard provision and enacted a provision against aggregating the causes of declining demand associated with a recession

2.12 *Unforeseen Developments*. The next element under the above guidelines is the presence of unforeseen developments and the effect of the tariff concession. The meaning of "unforeseen developments" in paragraph 1(a) was discussed in *Hatter's Fur*. The members of the Working Party in *Hatter's Fur*, except for the United States, agreed that "the term 'unforeseen development' should be interpreted to mean developments occurring after the negotiation of the relevant tariff concession which it would not be reasonable to expect that the negotiators of the country making the concession could and should have foreseen at the time when the concession was negotiated."[89] According to this view, "unforeseen" developments exist where they were "unforeseeable." However, later the Appellate Body took an apparently different view, making a distinction between the terms "unforeseeable" and "unforeseen."[90] A commentator discounted the importance of this phrase as a condition for the application of a safeguard measure since "all the benefit of doubt [concerning the existence of 'unforeseen developments'] goes to the party invoking it."[91]

2.13 The existence of "unforeseen developments" has been characterized as a "prerequisite" to an escape clause action. According to the Appellate Body, which reversed the previous Panel decision denying that the "unforeseen developments" clause creates any legal obligation, a Member applying a safeguard measure is obligated to demonstrate the existence of "unforeseen developments" as a matter of fact.[92] It is doubtful that the "unforeseen developments" clause should be interpreted as an affirmative legal requirement for the application of a safeguard measure. The question of the legal effect of this clause is rather significant since it ultimately determines what constitutes the disciplines on safeguards under the WTO. This issue of "unforeseen developments," therefore, is further discussed in Chapter 3.2.

2.14 Article XIX also states that import increases must result from "the effect of the obligations incurred" under the GATT. With respect to the phrase "effect of obligations incurred by a contracting party," the Appellate Body was of the view that the phrase only indicates that the increase in imports should be

---

(such as unemployment, reduced business expenditure, etc.) in the application of a safeguard measure. *See* the relevant discussions in Chapter 12.2 *infra*.

89 *Hatter's Fur, supra* note 82, para. 9.

90 *Korea – Dairy Products, supra* note 71, para. 84.

91 Jackson, *supra* note 78, at 563. In *Hatter's Fur*, the Working Party acknowledged that the change of fashion is foreseeable but not that *the degree to which the* change in fashion affected the competitive situation. *Hatter's Fur, supra* note 82, paras. 11, 12. Jackson suspected that it would be the case in *every* substantial increase in imports.

92 *Korea – Dairy Products, supra* note 71, para. 85. *See also United States – Steel Products, supra* note 71, para. 315 (noting that the "increased imports" must be an "effect or outcome" of the unforeseen development).

the result of obligations undertaken by the Member under the GATT 1994, including tariff concessions.[93] The phrase, therefore, does not impose any analytical obligation to be performed before the application of a safeguard measure. The SA does not include this phrase.

Application of MFN Principle. A question was also raised with respect to the applicability of the most-favored-nation (MFN) principle to a safeguard measure. The text of Article XIX neither specifically approves nor prohibits the selective application of a safeguard measure according to the sources of the product concerned. A specific MFN provision was included in the Charter of the ITO at the Havana meeting,[94] and the Contracting Parties generally understood that the MFN principle applied to safeguard measures, although the Charter had never acquired legal effect. The Contracting Parties of the GATT later confirmed the application of the MFN principle in subsequent panel cases.[95] The MFN principle is specified in Article 2.2 of the SA as discussed in Chapter 4. It was also pointed out that the authorization of a discriminatory measure applicable to the import only from a particular source would have been an invitation for a trade war between the importing country applying a safeguard measure and the affected exporting country.[96] **2.15**

Injury Test. Paragraph 1(a) also requires an injury test ("serious injury" or its "threat") as a prerequisite for the application of a safeguard measure. Article XIX does not provide any definition of serious injury. *Hatter's Fur* provides a discussion of the injury determination. It states: "Whether such a degree of adverse effect should be considered to amount to 'serious injury' is another question, on which the data cannot be said to point convincingly in either direction, and any view on which is essentially a matter of economic and social judgment involving a considerable *subjective* element. In this connection it **2.16**

---

93 The Appellate Body stated, "With respect to the phrase 'of the effect of the obligations incurred by a Member under this Agreement, including tariff concessions', we believe that this phrase simply means that it must be demonstrated, as a matter of fact, that the importing Member has incurred obligations under the GATT 1994, including tariff concessions. Here, we note that the Schedules annexed to the GATT 1994 are made an integral part of Part I of that Agreement, pursuant to paragraph 7 of Article II of the GATT 1994. Therefore, any concession or commitment in a Member's Schedule is subject to the obligations contained in Article II of the GATT 1994." *Korea – Dairy Products, supra* note 71, para. 84.

94 WTO, *Analytical Index, supra* note 85, p. 519.

95 *See Norway – Restrictions on Imports of Certain Textile Products*, GATT BISD 27S, 119 (1981). The GATT panel decision on Norway's safeguard measures on the import of certain textile products emphasized the requirement of a non-discriminatory application of a safeguard measure. The Panel "was of the view that that type of action chosen by Norway, i.e., quantitative restrictions limiting the importation of the nine textile categories in question, as the form of emergency action under Article XIX was subject to the provisions of Article XIII which provides for non-discriminatory administration of quantitative restrictions."

96 Bhala and Kennedy, *supra* note 87, p. 920.

may be observed that the Working Party naturally could not have the facilities available to the United States authorities for examining interested parties and independent witnesses from the United States hat-making areas, and for forming judgments on the basis of such an examination. Further, *it is perhaps inevitable that governments should on occasion lend greater weight to the difficulties or fears of their domestic producers than would any international body*, and that they may feel it necessary on social grounds, e.g., because of lack of alternative employment in the localities concerned, to afford a higher degree of protection to individual industries which in terms of cost of production are not economic ..." (emphasis added).[97]

2.17 This statement of the Working Party indicates that the determination of injury inevitably has certain elements of subjectivity and encompasses social as well as economic considerations. The Working Party refrained from engaging in *de novo* review of the national authorities' investigation and was also sympathetic about the need for protection on the part of the importing country for the social ramifications of the injury caused by increased imports. In an attempt to objectify the injury assessment, the SA provides a definition of injury and specifies injury factors.[98] In contrast to the attitude of the Working Party, deferring substantially to the national authorities for the injury determination,[99] the WTO Panels and the Appellate Body found that national authorities are obligated to provide reasoned explanations for their injury determination and have scrutinized the reasoning and explanations made by the national authorities for their decisions.[100]

2.18 *Form of Safeguard.* Paragraph 1(a) also stipulates that a safeguard measure is to "suspend the obligation in whole or in part or to withdraw or modify the concession." The measure may include various forms of import restrictions. For instance, contracting parties applied non-quantitative measures in the forms of increases in specific duties, increases in *ad valorem* duties, surcharges, surtaxes, imposition of a minimum value for duty, increases in compound duties, compensatory taxes, tariff quotas, and imposition of surtaxes and charges on products imported below a minimum price. They also applied non-tariff measures, including embargoes and bans on import licenses, global quotas, discretionary licensing, import deposit schemes, import authorization, and other import restrictions.[101]

---

97 *Hatter's Fur, supra* note 82, para. 30.

98 Refer to the relevant discussion in Chapter 5 *infra.*

99 *Hatter's Fur, supra* note 82.

100 *See* the relevant discussions in Chapters 4 and 5 *infra.*

101 WTO, *Analytical Index, supra* note 85, p. 522.

Duration and Extent. The phrase in paragraph 1(a), "... and to the extent and for such time as may be necessary to prevent or remedy serious injury ..." denotes the temporary nature of a safeguard measure and also requires proportionality between the measure applied and the injury. In *Hatter's Fur Case*, the Report concluded, "action under Article XIX is essentially of an emergency character and should be of limited duration. A government taking action under that Article should keep the position under review and be prepared to reconsider the matter as soon as this action is no longer necessary to prevent or remedy a serious injury. In the case under review, events that have occurred after it was decided to raise the duties would indicate that it would be desirable for the United States Government to follow the trends of consumption, production, and imports in the following months with a view to restoring the concession on hat bodies in whole or in part if and as soon as it becomes clear that its continued complete withdrawal cannot reasonably be maintained to be permissible under Article XIX."[102] Nonetheless, Article XIX did not specify the maximum duration of a safeguard measure. In contrast, the SA sets out the maximum duration.[103] If the importing country seeks a long-term modification of its concessions, the recourse has to be GATT Article XXVIII rather than safeguards. **2.19**

Protection of Preference. Paragraph 1(b) of Article XIX provides: **2.20**

> If any product, which is the subject of a concession with respect to a preference, is being imported into the territory of a contracting party in the circumstances set forth in subparagraph (a) of this paragraph, so as to cause or threaten serious injury to domestic producers of like or directly competitive products in the territory of a contracting party which receives or received such preference, the importing contracting party shall be free, if that other contracting party so requests, to suspend the relevant obligation in whole or in part or to withdraw or modify the concession in respect of the product, to the extent and for such time as may be necessary to prevent or remedy such injury.

This provision, although not clearly drafted, provides for the protection of preferential trade arrangements. It enables an importing country to apply a safeguard measure to protect the trade of a *third* country that is injured for the loss in whole or in part of a preference. For instance, suppose that country A has a free trade agreement with country B. Under the terms of this free trade agreement, country A imports product X from country B, tariff free. Country A also imports the like product X′ from country C with a 15 percent tariff on it. Country A subsequently provides a trade concession in a multilateral **2.21**

102 *Hatter's Fur, supra* note 82, para. 50.
103 Agreement on Safeguards, Article 7. Refer to the relevant discussion in Chapter 7.1 *infra*.

trade negotiation by reducing its tariff applicable to product X′ by 10 percent. Because of this concession, product X from country B may become less competitive in the market of country A because now its preference margin is relatively reduced, and its trade may be injured. Under the provision of paragraph 1(b), country A may apply a safeguard measure to product X at the request of country B.

2.22 The purpose of this provision is to ensure that preferential trading arrangements should be promoted and not endangered by the concessions made in multilateral trade negotiations. The protection of preferential trading arrangements may be justified as a way to promote the economic welfare of developing countries receiving economic benefit from such preferential treatment. It may also be justified in that preferential trade arrangements could eventually develop into a multinational framework, thereby giving the benefit of lower trade barriers to more countries as the number of participating countries increases.

2.23 There is no known application of this provision, and its significance is even less today since the tariff rates have been substantially reduced.[104] The application of this paragraph would also raise procedural problems as the SA does not provide any procedural guidelines for the application of a safeguard measure taken on behalf of a third country. These procedural problems are further examined in the next chapter in the context of the applicability of Article XIX after the implementation of the Agreement on Safeguards.

2.24 *Notification, Consultation, and Provisional Measure.* Paragraph 2 of Article XIX concerns the procedural requirements for the application of safeguards. It provides:

> Before any contracting party shall take action pursuant to the provisions of paragraph 1 of this Article, it shall give notice in writing to the CONTRACTING PARTIES as far in advance as may be practicable and shall afford the CONTRACTING PARTIES and those contracting parties having a substantial interest as exporters of the product concerned an opportunity to consult with it in respect of the proposed action. When such notice is given in relation to a concession with respect to a preference, the notice shall name the contracting party which has requested the action. In critical circumstances, where delay would cause damage which it would be difficult to repair, action

104 The tariff rates for non-primary products of industrial countries were reduced by 35–38 percent on average after each round of the eight trade negotiations since 1947. As a result, the average tariff rate of those countries after the Uruguay Round (1986–1994) fell to as low as 3.9 percent, rendering tariffs no longer a major trade barrier for non-primary products. Jackson, *supra* note 78, p. 74.

> under paragraph 1 of this Article may be taken provisionally without prior consultation, on the condition that consultation shall be effected immediately after taking such action.

Paragraph 2 of Article XIX requires a country proposing to apply a safeguard measure to provide advance written notice as well as an opportunity for consultation before applying the measure. This requirement of notification is to inform the countries to be affected by the proposed safeguard measure, thereby enabling them to review the proposed action in advance and prepare for its consequences to their trade. Consultations would facilitate the exchange of opinions and negotiations between affected exporting countries and the country proposing to apply the measure. Paragraph 2 also provides for provisional safeguard measures, which can be applied without prior consultations where delay would cause irreparable damage. The normal process, including consultations, must follow the provisional measure. Those requirements of notification, consultation, and provisional safeguard measure are also adopted in the Agreement on Safeguards with substantial elaborations.[105] 2.25

Compensation and Retaliation. Finally, Paragraph 3 of Article XIX concerns the important issues of compensation and retaliation. Paragraph 3(a) of the Article provides: 2.26

> If agreement among the interested contracting parties with respect to the action is not reached, the contracting party which proposes to take or continue the action shall, nevertheless, be free to do so, and if such action is taken or continued, the affected contracting parties shall then be free, not later than ninety days after such action is taken, to suspend, upon the expiration of thirty days from the day on which written notice of such suspension is received by the CONTRACTING PARTIES, the application to the trade of the contracting party taking such action, or, in the case envisaged in paragraph 1(b) of this Article, to the trade of the contracting party requesting such action, of such substantially equivalent concessions or other obligations under this Agreement the suspension of which the CONTRACTING PARTY do not disapprove.

Paragraph 3(b) further provides: 2.27

> Notwithstanding the provisions of sub-paragraph (a) of this paragraph, where action is taken under paragraph 2 of this Article without prior consultation and causes and threatens serious injury in the territory of a contracting party to the domestic producers of products affected by the action, that contracting party shall where delay would cause damage difficult to repair, be free to suspend, upon the taking of the action and throughout the period of consultation, such concessions or other obligations as may be necessary to prevent or remedy the injury.

105 *See* Chapter 6 *infra* for a discussion of the procedural requirements under the SA.

2.28 An application of a safeguard measure is bound to upset the balance of concessions between the exporting and importing countries. Since safeguard measures are applied irrespective of the existence of any unfair trade practice on the part of exporters, it is only reasonable that the balance of concessions should be restored by way of adequate compensation for the loss of trade. Compensation has taken the form of further concessions (tariff reductions) on the part of the importing country to the trade of the affected exporting countries.[106]

2.29 If parties fail to agree on compensation, paragraph 3(a) allows affected exporting countries to suspend their own concessions or other obligations to compensate for their loss of trade. The paragraph stipulates that any suspension should be substantially equivalent to the extent of the applied safeguard measure. There is a question as to the equivalency of the suspension, although an equivalent suspension would seem to be a suspension of the corresponding trade concessions that would yield roughly the same reduction in value in imports from the country applying the measure, as that caused by the application of the safeguard measure.[107] There is no restriction in the selection of products that can be subject to the suspension of concessions. Paragraph 3(b) also permits countries affected by provisional safeguard measures to suspend their concessions immediately where delay with the suspension would cause irreparable damage. The Agreement on Safeguards has made a significant modification in this area, as discussed in Chapters 3.3 and 8.3 below.

2.3 PROBLEMS OF ARTICLE XIX AND PROLIFERATION OF GRAY-AREA MEASURES

2.30 Article XIX provided rules for safeguards for the more than 40 years of the GATT regime. The lack of detailed substantive and procedural provisions in Article XIX inevitably caused problems in the discipline of safeguards. These problems included: (i) lack of procedural requirements for investigations causing no transparency in the process; (ii) no clear definition of serious injury allowing governments to make arbitrary decisions; (iii) inadequacy of the notification and consultation processes; (iv) lack of guidelines for the duration of safeguard measures; and (v) undisciplined gray-area measures that prevailed over safeguards.[108]

106 *See* WTO, *Analytical Index, supra* note 85, V. Notifications to the Secretariat of Actions under Article XIX pp. 539–559 for the safeguard measure applied during the GATT era.

107 The question of "equivalency" involves complicated issues as further explored in Chapter 8 *infra*.

108 GATT Secretariat, *Work Already Undertaken in the GATT on Safeguards*, GATT doc. No. MTN.GNG/NG9/W/1 (April 8, 1987). In addition, non-discriminatory application of safeguards was not clarified in Article XIX.

A series of efforts were made for the settlement of more precise and clearer disciplines on safeguards. Safeguard was a major issue in the Tokyo Round, which started in 1973. The Tokyo Round was successful in producing "codes" in the areas of anti-dumping and subsidies. However, despite significant efforts during negotiations, the participants failed to agree on the new rules on safeguards, as they could not come to agreement on certain key issues.[109] The key areas of disagreement included: authorization of a selective application of a safeguard measure according to the source of imports, introduction of a surveillance system, introduction of a dispute settlement mechanism, a definition of "serious injury," and the requirement of structural adjustment.[110] **2.31**

The positions of the major participants on those issues remained far apart throughout the negotiations, and they failed to bridge their differences. In general, developing countries demanded tougher rules on safeguards based on the MFN application, whereas developed countries preferred to reserve certain flexibility and to retain an ability to apply safeguards selectively according to the source of imports.[111] Some participants changed their positions, but it did not affect the outcome of the negotiations. For instance, a group of Nordic countries, including Finland, Iceland, Norway, and Sweden, departed from their initial negotiating position and agreed to adopt a non-discriminatory approach to the application of safeguards in the interest of trade liberalization.[112] However, the other European nations (EC[113] members) insisted on preserving some degree of selectivity in the application of safeguard measures. The areas of major disagreements are as follows.[114] **2.32**

---

109 GATT, *The Tokyo Round of Multilateral Trade Negotiations: Report by the Director-General of GATT* (April 1979), pp. 90–95 and *Supplementary Report of January 1980*, pp. 14–17.

110 *Id.*

111 According to Edwin Vermulst, this was the case particularly for the European Communities. Accounting for the reluctance of the EC to apply non-discriminatory safeguards, he notes that "in contrast to anti-dumping and anti-subsidy measures, (non-discriminatory) safeguards target fair trade and therefore amount to an admission by domestic industries that they cannot compete with fairly traded imports. Thus, safeguards tended to be viewed as an instrument for 'wimps.' For these reasons, safeguard actions were not popular with EC Member States and industries and few cases were brought in the past." Edwin Vermulst, Marta Pernaute, and Krista Lucenti, "Recent EC Safeguards Policy: 'Kill Them All and Let God Sort Them Out'?" (2004) 38(6) *Journal of World Trade* 955–984. However, departing from its early restraint from resorting to safeguards, the EC began to apply them from 2003. *Id.*

112 Statement Made by the Spokesman for Finland, Iceland, Norway and Sweden at the Meeting of Group "Safeguards" on December 13, 1978, GATT doc. MTN/SG/W/46 (December 14, 1978), p. 1.

113 The European Union (EU) was officially referenced as European Communities (EC) in the WTO for legal reasons until November 30, 2009. Thus in this book the EU is denoted as "EC" for the periods up to November 2009.

114 Terence P. Stewart (ed.), *The GATT Uruguay Round: A Negotiating History (1986–1992)* (The Hague: Kluwer Law and Taxation, 1993), pp. 1144, 1748–1752.

2.33 *MFN vs Selectivity*. This was the most important and debated issue in the Tokyo Round negotiations. The European Communities was a strong proponent of the selective applicability of a safeguard measure so that the measure could be focused on the exports from a few countries which were causing the most damage to their industries. Developing countries, the newly industrializing Asian countries in particular, strongly opposed the selective application, fearing that the selective measures would target exports from them.

2.34 *Compensation*. Developing countries generally favored compensation in return for the application of a safeguard measure. Developed countries, including the United States, argued that compensation is inconsistent with the temporary nature of a safeguard measure.

2.35 *Structural Adjustment*. Developing countries considered that safeguard measures should not substitute structural assistance and advocated the application of a safeguard measure only in conjunction with the requirement of structural adjustment. Developed countries, even if they acknowledged the need for structural adjustment, did not wish to be bound by such condition for the application of a safeguard measure.

2.36 *Preferential Treatment for Developing Countries*. Developing countries demanded certain preferential treatment to meet their development needs, including exemption of their products from the application of safeguard measures. Although developed countries were prepared to offer some preferential treatment to developing countries, these countries did not agree to the extent and conditions of the proposed preferential treatment to be included in the new rules.

2.37 *Injury Criteria*. Negotiators were in general agreement that there should be objective criteria for the determination of injury. While many developing countries demanded stringent injury criteria, developed countries preferred a certain flexibility in the assessment of injury. The draft text of 1978 included objective factors for injury determination such as "output, turnover, inventories, market share, profits, domestic employment and wages, utilization of productive capacity, productivity, and investment as well as the size of the market."[115]

2.38 *Notification and Consultation*. Developing countries considered that consultation should be required before the implementation of a safeguard measure.

---

115 *Draft Integrated Text on Safeguards*, GATT doc. No. MTN/SG/W/45 (December 11, 1978), p. 6.

Developed countries, in general, felt that the consultation should not amount to any pre-authorization of the application of a safeguard measure. The United States, however, stated that consultation-type procedures should rarely be bypassed.[116]

Surveillance Mechanism. Many delegations considered that a surveillance mechanism should be established to ensure that proper procedure is followed during the application of safeguard measures. Other delegations preferred the establishment of a more powerful, permanent body to determine the consistency of the measure with the relevant rules and to order compensation.[117] **2.39**

The impasse of the negotiations and the increasing economic difficulties at the end of the Tokyo Round had hardened the participants' positions on those issues discussed above, and compromise solutions were not found. However, efforts to create new rules on safeguards continued after the Tokyo Round. It should be noted that there was an inherent conflict in making the new rules on safeguards: on the one hand, the clear and detailed disciplines on safeguard measures had to be made; and on the other, countries would try to evade safeguard rules if those disciplines were too tight and compliance with them considered "too pricey" in comparison to other alternatives. Many countries complained at the start of the Tokyo negotiations that Article XIX was difficult to apply and did not meet their needs for effective protection without the burden of compensation or the danger of retaliation. Therefore, the new rules should resolve these difficulties, while maintaining the adequate level of scrutiny to prevent abuse. **2.40**

Proliferation of Gray-Area Measures.[118] The deficiency of the disciplines on safeguards also caused a growing dependency on so-called gray-area measures. The term "gray-area measure" refers to a voluntary restriction on trade agreed between the exporting and importing countries. Gray-area measures include voluntary export restraints (VERs), orderly marketing arrangements (OMAs), **2.41**

116 *United States Comments on Developing Country Safeguard Proposals*, GATT doc. No. MTN/SG/W/21 (February 14, 1977), p. 2 *cited in* Stewart, *supra* note 114, pp. 1751–1752.

117 Stewart, *supra* note 114, pp. 1751–1752.

118 *See* GATT Secretariat, *Uruguay Round – Group of Negotiation on Goods – Negotiating Group on Safeguards – Grey Area Measures – Background Note by the Secretariat* MTN.GNG/NG9/W/6 (September 16, 1987) for the description of the nature and background of gray-area measures. Ernst-Ulrich Petersmann's article "Grey Area Trade Policy and the Rule of Law" (1988) 22 *Journal of World Trade* 23–44 also provides an excellent account of the gray-area measures.

voluntary restraint agreements (VRAs),[119] and other similar bilateral agreements restraining trade.[120]

2.42 The substantial increase in exports from Asian countries such as Japan and Korea since the 1960s raised concern among competing domestic producers in European countries and the United States. Pressured by their domestic producers, the United States and Europe sought ways to limit imports from those Asian countries. The existing Article XIX measures were considered cumbersome, as Article XIX measures required an assessment of injury as well as compensation, and might result in retaliation absent agreement on compensation. Therefore, they negotiated gray-area measures outside the GATT which did not require injury assessment or compensation or involve a possibility of retaliation. Gray-area measures proliferated in the 1970s and 1980s as a means of restricting imports. In early 1991, 284 gray-area measures were known to be in existence, whereas only 24 safeguard measures under Article XIX were in force.[121]

2.43 The proliferation of gray-area measures raised serious concern for free trade. Economic inefficiency was an issue with gray-area measures. These measures disrupt a normal stream of trade and significantly diminish the economic gains that would have been obtained through unrestricted trade. By arbitrarily maintaining a reduced level of imports, domestic production and prices are kept at a higher level than they would be without restrictions on imports. As a result, the economic welfare of consumers is sacrificed for the benefit of selected domestic producers. As to the whole economy, the welfare loss to consumers resulting from the import restrictions is generally greater than the welfare gains to domestic producers, causing a net loss to the economy.[122] On the international plane, the quantity of trade is reduced, and there is a net loss to the global economy. Safeguard measures also restrict imports, but unlike gray-area measures, they are applied for a fixed term under the regulatory control of the SA, minimizing the possibility of abuse and economic loss.

---

119 The definitions of the terms "OMA," "VRA," and "VER" tend to be imprecise. For instance, under US foreign trade law, an "orderly marketing arrangement" is a formal bilateral trade agreement made by the US government under the provisions of sections 201–203 of the Trade Act of 1974. A VRA often requires the exporting country to apply the restraints, whereas an OMA allows the importing country to do so.

120 The forms of the trade restrictions placed by gray-area measures included: restrictions on the value (volume) of export sales; restrictions of market share; limits on the increase in export supplies; setting of the minimum export prices; restrictions on the conditions and timing of distribution. Michel M. Kostecki, "Marketing Strategies and Voluntary Export Restraints" (1991) 25 *Journal of World Trade* 87–99.

121 Stewart, *supra* note 114, pp. 1728–1729.

122 For the economic inefficiency of import restrictions, *see* Salvatore, *supra* note 30, pp. 222–228, 258–260. *See also* Sykes, *supra* note 30, pp. 35–46 and Rai, *supra* note 30, pp. 1–14.

Their inconsistency with the GATT provisions was another problem. Countries negotiated gray-area measures outside the GATT disciplines, and those measures arguably violated GATT Articles XI and XXIII, which generally prohibit quantitative restrictions as well as nullification or impairment of the benefit accruing to a contracting party under the GATT. Nevertheless, those measures were much less susceptible to legal challenges in the GATT, since neither the party accepting the restrictions nor a third party was likely to challenge them.[123] It was, therefore, necessary that this "outside" practice was somehow brought under the system. **2.44**

In addition, there was an issue with respect to the fairness of gray-area measures. Importing countries often demanded that unwilling exporting nations consent to gray-area measures. As the exporting countries depended upon their exports to the markets of the developed countries for their economic development, they had little choice but to accept such demands to avoid more severe restrictions on their trade. For instance, Japan accepted a voluntary restraint agreement on its exports of automobiles to the United States in the early 1980s under the threat of Congressional action for severe quota legislation against imports from Japan.[124] The EC,[125] the United States, and Canada accounted for nearly 90 percent of the gray-area measures taken, and those measures primarily targeted exports from the newly industrializing countries in Asia, including Korea and Japan.[126] The proliferation of gray-area measures, therefore, created inequitable conditions for the trade of exporting developing countries and became a serious impediment to free trade. **2.45**

In the final analysis, gray-area measures were inconsistent with the principal objective of the GATT, which was to promote free trade by preventing governments from arbitrarily interfering with international trade. In addition, the duration of gray-area measures was often uncertain, allowing the trade-distorting effect of those measures to continue without scrutiny. Accordingly, the danger existed that gray-area measures would turn the free trade promoted by the GATT into a system of trade regulated or "managed" by governments, as those measures were applied widely to a variety of products, **2.46**

---

123 Nonetheless, a third party may have an interest if exports are diverted to itself due to a gray-area measure. In the 1980s, the EC brought a case against the US–Japan semiconductor agreement before the GATT panel. *See Japan – Trade in Semi-Conductors* BISD 35S/116 (Report of the Panel adopted May 4, 1988). The GATT Panel found that the Japanese export monitoring system, as agreed with the United States, was inconsistent with GATT Article XI.

124 Kevin C. Kennedy, "Voluntary Restraint Agreements: A Threat to Representative Democracy" (1987) 11 *Hastings International and Comparative Law Review* 34–35.

125 *Supra* note 113.

126 GATT, *GATT Activities 1988* (1989), p. 45.

including textiles and clothing, agricultural products, steel products, electronic consumer products, and automobiles.[127]

2.47 As mentioned above, the efforts to settle new rules on safeguards were renewed after the Tokyo Round. The "GATT Work Programme," which was formed in 1979, recognized that the ongoing negotiations on safeguards are an essential element in the program,[128] although it was proved during the subsequent meetings that not much progress could be made on those issues, in particular on the selectivity issues. The Ministerial Declaration in November 1982 expressed concern about the lack of progress on safeguard negotiations, declaring that the contracting parties should "undertake, individually and jointly, to bring into effect expeditiously a comprehensive understanding on safeguards to be based on the principles of the General Agreement."[129]

2.48 A series of informal discussions and an examination of gray-area measures took place after the 1982 Declaration, but the participants were still unable to bridge their differences on the major issues. In 1983, the Director-General of GATT appointed an independent expert group to investigate problems facing the international trading system. In 1985, the group issued a report entitled "Trade Policies for a Better Future: Proposals for Action" (the Leutwiler Report), which included recommendations on safeguards. It recommended bringing gray-area measures into conformity with the GATT rules and eliminating those measures over a mutually agreeable time-period.[130] The Report also supported the non-discriminatory application of safeguard measures.[131] The Leutwiler Report, although it did not have any legal effect, made a significant impact on the subsequent Uruguay Round negotiations.

---

127 *See* Kostecki, *supra* note 120.

128 GATT doc. L/4884/Add.1/Annex VI, adopted on November 28, 1979, 26S/219, 220, para. 2.

129 GATT doc. L/5424, Ministerial Declaration adopted on November 29, 1982, 29S/9, 12, para. 7(vi).

130 GATT Secretariat, *Trade Policies for a Better Future: Proposals for Action* (1985), p. 38.

131 The group's ninth recommendation stated, "When emergency 'safeguard' protection for particular industry is needed, it should be provided only in accordance with the rules: it should not discriminate between different suppliers, should be time-limited, should be linked to adjustment assistance, and should be subject to continuing surveillance." *Id.*, p. 42. The group also noted, "We are in no doubt that safeguard rules of GATT must outlaw discrimination. Time and again the negotiation of voluntary export restraints with one supplier (the most 'disruptive' and therefore by definition the most competitive) has been followed by a proliferation of bilateral deals with *all* efficient suppliers who are not in a position to refuse, lending to virtual cartelization of world markets .... It is therefore untrue that 'selective' action helps to limit the extent of disruption of trade. Moreover, the process of discrimination against the most efficient suppliers contravenes the principle of comparative advantage and maximizes the cost to the world economy of the protection granted to the inefficient." *Id.*, p. 43.

2.4 NEGOTIATIONS IN THE URUGUAY ROUND AND THE AGREEMENT ON SAFEGUARDS

Multilateral negotiations on safeguards resumed in the Uruguay Round negotiations (1986–1994). The Ministerial Declaration in 1986, which launched the Uruguay Round negotiations, set the direction for the negotiations on safeguards. The Declaration provided that an agreement on safeguards (i) should be based on the basic principles of the GATT; (ii) should contain, *inter alia*, the following elements: transparency; objective criteria for action, including the concept of serious injury or threat thereof; temporary nature; degressivity (i.e., the measure should be relaxed regularly during its lifetime); structural adjustment; compensation and retaliation; notification; consultation; multilateral surveillance and dispute settlement; and (iii) should clarify and reinforce the disciplines of the General Agreement and should apply to all contracting parties.[132] **2.49**

The participants in the Uruguay Round negotiations began from the positions that they held in the previous negotiations, and the gap between those positions remained significant. Again, the issue of selectivity remained the most difficult and important one throughout the negotiations. The possibility of compromise arose as the EC, the strongest proponent of selective application, proposed that it might drop support for selectivity in return for flexibility in the allocation of quotas. A series of draft agreements were proposed from 1989 to 1991, as an attempt to build consensus and foster further negotiations. Through difficult negotiations and compromises, the historic agreement on safeguards was finally taking shape.[133] It should be noted that the Chairman of the Safeguard negotiation group, George Maciel, was instrumental in bringing success to the safeguards negotiations by producing proposed drafts consistently, which progressively narrowed differences among the participants. The progress of the negotiation and the final outcome in the major issues are as follows. **2.50**

Selectivity. Many developing countries, including India and the Pacific Rim countries (Australia, Hong Kong, Korea, New Zealand, Japan, and Singapore), concerned that their exports would be the target of selective application of protective measures, consistently supported the adoption of the MFN principle **2.51**

---

132 *Ministerial Declaration on the Uruguay Round*, GATT doc. GATT/MIN.DEC 86-1572, section 1.D (September 6, 1986), 33S/19, 24–25.

133 The final text agreement on safeguards was included in the GATT Director-General, Dunkel's package put out in December 1991. *Draft Final Act Embodying the Results of the Uruguay Round of Multilateral Trade Negotiations*, GATT doc. MTN.TNC/W/FA (December 20, 1991).

in the application of safeguard measures.[134] The EC, on the other hand, held to its previous position in support of the selective application of safeguard measures.[135] The United States also supported the application of selective safeguards.[136] Proponents of selective application reiterated that it would be reasonable to restrain imports that hurt domestic industries the most and to leave the others unaffected by the safeguard measure.

2.52 As mentioned above, the EC expressed its intention to accept the MFN principle in return for a certain flexibility in the quota allocation. In the final compromise, the MFN principle was adopted in the Agreement on Safeguards, thereby prohibiting the application of safeguards on a selective basis in principle (SA Article 2.2). However, selectivity was also accommodated to the extent that a Member is permitted to deviate from the MFN principle in allocating quotas where imports from certain Members have increased disproportionately in relation to the total increase of imports of the product concerned during the representative period (SA Article 5.2(b)).[137]

2.53 *Gray-Area Measures.* The United States submitted a position paper on safeguards to the negotiating group in 1987 entitled, "US Thoughts on Safeguards."[138] In the paper the United States introduced five possible options, ranging from the total elimination of gray-area measures to the legitimatization of the measures, subject to more clear and precise disciplines. Developing countries generally favored the elimination of the measures.[139] By November 1989, most countries supported phasing out gray-area measures or bringing such measures into conformity with the new safeguards agreement.[140] Article 11 of the SA prohibits all gray-area measures.[141]

2.54 *Compensation and Retaliation.* During the Uruguay Round negotiations, most countries supported preserving the right to compensation and retaliation in some form. On the other hand, the participants were also aware that the requirement of compensation and the authorization of suspension of conces-

---

134 Stewart, *supra* note 114, pp. 1761–1762.

135 *Id.*, p. 1764.

136 *Id.*, pp. 1768–1769.

137 *Id.*, pp. 1795–1796. Article 5.2(a) of the SA requires Members to allocate quotas among exporting countries based on their share during a previous representative period. The provision authorizing deviation from MFN principles under Article 5.2(b) is designed to ensure that the countries that contributed to the problem significantly by increasing their exports rapidly in recent years are not rewarded by receiving a large quota share.

138 *United States Thoughts on Safeguards*, MTN.GNG./NG9/W/12 (December 9, 1987).

139 Stewart, *supra* note 114, p. 1771.

140 GATT doc. MTN.GMG/NG9/13 (December 12, 1989).

141 Refer to the relevant discussion in Chapter 9.1 *infra*.

sions under Article XIX had been an important reason for countries to deviate from safeguards and adopt gray-area measures. In order to provide an incentive for countries to comply with the rules on safeguards and not to resort to measures outside the safeguard mechanism, the negotiators agreed to suspend the right to retaliation for the first three years of the application of a safeguard, provided that the measure conforms to the agreement and that it is also based on an absolute, rather than relative, increase in imports (SA Article 8.3).[142]

Injury Criteria. As in the previous Tokyo Round, developing countries pressed for tougher criteria for injury determination and argued that the injury determination should be made conditional on findings of a direct causal link between increased imports and of an overall decline in the condition of domestic producers.[143] However, the EC and United States preferred to retain flexibility in the determination of injury. **2.55**

A series of injury criteria, including increases in imports, market share taken by imports, sales, production, productivity, capacity utilization, profits and losses, and employment, were included in the text (SA Article 4.2(a)). The United States emphasized that neither of the listed factors, nor even several factors, may necessarily be decisive in the injury determination, and that the relevant factors to be considered might differ from case to case.[144] The requirement for the causal link between increased imports and the injury was also included (SA Article 4.2(b)). **2.56**

Structural Adjustment. The participants generally considered that safeguard measures should not be a substitution for structural adjustment. Many developing countries considered that the implementation of a structural adjustment plan by the industry seeking relief should be required in conjunction with a safeguard measure. Developed countries, including the United States and Japan, opposed the inclusion of the structural adjustment requirement, which would encourage governments to invest financially in their domestic industries.[145] **2.57**

In the final compromise, the text would note the facilitation of structural adjustment as the objective of a safeguard measure in the Preamble, but there would be no specific requirement of structural adjustment. The evidence of **2.58**

142 Stewart, *supra* note 114, p. 1798.

143 *Communication from Australia, Hong Kong, Korea, New Zealand, and Singapore*, GATT doc. MTN.GNG/NG9/W/4 (May 25, 1987).

144 *Submission by the United States*, GATT doc. MTN.GNG/NG9/W/23 (June 13, 1989), p. 3.

145 Stewart, *supra* note 114, pp. 1774–1775.

structural adjustment would be required for an extension of the measure (SA Article 7.2).[146]

2.59 *Special Rules for Developing Countries.* The negotiators were generally prepared to offer some preferential treatment to accommodate the development needs of developing countries. A longer period for the application of safeguard measures and a lower injury standard were proposed to afford preferential treatment to developing countries.[147] Developed countries were reluctant to relax the general conditions for the application of safeguards (e.g., lowering the injury criteria) for the benefit of developing countries.

2.60 The participants agreed that safeguard measures are not to be applied to products originating from a developing country where both the market share of the product from that particular developing country and the aggregate market share of such product from the other developing countries were below specified levels (SA Article 9.1). It was also agreed that developing countries could maintain safeguard measures for a longer period (SA Article 9.2). However, they did not adopt a proposal to entirely exempt the least-developed countries from safeguard measures.[148]

2.61 *Procedural Issues.* The participants were in favor of more precise and transparent procedures regarding the application of safeguards. The United States stressed that safeguard measures should be transparent, temporary, degressive, and subject to review and termination when no longer necessary.[149] The negotiators agreed to adopt elaborate procedural requirements for investigation (SA Article 3). The text would also provide for a mid-term review (SA Article 7.4); detailed notification requirements and a consultation process (SA Article 12); and a monitoring system to ensure proper application of safeguard measures (SA Article 13). It bears mentioning that the United States was instrumental in bringing new concepts to the disciplines on safeguards, based on its own safeguard provisions.[150] Those concepts included: (i) injury criteria; (ii) procedures to ensure transparency; (iii) a durational limit to a safeguard measure; and (iv) the liberalization requirement for a measure extending over one year.[151]

---

146 *Draft Final Act Embodying the Results of the Uruguay Round of Multilateral Trade Negotiations*, GATT doc. MTN.TNC/W/FA (December 20, 1991).

147 Stewart, *supra* note 114, p. 1775.

148 Complete exemption should be offered to the imports from the least-developed countries in consideration of their dire economic needs. *See* Chapter 15.1 *infra* for the relevant discussion.

149 Stewart, *supra* note 114, pp. 1764–1765.

150 Chapter 12 introduces the US safeguard provisions ("Section 201 measure").

151 *Statement of Administrative Action for the Uruguay Round Agreement on Safeguards, Message from the President of the United States Transmitting the Uruguay Round Trade Agreements, Texts of Agreements Implementing Bill, Statement of Administrative Action on Required Supporting Statements*, H.R. Doc. No. 316 vol. 1, 103rd Cong., 2nd Sess. 956–957 (September 27, 1994).

PART II

AGREEMENT ON SAFEGUARDS

3

ARTICLE XIX AND AGREEMENT ON SAFEGUARDS

3.1 A LONG-AWAITED AGREEMENT

3.01 Difficult negotiations had continued for decades and failures had been repeated before the world finally saw the Agreement on Safeguards at the end of the Uruguay Round negotiations. In the meantime, the disciplines on safeguards crumbled due to the noted deficiency of Article XIX.[152] Rule-evading gray-area measures had proliferated, undermining the objective of free trade in the process. Therefore, no matter how difficult it had proved time and again, it was essential to agree upon new rules on safeguards, and it was finally achieved in the Uruguay Round negotiations.

3.02 The delicate balance and compromises of the conflicting interests between developed and developing countries are found in the text of the new Agreement. For instance, the SA declares the principle of the non-discriminatory application of a safeguard measure and prohibits all gray-area measures. At the same time, it also accommodates the need to focus on imports from certain Members where such imports have increased disproportionately in relation to the total imports, by allowing the importing countries to deviate from the MFN allocation of quota.

3.03 The Agreement on Safeguards, composed of 14 Articles in total, provides detailed substantive and procedural requirements for the application of a safe-

152 *See* Chapter 2.3 *supra* for the relevant discussion.

guard measure. The Agreement, hailed as "a heroic statement of principle,"[153] has objectives of re-establishing multilateral control over safeguards and eliminating measures that escape such control.[154] It also emphasizes the importance of structural adjustment and the need for a comprehensive agreement. That the SA establishes rules for the application of safeguard measures is also clarified.[155]

This chapter discusses the applicability of Article XIX after the implementation of the SA in 1995. The remaining chapters in Part II introduce and analyze the provisions of the SA in the following order: Article 2—general conditions (including standard of review and burden of proof); Article 4—injury and causation; procedural requirements (Articles 3 and 12); application of safeguard measure (Articles 5 and 7); compensation and retaliation (Article 8); prohibition of gray-area measures (Article 11); and the remaining issues, including provisional measures (Article 6), differential treatment (Article 9), surveillance (Article 13), and the final assessment of the SA ("Is the Safeguards Agreement Working?"). The discussion of SA provisions accompanies proposals to modify the existing provisions where deemed necessary to improve the clarity and effectiveness of the disciplines on safeguards.[156] **3.04**

3.2 "UNFORESEEN DEVELOPMENTS" CLAUSE[157]

The Old and the New: GATT and WTO. The success of the Uruguay Round in 1994 and the subsequent beginning of the WTO marked an end to the five decades of the GATT regime. The old GATT provisions were preserved and incorporated into Annex 1A of the WTO Agreement as "GATT 1994." This incorporation means that the rules of GATT comprise part of the WTO disciplines to the extent that there is no conflict with the new rules agreed in **3.05**

153 Jackson, *supra* note 78.

154 Preamble of the SA. *See infra* Appendix 3 for the full text of the SA.

155 Article 1 of the Agreement provides that "[t]his Agreement establishes rules for the application of safeguard measures which shall be understood to mean those measures provided for in Article XIX of GATT 1994."

156 *See also* Annex 4, Proposed Modifications of Agreement on Safeguards, for the specific proposal for the modifications.

157 For Chapters 3.2 and 3.3, extensive references are made to the author's previous works, "Critical Issues in the Application of the WTO Rules on Safeguards – In the Light of the Recent Panel Reports and the Appellate Body Decisions" (2000), *supra* note 1 and "Destabilization of the Discipline on Safeguards? – Inherent Problems with the Continuing Application of Article XIX after the Settlement of the Agreement on Safeguards" (2001), *supra* note 1.

the Uruguay Round.[158] According to this framework, one might consider that GATT Article XIX still applies after the implementation of the SA.[159]

3.06 Nevertheless, the long negotiation process for the conclusion of the Agreement on Safeguards, as well as the comprehensive nature of the Agreement,[160] makes it fairly evident that this new Agreement on Safeguards is meant to replace the outdated provisions of Article XIX and provide all the substantive and procedural rules for the application of safeguards. The negotiators of Article XIX did not intend to keep the provisions of Article XIX as additional disciplines on safeguards to those of the SA.[161] Members had long sought to replace the archaic provisions of Article XIX with more detailed and comprehensive rules on safeguards, and finally achieved this objective with the conclusion of the SA.[162]

3.07 *Unforeseen Developments.*[163] The question of whether the new Agreement is indeed a sole authority of safeguards was raised in the first WTO panel cases on safeguards, *Korea – Dairy Products* and *Argentina – Footwear*. The specific question was whether a particular clause in Article XIX that is apparently omitted from the SA constitutes a legal requirement for the application of a safeguard measure.[164] Article XIX:1(a) provides:

---

158 A general interpretative note to Annex 1A provides, "In the event of conflict between a provision of the General Agreement on Tariffs and Trade 1994 and a provision of another agreement in Annex 1A to the Agreement Establishing the World Trade Organization, the provision of the other agreement shall prevail to the extent of the conflict."

159 The Panel in *Korea – Dairy Products* stated, "It is now well established that the WTO Agreement is a 'Single Undertaking' and therefore all WTO obligations are generally cumulative and Members must comply with all of them simultaneously unless there is a formal conflict between them" (footnote omitted). *Korea – Dairy Products, supra* note 70, para. 7.38.

160 The SA repeats and incorporates provisions in Article XIX with substantial modifications and elaborations.

161 Thus, the Panel in Argentina determined that safeguard measures that conform to the provisions of the SA are also consistent with Article XIX. *Argentina – Footwear, supra* note 70, para. 8.69.

162 Refer to the discussion of the history of negotiations on safeguards in Chapter 2 *supra*. The remainder of Chapter 3.2 provides arguments in support of the sole authority of the SA.

163 The author does not support the Appellate Body's decision to hold the demonstration of "unforeseen developments" under Article XIX as a legal condition for the application of safeguard. *See also* Jacques Bourgeois, "Article 1 SA," *in* Rüdiger Wolfrum, Peter-Tobias Stoll, and Michael Koebele (eds.), *WTO: Trade Remedies*, Max Planck Commentaries on World Trade Law (Leiden: Martinus Nijhoff, 2008), pp. 260–261. For a dissenting view, *see* Felix Mueller, "Is the General Agreement on Tariffs and Trade Article XIX 'Unforeseen Developments Clause' Still Effective Under the Agreement on Safeguards?" (2003) 37(6) *Journal of World Trade* 1119–1151. *See also* Weihuan Zhou and Mandy Meng Fang, "Unforeseen Developments' Before and After US – Safeguard Measure on PV Products: High Standard or New Standard?" (2023) 22(5) *World Trade Review* 541–561.

164 *Korea – Dairy Products, supra* note 70, paras. 4.142–4.254. *Argentina – Footwear, supra* note 70, paras. 5.1–5.66.

> If, *as a result of unforeseen developments* and of the effect of the obligations incurred by a contracting party under this Agreement, including tariff concessions, any product is being imported into the territory of that contracting party in such increased quantities and under such conditions as to cause or threaten serious injury to domestic producers in that territory of like or directly competitive products, the contracting party shall be free, in respect of such product, and to extent and for such time as may be necessary to prevent or remedy such injury, to suspend the obligation in whole or in part or to withdraw or modify the concession (emphasis added).

The general conditions for the application of a safeguard measure under the SA do not include the "unforeseen developments" clause. Article 2.1 of the SA reads as follows: **3.08**

> A Member may apply a safeguard measure to a product only if that Member has determined, pursuant to the provisions set out below, that such product is being imported into its territory in such increased quantities, absolute or relative to domestic production, and under such conditions as to cause or threaten to cause serious injury to the domestic industry that produces like or directly competitive products. (footnotes omitted)

In the first safeguard cases cited above, the European Communities[165] argued that the clause in question requires Members to establish the existence of "unforeseen developments" that led to increases in imports, although that particular clause is not found in the SA.[166] According to this argument, the cumulative applicability of both Article XIX and the SA justifies the legal requirement that is included in Article XIX but not in the SA. This argument faced an objection that the omission of the clause from the SA was intentional; thus, there is a conflict between the provisions of Article XIX:1(a) and those of the SA, the latter of which should prevail.[167] **3.09**

The provisions of the SA do not clarify the legal relationship between Article XIX and the SA.[168] The Panel in *Korea – Dairy Products* found that Article **3.10**

---

165 *Supra* note 113.

166 *Korea – Dairy Products*, *supra* note 70, paras. 4.142–4.146 and 4.149–4.168.

167 *Id.*, paras. 4.142–4.146 and *Argentina – Footwear*, *supra* note 70, paras. 5.1–5.5. Fernando Piérola-Castro, a senior counsel at the Advisory Center on WTO Law, also opined that the negotiation history "suggests an intent to omit the notion [of unforeseen development] contained in Article XIX:1(a)." Fernando Piérola-Castro, *WTO Agreement on Safeguards and Article XIX of GATT: A Detailed Commentary* (New York: Cambridge University Press, 2022), p. 22.

168 Article 1 states that the Agreement provides rules for the application of safeguard measures "provided for in Article XIX of GATT 1994." The provision does not clarify the legal relationship between Article XIX and the SA. In contrast, Article 1 of the Agreement on Implementation of Article VI of the GATT 1994 specifies the legal relationship between that Agreement and the relevant provisions of the GATT: "[A]n antidumping measure shall be applied only under the circumstances provided for in Article VI of GATT 1994 and pursuant to investigations initiated and conducted in accordance with this Agreement. The following provisions govern the application of Article VI of GATT 1994 in so far as action is taken under antidumping legislation or regulation."

XIX:1 is still generally applicable, and there is no formal conflict between the provisions of Article XIX:1 and Article 2.1 of the SA.[169] However, it rejected the argument that the "unforeseen developments" clause creates any legal obligation.[170] It considered the clause to be "an explanation of why an Article XIX measure may be needed, taking into account the fact that at the time (1947) the CONTRACTING PARTIES had just agreed (for the first time) on multilateral tariff bindings and on a general prohibition against quotas."[171]

3.11 The Panel in *Argentina – Footwear* also arrived at the same conclusion. It determined that it was "unrealistic to assume that the practice of non-enforcement of the unforeseen developments condition was unknown when the new Safeguards Agreement was negotiated during the Uruguay Round. If it had been the object and purpose of the Safeguards Agreement to clarify and reinforce the disciplines of Article XIX and to re-establish multilateral control over safeguard measures also with respect to the unforeseen developments condition, the need for clear rules, detailed definitions and refined procedures regarding this condition would have been of particular importance. To put it differently, if the reinforcement of the unforeseen developments condition had been one of the objectives of the new Safeguards Agreement, one would expect to find detailed provisions concerning it in the new agreement, rather than an express omission of that criterion."[172] The Panel subsequently held that safeguard measures consistent with the requirements of the Safeguards Agreement also satisfy the requirements of Article XIX.[173]

3.12 This ruling acknowledged the sole authority of the Agreement on Safeguards, although neither of the Panels in *Korea – Dairy Products* and *Argentina – Footwear* stated that the SA replaces Article XIX. Those Panel decisions were appealed to the Appellate Body. The Appellate Body concurred with the Panel in *Korea – Dairy Products* that both the Agreement on Safeguards and Article XIX apply to the application of safeguards, but did not consider the "unforeseen developments" clause to be merely explanatory. The Appellate Body did not find that this clause "establish[ed] independent conditions for the application of a safeguard measure, additional to the condition set forth in the second clause of that paragraph," but nevertheless determined that it

---

169 *Korea – Dairy Products*, *supra* note 70, para. 7.39. This conflict issue was not closely examined by the Appellate Body when it determined that the unforeseen developments clause in Article XIX:1(a) constitutes a legal requirement for the application of a safeguard. *Korea – Dairy Products*, *supra* note 71, paras. 68–90.

170 *Korea – Dairy Products*, *supra* note 70, para. 7.42.

171 *Id.*

172 *Argentina – Footwear*, *supra* note 70, para. 8.66.

173 *Id.*, para. 8.69.

"*describes certain circumstances which must be demonstrated as a matter of fact for a safeguard measure to be applied consistently with the provisions of Article XIX of the GATT 1994*" (emphasis added).[174]

It is unclear from the Appellate Body decision what distinguishes "an independent condition" from "circumstances which must be demonstrated as a matter of fact." A subsequent Panel found that the latter term could be read to imply a lesser threshold than the former.[175] Regardless of whether it is a greater or lesser threshold, the Appellate Body decision made this particular clause in Article XIX a legal requirement for the application of a safeguard measure, as the Appellate Body determined that the existence of unforeseen developments is "a prerequisite" that must be demonstrated "in order for a safeguard measure to be applied."[176] **3.13**

Adding a legal requirement that is not included in the SA causes significant problems for the disciplines on safeguards. First, the addition of such a requirement does not seem consistent with the intent of the negotiators in the Uruguay Round.[177] The Panel statement in *Argentina – Footwear* cited above makes this point clearly. In fact, the negotiation history of safeguards reveals that the SA was intended to be the sole legal authority on safeguards: e.g., the earlier version of the draft agreement on safeguards did contain the "unforeseen developments" clause. By mid-1990, however, the clause was omitted from the draft, while other conditions of Article XIX were repeated almost verbatim.[178] Pierre Didier accounts that "a 1990 draft of an agreement included ['unforeseen developments'] and amplified it by imposing the obligation to establish an 'unforeseen, sudden and significant increase'. Both the United States and the EC rejected this terminology as being too difficult or restrictive to apply."[179] **3.14**

Therefore, it is only reasonable to conclude that this omission was intentional.[180] In addition, the exclusion of the clause would have been consistent with **3.15**

174 *Korea – Dairy Products, supra* note 71, para. 85. *Argentina – Footwear, supra* note 71, para. 92. *See also* the Panel decision in *Ukraine – Passenger Cars, supra* note 70, para. 7.52 (noting "[c]ircumstances" are distinguished from "conditions").

175 *United States – Lamb Meat, supra* note 70, para. 7.19.

176 *United States – Lamb Meat supra* note 71, para. 71.

177 *See also* Lee (2000), *supra* note 1, p. 136.

178 GATT Doc. MTN.GNG/NG9/W/25 (June 27, 1989).

179 Pierre Didier, *Les principaux accords de L'OMC et leur transposition dans le Communaute Europeene* (1997), pp. 271–272.

180 Piérola-Castro, *supra* note 167.

prevalent practices among Members at the time of the decision.[181] Academia, in general, seems to agree that the existence of "unforeseen developments" is not a substantive requirement.[182] The Preamble of the SA also indicates the intent of the Uruguay Round negotiators to this effect: it states in relevant part, "Recognizing further that … *a comprehensive agreement*, applicable to all Members and based on the basic principles of GATT 1994, is called for" (emphasis added), affirming that the SA is indeed a comprehensive agreement, including all the conditions and requirements for the application of a safeguard measure.

3.16 Secondly, the clause is too ambiguous to be an objective legal requirement.[183] The meaning of the "unforeseen developments" clause was first examined in an early GATT panel case, *Withdrawal by the United States of a Tariff Concession under Article XIX of the General Agreement ("Hatter's Fur Case")*, where the members of the Working Party except the United States agreed "that the term 'unforeseen development' should be interpreted to mean developments occurring after the negotiation of the relevant tariff concession which it would not be reasonable to expect that the negotiators of the country making the concessions could and should have foreseen at the time when the concession was negotiated."[184] According to this interpretation, the reasonableness of the foresight, that is, the *foreseeability* of those developments, should be the standard to determine the existence of "unforeseen developments."

3.17 The Appellate Body took a different view. Unlike the GATT panel, it emphasized the distinction between "unforeseen" and "unforeseeable," and determined that the clause would mean the former rather than the latter.[185]

---

181 A survey showed that the demonstration of unforeseen developments had been omitted in the vast majority of safeguard applications after the implementation of the SA. Among 28 surveyed safeguard applications since 1995, only five showed any discussion of unforeseen developments, suggesting that many Members had not perceived the demonstration of "unforeseen developments" as a legal requirement for the application of a safeguard measure. Cliff Stevenson, "Are World Trade Organization Members Correctly Applying World Trade Organization Rules in Safeguard Determinations?" (2004) 38 *Journal of World Trade* 324–327.

182 *See* M. Bronckers, "Voluntary Export Restraints and the GATT 1994 Agreement on Safeguards," *in* J.H.J. Bourgeois, F. Berrod and E. Fournier (eds.), *The Uruguay Round Results: A European Lawyers' Perspective* (European University Press, 1995), p. 275, and M. Trebilcock and R. Howse, *The Regulation of International Trade* (Routledge, 2nd ed., 1999), p. 228. *See also* Tilottama Raychaudhuri, "The Unforeseen Developments Clause in Safeguards under the WTO: Confusions in Compliance" (2010) 11(1) *The Estey Centre Journal of International Law and Trade Policy* 302–320; Rai, *supra* note 30, pp. 32–49; Sykes, *supra* note 30, pp. 102–106; Bourgeois, *supra* note 163.

183 *See* Lee (2000), *supra* note 1, p. 135.

184 GATT Panel Report in *Withdrawal by the United States of a Tariff Concession under Article XIX of the General Agreement*, GATT/CP/106, report adopted on October 22, 1951, GATT/CP.6/SR.19, Sales No. GATT/1951-2, p. 10, para. 9.

185 *Korea – Dairy Products*, *supra* note 71, para. 84.

The difference between the views of the GATT panel and the Appellate Body demonstrates the equivocal and ambiguous nature of the clause. The absence of foresight is a question of subjective knowledge and therefore difficult to prove as a matter of fact. What evidence should be sufficient to demonstrate the absence of foresight? If evidence is needed to establish that such developments could not have been foreseen, it becomes a *foreseeability* test, from which the Appellate Body made a clear distinction. If, on the other hand, nothing more than the Member's claim would be sufficient, it would make the requirement virtually a nullity. The Panel in *United States – Lamb Meat* found that the term "unforeseen" implies a lesser threshold than "unforeseeable,"[186] but this distinction does not provide any clear standard for the demonstration of "unforeseen developments."[187]

The subsequent Panel in *United States – Steel Products* considered that there is an objective element in the standard for determining "unforeseen developments." The Panel was of the view that the appropriate focus is on what *should or could have been* foreseen in light of the circumstances and that the standard is not "what the specific negotiators had in mind but rather what they could (reasonably) have had in mind."[188] The *Steel* Panel suggested a test to determine whether the developments in question were *unforeseeable* rather than *unforeseen*, going back to the approach taken by the earlier GATT panel as discussed above.[189] However, the Appellate Body had taken a different view and made a distinction between "unforeseen" and "unforeseeable."[190] **3.18**

186 *United States – Lamb Meat*, *supra* note 70, para. 7.22.

187 The ambiguity of the requirement led to a disagreement between the Appellate Body and a subsequent Panel. The Panel in *Argentina – Preserved Peaches* stated that it "did not agree with the statement by the Appellate Body in *Argentina – Footwear (EC)* that the increased quantities of imports should have been 'unforeseen' or 'unexpected'. The text of Article XIX:1(a), together with the Appellate Body's own discussion of it and earlier conclusion regarding the logical connection between the circumstances in the first clause of Article XIX:1(a) – including unforeseen developments – and the conditions in the second clause – including an increase in imports – show that this is not a requirement for the imposition of a safeguard measure" (footnote omitted). *Argentina – Preserved Peaches*, *supra* note 70, para. 7.24. For a further discussion of disagreements between panels and the Appellate Body in the WTO safeguards jurisprudence, *see* Dukgeun Ahn and Hyerim Kim, "Judicial Conflicts between Panels and the Appellate Body in the WTO Safeguard Jurisprudence" (2020) 54(6) *Journal of World Trade* 961–982.

188 *United States – Steel Products*, *supra* note 70, para 10.43.

189 The Panel cited the decision by the GATT Panel and stated that the Panel's point was "recognized early in GATT by the *US – Fur Felt Hats* decision, which characterized unforeseen developments as 'developments [...] which it would not be reasonable to expect that the negotiators of the country making the concession could and should have foreseen at the time when the concession was negotiated'." *Id.*

190 *Korea – Dairy Products*, *supra* note 71, para. 84. The Appellate Body in *United States – Steel Products* noted that the increased imports must be an effect or outcome of the unforeseen development, reiterating its earlier position. *United States – Steel Products*, *supra* note 71, para. 315.

3.19 Thirdly, the reading of the relevant provisions of the SA supports the position that the Agreement constitutes a comprehensive set of rules on the application of safeguards.[191] The Appellate Body determined that the references to Article XIX made in Articles 1 and 11.1(a) indicate the continuing applicability of Article XIX.[192] Article 1 provides, "This Agreement establishes rules for the application of safeguard measures which shall be understood to mean those measures provided for in Article XIX of GATT 1994." The relevant phrase in Article 11.1(a) provides, "A Member shall not take or seek any emergency action on imports of particular products as set forth in Article XIX of GATT 1994 unless such action conforms with the provisions of that Article applied in accordance with this Agreement."

3.20 Despite the position held by the Appellate Body, the references to Article XIX in those phrases do not necessarily mean that every clause in Article XIX, such as the "unforeseen developments" clause, should be given legal effect. On the contrary, the controlling phrase in Article 1 is "This Agreement establishes rules for the application of safeguard measures…," and that in Article 11.1(a) is "… shall not take or seek any emergency action on imports … unless such action conforms with the provisions of that Article *applied in accordance with this Agreement*" (emphasis added). These clauses indicate that the SA sets the comprehensive rules for the application of a safeguard measure. Therefore, the old phrase in Article XIX, not included in the new rules, cannot be considered a requirement for the application of a safeguard measure. The same indication is made in the Preamble of the SA that recognizes that "a comprehensive agreement … is called for."[193] If the SA is not this comprehensive agreement, including all the substantive and procedural requirements for the application of a safeguard measure, what is?

3.21 The general conditions for the application of a safeguard measure, provided in Article 2.1 of the SA, neither include the "unforeseen developments" clause nor make any reference to the relevant provisions in Article XIX. It is difficult to concede that the Article would repeat all the other conditions of Article XIX almost verbatim while omitting the "unforeseen developments" clause if the clause was to be considered part of the general requirement. The provision of Article 8.3 also suggests that the SA includes all the legal requirements. Under Article 8.3, the right of retaliation is suspended for three years where

---

191 *See* Lee (2000), *supra* note 1, pp. 135–136.

192 *Korea – Dairy Products*, *supra* note 71, para. 77.

193 The relevant part of the Preamble provides, "Recognizing further that, for these purposes, a comprehensive agreement, applicable to all Members and based on the basic principles of GATT 1994, is called for."

a safeguard measure is based on an absolute increase in imports and *conforms to the provisions to the Agreement* (emphasis added). If Article XIX was to preserve any requirement that is not included in the Agreement on Safeguards, this three-year bar to retaliation should have been made inapplicable to a safeguard measure that is inconsistent with *either* the provisions of the Agreement *or* those of Article XIX, but Article 8.3 makes no reference to Article XIX. Such a reference would have been made should the provisions of Article XIX still be applicable.

In addition, the requirement of "unforeseen developments" does not seem to serve any useful purpose.[194] It is unlikely that any Members would have granted import concessions to the extent that they did had they foreseen any developments that would lead to serious injury or threat thereof to their own domestic industry. Even in the unlikely circumstance that they did, there seems to be no reason to prohibit them from applying safeguard measures. Suppose that a Member foresaw possible developments that may cause injury to their domestic industry but nevertheless proceeded with granting import concessions, believing that safeguard measures would be available should they need them. The granting of import concessions in reliance on future availability of a safeguard measure is positive for the promotion of free trade since the Member may not even have considered the import concessions without possible recourse to safeguard measures. This shows that the requirement of "unforeseen developments" serves no useful purpose and may even discourage Members from making more concessions. Therefore, the clause should be removed from the disciplines on safeguards. **3.22**

The Appellate Body stated that had the Uruguay Round negotiators intended to *expressly omit* the "unforeseen developments" clause, they would and could have said so in the *Agreement on Safeguards*.[195] On the contrary, the WTO agreements, including the SA, do not make an express statement about the intent of the Uruguay Round negotiators every time they modify or revise the relevant GATT provisions. Such an intent is often understood in the context of the new provisions. Nevertheless, perhaps a specific provision in the SA that affirms the sole authority of the SA might be necessary in order to clarify the intent of the Uruguay Round negotiators. **3.23**

How to Meet the Current Requirement? As ambiguous and dubious as this requirement may be, a Member proposing to apply a safeguard measure would **3.24**

194 *See also* Lee (2001), *supra* note 1, pp. 1236–1242.
195 *Argentina – Footwear*, *supra* note 71, para. 88.

have to demonstrate "unforeseen developments" as required by the Appellate Body decisions. First, Members would have to identify certain developments that have led to the increase in imports causing or threatening to cause serious injury to the domestic industry.[196] Then Members would have to proceed to answer the following two questions: *why* were certain developments not "foreseen" and *how* did these unforeseen developments lead to the injurious increase in imports?[197] The Appellate Body affirmed that the national authorities would have to provide a reasoned explanation of their conclusion about the "unforeseen developments" subject to the same standard of review previously set out by Panels and the Appellate Body.[198]

3.25 A previous Panel determined that the investigation report must specifically examine these "unforeseen developments."[199] The Panel stated that "it must be clear from the published report that the investigating authorities examined the existence of unforeseen developments and came to a reasoned conclusion in this regard."[200] The Appellate Body affirmed the Panel's decision that the demonstration of the "unforeseen developments" must be documented in the published report of the investigating authorities.[201] If the published report does not discuss or offer any explanation as to *why* certain factors mentioned are regarded as "unforeseen developments," then the report does not demonstrate that the safeguard measure has been applied as a result of "unforeseen developments."[202]

196 Thus, the Panel in *Dominican Republic – Polypropylene Bags and Tubular Fabric* examined, as the first step of the analysis, whether the investigating authority (European Commission) identified any unforeseen development. *Dominican Republic – Polypropylene Bags and Tubular Fabric, supra* note 70, paras. 7.88–7.95.

197 *United States – Steel Products, supra* note 70, para. 10.69. *See also Dominican Republic – Polypropylene Bags and Tubular Fabric, supra* note 70, paras. 7.96–7.141.

198 *United States – Steel Products, supra* note 71, para. 279. *See* Chapter 4.1 *infra* for the relevant discussion of the standard of review.

199 Article 3.1 of the SA provides that "[t]he competent authorities shall publish a report setting forth their findings and reasoned conclusions reached on all pertinent issues of fact and law." *See* Chapter 6.1 *infra* for a discussion of investigation report.

200 *United States – Lamb Meat, supra* note 70, para. 7.29. The Panel also stated, "In our view, this substantive requirement of GATT Article XIX:1 could be fulfilled even if the conclusion in question did not use the precise terminology 'unforeseen developments.' Nevertheless, no matter how such a conclusion is presented in an authority's determination, there needs to be a conclusion that makes clear that changes that had not been anticipated had taken place in the market, and that these changes had resulted in a situation in which increased imports was causing or threatening to cause serious injury." *Id.*, para. 7.31. The Panel in *Dominican Republic – Polypropylene Bags and Tubular Fabric* also affirmed that it is in the published report of the competent authority that this Panel must examine whether the authority provided findings and reasoned conclusions concerning the existence of unforeseen developments in accordance with Article XIX:1(a) of the GATT 1994. *Dominican Republic – Polypropylene Bags and Tubular Fabric, supra* note 70, para. 7.141.

201 *United States – Lamb Meat, supra* note 71, para. 72.

202 *Id.*, para. 73.

The importance of adequate reasoning was reiterated in *Chile – Agricultural Products*. Chile contended that the Chilean Distortions Commission (Chilean national authority: CDC) made its findings and reasoned conclusions relating to the requirement of "unforeseen developments" in the Minutes of Session No. 193, in which it states that "[t]he increase in imports, and the potential for further substantial increases, has occurred at a time when international prices of the products investigated have been subject to sizeable and rapid decreases." Nevertheless, the Panel found that the CDC did not discuss or offer any explanation in its report as to *why* the reported "sizeable and rapid decrease in international prices" could be regarded as an unforeseen development. Based on this finding, the Panel also determined that Chile violated Article 3.1 of the SA regarding unforeseen developments.[203] The Panel in *Argentina – Preserved Peaches* also determined that Article XIX:1(a) requires, as a minimum, some discussion by the competent authorities as to why the developments were unforeseen at the time the relevant obligation was negotiated, and why conditions in the second clause of Article XIX:1(a) occurred "as a result" of circumstances in the first clause.[204] 3.26

The Panel in *United States – Steel Products* also emphasized the importance of the logical connection between unforeseen developments and the increase in imports.[205] It determined that the national authorities must support their conclusion with specific data that the unforeseen developments led to the increase in imports causing or threatening to cause serious injury to the domestic industry.[206] Additionally, the Panel found that the national authorities are obligated to demonstrate "unforeseen developments" with respect to each product that is subject to the safeguard.[207] The Appellate Body subsequently affirmed these Panel decisions.[208] In *European Union – Steel Products*, the Panel reiterated that the investigating authorities must provide evidence to support the connection between unforeseen developments and injurious imports.[209] Again, it is doubtful that this old clause from Article XIX should be considered to be a legal requirement.[210] Nonetheless, since the Appellate Body decision remains 3.27

---

203 *Supra* note 199. *Chile – Agricultural Products, supra* note 70, paras. 7.135–7.138.

204 *Argentina – Preserved Peaches, supra* note 70, paras. 7.23–7.28.

205 *United States – Steel Products, supra* note 70, para. 10.104.

206 *Id.*, paras. 10.121–10.123.

207 *Id.*, paras. 10.124–10.126.

208 *United States – Steel Products, supra* note 71, paras. 316, 326, 329.

209 *European Union – Steel Products, supra* note 70, para. 7.130.

210 Upholding the previous Appellate Body decisions on the "unforeseen developments" clause, the Panel in *Dominican Republic – Polypropylene Bags and Tubular Fabric* opined, "The dispute settlement system of the WTO does not establish a system of precedents, and therefore the reasoning of the Appellate Body in a particular case is not binding on panels set up to examine other cases. However, the reports adopted by the

unchanged and applicable to future safeguard cases, Members are obligated to demonstrate the existence of unforeseen developments.[211]

3.3 APPLICABILITY OF ARTICLE XIX

3.28 Beyond the "unforeseen developments" clause in Article XIX:1(a) discussed above, the general applicability of Article XIX needs to be examined, since this issue has significant theoretical and practical implications, going to the important question of what constitutes disciplines on safeguards. Previous Panels and the Appellate Body have already affirmed that the provisions of Article XIX are applied,[212] but its application would not affect the disciplines on safeguards established by the SA as long as it does not create a separate legal obligation or alter legal relations between Members, independently of the provisions of the SA. The text of the SA repeats and elaborates on most provisions of Article XIX, but not every one of them. Are those "missing" provisions remaining in Article XIX still applicable, independently of the SA?

3.29 *Paragraph 1(b)*. As discussed in Chapter 2.2 above, paragraph 1(b) of Article XIX authorizes the application of a safeguard measure applied on behalf of a third party benefiting from a preferential arrangement. The SA does not include any provision for the application of a safeguard measure taken on behalf of a third party. If the same rationale as the Appellate Body adopted

---

Dispute Settlement Body create legitimate expectations among the Members of the WTO. As the Appellate Body has pointed out, 'following the Appellate Body's conclusions in earlier disputes is not only appropriate, but is what would be expected from panels, especially where the issues are the same'. In the present dispute, the Dominican Republic does not offer any convincing arguments why the Panel should depart from the interpretation adopted by the Appellate Body" (footnotes omitted). *Dominican Republic – Polypropylene Bags and Tubular Fabric, supra* note 70, para. 7.129. It is hoped that future Panels and the Appellate Body will find that several grounds put forward in this chapter provide justification to depart from the previous decisions affirming the "unforeseen development" clause as constituting a legal requirement.

211 *United States – Washers, supra* note 70, para. 7.20 (noting that nothing in SA Article 3.1 suggests a narrow reading of it so as "to exclude the circumstances set out in the first clause of Article XIX:1(a)") and paras. 7.26–7.27 (requiring explanations for the existence of the unforeseen developments that led to the increase in imports). The Panel in *India – Iron or Steel Product* accepted the developments identified by the investigating authorities as unforeseen, based on the view that negotiators "could not reasonably have expected this confluence of events when India negotiated its concessions." *India – Iron or Steel Products, supra* note 70, para. 7.97. The Panel in *United States – Photovoltaic Products* noted that "unforeseen developments" have both subjective ("unforeseen") and objective ("unforeseeable") elements but without clarifying which of these elements should control in the determination of "unforeseen developments" and why. *United States – Photovoltaic Products, supra* note 70, para. 7.15. In *European Union – Steel Products*, the Panel examined (i) whether the importing country identified any unforeseen developments; (ii) whether the developments were unforeseen; and (iii) whether the importing country established that the increase in imports was "as a result of" the unforeseen developments, in the assessment of the "unforeseen development." *European Union – Steel Products, supra* note 70, paras. 7.88–7.153.

212 Refer to the relevant discussion in the preceding chapter.

concerning the "unforeseen developments" clause was to apply here, the provision of paragraph 1(b) would still be effective, as the SA does not specifically prohibit the application of a safeguard measure on behalf of a third party.

Just as in the case of the "unforeseen developments" clause, the SA simply "omits" provisions for the measure for a third party. If the rationale for adopting the "unforeseen developments" clause as a legal requirement were correct, and if a Member is therefore allowed to invoke paragraph 1(b) and apply a safeguard measure on behalf of a third party, there would be procedural chaos.[213] For instance, who should investigate the domestic industry of a third party: one applying the measure or the one requesting it? Could the negotiators in the Uruguay Round ever have intended that they would leave any effective provision of Article XIX to a procedural vacuum or omit an important general condition from Article 2.1 of the SA? The participants of the Uruguay Round most likely considered neither the "unforeseen developments" clause nor paragraph 1(b) applicable. **3.30**

Paragraph 3(b). The continuing application of Article XIX also creates a problem with respect to the provision of paragraph 3(b), which authorizes immediate retaliation against provisional measures where a delay in retaliation would cause irreparable damage to the exporting Member.[214] Again, there is no specific prohibition in the SA against this type of "emergency" retaliation. On the other hand, Article 8.3 of the SA suspends the right to retaliation for three years when the safeguard is applied based on an absolute increase in imports and conforms to the provisions of the SA. The same questions are raised here: i.e., is it reasonable to believe that the negotiators in the Uruguay Round could have agreed to a three-year bar on the retaliation as an incentive for the importing Member applying a safeguard measure and then intended to leave this immediate retaliation still effective, without any provision in the SA? Is the immediate retaliation under paragraph 3(b) compatible with the policy under Article 8.3 to suspend retaliation and provide incentive for the importing Member applying a safeguard measure in compliance with the provisions of the SA for a shorter period?[215] Article 8.3 does not mention any exception to the suspension of retaliation based on the irreparability of damage to the exporting country. **3.31**

---

213 Lee (2001), *supra* note 1, pp. 1242–1245.
214 Refer to the relevant discussion in Chapter 2.2 *supra.*
215 *See* Chapter 8 for the discussion of the provision of Article 8.3.

3.32 It has been suggested that the immediate retaliation under paragraph 3(b) may be considered fair, given that the provisional measures are also taken without any prior consultation.[216] Nevertheless, this issue needs to be considered in the context of the *modification* of the retaliatory rights of the exporting Members, as a result of the Uruguay Round negotiations. The new policy under Article 8.3 has reset the rights and obligations of the Members with respect to retaliation, and the validity of paragraph 3(b) needs to be reassessed in light of this new policy. It is difficult to conceive that the Uruguay Round negotiators would have omitted the provision authorizing immediate retaliation, which would frustrate the policy of suspension under Article 8.3, had they intended to maintain it in the disciplines on safeguards.

3.33 As history has shown,[217] the lack of clear and detailed rules for the application of safeguards made the settlement of the new set of rules inevitable. The SA adopts the concept of safeguards from Article XIX and builds on it, providing the detailed substantive and procedural rules for the application of safeguards. The progressive and comprehensive nature of the SA does not make itself supplementary to the outdated rules of Article XIX, but rather replaces the old regime as a complete set of disciplines governing the application of safeguards.

3.34 Nonetheless, Appellate Body decisions have denied the sole authority of the SA in the application of safeguards and affirmed the continuing applicability of the provisions of Article XIX. The application of Article XIX provisions that are neither expressly adopted nor modified by the new Agreement, such as the "unforeseen developments" clause, paragraph 1(b), and paragraph 3(b), would create problems in the disciplines on safeguards.

3.35 The other provisions of Article XIX have been replaced by the provisions of the SA for all practical purposes:[218] Article XIX:1(a), other than the "unforeseen developments" clause, has been absorbed into the provisions of Article 2.1;[219] the notice and consultation requirements in paragraph 2 are replaced with more detailed provisions of Article 12 of the SA, which cover the timing, contents, and manner of notifications and consultations; the provision of provisional safeguard measures in paragraph 2 is also replaced with the new

216 Bhala and Kennedy, *supra* note 87, pp. 930–931.

217 *See* the relevant discussion of Chapter 2.3 *supra.*

218 Chapters 4–9 *infra* provide a discussion of the provisions of the SA.

219 Another clause in Article XIX:1(a), "of the effect of the obligations incurred by a contracting party under this Agreement," is also missing from the SA. The Appellate Body opined that this phrase "simply means that it must be demonstrated, as a matter of fact, that the importing Member has incurred obligations under the GATT 1994, including tariff concessions." The clause does not seem to impose an analytical obligation to be performed before the application of a safeguard measure. *Korea – Dairy Products, supra* note 71, para. 84.

provision of Article 6, which sets the time limit and regulates the form of a provisional safeguard measure; and paragraph 3(a) governing compensation and retaliation is also substituted and modified by the provisions of Article 8 of the SA.

In conclusion, despite the Appellate Body ruling that Article XIX is still alive, the Agreement on Safeguards controls the application of safeguards subject only to one exception created by the Appellate Body decision, the "unforeseen developments" clause. Paragraphs 1(b) and 3(b) have never been invoked since the implementation of the SA, and it would seem unlikely that they will be invoked in the future.[220] Again, the creation of such an exception can destabilize the disciplines on safeguards and runs counter to the intention of the Uruguay Round participants.C **3.36**

220 For instance, it is unlikely that a Member will apply a safeguard measure on behalf of a third country under paragraph 1(b), a provision that has never been invoked. Members have also refrained from adopting the immediate retaliatory measures since the implementation of the SA.

4

ARTICLE 2 – GENERAL CONDITIONS

4.1 PRELIMINARY ISSUES: STANDARD OF REVIEW[221] AND BURDEN OF PROOF

4.01 The standard of review and the burden of proof which are to be applied by dispute settlement panels in specific dispute cases are preliminary but important issues. By setting the bounds of review applied to national investigations and applications of safeguards, the standard of review not only provides the panels with a benchmark for their review but also affects the conduct of national authorities in the investigation and application of a safeguard measure. The standard of review can determine the amount of discretion that the national authorities enjoy in the application of a safeguard, thereby affecting the extent of control that the WTO disciplines have on safeguard investigations and applications. It is also important to determine which party bears the burden of proof to establish a *prima facie* case. This chapter begins with a discussion of the standard of review and the burden of proof, then proceeds to examining the general conditions for the application of a safeguard measure under SA Article 2.

221 *See also* Lee (1999), *supra* note 1, pp. 33–34. For a more comprehensive discussion of the standard of review in the WTO jurisprudence generally, *see* M. Oesch, *Standards of Review in WTO Dispute Resolution* (Oxford University Press, Oxford, 2003); Andrew T. Guzman, "Determining the Appropriate Standard of Review in WTO Dispute Resolution" (2009) 42 *Cornell Journal of International Law* 45–76; Ross Becroft, *The Standard of Review in WTO Dispute Settlement: Critique and Development* (Edward Elgar, 2012).

Standard of Review. The applicable standard of review has been a contentious issue. Unlike the Anti-Dumping Practices Agreement,[222] the Agreement on Safeguards does not specify the applicable standard of review. The Panel in *Korea – Dairy Products*, referring to the Appellate Body's findings in *European Communities – Hormones*, ruled that the provisions of Article 11 of the Understanding on Rules and Procedures Governing the Settlement of Disputes (DSU) are applicable if the relevant WTO multilateral trade agreement does not provide for a specific standard of review.[223] Article 11 provides that "a panel should make an objective assessment of the matter before it, including an objective assessment of the facts of the case and the applicability and conformity with the relevant covered agreements." The Panel in *Dominican Republic – Polypropylene Bags and Tubular Fabric* confirmed that the obligation imposed by Article 11 of the DSU includes the consideration of all aspects of the matter, both factual and legal, and implies *inter alia* that the panel should consider the issues raised by the parties, without overstepping its terms of reference.[224] **4.02**

Panels have repeatedly emphasized that they would not engage in a *de novo* review of national authorities' investigations, although it would not completely defer to the findings of national authorities either.[225] While national authorities have discretion to make substantive findings and conclusions under the SA, the panel would nevertheless examine whether: (i) the national authorities examined all the facts in their possession, as well as those which they should have obtained; (ii) adequate explanation was provided of how the facts as a whole supported the determinations made; and, consequently, (iii) the **4.03**

---

222 Article 17.6 of the Agreement on Implementation of Article VI of the General Agreement on Tariffs and Trade 1994 provides, "In examining the matter referred to in paragraph 5: (i) in its assessment of the facts of the matter, the panel shall determine whether the authorities' establishment of the facts was proper and whether their evaluation of those facts was unbiased and objective. If the establishment of the facts was proper and the evaluation was unbiased and objective, even though the panel might have reached a different conclusion, the evaluation shall not be overturned; (ii) the panel shall interpret the relevant provisions of the Agreement in accordance with customary rules of interpretation of public international law. Where the panel finds that a relevant provision of the Agreement admits of more than one permissible interpretation, the panel shall find the authorities' measure to be in conformity with the Agreement if it rests upon one of those permissible interpretations."

223 *Korea – Dairy Products, supra* note 70, para. 7.26. The position is also affirmed by subsequent Panels. *Dominican Republic — Polypropylene Bags and Tubular Fabric, supra* note 70, para. 7.4.

224 *Dominican Republic — Polypropylene Bags and Tubular Fabric, supra* note 70, para. 7.5.

225 *Korea – Dairy Products, supra* note 70, para. 7.30. and *Argentina – Footwear, supra* note 70, para. 8.124. The Appellate Body affirmed this approach, and the subsequent panels also followed it. *United States – Argentina, supra* note 71, paras. 116–122; *United States – Wheat Gluten, supra* note 70, para. 8.5; *United States – Lamb Meat, supra* note 70, para. 7.3; *Dominican Republic — Polypropylene Bags and Tubular Fabric, supra* note 70, para. 7.7; *United States — Photovoltaic Products, supra* note 70, para. 7.4; *United States – Washers, supra* note 70, para. 7.2.

determination made was consistent with the international obligations of the Member applying a safeguard measure.[226] Concurring with this position, the Appellate Body in *United States – Lamb Meat* stated, "[A] panel's application of the appropriate standard of review of the competent authorities' determination has two aspects. First, a panel must review whether the competent authorities have, as a *formal* matter, evaluated *all relevant factors* and, second, a panel must review whether those authorities have, as a *substantive* matter, provided a *reasoned and adequate explanation* of how the facts support their determinations."[227]

4.04 *Adequacy of Reasoning*. According to those guidelines, Panels have reviewed both the adequacy of the national authorities' reasoning for their decisions and the scope of facts examined. This practice has created certain ambiguities and difficulties in the application of safeguard measures. First, the above guidelines do not specify how the adequacy of a national authority's reasoning should be determined. The determination of the adequacy of reasoning is inherently a subjective task, and it is difficult to set the objective criteria for such a determination. The Appellate Body emphasized the need for close scrutiny of the national authorities' reasoning. It determined that panels are obligated to examine the adequacy of national authorities' reasoning closely and examine it in light of alternative arguments. It found that the Panel had failed to apply a standard of review where it was deemed to have conducted only a cursory examination of the national authorities' reasoning.[228]

4.05 The adequacy of reasoning would also be an issue where two different conclusions can reasonably be drawn from the same set of facts.[229] The Appellate Body in *United States – Lamb Meat* found that "A panel must find, in particular, that an explanation is not reasoned, or is not adequate, if some *alternative explanation* of the facts is plausible, and if the competent authority's explanation does not seem adequate in the light of that alternative explanation."[230] According to this finding, an explanation for the national authority's decision would have to be rejected if it is refuted by alternative reasoning. In addition, a previous Panel decision indicated that a national authority's explanation and reasoning for its conclusion would not be accepted unless they are included in the original investigation report.[231]

---

226 *Korea – Dairy Products, supra* note 70, para. 7.30.

227 *United States – Lamb Meat, supra* note 71, para. 141.

228 *United States – Lamb Meat, supra* note 71, para. 148.

229 *See also* Lee (1999), *supra* note 1, p. 39.

230 *United States – Lamb Meat, supra* note 71, para. 106.

231 *Korea – Dairy Products, supra* note 70, para. 7.72. *See also United States — Photovoltaic Products, supra* note 70, para. 7.5; *United States – Washers, supra* note 70, para. 7.3.

These decisions mean that national authorities would have to consider every possible reasoning and conclusion that can be drawn from the given facts and then justify their conclusion in the investigation report against all the other alternative reasoning. This is onerous on the authorities and in contrast to the standard of review stipulated in the Anti-Dumping Practices Agreement that allows the evaluation of the national authority to stand, even though the panel (or the complainant) might have reached a different conclusion, as long as the authority's establishment of the facts was proper and the evaluation was unbiased and objective.[232] It is only fair that Members defending their measure should be given the opportunity to justify their conclusion with supplementary reasoning, if necessary, before their explanations and reasoning are rejected due to the alternative reasoning brought forward by the complainant in the panel process. Such opportunity was denied in a previous Panel case.[233] **4.06**

In rendering its decision cited above, the Appellate Body in *United States – Lamb Meat* seems to have presumed that all the arguments raised by the complainant in the panel process had also been presented to the national authorities during the investigation, and therefore, should have been known to them before the conclusion of the investigation. The Appellate Body opined that WTO Members cannot improperly withhold arguments from the competent authorities with a view to raising those arguments later before a panel and that it is unlikely that a Member would do so.[234] Nonetheless, the national authorities may not always have a chance to hear all the arguments before the panel process begins, since the complainant may provide an additional argument later. During the Panel proceedings, the complainant may raise new counter-arguments to the authority's reasoning for its decision, and therefore, Members should be given the opportunity to support its determination with supplementary explanations, if necessary. **4.07**

Sufficiency of Data. Secondly, the panel review would also determine whether the national authorities examined all the facts in their possession and those which they should have obtained.[235] The national authorities would have to examine all relevant factors based on the data pertaining to the condition of **4.08**

232 Anti-Dumping Practices Agreement, Article 17.6, *supra* note 222. Consideration should be given to revising the relevant SA provision to clarify the applicable standard of review. *See* Appendix 4 for an example.

233 In *Korea – Dairy Products*, the Panel did not accept Korea's justifications for many of its findings since they were not included in its investigation report. *See* Lee (1999), *supra* note 1, p. 39.

234 *United States – Lamb Meat*, *supra* note 71, para. 115.

235 In *Korea – Dairy Products*, the Panel stated, "For us, an objective assessment entails an examination whether the KTC (the Korean investigation authority) had examined all facts in its possession or *which it should have obtained* in accordance with Article 4.2 of the Agreement on Safeguards ..." (emphasis added). *Korea – Dairy Products*, *supra* note 70, para. 7.30.

the industry. The collection and use of the relevant data raise a particular issue. Collecting data is often a difficult task, particularly in developing countries with a limited availability of industrial statistics, to which discerning the precisely relevant data may be even more onerous.[236]

4.09 Should certain discrepancies in data be accepted in consideration of a limited availability of statistics? The Panel in *Korea – Dairy Product* did not seem to allow for such a discrepancy.[237] Furthermore, the *Dairy* Panel not only required that national authorities examine all available data, but also demanded that they make a reasonable estimate where actual data are not available due to a lack of statistics.[238] Notwithstanding the reliability of such an estimate, the requirement for such an estimation seems tantamount to directing national investigating authorities how to conduct their own investigations, a role which Panels have repeatedly declined to assume.[239]

4.10 The issue of the collection and examination of data was addressed again in *United States – Wheat Gluten*. The Panel stated, "It is not our role to collect new data, nor to consider evidence which could have been presented to the United States International Trade Commission (USITC) by interested parties in the investigation, but was not." The decision meant that national authorities' decisions would not be considered inadequate for failing to consider evidence and facts that had not been presented to them.[240] However, the Appellate Body reversed this decision and found that the national authorities should not rely solely on information submitted by the parties and that they should seek out pertinent information necessary to assess the injury to the domestic industry.[241] This Appellate Body decision is justified, as it is the national authorities' responsibility and not the interested parties' to ensure proper assessment of the condition of domestic industry based on all pertinent information.

4.11 The Appellate Body in *United States – Lamb Meat* provides guidelines on the sufficiency of data. It found that the data before the competent authorities must be sufficiently representative to give a true picture of the domestic indus-

---

236 In *Korea – Dairy Products*, the Panel considered Korea's analysis of the domestic industry's profits and losses inadequate since, *inter alia*, the data used by the Korean investigating authorities were "too broad," as it included profits and losses from businesses other than those related to the production and sale of domestic products. *Korea – Dairy Products*, *supra* note 70, para. 7.71.

237 *Id.*

238 *Id.*, para. 7.82.

239 *See also* Lee (1999), *supra* note 1, p. 40.

240 *United States – Wheat Gluten*, *supra* note 70, para. 8.6.

241 *United States – Wheat Gluten*, *supra* note 71, paras. 53–55.

try.[242] It acknowledged that collecting data that includes all domestic producers might not be practical in many instances. It also determined that what is sufficient in any given case would depend on the "particularities" of the domestic industry at issue.[243] The decision indicates that the data collected and used for the examination needs to be a statistically valid sample; otherwise, there should be some other plausible explanation as to why presented data would be representative of the industry.

Multiple Explanations. The Appellate Body made an interesting ruling where a national authority provided more than one explanation that cannot be reconciled with each another. In *United States – Steel Products*, the Panel noted that the USITC Commissioners made divergent findings that are, in the view of the Panel, impossible to reconcile given that they were based on differently defined products.[244] (Some Commissioners found that certain steel products should be included and considered together in a larger category of products, and the others considered them separate products. They were also divergent on injury determinations.) The Panel determined that a Member is not allowed to base a safeguard measure "on a determination supported by a set of explanations each of which is different and impossible to reconcile with the other."[245] **4.12**

The Appellate Body disagreed with the Panel and reversed its decision, concluding that the affirmative findings based on different product groupings are not necessarily mutually exclusive.[246] The Appellate Body was of the view that nothing in the SA prevents a national investigating authority from setting out multiple findings to support its determination and that it is the Panel's obligation to consider each of them to assess if any one of them provides a reasoned and adequate explanation of its final determination.[247] **4.13**

This Appellate Body decision raises doubt as to the proper examination of a national authority's determination in the presence of divergent opinions **4.14**

---

242 *United States – Lamb Meat*, *supra* note 71, para. 132.

243 *Id.*

244 *United States – Steel Products*, *supra* note 70, para. 10.194. The Panel further explained, "For the purposes of the Agreement on Safeguards, with regard to, for instance, the question of whether imports have increased, it makes a difference whether the product at issue is tin mill or a much broader category called CCFRS and containing tin mill products. The difference is that the import numbers for different product definitions will not be the same." *Id.*, para. 10.195.

245 *Id.*, paras. 10.195, 10.262.

246 The Appellate Body stated, "We do not believe that an affirmative finding with respect to a broad product grouping, on the one hand, and an affirmative finding with respect to one of the products contained in that broad product grouping, on the other hand, are, necessarily, mutually exclusive." *United States – Steel Products*, *supra* note 71, para. 413.

247 *Id.*, para. 414.

within a national authority. The Appellate Body considered that the relevant provisions in the SA do not necessarily prevent a presentation of multiple explanations on the part of a national authority.[248] Nevertheless, the subject of the panel assessment is the explanation offered by the national investigating authority to support its own determination, not that of each individual Member within the authority. It is difficult to understand how a national investigating authority can offer an adequate and reasonable explanation if it fails to reconcile divergent views within its own body and presents multiple explanations that cannot be reconciled with one another. It is the national investigating authority's responsibility, and not the Panel's, to provide an explanation that is adequate and reasonable to support its determination. For this, national authorities would have to coordinate and reconcile internal disagreements and present a coherent explanation.

4.15 *Applicability of the SA.* The Appellate Body also held that a panel is required to assess not only the facts of the case but also the *applicability* of the relevant covered agreement invoked by a complaint.[249] In *Indonesia – Safeguard on Certain Iron or Steel Products*, the Panel determined that Indonesia's measures did not constitute a safeguard measure under the provisions of the SA where the parties did not dispute their applicability.[250] The Appellate Body found that "Article 11 of the DSU requires panels to undertake an 'objective assessment of the matter before it, including an objective assessment of the facts of the case and the applicability of and conformity with the relevant covered agreements.'"[251] According to the Appellate Body decision, the panel's standard of review includes an assessment of the SA's applicability of disputed measures where the SA is invoked by a complainant, even if the other party to the dispute does not raise any issue about its applicability.

4.16 *Burden of Proof.* A question has also been raised as to who bears the burden of proof should an application of a safeguard measure be challenged.[252] The SA is silent about this issue, and therefore, this question has to be addressed with reference to the relevant jurisprudence, including the Panel and Appellate Body rulings on this issue.

---

248 The Appellate Body stated in *Steel Products*, "the Panel should have continued its enquiry by examining the divergent views of the Commissioners *separately*, in order to *ascertain* whether one of these sets of findings contained a reasoned and adequate explanation for the USITC's single institutional determination" (emphasis added). *Id.*, para. 416.

249 *Indonesia – Safeguard on Certain Iron or Steel Products*, *supra* note 71, paras. 5.31 and 5.33.

250 *Id.*, para. 5.24.

251 *Id.*, para. 5.31.

252 *See*, *Korea – Dairy Products*, *supra* note 70, paras. 4.43–4.106.

The principle of jurisprudence in many civilized legal systems generally indicates that a complainant is obligated to found their own claim: i.e., the burden of proof rests with the complainant. The Panel in *Korea – Dairy Products* confirmed this principle, finding that "as a matter of law the burden of proof rests with the European Communities, as complainant, and does not shift during the panel process."[253] The Panel also ruled that once the EC made a *prima facie* case, Korea had to provide an effective refutation of it.[254] The Panel also said that at the end of the process, it would assess and weigh the evidence and arguments of both parties to determine whether the complainant's claims were well founded. **4.17**

This decision indicates that a complainant should first establish a *prima facie* case. If the complainant has not met the standard for a *prima facie* case, then its complaint is dismissed. The question has been raised as to an appropriate standard (threshold) for the establishment of a *prima facie* case. The Panel in *Korea – Dairy Products* considered this issue. Following the previous Appellate Body decision,[255] the Panel defined a *prima facie* case as "one which, in the absence of effective refutation by the defending party, requires a panel, as a matter of law, to rule in favour of the complaining party presenting the *prima facie* case."[256] The Panel's ruling of the *prima facie* case was subsequently affirmed by the Appellate Body.[257] **4.18**

In *United States – Line Pipe*, the minimum standard for the establishment of a *prima facie* case was at issue. In this case, the complainant argued that the United States violated Articles 2 and 4 of the *Agreement on Safeguards* by excluding Mexico and Canada from the application of the safeguard measure where it included imports from these countries in its injury assessment.[258] The United States argued that it considered the injurious impact of the imports from sources other than Canada and Mexico in a note included in the relevant USITC Report.[259] **4.19**

---

253 *Id.*, para. 7.23. The Panel in *United States — Photovoltaic Products* also affirms that "the general allocation of the burden of proof in WTO dispute settlement requires that the complaining party assert and prove its claim." *United States — Photovoltaic Products*, *supra* note 70, para. 7.7. *See also United State – Washers*, *supra* note 70, para. 7.5.

254 *Korea – Dairy Products*, *supra* note 70, para. 7.24. *See also United States – Washers*, *supra* note 70, para. 7.5.

255 *European Communities – Measures Concerning Meat and Meat Products*, WT/DS26/AB/R (January 16, 1998) ("*European Communities – Hormones*").

256 *Korea – Dairy Products*, *supra* note 70, para. 7.24.

257 *Korea – Dairy Products*, *supra* note 71, paras. 142–150.

258 For a discussion of the substantive issue, *see* Chapter 4.4 *infra*.

259 *Lamb Meat*, USITC Pub. No. 3176 (April 1999), pp. I-26/27. The note stated, "We note that we would have reached the same result had we excluded imports from Canada and Mexico from our analysis. Imports from non-NAFTA sources increased significantly over the period of investigation, in absolute terms and as

4.20 The Panel concluded that the specificity of the complainant's claim would determine whether it had established a *prima facie* case. It found that the complainant must address and rebut *specific* information set out in the national authority's investigation report, in this case the contents of the relevant note, in order to establish a *prima facie* case.[260] However, the Appellate Body found that the Panel's requirement would impose an impossible burden on the complainant since, as an exporting country, the complainant would not have the relevant data to conduct its own analysis as importing countries could do.[261] In this case, the Appellate Body determined that the complainant established a *prima facie* case where it demonstrated, although it did not address and rebut the specific information (the contents of the note) in the investigation report, that the United States considered imports from all sources in its injury determination but excluded imports from Canada and Mexico from its safeguard measure, thereby violating Articles 2 and 4 of the SA.[262]

4.21 The Appellate Body found that the note provided a "*finding*" that imports from non-NAFTA sources increased significantly over the period of investigation and the "*basis for a finding*" that imports from non-NAFTA sources caused serious injury to the relevant domestic industry.[263] Nevertheless, it concluded that the United States had failed to rebut the *prima facie* case made by Korea since the note and other parts of the USITC Report addressing the imports from NAFTA countries did not establish explicitly, through a reasoned and

---

a percentage of domestic production. Non-NAFTA imports fell from *** tons in 1994 to *** tons in 1996, but then rose sharply to *** tons in 1997 and *** tons in 1998. While non-NAFTA imports fell from *** tons in interim 1998 to *** tons in interim 1999, they remained at a very high level in interim 1999, exceeding in just 6 months the level of *full* year 1995 and 1996 imports. These imports also increased significantly in terms of market share at the end of the period of investigation, rising from *** percent in 1996 to *** percent in 1998, and from *** percent in interim 1998 to *** percent in interim 1999. Moreover, the non-NAFTA imports were among the lowest-priced imports. Except for 1994, the average unit value of imports from Canada exceeded the average import unit value throughout the period of investigation, and the volume of imports was relatively small. The average unit value of imports from Mexico exceeded the average for all imports in 1998 and interim 1999, the period in which the serious injury occurred, and the volume of imports from Mexico declined during this period. Moreover, in the 244 possible product-specific price comparisons, non-NAFTA imports undersold domestic line pipe in 194 instances (about 80 percent), and Korean product accounted for by far the largest number of instances of underselling (95 of the 194). Data are based on those in Table C-1 adjusted to exclude certain imports of Arctic-grade and alloy line pipe." *Id.*

260 *United States – Line Pipe, Korea – Dairy Products, supra* note 70, para. 7.171. The Panel considered that the complainant did not establish a *prima facie* case by failing to address and rebut specific information in the USITC Report (the contents of note 168). The Panel also noted, "In doing so, we do not find that note 168 is sufficient for the purposes of Articles 2.1 and 4.1. We merely find that Korea has failed to establish a *prima facie* case that the United States violated those provisions." *Id.*, note 148.

261 *United States – Line Pipe, supra* note 71, para. 187.

262 *Id.*, paras. 186 and 187.

263 *Id.*, para. 193.

adequate explanation, that increased imports from non-NAFTA sources by themselves caused serious injury or threat of serious injury.

According to the Appellate Body decision, the complainant may establish a *prima facie* case by demonstrating a violation of the legal requirement on the part of the respondent, and the complainant is not required to address and rebut specific information included in the investigation report which may be inconsistent with the complainant's claim. The respondent, nevertheless, should explicitly rebut the *prima facie* case made by the complainant with a reasoned explanation. **4.22**

The position of the Appellate Body seems reasonable in that evidence for a *prima facie* case need not be conclusive. Many national practices also recognize that a *prima facie* case is established as long as the evidence presented *tends to* support the claim made, although the evidence may not be conclusive.[264] In line with this position, the Panel in *Argentina – Preserved Peaches* stated that it "will follow consistent practice in relation to the burden of proof, according to which the party who asserts a fact, or the affirmative of a particular claim or defense, whether the complainant or the respondent, bears the burden of proof of that fact, or the affirmative of that claim or defense. If that party adduces evidence sufficient to raise a presumption that what is asserted is true, the burden then shifts to the other party, who will fail unless it adduces sufficient evidence to rebut the presumption" (footnote omitted).[265] **4.23**

These Panel and Appellate Body decisions indicate that the threshold for a *prima facie* case is met if the evidence presented is sufficient to demonstrate the complainant's claim generally, and the rebuttal of the specific information, which may not support the claim of a *prima facie* case, is not necessary. This means that Members proposing to apply a safeguard measure should be prepared to defend their case with stronger evidence and arguments once the complainant makes a *prima facie* case by indicating the violation of the rule with *some* evidence, which may not necessarily be conclusive.[266] **4.24**

264 *See* US judicial cases, *State v. Harenza*, 213 Kan. 201, 515 P.2d 1217, 1222 (November 3, 1973), *Godesky v. Provo City Corp.*, Utah, 690 P.2d 541, 547 (September 12, 1984) and *Mitsui Petrochemicals (America) v. US*, 21 C.I.T. 882, 885, 1997 WL 438840, 3 (July 3, 1997).

265 *Argentina – Preserved Peaches, supra* note 70, para. 7.8. The Panel in *Dominican Republic — Polypropylene Bags and Tubular Fabric* also followed this position. *Dominican Republic — Polypropylene Bags and Tubular Fabric, supra* note 70, paras. 7.16–7.18.

266 Thus, the Panel in *United States – Washers* found that the complainant (Korea) made a *prima facie* case when it noted Korea's argument that the investigating authority (USITC) did not evaluate and explain the trends in import volumes over the period of investigation. *United States – Washers, supra* note 70, para. 7.95.

4.2 INCREASED IMPORTS[267]

4.25 *Provision of Article 2.1.* Article 2.1 of the SA prescribes the general conditions for the application of a safeguard measure. It provides:

> A Member may apply a safeguard measure to a product only if that Member has determined, pursuant to the provisions set out below, that such product is being imported into its territory in such increased quantities, absolute or relative to domestic production, and under such conditions as to cause or threaten to cause serious injury to the domestic industry that produces like or directly competitive products.

4.26 Those general conditions have been adopted from the provisions of GATT Article XIX: (i) increase in imports; (ii) that causes or threatens to cause; (iii) serious injury to domestic producers of like or directly competitive products.[268]

4.27 Safeguard measures are predicated on an *increase in imports* that causes serious injury or threat thereof to a domestic industry. Therefore, Members contemplating a safeguard measure should first establish the requisite increase in imports. It can be *either* an absolute *or* a relative increase (i.e., Members are allowed to apply a safeguard measure where the amount of imports has actually decreased, albeit less than the decrease in domestic production),[269] but it must be an *actual* increase; a mere threat of an increase is not sufficient.[270] The increase in imports is also one of the eight injury factors under Article 4.2.[271]

4.28 *Pace of Increase.* The pace of increase in imports has been an important issue. Safeguard measures are an emergency device, designed to relieve a domestic industry of an acute injury caused by radical increases in imports. Gradual increases in imports over a long period of time are unlikely to put a domestic industry in a situation that justifies an emergency remedy such as a safeguard. The Appellate Body supported this position. It ruled that the increase in imports "must have been recent enough, sudden enough, sharp enough and significant enough, both quantitatively and qualitatively, to cause or threaten to cause serious injury."[272] The Appellate Body also determined that the wording of the relevant phrase in Article 2.1, "such product is *being* imported" (emphasis added) supports its conclusion. It interpreted the phrase as the description of a current, on-going increase in imports.

---

267 *See also* Lee (2002), *supra* note 1, pp. 650–651.

268 Paragraph 1(a) of the GATT Article XIX.

269 *See* Chapter 2.2 *supra* for the relevant discussion of relative increase in imports.

270 *Chile – Agricultural Products*, *supra* note 70, para. 7.161.

271 *See* Chapter 5.1 *infra* for the relevant discussion of the injury factors.

272 *See* the Appellate Body decision, *Argentina – Footwear*, *supra* note 71, para. 131. The decision was also followed in *United States – Wheat Gluten*, *supra* note 70, para. 8.31.

4.29 In line with the Appellate Body decision, the Panel in *India – Iron or Steel Products* reiterated the importance of conducting both a quantitative and qualitative analysis of import trends based on objective data.[273] The Panel in *European Union – Steel Products* also found that the complainant is obligated to "adduce the reference point or benchmark against which to ascertain what may or may not be 'enough.'"[274] The Panel observed the concept of "enough" as relational: "Something is 'enough' in relation to something else. What qualifies as 'enough' cannot exist in the abstract untethered from some reference point or benchmark for ascertaining what is 'enough.'"[275]

4.30 *Identification of Increase in Long-Term Trends.* Critics have pointed out that competent national authorities will be able to "create" an increase in import through statistical manipulations by, for instance, choosing the "right" periodical reference points that will yield an increasing trend. However, such a "manipulation" would now be more difficult to pass because of the Appellate Body decision that found a mere comparison of the selective periodical reference to be insufficient to meet the necessary standard of an increase in imports.[276] National investigating authorities would have to establish that the increase is current and radical enough to warrant the application of an emergency import restriction.

4.31 On the other hand, a Panel also found that discrepancies in the increasing trend at some point of the reference period, particularly early in that period, do not necessarily negate the claim of the increase in imports, as long as a recent,

---

273 *India – Iron or Steel Products*, *supra* note 70, paras. 7.149–7.150.

274 *European Union – Steel Products*, *supra* note 70, para. 7.183.

275 *Id.* A commentator criticized that qualitative guidance is not particularly helpful. Sykes, *supra* note 30, p. 126. There is inherent ambiguity with the elements of qualitative analysis under Article 2.1, and panels have tried to set parameters. For example, the Panel in *United States – Washers* found that the analysis of increased imports under Article 2.1 does not require consideration of increased domestic consumption where the complainant argued that the latter is required to assess the qualitative significance of increased imports. *United States – Washers supra* note 70, para. 7.87. The Panel in *Ukraine – Passenger Cars* also concluded that the conditions under which imports occur do not have a bearing on the analysis of increased imports under Article 2.1. *Ukraine – Passenger Cars*, *supra* note 70, para. 7.190. The Panel opined that "Article 2.1 contains the phrase 'such product is being imported into its territory in such increased quantities … and under such conditions as to cause or threaten to cause serious injury to the domestic industry…'. In our view, this phrase identifies two distinct elements. The first element refers to increased quantities of imports, while the second refers to the conditions under which they occur, which must be such as to make it possible for those increased quantities to cause serious injury or threat thereof. The 'conditions' under which imports occur in our view have no bearing on whether or not there have been increased quantities of imports. Consequently, we do not consider that an analysis of the 'conditions' under which imports occur forms an integral part of the analysis of the quantities in which imports occur." *Id.* For a further analysis of this case, *see* Arevik Gnutzmann-Mkrtchyan and Simon Lester, "Does Safeguards Need Saving? Lessons from the Ukraine–Passenger Cars Dispute" (2017) 16(2) *World Trade Review* 227–251.

276 *Argentina – Footwear*, *supra* note 71, paras. 129–131.

sharp, and substantial increase in imports is demonstrated to the end of the period.[277] The subsequent Appellate Body in *United States – Lamb Meat* also affirmed that the real significance of short-term trends in the most recent data should be assessed in the light of long-term trends. It found that the evaluation of the most recent data in isolation may result in a "misleading" picture of the domestic industry.[278] The recent increase in imports may be a result of a regular business cycle, causing increased demands for domestic products as well as imports in regular intervals.[279]

4.32 *Methodology.* The Panel decision in *United States – Line Pipe* gave substantial deference to the national investigating authorities on the determination of the increase in imports.[280] The Panel found that competent national authorities may choose such methodology to determine the increase in imports as they consider fit, as long as the methodology chosen was not "inherently biased" or would have precluded the investigating authorities from "performing a reasonable evaluation of the facts in the investigation."[281] The Panel affirmed that the recent imports have to be examined, but it did not believe that the investigating authorities are obligated to examine the imports during the period immediately preceding their decision. The six-month gap between the decision and the end point of the investigation was considered acceptable.[282]

4.33 The Panel also found that the period of investigation and its breakdown for periodical comparison is left to the discretion of the investigating authorities. In this case, the USITC examined a five-year period from 1994 to 1998 as well as the first semester of 1999. In its investigation, the USITC compared the figures for each full year with the preceding year, and the figures for interim 1999 with those of the first semester of 1998, for its December 1999 decision.[283] The Panel determined that the USITC's choice of the investigation period was proper since it allowed the USITC to focus on the recent imports, and the period selected was long enough to allow the appropriate conclusions to be drawn with respect to the condition of the domestic industry.[284]

---

277 *United States – Wheat Gluten, supra* note 70, para. 8.33.

278 *United States – Lamb Meat, supra* note 71, para. 138.

279 The Panel in *Preserved Peaches* also warned, "if the most recent data is evaluated in isolation, the resulting picture of the domestic industry may be quite misleading." *Argentina – Preserved Peaches, supra* note 70, para. 7.106.

280 *United States – Line Pipe, supra* note 70, paras. 7.186–7.217.

281 *Id.*, para. 7.206.

282 *Id.*, para. 7.207.

283 *Id.*, paras. 7.199–7.200.

284 *Id.*, para. 7.204.

From the facts of this case, it is not altogether clear whether the Panel's treatment of this issue was consistent with the previous Appellate Body position. A comparison of the first semester of 1998 and the first semester of 1999 revealed a decline in imports.[285] Therefore, the examination of the more current time periods such as the second semester of 1998, and even the period after the first semester of 1999, would have been essential in determining the significance of the latest decline in imports.[286] The Panel accepted the methodology adopted by the United States, which did not involve the comparison of the current time periods, and did not consider whether such comparison was necessary. Arguably, the Panel decision gave overly broad deference to the national authority and did not properly review whether the United States provided adequate, reasoned explanations as to the existence of the requisite increase in imports under the required standard of review.[287] **4.34**

The Appellate Body did not rule on this issue, since the Panel decision on this point was not appealed. Where the amount of imports decreased for a significant period of time toward the end of the investigation period, the application of a safeguard measure in the presence of such a decline may not be consistent with the requirement of "sudden" and "recent" increase in imports, as set out by the previous Appellate Body decision. Therefore, it is important that the national investigating authorities determine whether the decrease was only a temporary fluctuation from the overall increase in imports that would still justify the application of a safeguard measure, or whether it was the beginning of a significant downturn where the application of a safeguard may not be necessary. **4.35**

Recent Decline in Imports. The Panel was more critical in the evaluation of increased imports in a subsequent case, *Chile – Agricultural Products*. The Panel rejected Chile's claim of an increase in imports where imports of the product concerned actually fell significantly in the period immediately preceding the investigation.[288] The Panel did not find the existence of increased imports where imports fluctuated and no identification of a discernible upward trend in imports could be made.[289] The Panel also determined that even if a significant **4.36**

---

285 *Id.*, para. 7.209.

286 The United States argued that even if there had been a decline in the absolute amount of imports, the application of a safeguard measure would still have been justifiable based on the increase in the amount of imports relative to domestic production under the provision of Article 2.1. However, the existence of the relative increase in imports in 1999 interim was also disputed. *Id.*, para. 7.216.

287 *See* Chapter 4.1 *supra* for a discussion of the standard of review.

288 *Chile – Agricultural Products*, *supra* note 70, para. 7.155.

289 *Id.*, para. 7.156.

import increase was observed between certain time periods, national authorities would still have to provide a reasoned analysis about the significance of the import volumes, where such volumes were lower than import volumes in a preceding time period.[290]

4.37 The increase in imports was also an important issue in a highly publicized case, *United States – Steel Products.* With respect to increased steel imports, the Panel decided that the increase must indicate "a certain degree of recentness, suddenness, sharpness and significance," following the previous decision in *Argentina – Footwear.*[291] Nonetheless, the *Steel* Panel, in agreement with the Panel's view in *United States – Line Pipe*, also determined that the increase in imports need not continue up to the period immediately preceding the investigating authority's determination, nor up to the very end of the investigation period, although the increase still has to be "recent."[292] The Panel determined that the question as to whether a decrease in imports at the end of the period of investigation prevents a finding of increased imports would depend on the duration and the degree of the decrease at the end of the relevant period of investigation, as well as the nature of the increase that intervened beforehand reflected by, for instance, its sharpness and its extent.[293] The Panel also found that the national investigating authority is not obligated to consider the data made available *after* its determination of increased imports.[294]

4.38 The Panel in *US Steel Safeguards* made measure-by-measure assessments on the USITC determinations with respect to each specific product.[295] Regarding

290 *Id.*, para. 7.157. The importance of the qualitative evaluation of import trends was again emphasized in *Argentina – Preserved Peaches.* Following the Appellate Body rulings in *Argentina – Footwear*, the Panel found that an identification of a mathematical increase in imports is insufficient. In other words, the national investigating authorities must establish an increase in imports through q*ualitative* evaluation of overall import trends. *Argentina – Preserved Peaches, supra* note 70, para. 7.54. The Panel did not believe that consideration of an increase in imports without regard to the entire import trends was sufficient where imports had increased toward the end of the investigation period but had decreased substantially up to an earlier point in the period. *Id.*, paras. 7.53–7.69. According to the Panel, the import increase should have been considered in the context of the previous substantial decline of imports. *Id.*, para. 7.61

291 *United States – Steel Products, supra* note 70, para. 10.167. The Appellate Body subsequently upheld this Panel position. *United States – Steel Products, supra* note 71, para. 361.

292 *United States – Steel Products, Report of the Panel, supra* note 70, para. 10.162.

293 *Id.*, para. 10.163.

294 *Id.*, para. 10.173. However, the Panel in *Ukraine – Passenger Cars* found that the two-year gap between the end of the investigation period and the decision to apply the safeguard measure called into question the recentness of increased imports while the 18-month time gap did not. *Ukraine – Passenger Cars, supra* note 7 0, paras. 7.182 and 7.184.

295 The United States applied safeguard measures to slabs, flat steel, hot-rolled bar, cold-finished bar, rebar, certain welded tubular products, carbon and alloy fittings, stainless steel bar, stainless steel rod, tin mill products and stainless steel wire. These measures were announced in Proclamation 7529 of March 5, 2002 – To Facilitate Positive Adjustment to Competition from Imports of Certain Steel Products ("Proclamation")

certain carbon flat-rolled steel (CCFRS), hot-rolled bar, and stainless steel rod, the Panel noted the decreasing import trends toward the end of the investigation period, particularly the significant drop in the interim 2001, and did not consider the claimed increases in imports during the investigation period to be recent enough.[296] The Appellate Body, emphasizing the national investigating authority's responsibility to examine import trends, agreed with the Panel findings with respect to those products.[297]

On the other hand, the Panel found that the USITC provided an adequate and reasoned explanation of increased imports with respect to cold-finished bar, rebar, welded pipe, fittings, flanges and tool joints (FFTJ), and stainless steel bar where there were significant increases in imports in the recent period prior to the determination, as identified by the overall trends (e.g., sharp increases followed by relatively insignificant drops).[298] In addition, the Panel emphasized that the fulfillment of the requirement of increased imports under Article 2.1 does not mean that such increases are sufficient to *cause* serious injury to a domestic industry. The Panel was of the view that this question should be treated in the context of causation under Article 4.2(b).[299] **4.39**

The Panel in *Dominican Republic – Polypropylene Bags and Tubular Fabric* confirmed that the decrease in imports toward the end of the investigation period does not necessary negate the determination of an increase in imports where imports did recover in the subsequent months.[300] The Panel also found that if multiple products are investigated, Article 2.1 does not require separate **4.40**

---

and the Memorandum of March 5, 2002 – Action Under Section 203 of the Trade Act of 1974 Concerning Certain Steel Products by the President of the United States of America ("Memorandum"), *Federal Register* Vol. 67, No. 45 (Mar. 7, 2002). *See* Chapter 14 *infra* for more discussions of the US Steel Safeguards.

296 *United States – Steel Products,* Report of the Panel, *supra* note 70, paras. 10.178–10.187, 10.201–10.210, 10.264–10.277.

297 *United States – Steel Products, supra* note 71, paras. 369, 376, 383, 399. The Appellate Body did not agree to a particular aspect of the Panel conclusion with respect to stainless steel rod, but it nonetheless supported the Panel finding that the United States failed to provide a reasoned and adequate explanation of how the facts supported its determination of increased imports of this product. *Id.,* paras. 395–399.

298 *United States – Steel Products, supra* note 70, paras. 10.214–10.215, 10.224, 10.233, 10.244, 10.253–10.254.

299 *Id.,* para. 10.255.

300 *Dominican Republic — Polypropylene Bags and Tubular Fabric, supra* note 70, paras. 7.231–7.234. According to the Panel, "an increase in imports of 1,160,748.39 kg (60.76 percent) was observed at the beginning of the [investigation] period (2006–2007) and an increase of 288,747.63 kg (9.40 percent) during the intermediate period (2007–2008), so that imports increased continuously in two out of three annual comparisons, including a significant increase between the years 2006 and 2007. It also identified a decrease in imports of 493,096.13 kg (14.68 percent) at the end of the period (2008–2009). In the Preliminary Technical Report it was indicated that the decrease in question could be attributed to an overall reduction in Dominican Republic imports in 2009. In the final phase of the investigation, reference was also made to the fact that in the first half of 2010, in particular in the months of February, March and June of that year, imports recovered, in some cases reaching levels higher than those recorded during 2009," *Id.,* para. 7.231.

evaluations of each product to determine an increase in imports.[301] The Panel in *European Union – Steel Products* also confirmed that fluctuations in import levels observed for individual product categories do not necessarily negate the investigating authority's finding of increased imports for the product as a whole.[302]

4.41 *Conclusion.* The examination of Panel and Appellate Body decisions in increased imports leads to certain conclusions. First, the significant increase in imports has to be identified in overall trends rather than isolated periods. Secondly, fluctuations in imports do not necessarily negate a claim of the increase in imports, but those significant enough to frustrate the overall increasing trends will do so. Finally, the increase in imports needs to be sufficiently recent, and a significant decrease toward the end of the investigation period should be considered carefully, as it can be a beginning of a downward trend in imports – the examination of import trends in more recent periods may be necessary to determine this.

4.3 "LIKE OR DIRECTLY COMPETITIVE PRODUCTS"

4.42 *Definition of Protected Domestic Industry.* As safeguard measures protect the domestic industry that produces "like or directly competitive products" to the imports (Article 2.1), it would be necessary to identify the domestic industry subject to the protection. Article 4.1(c) of the SA defines "domestic industry" as "the producers as a whole of the *like or directly competitive products*, operating within the territory of a Member, or those whose collective output of the *like* or *directly competitive products* constitute a major proportion of the total domestic production of those products" (emphasis added).[303] According to this

301 *Dominican Republic — Polypropylene Bags and Tubular Fabric, supra* note 70, paras. 7.236–7.237. The complainants argued that the determination of the increase in imports is invalid because there was no separate determination of the increase in imports of tubular fabric and polypropylene bags. The Panel did not consider that the increase in imports should have been demonstrated separately with respect to each of these products. *Id.*, para. 7.236.

302 *European Union – Steel Products, supra* note 70, paras. 7.177–7.181. The Panel found that "the central analysis conducted by the European Commission related to the product as a whole, the analysis of product categories and product families was supplemental, and this granular analysis still disclosed trends that were similar to those observed for the product as a whole, we do not consider that Turkey has established that the European Commission did not provide a reasoned and adequate explanation of its finding of increase in imports in light of the fluctuations in import levels observed for certain individual product categories and product families." *Id.*, para. 7.181. The Panel also found that the scope of product for initial investigation does not have to be identical to the scope of product for the application of a safeguard measure as long as the national authority does not include the excluded product in its analysis. *Id.*, para. 7.73.

303 Note that the nationality of the producers is immaterial. Foreign producers are also considered part of the domestic industry as long as they produce within the national border of a Member applying a safeguard measure.

definition, the determination of injury must be based on the condition of the domestic industry that produces "like or directly competitive products" and those products only. In fact, it would hardly be justifiable to restrict imports that do not affect the position of the domestic industry concerned. Therefore, the identification of "like or directly competitive products" is necessary to identify the domestic industry. However, the SA does not provide a methodology or criteria for the determination of like or directly competitive products.

Like Product. What would be the criteria for the determination of "like or directly competitive products"? With respect to the "like" product, a similarity in the physical characteristics and the product usage is a determining factor.[304] A Panel decision considered the determination of a "like" product. In *United States – Lamb Meat*, the Panel found that "like" products mean like "end" products.[305] In this case, the Panel concluded that the feeders and growers of live lambs were not included in the domestic industry since imports – lamb meat – and the domestic product in question – live lambs – could not have been like products.[306] The degree of vertical integration in the production process involving two products (i.e., obviously live lambs are processed into lamb meat) was found irrelevant in the determination of like products. **4.43**

Directly Competitive Product. The question of a "directly competitive product" was not examined in *United States – Lamb Meat*, as the USITC's consideration was explicitly limited to "like" product and not "directly competitive product." The concept of "directly competitive product" expands the range of protected domestic products and protects domestic products which may not bear any physical similarity to the imported products in question. An essential element of directly competitive products would be a degree of market competition between domestic and imported products. In *United States – Lamb Meat*, it was conceivable that the close commercial relationship and a high degree of substitutability between live lambs and lamb meat would have rendered them "directly competitive products." In *Korea – Dairy Products*, where the safeguard measure was applied to imports of certain skimmed milk powder products (SMPPs), raw milk was included in the extent of domestic industry, despite physical dissimilarities between raw milk and SMPPs.[307] The significant overlap between the end use of raw milk and that of SMPPs was the reason **4.44**

304 For an overview of "like product" in WTO law, *see* Won-Mog Choi, *"Like Products" in International Trade Law: Towards a Consistent WTO Jurisprudence* (Oxford University Press, 2003).

305 *United States – Lamb Meat, supra* note 70, para. 7.109.

306 *Id.*, paras. 7.105–7.107.

307 *See* Paragraph III.2 of the Notification of April 1, 1998, G/SG/N/10/KOR/1/Suppl.1 (Exhibit EC-10).

for the inclusion of raw milk, and this determination was not challenged in the subsequent Panel proceedings.[308]

4.45 It has also been suggested that a comparison and contrast of the relevant product characteristics such as sizes, designs, inputs, add-on components, direct and derivative uses, wholesale and retail costs, manufacturing methodologies, and a range of other features of the two products should be permitted in the determination of like or directly competitive products.[309] Since the purpose of the application of a safeguard measure is to protect the relevant domestic industry competing with imports, the key for the determination of like or directly competitive products is to identify domestic products that are being displaced by the imports in question due to market competition. The relevant economic indicators, such as the "cross-elasticity of demand"[310] would be useful in assessing market competition between the domestic products and imports.

4.46 An interesting question has been raised where imports not only compete with certain domestic end products but also adversely affect the position of those domestic producers who supply parts for those end products. Should those producers of parts also be included in the domestic industry? As mentioned above, the degree of integration in the production process involving two products was found irrelevant in the determination of like products. Therefore, it is unlikely that those "parts" would be considered "like products." Alternatively, would they be considered "directly competitive products"? For instance, there are many part producers involved in the production of an automobile. Should they all be included in the domestic producers entitled to protection where their market performance is adversely affected by the imports? Again, the key for this determination is the degree of market substitutability, because the domestic products in question would not be "directly" competing with imports unless there is a significant degree of market substitutability between them. In the above automobile example, the producers of car windshields are less likely to be considered domestic producers because the degree of substitutability between imported automobiles and domestic windshields would be low.

4.47 Also, the Panel found a restriction on the determination of the directly competitive product based on the production process unjustified. In *Dominican*

308 *Korea – Dairy Products*, *supra* note 70, para. 4.294.

309 Bhala and Kennedy, *supra* note 87, p. 911.

310 The cross-elasticity of demand is the change of quantity in one good occurring as a result of a unit change of the price in the other good. If it is positive, there exists positive substitutability between two products.

Republic – Polypropylene Bags and Tubular Fabric, the Panel held that the directly competitive product should not be restricted to the product manufactured from a particular stage of production (the processing of virgin resin) where the product under investigation on which the safeguard measures were imposed is tubular fabric and polypropylene bags in general.[311]

In determining the likeness or direct competitiveness between domestic and imported products subject to the safeguard, the obligation of national authorities to provide reasoned conclusions has been emphasized.[312] In *Chile – Agricultural Products*, Chile asserted that wheat and wheat flour are directly competitive products. It also contended that the reasoning was included in the CDC (Chilean Distortions Commission) reports, which states: "wheat flour represents an alternative way of importing wheat if direct imports prove to be more costly or are subject to a higher tariff, so it is necessary to apply a treatment similar to that applicable to wheat." The Panel determined that this comment relates to a possible relationship of likeness or direct competitiveness between imported wheat and imported wheat flour, but not between domestic wheat or wheat flour and the imported wheat flour.[313] **4.48**

4.4 NON-DISCRIMINATORY APPLICATION OF SAFEGUARD MEASURES[314]

Under the SA, safeguard measures are applied non-discriminatorily. Article 2.2 provides, "A safeguard measure shall be applied to a product being imported irrespective of its source." The Article expressly requires that Members apply safeguard measures on the MFN basis, thus incorporating the result of long negotiations on this issue.[315] **4.49**

Price Discrimination. Concern was raised that the importing Member may evade the MFN requirement by price discrimination: that is, applying a safeguard measure to a product below a certain price.[316] Obviously, price discrimination would hurt relatively inexpensive exports from developing country **4.50**

311 *Dominican Republic — Polypropylene Bags and Tubular Fabric*, *supra* note 70, paras. 7.183–7.201.
312 *Chile – Agricultural Products*, *supra* note 70, para. 7.146.
313 *Id.*, paras. 7.144–7.145.
314 The discussions of Chapter 4.4 draw extensively from the author's previous work, "Safeguard Measures: Why Are They Not Applied Consistently With the Rules? – Lessons for Competent National Authorities and Proposal for the Modification of the Rules on Safeguards" (2002) *supra* note 1.
315 *See* Chapters 2.3 and 2.4 *supra*.
316 Bhala and Kennedy, *supra* note 87, p. 918. For the cases of price discrimination, *see* WTO, *Analytical Index*, *supra* note 85, p. 521.

Members where low production costs, such as labor costs, tend to keep prices down.

4.51 Would price discrimination be compatible with the MFN provision of Article 2.2? The provision does not specifically prohibit price discrimination. It requires that safeguard measures be applied to a product "irrespective of its sources."[317] It is, therefore, arguable that as long as price discrimination applies to a product being imported from all Members on equal terms, it is consistent with the requirement of Article 2.2. On the other hand, even if price discrimination applies across the board, it could be a *de facto* discrimination against products from a certain group of Members, in particular, developing country Members where production costs tend to be lower, and therefore, so does the price. The key phrase of Article 2.1, "… shall be applied to a product being imported …" stipulates *how* Members must apply a safeguard measure, and it does not authorize any discrimination, including discrimination based on price, for the application of a safeguard measure. Hence, arguably, the Article does not authorize a measure applied selectively according to the price of a product.

4.52 *Parallelism.* In some safeguard cases, imports originating from the members of free trade areas or customs unions[318] have been exempted from the application of safeguards. A customs union may adopt a policy so as to restrict a member State from applying a safeguard measure on imports from the other member States,[319] and the question is whether a member of a customs union is authorized to exempt imports from the other member States from its application of a safeguard measure.

4.53 In *Argentina – Footwear*, the Panel found that a member of a customs union is not allowed to exempt imports from the other member countries where it made injury determination based on the examination of imports from all sources,

317 Article 2.2 of the SA.

318 The term "customs union" includes "free trade area" unless indicated otherwise.

319 For instance, Section 301(a) of the USMCA (United States–Mexico–Canada Agreement) Implementation Act (formerly Section 311(a) of the NAFTA Implementation Act) provides that if the USITC makes an "affirmative injury determination" in an investigation under Section 202 of the United States Trade Act, the Commission is also required to find "whether (1) imports of the article from a USMCA country, considered individually, account for a substantial share of total imports and (2) imports of the article from a USMCA country, considered individually or, in exceptional circumstances, imports from USMCA countries considered collectively, contribute importantly to the serious injury, or threat thereof, caused by imports." A USMCA country is not to apply a safeguard measure to imports from the other USMCA countries unless both conditions (1) and (2) above are met. A critic argued that the exclusion of products from the members of preferential trade agreements (PTAs) from the application of safeguard measures represented explicit discrimination against the non-members. Chad P. Bown and Rachel McCulloch, "Nondiscrimination and the WTO Agreement on Safeguards" (2003) 2(3) *World Trade Review* 333.

including those from member countries. This required consistency between the scope of safeguard application and that of injury assessment is called "parallelism," and this parallelism was emphasized in *Argentina – Footwear*.[320] The Appellate Body subsequently affirmed the Panel decision but did not address the question of whether a member of a customs union may exclude the other member countries from its application of a safeguard measure *if its injury determination is based on the analysis of imports from non-member countries only*.[321] The issue was reiterated in *United States – Wheat Gluten* where the Panel did not approve of excluding imports from Canada, a member of the NAFTA, where the injury determination was made based on imports from all sources.[322]

In *United States – Wheat Gluten*, the United States conducted a separate analysis of the causal effect of the imports from Canada on serious injury to the domestic industry and subsequently determined that the imports from Canada did not reach a "substantial share" and did not "contribute importantly" to the injury.[323] The Panel found that once an injury determination is made based on the imports from all sources, a safeguard measure must be applied to the imports from all sources regardless of the result from such an analysis because imports from different sources may have *collectively* caused the injury, and therefore, the exclusion of the imports from a particular source from the application of a safeguard measure would not be warranted.[324] **4.54**

Would a member of a customs union be allowed to exclude imports from other members from its application of a safeguard measure if it makes an injury determination based on imports from the non-member countries only? The subsequent Panel in *United States – Line Pipe* considered this question. It found that the provision in Article XXIV of GATT allows a member of the customs union to exclude imports from the other members if the injury determination is based on imports from the non-member States of a customs union only. According to the Panel, the provisions in Article XXIV that authorize the elimination of duties and other restrictive regulations of commerce among the members of a customs union can also be used to exempt imports from the other members in the application of a safeguard measure.[325] **4.55**

---

320 *Argentina – Footwear*, *supra* note 70, paras. 8.72–8.92.

321 *Argentina – Footwear*, *supra* note 71, paras. 99–114.

322 *United States – Wheat Gluten*, *supra* note 70, para. 8.178.

323 Then, by operation of the relevant NAFTA provisions, the United States was not allowed to apply safeguard measures to another member State of NAFTA. *Supra* note 319.

324 *United States – Wheat Gluten*, *supra* note 70, para. 8.176. The Appellate Body also upheld the Panel findings. *United States – Wheat Gluten*, *supra* note 71, paras. 98–100.

325 *United States – Line Pipe*, *supra* note 70, paras. 7.135–7.163.

4.56 The Appellate Body ruled that any gap between the scope of injury assessment and the scope of safeguard measure is justified *only if* the Member explicitly establishes that imports from sources covered by the measure satisfy the conditions for the application of a safeguard measure as set out in Article 2.1.[326] In *Line Pipe*, the United States contended that it had considered the injurious effects of imports from non-NAFTA countries, and pointed out a note in the relevant USITC Report as the evidence of this consideration.[327] However, the Appellate Body found that the note included only conclusions about such injurious effects and that the United States had failed to provide a reasoned and adequate explanation[328] that established explicitly that imports from non-NAFTA sources satisfied the conditions for the application of safeguard measures.[329] The Appellate Body decision affirmed the requirement of *parallelism* under the provisions of Article 2, which requires that the scope of imports considered for injury determination should be identical to that subject to the safeguard.

4.57 In *United States – Steel Products*, there was debate as to what amounts to a finding[330] that establishes explicitly that imports from sources covered by the measure satisfy the conditions for a safeguard measure.[331] The United States indicated that the competent authorities' formal conclusion is sufficient and an "explicit" recitation of each step of the analytical process leading to that conclusion is not required.[332] The Panel disagreed and determined that the competent authorities must provide a reasoned and adequate explanation of how the facts support the determination that the products covered in the measure have alone caused serious injury to the domestic industry.[333]

4.58 The Panel made measure-by-measure assessments to determine whether the United States fulfilled the requirement of parallelism. With respect to all product categories, the Panel found that the United States failed to establish explicitly that imports from the sources included in the application of these measures fulfilled the conditions for the application of a safeguard measure: i.e., it did not take the required analytical steps under the SA to establish

---

326 *United States – Line Pipe*, Report of the Appellate Body, *supra* note 71, para 181, quoting its previous decision in *United States – Wheat Gluten*, *supra* note 71, para 98.

327 *Supra* note 259.

328 The national authorities must provide findings and *reasoned* conclusions on all pertinent issues of fact and law (Article 3.1).

329 *United States – Line Pipe*, *supra* note 71, paras. 197–199.

330 *Supra* note 328.

331 *United States – Steel Products*, *supra* note 70, para. 10.594.

332 *Id.*

333 *Id.*, paras. 10.195–10.196.

that the imports not exempted from the safeguards alone caused injury to the domestic industry. A few paragraphs in the Second Supplementary Report commenting on the effect of the exclusion were considered insufficient and rather inconclusive, lacking adequate reasoning and explanations.[334] The Panel determined, in particular, that the causal effects of excluded imports were not adequately addressed under Article 4.2(b) of the SA.[335]

On appeal, the United States argued that nothing in the SA requires a distinct or explicit analysis of imports from sources *not* subject to the measure.[336] The Appellate Body affirmed the Panel position, stating that the imports excluded from the application of the safeguard measure must be considered a factor "other than increased imports" within the meaning of Article 4.2(b).[337] The Appellate Body found that the possible injurious effects that these excluded imports may have on the domestic industry must not be attributed to the imports included in the safeguard measure pursuant to Article 4.2(b).[338] The Appellate Body was also of the view that the Member must make *a single joint determination*, rather than making separate and partial determinations of the injurious impact of the imports included in the measure, *although imports from some of those countries are very small and almost non-existent.*[339] **4.59**

These Panel and Appellate Body decisions impose considerable analytical tasks on a Member proposing to apply a safeguard measure with the exemption of imports from some of its trading partners. Nonetheless, it appears from the relevant Panel and Appellate Body decisions that a Member may in fact exempt imports from other members of the customs union as long as the requirement of parallelism is met, as discussed above. **4.60**

334 With respect to CCFRS, the Panel noted analytical flaws in the USITC report. First, the causal effects of the excluded products were not adequately considered. Secondly, the USITC discussion of "non-NAFTA imports" still included the imports from Israel and Jordan, which were excluded from the steel safeguards, and therefore, should have been excluded along with NAFTA imports in the USITC analysis. *Id.*, paras. 10.601–10.609. The Panel made the same conclusions with respect to the other eight product categories. *Id.*, paras. 10.623, 10.633, 10.643, 10.653, 10.660, 10.670, 10.680, 10.692. The split of opinions among the USITC Commissioners with respect to tin mill products and stainless steel wire was also noted.

335 Article 4.2(b) of the SA provides, "The determination referred to in subparagraph (a) (injury determination) shall not be made unless the investigation demonstrates, on the basis of objective evidence, the existence of the causal link between increased imports of the product concerned and serious injury or threat thereof. When factors other than increased imports are causing injury to the domestic industry at the same time, such injury shall not be attributed to increased imports" (explanation added). The issue of causation will be discussed in Chapter 5.2 *infra.*

336 *United States – Steel Products, supra* note 71, para. 447.

337 *Id.*, para. 450. *See also supra* note 335.

338 *Id.*

339 *Id.*, para. 468.

4.61 *FTA and Exclusion.* The Panel in *Line Pipe* considered that the authorization of a free trading area under GATT Article XXIV is a legal ground for exclusion of intra-FTA[340] imports from a safeguard measure, indicating that the exclusion is permissible among members of a customs union.[341] Article XXIV authorizes the establishment of a customs union and enables its members to provide preferential treatment for each other by eliminating duties and other restrictive regulations of commerce, with respect to "*all*" or "*substantially all*" trade within the territory of the customs union (Article XXIV:8(a)(i)). Article XXIV also requires that substantially the same duties and other regulations of commerce be applied by each of the members of the union to the trade of territories not included in the customs union (Article XXIV:8(a)(ii)).

4.62 The author previously expressed doubt about the position that the provisions of Article XXIV provide defense to the selective application of safeguards in favor of the other member States of a customs union, as it is not clear that the authorization of the *permanent* elimination of trade barriers among members of a customs union under Article XXIV extends to the different circumstances in which a Member applies a temporary trade barrier such as a safeguard measure, to remedy or prevent serious injury to a domestic industry.[342] In addition, where a single member of a customs union imposes a safeguard measure to a product, the duties and other regulations of commerce applied by the other union members will not be the same with respect to the product in question, despite the requirement of Article XXIV:8(a)(ii).

4.63 This rationale is consistent with the provisions of Article XXIV:8. Nevertheless, should this rationale be applied to prohibit the exemption of imports from the other member States of a customs union, it would frustrate the policy within customs unions that may require the exemption of imports from the member States from a safeguard measure. Footnote 1 of Article 2 authorizes a customs union to apply a safeguard measure *on behalf of a member State.*[343] It also provides that in such cases the measure shall be limited to that member State.

---

340 FTAs in the context of this book are understood to include all bilateral or multilateral agreements to create free trade relations among the participants.

341 *United States – Line Pipe, supra* note 70, paras. 7.135–7.163.

342 Lee (2002), *supra* note 1, p. 649.

343 Footnote 1 of Article 2 provides, "A customs union may apply a safeguard measure as a single unit or on behalf of a member State. When a customs union applies a safeguard measure as a single unit, all the requirements for the determination of serious injury or threat thereof under this Agreement shall be based on the conditions existing in the customs union as a whole. When a safeguard measure is applied on behalf of a member State, all the requirements for the determination of serious injury or threat thereof shall be based on the conditions existing in that member State and the measure shall be limited to that member State. Nothing in this Agreement prejudges the interpretation of the relationship between Article XIX and paragraph 8 of Article XXIV of GATT 1994."

Should this limitation mean that the safeguard is applied to imports from the other member States as well as from non-member States?

It is difficult to conceive that a safeguard measure of a customs union applied on behalf of a member State should, although temporarily, erect trade barriers among the member States which have been removed permanently under the authorization of Article XXIV. If the imports from the other member States may be exempted from a safeguard measure where a customs union applies it on behalf of a member State under this provision, there seems no reason to deny the same exemption where an individual member State applies a safeguard measure. The requirement of *parallelism* should be observed whether a safeguard measure is applied by a customs union or by an individual member State. **4.64**

The Appellate Body avoided making any definitive ruling on this issue by stating that it did not want to "prejudge" the Article XXIV issue.[344] Nevertheless, if the previous Article XXIV analysis by the *Line Pipe* Panel was ultimately to be correct, the exclusion of imports from a country with which the importing country has no FTA can be considered to be violating the parallelism requirement under Article 2.2 because it would not have Article XXIV justification. In fact, permitting selective application of safeguard measures against imports from certain countries without any justifying apparatus such as an FTA authorized by Article XXIV would undermine the MFN application of safeguards, which was finally agreed after decades of debates and negotiations.[345] **4.65**

Finally, it is to be noted that the Panel in *Dominican Republic – Polypropylene Bags and Tubular Fabric* confirmed that the exemption of products from certain developing countries under Article 9.1 is an exception to the requirement of parallelism, and it would not be necessary to undertake a new analysis of the increase in imports, the injury, and causation.[346] **4.66**

---

344 *United States – Line Pipe, supra* note 71, para. 198. Nonetheless, it appears that the Appellate Body approved the exemption provided that the requirement of parallelism is met, by ruling that any gap between the scope of injury assessment and the scope of safeguard measure is justified if the Member establishes explicitly that imports from sources covered by the measure satisfy the conditions for the application of a safeguard measure as set out in Article 2.1. *United States – Line Pipe, supra* note 71, para. 181, quoting its previous decision in *United States – Wheat Gluten, supra* note 71, para. 98.

345 *See* Chapter 2 *supra* for a discussion of long negotiation process of the SA. A study described various ways in which a member of a regional trade agreement may determine injury and apply a safeguard measure with respect to imports from the other members of the agreement. Joost Pauwelyn, "The Puzzle of WTO Safeguards and Regional Trade Agreements" (2004) 7 *Journal of International Economic Law* 141–142.

346 *Dominican Republic – Polypropylene Bags and Tubular Fabric, supra* note 70, para. 7.385. SA Article 9.1 exclude products originating from certain developing country Members from the coverage of a safeguard measure under two requirements: the individual share of the developing country Member which it is sought to exclude from the application of the measure shall not exceed 3 percent of the imports of the Member applying the measure; and the collective share of the developing countries that meet the first requirement shall not exceed 9 percent of total imports of the product concerned. *Id.*, para. 7.373.

5

ARTICLE 4 – INJURY AND CAUSATION

5.1 INJURY DETERMINATION

5.01 The injury determination constitutes a core stage in the investigation for a safeguard measure, as safeguard measures remedy or prevent *serious injury* to the domestic industry (Article 2.1). Article 4.1 provides a series of definitions for the terms relevant to the injury determination. For instance, "serious injury" is defined as "a significant overall impairment in the position of a domestic industry" (Article 4.1(a)) and "threat of serious injury" as "serious injury that is clearly imminent, in accordance with the provisions of paragraph 2" (Article 4.1(b)).[347]

5.02 These brief definitions do not remove the inherent subjectivity in the injury determination. It is left to the national authorities to assess whether the investigated injury constitutes "an overall impairment in the position of the domestic industry" and, in the case of a threat, whether the injury is "imminent." Injury determination is an art, rather than a precise science, and a certain degree of subjectivity is inevitable. Nevertheless, in conjunction with the specific injury factors specified in Article 4.2(a) and the reasoned explanations and analysis required for the injury determination under Articles 3 and 4.2(c),[348] these provisions of the SA reduce the arbitrariness of the injury assessment.

---

347 The term "injury" includes the concepts of both "serious injury" and "threat of serious injury" to domestic industry unless indicated otherwise.

348 Article 4.2(c) provides, "The competent authorities shall publish promptly, in accordance with the provisions of Article 3, a detailed analysis of the case under investigation as well as a demonstration of the relevance of the factors examined." *Korea – Dairy Products*, *supra* note 70, para. 7.55. *Argentina – Footwear*, *supra* note 70, para. 8.206 and *supra* note 71, para. 136.

Consideration of Injury Factors. Article 4.2(a) specifies injury factors to be considered in the assessment of injury. The Article provides in relevant part, 5.03

> [T]he competent authorities shall evaluate all relevant factors of an objective and quantifiable nature having a bearing on the situation of that industry, in particular, *the rate and amount of the increase in imports of the product concerned in the absolute and relative terms, the share of the domestic market taken by increased imports, changes in the level of sales, production, productivity, capacity utilization, profits and losses, and employment* (emphasis added).

The Article establishes objective criteria for the assessment of injury by listing eight injury factors. Panel and Appellate Body decisions have provided certain guidelines for the injury assessment under Article 4.1(a). First, the examination of *every* listed factor is mandatory. In *Korea – Dairy Products*, the Panel did not believe that all eight factors would be important in the injury assessment in every case. Nevertheless, it required a Member proposing to apply a safeguard measure to consider each and every factor listed under Article 4.2(a) before dismissing any of them as not having a bearing on the situation of that industry.[349] This position was also supported by the Appellate Body.[350] 5.04

There is a question *why* consideration of those listed factors should be made mandatory where some of them may have little or no relevance to the situation of the domestic industry.[351] Arguably, it makes little sense to require national authorities to explain why certain factors are not relevant: the point of review should be whether an injury assessment demonstrates an overall impairment in the position of the domestic industry, and not the number of factors considered by the authorities. 5.05

Nevertheless, there is practical concern that if the national authority is not required to consider all the factors, this discretion may lead to an arbitrary injury determination based on the examination of only a few factors which support the determination and not of other factors which do not. Under the relevant standard of review, the panel may not conduct a *de novo* review of the national authorities' investigations.[352] Therefore, the current list of injury 5.06

---

349 *Korea – Dairy Products, supra* note 70, para. 7.55.

350 *Argentina – Footwear, supra* note 71, para. 136.

351 For instance, capital utilization is one of the eight injury factors listed in Article 4.2(a), but this factor may not always be relevant. For instance, in a dairy industry where capital utilization can be measured in terms of the number of cows to be milked at a given time, capital utilization would always be close to 100 percent regardless of the conditions of the domestic industry. It is because those cows have to be milked at regular intervals to avoid contracting udder disease.

352 A *de novo* review will be outside the standard of review. *See* Chapter 4.1 *supra* for a discussion of the standard of review.

factors, though not all of them may be relevant in every case, provides a benchmark for the panel review.

5.07 In addition, the Appellate Body held that an examination by the national authorities should not be limited to the eight listed injury factors. The national authorities must analyze *all* factors that they consider relevant.[353]

5.08 *Explanation Required for Injury Determination.* Competent national authorities are obligated to provide an adequate explanation as to how the factor considered supports or detracts from a finding of serious injury.[354] Article 4.2(c) provides, "The competent authorities shall publish promptly, in accordance with the provisions of Article 3, a detailed analysis of the case under investigation as well as a demonstration of the relevance of the factors examined."[355] As mentioned, injury determination is not a precise science, and the provision of the SA does not provide a numeric threshold for injury determination (e.g., what percentage decline of employment should be regarded indicative of serious injury). What is required is a demonstration of the national authorities' consideration of those injury factors by providing a reasonable explanation for their decision.[356] The question is *to what extent* the authorities must explain their decisions. In the absence of any quantitative threshold for serious injury, which would at any rate be difficult to set, it would be impossible to remove

353 *United States – Wheat Gluten, supra* note 71, para. 55. While the Panel in *United States – Wheat Gluten* ruled that competent authorities are required to consider the listed injury factors under Article 4.2(a) and other factors that are clearly raised before them as relevant by the interested parties in the domestic investigation, the Appellate Body reversed this decision and required national authorities to examine other factors that they consider relevant irrespective of whether they had been clearly raised by the interested parties. In consideration of the relevant factors, the Panel in *Dominican Republic – Polypropylene Bags and Tubular Fabric* did not support the national authority's finding of serious injury where only four injury factors (cash flow, costs, profits and losses, and inventories) were shown to have performed negatively as compared with the evidence that seven factors (including important elements indicative of the position of the domestic industry, such as production, sales, installed capacity and capacity utilization, and production's share of domestic consumption) performed positively. *Dominican Republic – Polypropylene Bags and Tubular Fabric, supra* note 71, paras. 7.273–7.278 and paras. 7.304–7.313.

354 *Korea – Dairy Products, supra* note 70, para. 7.58. *Argentina – Footwear, supra* note 70, para. 8.221.

355 It has been suggested that the literal interpretation of the text of Article 4.2(c) may require publication of injury assessment before the issuance of the final report under Article 3.1. *See* Bhala and Kennedy, *supra* note 87, p. 927. The publication under Article 4.2(c) is to be made in accordance with Article 3, and previous Panels and the Appellate Body did not distinguish the publication required under Article 4.2(c) from the report under Article 3. The Appellate Body in *Wheat Gluten* stated, "We recall that, under Article 3.1 of *the Agreement on Safeguards, the competent authorities* must 'publish a report' which provides 'reasoned conclusions' on 'all pertinent issues'. (emphasis added) Under Article 4.2(c), that report must also contain 'a detailed analysis', including 'a demonstration of the relevance of the factors examined'." According to this finding, as Article 3.1 must also include the analysis required under Article 4.2(c), a separate report does not seem necessary. *United States – Wheat Gluten, supra* note 71, para. 160.

356 For example, where Korea chose to disregard certain increases in the production of the domestic industry, the Panel required an explanation for its decision to disregard those increases. *Korea – Dairy Products, supra* note 70, para. 7.67.

the inherent subjectivity of injury determination. For instance, would it be possible to explain why a decrease in employment of a given percentage, say, 10 percent, should be considered indicative of serious injury? Are national authorities required to make such an explanation?

In *Argentina – Footwear*, a literal interpretation of the Panel decision may indicate that the national authorities are indeed required to do so. The Panel determined that the national authorities had to explain, *inter alia*, "why, for example, an employment decline of a given percentage supports a finding of serious injury or threat to the particular industry being considered."[357] This Panel decision should be understood in the factual context of the case, in which there was a significant discrepancy in the employment data presented by Argentina. It appears that the Panel demanded the explanation in light of this discrepancy: e.g., which data is the basis for the national authority's decision and why.[358] **5.09**

In contrast, where there was no question about the consistency of the data, the Panel did not demand such an explanation as to why the national authority would consider a certain decrease in an injury factor to be an indication of injury. In *Korea – Dairy Products*, Korea considered certain changes in the level of sales, one of the listed injury factors, to be indicative of injury on the basis of the figures included in its investigation report (domestic milk powder: 12,191 tons for 1993, 12,468 tons for 1994, 10,690 tons for 1995 and 2,741 tons for the January–April period of 1996; domestic raw milk: 1,844,463 tons in 1993, 1,947,128 tons in 1994, 1,947,965 tons in 1995, and 984,934 tons in the January–June period of 1996).[359] The EC argued that the level of sales in domestic raw milk was "remarkably stable" and questioned Korea's claim of a decrease in the sales of raw milk in 1996.[360] Nevertheless, the Panel accepted that this decline could support the Korean authority's finding of serious injury **5.10**

357 *Argentina – Footwear*, *supra* note 70, para. 8.221.

358 According to the Panel, the discrepancy was as the following: "on employment, Act 338 refers to a representation by the petitioners that employment declined by 34 percent between 1991 and 1995, but also indicates that questionnaire results reflected a 5 percent decline. In response to a Panel question, Argentina stated that the questionnaire data showed a 13 percent decline, and referred as well to employment data from the Argentine Industrial Union showing a 21 percent decline. Upon questioning by the Panel as to how these different data could be reconciled, Argentina replied that all of the data showed declines, and only then provided the explanation noted above as to the different compositions of the questionnaire responses included in the calculations of the 5 percent and 13 percent declines." *Id.*, para. 8.220.

359 *Investigation Report on Industrial Injury Related to the Increase of Certain Dairy Products Imports* ("The OAI Report"), Office of Administration and Investigation, Korean Trade Commission (October 23, 1996), pp. 38–45.

360 *Korea – Dairy Products*, *supra* note 70, para. 4.302.

to the domestic industry and did not require Korea to *justify why* those specific decreases in sales should be regarded as indicative of a serious injury.[361]

5.11 In conclusion, reasoning and explanation seems particularly important where national authorities decide to disregard certain aspects of a particular injury factor or use data that reveal significant discrepancies. For instance, where Korea chose to disregard the increases in the production of the domestic industry, the Panel required reasoning for its decision to disregard those increases.[362] It would be important to provide convincing reasoning and explanations particularly where alternative reasoning was put forward, the application of which could have altered the outcome of the analysis, or where national authorities claim the existence of injury based on a minute decrease in injury factors.[363]

5.12 The Appellate Body in *United States – Lamb Meat* once again emphasized the importance of qualitative evaluation and reasoning in injury determination, stating that the list of relevant factors to be evaluated is not a mere "check list." It ruled that competent authorities must conduct a substantive evaluation of the "bearing," or the "influence" or "effect" or "impact," that the relevant factors have on the "situation of the domestic industry."[364] This confirms the point made by the previous Panel and Appellate Body decisions that it would be insufficient to simply state the observed changes in injury factors to support injury determinations, and the national authorities would have to explain how those changes support or detract from the injury determination.

5.13 *Price Analysis Required?* Is an injury factor for mandatory consideration found elsewhere in the SA other than Article 4.2(a)? Article 2.1 provides, "A Member may apply a safeguard measure, pursuant to the provisions set out

361 *Id.*, paras. 7.64–7.66.

362 *Id.*, para. 7.67. Similarly, the Panel in *Dominican Republic — Polypropylene Bags and Tubular Fabric* ound that the national authority failed to provide a reasoned and adequate explanation for its conclusions. The national authority had concluded that production contracted and the share of imports increased when value per production volume decreased, but production recorded a cumulative increase of 91 percent over the period of investigation. The national authority had also observed that production by value increased by 63 percent, and the share of imports increased for only one year and then steadily decreased: the share of imports in the domestic consumption increased from 61 percent in 2006 to 67 percent in 2007 but decreased to 64 percent in 2008 and 57 percent in 2009. *Dominican Republic — Polypropylene Bags and Tubular Fabric, supra* note 70, paras. 7.273–7.278 and paras. 7.292–7.299.

363 Thus, an injury claim based on a nominal decrease in injury factors may well prompt a panel to review the authorities' reasoning for the injury decision in order to prevent the abuse of a safeguard measure.

364 *United States – Lamb Meat, supra* note 71, para. 104. The Panel in *Dominican Republic — Polypropylene Bags and Tubular Fabric* also held that merely providing information on the trend in inventories with respect to the end points of the period of investigation (the beginning and end), without offering any reasoned additional explanation of how this information tied in with its conclusion, is not sufficient. *Dominican Republic — Polypropylene Bags and Tubular Fabric, supra* note 70, paras. 7.279–7.284.

below, that such product is being imported into its territory ... *under such conditions* as to cause or threaten to cause serious injury to the domestic industry ...." With respect to the clause "under such conditions" included in Article 2.1, a question arose as to whether this clause requires Members to perform a price analysis of the imported products to examine the conditions under which the relevant products were imported. Previous Panels found that the phrase does not create an additional criterion or analytical requirement to be performed and that Members, therefore, are not obligated to conduct a price analysis under this phrase.[365]

Methodology.[366] A particular methodology adopted by the authorities for collecting data or injury assessment, and the weight accorded to each factor by the authorities for purposes of the final determination of serious injury, is within the discretion of the national authorities. In the injury assessment, national authorities need not demonstrate that injury was found in the analysis of every injury factor. Some factors may show decline, supporting a claim of injury, and some may not. However, the overall analysis of all the relevant factors should demonstrate a significant impairment of the position of the domestic industry.[367] **5.14**

In *United States – Line Pipe*, questions were raised with respect to the methodology of injury assessment. Korea challenged the USITC's allocation of company-wide fixed costs on line pipe based on its turnover where the company produces other products as well. The Panel found that such allocation was inevitable, since a cost analysis is required under the provision of Article 4.2(a).[368] This position seems to be in conflict with the previous Panel decision in *Korea – Dairy Products*, which did not accept Korea's profit/loss analysis of its domestic industry, since the Panel determined that those examined producers were also involved in other lines of production.[369] **5.15**

The *Line Pipe* Panel also stated that it would only consider rejecting the methodology adopted by the USITC if Korea proposed an alternative method.[370] According to this decision, the methodology adopted by the national authorities for injury assessment would be accepted unless countered by the complainant with an alternative methodology. This position is not consistent with **5.16**

365 *Korea – Dairy Products, supra* note 70, paras. 7.51–7.52; *Argentina – Footwear, supra* note 71, para. 8.108.
366 Lee (2002), *supra* note 1, pp. 652–653.
367 *Argentina – Footwear, supra* note 71, paras. 138 and 139.
368 *United States – Line Pipe, supra* note 70, para. 7.228.
369 *Supra* note 233.
370 *United States – Line Pipe, supra* note 70, para. 7.228.

the standard of review established in previous cases and used by this Panel,[371] and the appropriateness of the national authorities' investigation should not be determined by the availability of an alternative proposal made by the complainant.

5.17 The Panel also approved of the USITC's attribution of certain costs to the line pipe production where the cost was allegedly associated with the production of other products as well as with the temporary closure of factories.[372] The Panel upheld the investigating authority's decision on the ground that the complainant's challenge against the USITC's decision failed to demonstrate that such attribution was improper. The standard of review, as affirmed by the Appellate Body, requires the panel to examine the national authorities' reasoning critically.[373] Nevertheless, the Panel did not inquire into the legitimacy of such allocation. The Panel decision seems inconsistent with the previous Appellate Body decision.

5.18 *Currency of Injury*. A Panel decided that *current* serious injury should be found to exist, "up to and including the very end of the period of investigation."[374] The currency of injury was also called into question in *United States – Line Pipe*. The complainant argued that the deterioration of the US domestic industry was only temporary since the relevant factors, such as investment, capital expenditure, price, and demand, all increased toward the end of the investigation period.[375] In disagreement, the United States contested that the increase in capital investment reflected pre-import surge decisions and that the price increases were not driven by the improving condition of the domestic industry, but by increasing input costs.[376]

5.19 The Panel rejected the complainant's argument for the reason that the increases in those factors did not necessarily negate the claim of injury. The Panel emphasized that the onus was on the complainant to prove its case and found that Korea had failed to do so.[377] However, the Panel seems to have applied a test that is inconsistent with the previous decision that a complainant only needs to establish a *prima facie* case.[378] Once a *prima facie* case is established, it is then up to the defendant to refute the case made by the complainant. Korea

---

371 Refer to the discussion of the standard of review in Chapter 4.1 *supra*.

372 *United States – Line Pipe*, *supra* note 70, para. 7.237.

373 *United States – Lamb Meat*, *supra* note 71, para. 106. *See also* Chapter 4.1 *supra* for the relevant discussion.

374 *United States – Wheat Gluten*, *supra* note 70, para. 8.81.

375 *United States – Line Pipe*, *supra* note 70, paras. 7.246–7.248.

376 *Id.*, paras. 7.249–7.251.

377 *Id.*, para. 7.258.

378 *See* the relevant discussion of the *prima facie* case in Chapter 4.1 *supra*.

seems to have established a *prima facie* case by demonstrating the decreasing trend in injury factors, and therefore, the Panel should have critically examined whether the United States had provided an adequate and reasoned explanation for its injury determination under the standard of review.[379]

Consideration of the Changes in Other Factors. The assessment of an individual factor should be made in conjunction with other factor(s). For instance, the adoption of a labor-saving production or management technology may improve the competitiveness of a given domestic industry, resulting in improved productivity. Nevertheless, it may also result in a decrease in employment in that industry. In such a case, a decline in employment should not be considered to be an indication of injury. Members should also note that an increase in imports, one of the injury factors under Article 4.2(a), must be evaluated in both *absolute* and *relative* terms.[380] **5.20**

Considering Segments of Domestic Industry. In assessing injury, Members may make an analysis of distinct segments of the domestic industry, but they should either consider all segments, or provide an explanation of how the chosen segments represent the whole industry.[381] The same requirement applies to the selection of individual producers for injury assessment. If the authorities do not examine all producers, they should provide an adequate explanation of how the selection of the particular producers renders an objective picture of the whole domestic industry.[382] **5.21**

Sufficiency of Data for Injury Assessment. The Appellate Body in *United States – Lamb Meat* provided guidelines for determining the sufficiency of data for an injury determination. It held that the data used by the competent authorities must be sufficiently representative to provide a true picture of the domestic industry.[383] The Appellate Body acknowledged that the collection of data that includes all domestic producers might not be practical in many instances. It also considered that sufficiency might vary based on the "particularities" of the domestic industry.[384] This indicates that the data collected and used for the examination needs to be a statistically valid sample; otherwise, there must be a plausible explanation as to why the chosen data would represent the condition of the industry. In addition, the Appellate Body decision held **5.22**

379 *See* Chapter 4.1 *supra* for a discussion of the standard of review.
380 *Chile – Agricultural Products, supra* note 70, para. 7.160.
381 *Korea – Dairy Products, supra* note 70, para. 7.59.
382 *Id.*, para. 7.73.
383 *United States – Lamb Meat, supra* note 71, para. 132.
384 *Id.*, para. 132.

that competent national authorities cannot merely depend on the information submitted by the interested parties. The authorities should actively seek out all relevant information pertaining to the condition of the domestic industry.[385]

5.23 *Threat of Serious Injury.* A safeguard measure is also applicable based upon the threat of serious injury. Article 4.1(b) provides that threat of serious injury "shall be understood to mean serious injury that is *clearly imminent*[386] … A determination of the existence of a threat of serious injury shall be based on *facts and not merely on allegation, conjecture or remote possibility* …" (emphasis added).[387] The SA does not provide any particular methodology to be followed for the determination of a threat of injury.[388]

5.24 A Panel decision set forth the guidelines for conducting a threat analysis as follows: "(i) that a threat determination needs to be based on an analysis which takes objective and verifiable data from the recent past (i.e., the latter part of an investigation period) as a starting-point so as to avoid basing a determination on allegation, conjecture or remote possibility; (ii) that factual determination from the recent past complemented by fact-based projections concerning developments in the industry's condition, and concerning imports, in the imminent future needs to be taken into account in order to ensure an analysis of whether a significant overall impairment of the relevant industry's position is imminent in the near future; (iii) that the analysis needs to determine whether injury of a serious degree will actually occur in the near future unless safeguard action is taken."[389]

5.25 The relevant Panel and the Appellate Body decisions also held that in determining the immediacy of injury, the focus of the national authorities' examination should be on the most recent data.[390] The Appellate Body also emphasized that the recent data should be evaluated in the context of an extended trend

385 *United States – Wheat Gluten, supra* note 71, para. 55.

386 According to the Appellate Body, the phrase "clearly imminent" indicates that the domestic industry is on the brink of suffering serious injury. *United States – Lamb Meat, supra* note 71, para. 125.

387 The Panel in *Argentina – Preserved Peaches* once again emphasized that the competent authorities' determination of a threat of serious injury must be based on facts and not on remote possibility. *Argentina – Preserved Peaches, supra* note 70, paras. 7.83–7.134. The Panel in *European Union – Steel Products* also found that the national authority's injury findings must be "based on facts." *European Union – Steel Products, supra* note 70, para. 7.242.

388 The Panel in *Lamb Meat* also considered that the SA provides no explicit guidance on a particular methodology to be followed. *United States – Lamb Meat, supra* note 70, para. 7.127. The Appellate Body subsequently shared the Panel's consideration. *United States – Lamb Meat, supra* note 71, para. 137.

389 *See United States – Lamb Meat, supra* note 70, para. 7.129.

390 The Panel and the Appellate Body found that the most recent evidence would provide the strongest evidence of the future state of the domestic industry. *United States – Meat Lamb*, Report of the Panel, *supra* note 70, para. 7.132 and Report of the Appellate Body, *supra* note 71, para. 137.

(i.e., the decline toward the end of the investigation period may be part of a normal economic cycle).[391]

National authorities must also conduct a careful evaluation of the relevant injury factors under Article 4.1(a) in the assessment of the threat of injury, as in the case of actual injury. Based on an analysis of all relevant factors, the overall impact on the domestic industry must also be assessed. By conducting a substantive evaluation of the relevant factors, competent authorities are able to make a proper overall determination as to whether the domestic industry is threatened with serious injury.[392] **5.26**

In *European Union – Steel Products*, the domestic industry's performance was improved toward the end of the period of investigation.[393] The Panel opined that the SA does not establish "a categorial rule that precludes authorities from finding a threat of serious injury whenever data show positive trends in the domestic industry's performance" at a given point of the period of investigation; if the evidence "indicates that serious injury is 'clearly imminent' despite clear improvements in the domestic industry's performance, an authority may find a threat of serious injury."[394] The Panel observed that the improvement could be "fleeting or illusory and that the domestic industry will continue to be at a competitive disadvantage *vis-à-vis* imports once the short-lived improvement recedes."[395] **5.27**

Distinction between Injury and Threat. In *United States – Line Pipe* the USITC made a finding of "serious injury or the threat of serious injury," without any distinction between the two. In the opinion of the United States, the distinction is not important, as serious injury and its threat are not mutually exclusive of each other – they are only different "labels" addressing the timing of the injury and neither of them indicates the precise state of the domestic industry.[396] **5.28**

The Panel disagreed and subsequently found that both "serious injury" and "threat of serious injury" refer to distinctively different states of the domestic industry – the former being "a significant overall impairment in the position of a domestic industry" (Article 4.1(a)) and the latter, "serious injury that is **5.29**

---

391 *Id.*, para. 138.
392 *United States – Lamb Meat*, *supra* note 71, para. 104.
393 *European Union – Steel Products*, *supra* note 70, para. 7.208.
394 *Id.*, para. 7.206.
395 *Id.* The Panel found that the European Union failed to demonstrate that the improved performance of its domestic industry toward the end of the period of investigation was of such a nature and determined that its definitive safeguard measure was inconsistent with Article 4.1(b) of the SA. *Supra* note 387.
396 *United States – Line Pipe*, *supra* note 70, para. 7.261.

clearly imminent" (Article 4.2(b)) but no present serious injury. These two terms, therefore, cannot be used interchangeably.[397] The Panel found that the failure to make a discrete decision between "serious injury" and "threat of serious injury" violates the requirement to provide an adequate explanation as to the condition of the domestic industry under the provisions of Article 3.1 and Article 4.2(c).

5.30 On appeal, the Appellate Body reversed the Panel decision. The Appellate Body recognized the conceptual distinction between "serious injury" and "threat of serious injury," but found that the distinction does not necessarily require national authorities to make a discrete decision between these two.[398] According to the Appellate Body, serious injury is often the realization of a threat of serious injury and the precise point where "a threat of serious injury" becomes "serious injury" may sometimes be difficult to discern.[399] Therefore, it found that national authorities should not be precluded from finding both serious injury and its threat since a Member obtains a right to apply a safeguard measure where there is *at least* a threat of serious injury. The threat only indicates a lower threshold for the application of a safeguard measure.[400]

5.31 It is questionable whether national authorities should be allowed to apply a safeguard measure without a definite and discrete determination of the state of its own domestic industry. Although a Member may apply a safeguard measure based on either serious injury or its threat, it has an obligation under Articles 3.1 and 4.2 to examine the condition of its domestic industry and provide a reasoned conclusion of its injury assessment.[401] As the Appellate Body found, there may be a continuum between a threat of serious injury and its realization. Nevertheless, both refer to the apparently different conditions of a domestic industry that could not have occurred at the same time. Therefore, making an indiscrete decision about the condition of domestic industry between serious injury and its threat indicates, arguably, an absence of reasoned conclusions about the state of the domestic industry. Thus, the indiscrete determination contravenes the requirements of Articles 3.1 and 4.2(c) of the SA.

5.32 The national authorities fail to establish a clear basis for the application of a safeguard measure if they cannot determine whether their domestic industry has sustained actual injury or is facing a threat. The application of

397 *Id.*, paras. 7.264–7.266.
398 *United States – Line Pipe*, *supra* note 71, para. 167.
399 *Id.*, para. 168.
400 *Id.*, paras. 169–170.
401 Articles 3.1 and 4.2(c) of the SA.

emergency import restrictions such as safeguards is hardly justifiable if the national authorities have not even identified the condition of the domestic industry clearly. The Appellate Body relied in its decision, *inter alia*, on the current wording of Article 4.2(a), in particular, the use of "or" in the phrase.[402] Therefore, it seems necessary to modify the wording of the Article to ensure the national authorities' responsibility to make a discrete determination on the condition of the domestic industry.

5.2 CAUSATION

The SA requires the establishment of a causal link between the increased imports and injury for the application of a safeguard measure. Neither significant increases in imports, nor injury to the domestic industry, would be sufficient to justify a safeguard measure unless the injury to the domestic industry is attributed to the increase in imports. Article 4.2(b) provides: **5.33**

> The determination referred to in subparagraph (a) shall not be made unless this investigation demonstrates, *on the basis of objective evidence*, the existence of the causal link between increased imports of the product concerned and serious injury or threat thereof when factors other than increased imports are causing injury to the domestic industry at the same time, such injury shall not be attributed to increased imports (emphasis added).

Test for Causation. The Panel in *Argentina – Footwear* prescribed a three-pronged test for the determination of causation.[403] The first prong is whether an upward trend in imports coincides with downward trends in the injury factors, and if not, whether a reasoned explanation is provided as to why the data nevertheless shows causation. The second is whether the condition of competition in the domestic market between imported and domestic products, based on objective evidence, demonstrates a causal link between the imports and the injury. The third prong is whether other relevant factors have been analyzed and whether it is established that the injury caused by factors other than the imports has not been attributed to them.[404] **5.34**

---

402 The relevant provision states, "In the investigation to determine whether increased imports have caused *or* are threatening to cause serious injury to a domestic industry under the terms of this Agreement ..." (emphasis added).

403 *Argentina – Footwear, supra* note 70, para. 8.229. The Appellate Body affirmed this test. *Argentina – Footwear, supra* note 71, paras. 140–146. The test was also followed by the subsequent Panels in *United States – Wheat Gluten, supra* note 70, para. 8.91, *United States – Steel Products, supra* note 70, para. 10.285, and *Dominican Republic — Polypropylene Bags and Tubular Fabric, supra* note 70, para. 7.346.

404 In applying this three-prong test, the Panel in *United States – Steel Products* concluded that all product categories but one failed to meet this test. The Panel considered that the USITC failed to establish a coincidence between the increasing trends in imports and the decreasing trends in the injury factors. It also failed to provide any other compelling argument as to *why* the causal link nevertheless existed. The USITC's analysis

5.35 The examination of causation often requires a complicated analysis that includes legal and economic aspects.[405] The first prong of the test can be met by comparing the trend of imports with that of domestic production. In *United States – Wheat Gluten*, the Panel held that the general and overall coincidence of an upward trend in increased imports and a negative trend in injury factors over the period of investigation would be sufficient to meet the first requirement, and that precise coincidence in every injury factor would not be required.[406]

5.36 The second prong requires an analysis of market competition between imports and domestic products. A mere coincidence of time between the upward trend in increased imports and the negative trend in injury factors would not be sufficient evidence for a causal link. The existence of market competition between imports and domestic products would show a possible causal relationship between imports and the injury, since it indicates that increased imports would displace competing domestic products. The relevant economic measurements, such as the "cross-elasticity of demand,"[407] can be used to determine the degree of market competition between imports and domestic products. A commentator opined that while there is no requirement to conduct a price-based comparison between imported and domestic products, such an examination can nevertheless be helpful to provide a reasoned and adequate explanation of the causation, but an improperly explained analysis of price depression or price suppression in the causation analysis may lead to an inconsistency with Article 4.2(b) of the SA.[408]

---

of competition between imports and domestic products was not adequate. It also failed to properly separate and assess the nature and extent of the injurious effects of factors other than increased imports because it improperly dismissed a number of factors (i.e., declining domestic demand, domestic capacity increases, intra-industry competition and legacy costs) in its non-attribution analysis although it acknowledged that those factors were also causing injury to the industry. *United States – Steel Products*, *supra* note 70, paras. 10.278–10.586. For a measure-by-measure analysis, *see id.*, paras. 10.361–10.586.

405 The analysis of causation often entails both factual and legal examinations. The econometric tests such as the "Granger causality test" may be used to determine the economic impacts of the increased imports on domestic industry. *See* Lee, Y.S. and Jai S. Mah, "Reflections on the Agreement on Safeguards in the WTO" (1998) 21(6) *World Competition* 29 for a discussion of the Granger test. A suggestion was also made to apply the *conditio sine qua non* theory to facilitate the assessment of causation. David Leys, "Does a Theory of Causation Exist under the WTO Safeguards Agreement?" (2014) 9(1) *Global Trade and Customs Journal* 10–19. *See also* Pratik Tayal, "A New World of Causation in Safeguards: Application of the 'But for' Test" (2015) 10(10) *Global Trade and Customs Journal* 355–363.

406 *United States – Wheat Gluten*, *supra* note 70, paras. 8.97–8.102. *See also United States — Photovoltaic Products*, *supra* note 70, para. 7.189.

407 *Supra* note 310.

408 Piérola-Castro, *supra* note 167, pp. 169-170. *See also United States – Washers*, *supra* note 70, paras. 7.161–7.173, 7.181, 7.146.

The third prong examines possible causes other than increased imports. There has been a question as to whether a causal link is established where factors other than the increase in imports simultaneously contribute to the injury to the domestic industry.[409] Article 4.2(b) states, "When factors other than increased imports are causing serious injury to the domestic industry at the same time, such injury *shall not be attributed to increased imports*" (emphasis added). A literal interpretation of this phrase may lead to a conclusion that the causal link is not established (i.e., injury is not attributed to the increase in imports) where factors other than the increase in imports contribute to the injury at the same time. **5.37**

The problem is that, in reality, there would almost always be some other factors that may have contributed to the declining condition of the domestic industry. The Panel in *United States – Wheat Gluten* found that the increased imports need not be the sole cause but should be a sufficient cause of the injury, capable of causing the injury "*in and of themselves.*"[410] The Appellate Body held a different view and subsequently found that a causal link is established as long as the increased imports have contributed to the injury, and such contribution is sufficiently clear.[411] It did not believe that increased imports "in and of themselves" should be sufficient to cause serious injury.[412] According to the Appellate Body, national authorities would be able to establish a causal link where they find "a genuine and substantial relationship of cause and effect" between the increased imports and injury after separating and examining the injurious effects of other factors.[413] **5.38**

Would a causal link be established where it is difficult to discern the effects of the increase in imports from those of the other factors? The Appellate Body in *United States – Wheat Gluten* found that the non-attribution requirement of Article 4.2(b) presupposes the separation and examination of the injurious effects of the other factors. Therefore, the requirement of Article 4.2(b) is not fulfilled in cases where the injurious effects of the increase in imports cannot be assessed separately from those of the other factors. It stated, "the final determination about the existence of 'the causal link' between increased imports and serious injury can only be made *after* the effects of increased imports have been properly assessed, and this assessment, in turn, follows the separation of **5.39**

409 *See* Lee (2000), *supra* note 1, pp. 140–142.
410 *United States – Wheat Gluten, supra* note 70, para. 8.138.
411 *United States – Wheat Gluten, supra* note 71, para. 67.
412 *Id.*, para. 70.
413 *Id.*, para. 69.

the effects caused by all the different causal factors."[414] The Appellate Body in *United States – Line Pipe* reiterated, "competent national authorities must separate and distinguish the injurious effects of the increased imports from the injurious effects of the other factors."[415]

5.40 The Appellate Body sought guidance in the interpretation of the causation clause from an anti-dumping case that also involved the non-attribution issue.[416] Article 3.5 of the Anti-Dumping Practices Agreement provides in relevant part:

> It must be demonstrated that the dumped imports are, through the effects of dumping, as set forth in paragraphs 2 and 4, causing injury within the meaning of this Agreement. The demonstration of a causal relationship between the dumped imports and the injury to the domestic industry shall be based on an examination of all relevant evidence before the authorities. The authorities shall also examine any known factors other than the dumped imports which at the same time are injuring the domestic industry, and the injuries caused by these other factors must not be attributed to the dumped imports ....[417]

5.41 Interpreting the non-attribution clause in the Article, the Appellate Body repeated its previous position and stated, "In order that investigating authorities ... are able to ensure that the injurious effects of the other known factors are not 'attributed' to dumped imports, they must appropriately assess the injurious effects of those other factors. Logically, such an assessment must involve separating and distinguishing the injurious effects of the other factors from the injurious effects of the dumped imports."[418] The Appellate Body acknowledged the practical difficulty in separating and assessing the injurious effects of the factors other than the increased imports, but it was fortified in the position that such a separate assessment was envisaged by the non-attribution requirement.[419] The Panel in *United States – Photovoltaic Products* also found that there is no obligation to conduct a collective assessment of all of the other factors although the latter must be identified individually.[420]

---

414 *United States – Lamb Meat, supra* note 71, para. 180.

415 *Id.*, para. 215.

416 *Id.*, para. 214.

417 Anti-Dumping Practices Agreement, Article 3.5.

418 *United States – Hotrolled Steel Products from Japan* ("*United States – Hotrolled Steel Products*"), Report of the Appellate Body, WT/DS184/AB/R (July 24, 2001), para. 223.

419 *Id.*, para. 228. In interpreting the causation provision in the Anti-Dumping Practices Agreement, the Appellate Body also acknowledged that the Panel and its own decisions in safeguard cases can provide guidance. *Id.*, para. 230.

420 *United States – Photovoltaic Products, supra* note 70, para. 7.288.

The language of the non-attribution provision of Article 4.2 seems ambiguous, and such an ambiguity has caused repeated disagreements between previous Panels and the Appellate Body on the interpretation of this provision, pertaining to the sufficiency of causation – whether increased imports *in and of themselves* should have caused the injury.[421] The Appellate Body decision cited above seems to have a better justification, since when multiple factors are contributing to the injury at the same time it may be difficult to prove whether increased imports alone would have caused the injury, but these increased imports may still have been an essential factor in causing the injury. In this case, a safeguard measure would be able to remedy or prevent the injury by suppressing the increase in imports. 5.42

Concerning the criteria for causation, it is still not clear exactly what the Appellate Body meant in its phrases such as "a genuine contribution" to the result, or "a genuine and substantial relationship of cause and effect." Although increased imports need not be the sole cause, the negotiators in the Uruguay Round could not have intended to authorize the application of a safeguard measure where the increase in imports is only a minor factor. The modification of Article 4.2(b) may, therefore, be necessary to resolve this confusion about the criteria for causation in the presence of multiple causal factors. Such a clarification should indicate that increased imports must be a *major* factor of the injury. 5.43

On a final note, Sykes argued that the current causation provision in the SA is problematic in that it is not increased imports that cause injury to the domestic industry but some other exogenous factors.[422] For example, if lower prices of imports cause domestic consumers to buy more of imports and less of competing domestic products, causing serious injury to the domestic industry, the cause for the injury is the relatively lower prices of imports *vis-à-vis* domestic products, and the increase in imports is an incidental outcome of this, not a cause for the injury. 5.44

It is a plausible view from economics, and one way to reconcile this with the current SA provision is that the term "increased imports" in the context of causation may be considered shorthand or a proxy for the underlying factors 5.45

421 The Panel in Lamb Meat arrived at an apparently different conclusion from the Appellate Body's previous decision on the interpretation of the non-attribution provision. The Panel's position that the increased imports alone should be capable of causing the injury, was consistent with the previous Panel decision in Wheat Gluten, which was subsequently rejected by the Appellate Body. *United States – Lamb Meat, supra* note 70, paras. 7.238 and 7.241.

422 Sykes, *supra* note 30, p. 157.

that drive imports and not just imports which, as Sykes correctly observed, is the difference between consumption and local supply at given prices.[423]

5.46 Sykes also opined that certain kinds of economic development that leads to an increase in imports, such as an upward shift of import supply curve, may be considered a legitimate cause,[424] but the current rule does not exclude specific types of economic development that lead to an increase in imports from consideration of causation.[425] For example, there seems no reason to exclude some other developments, such as an upward shift of a demand curve for imports which may be caused by an increased consumer taste and preference for imports and, in turn, leads to an increase in imports, from a safeguard measure.

5.47 The current test, which requires not only correlation between increased imports and injury but also the existence of competition between them, is useful to determine causation.[426] While other factors that cause injury to the domestic industry may also lead to an increase in imports, as Sykes correctly argues, the current Appellate Body ruling does not preclude the finding of causation when those factors are present as long as the increased imports have contributed to the injury and when such contribution is sufficiently clear.[427] As noted above, the Appellate Body did not require that increased imports "in and of themselves" should be sufficient to cause serious injury.[428]

---

423 The author previously opined that the legal causation, as stipulated in the Agreement on Safeguards, is a normative, not necessarily an economic assessment, which decides where to stop in the presence of multiple layers of factors with one leading to another. *See* Yong-Shik Lee, "Not Without a Clue: Commentary on 'The Persistent Puzzles of Safeguards'" (2006) 40 *Journal of World Trade* 385–404, at 397. Increased imports, when considered from the perspective of domestic producers who have to compete with imports, displace their products and cause injury, regardless of what underlying economic factor may have led to the increases in imports. Thus, increased imports may well be stipulated as a legal cause in the SA that attempts to remedy injury to the domestic industry. *Id.* An analogy can be made to the relationship between drunk driving and an accident that it causes. Certainly drunk driving can be analyzed as an outcome, rather than a cause, from the dynamics among individual factors causing drunk driving, such as reckless character of the driver who became drunk before driving, effectiveness of police checks and strength of penal penalty against drunk driving, presence of due care and contributory fault on the part of pedestrians, etc. However, from the perspective of a victim whom a law may seek to protect, drunk driving or whatever factor may have caused drunk driving in the first place, is considered a cause for his or her injury. Drunk driving is, therefore, stipulated as a cause by traffic laws that attempt to protect the public from drunk driving. *Id.*, footnote 59.

424 Gene M. Grossman and Alan Sykes, "United States – Definitive Safeguard Measures on Imports of Certain Steel Products" (2007) 6(1) *World Trade Review* 89–122, at 121.

425 Lee, *supra* note 423, pp. 397–403.

426 *Id.*

427 *United States – Wheat Gluten*, *supra* note 71, para. 67.

428 *Id.*, para. 70. The attribution is a potentially complex issue, and Petros Mavroidis opined that the multivariate method adopted by Grossman is a way to approach this issue, where in principle the decomposition method developed by Irwin and the calibration method by Kelly also help. For details of these methods, *see* Gene M. Grossman, "Imports as a Cause of Injury: The Case of the U.S. Steel Industry" (1986) 20 *Journal of International Economics* 201–222; Douglas A. Irwin, "Causing Problems? The WTO Review of Causation

5.3 CONCLUSION

Injury and causation are issues of essential importance in the application of safeguards, as their determination constitutes the core of safeguard investigations. While it is not possible to remove the inherent subjectiveness and arbitrariness in the determination of injury and causation, the Safeguards Agreement sets analytical steps that improve the objectiveness of the process compared to Article XIX. These steps include the evaluation of specific injury factors, particularly those listed in Article 4.2(a), and the final injury determination based on this evaluation. **5.48**

The issue of causation has been complex and controversial, particularly where multiple causal factors are contributing to the injury. The requirement to conduct a separate evaluation of potential causal factors other than increased imports would impose a considerable analytical burden on Members.[429] This causal analysis is all the more significant since an Appellate Body decision held that only *a portion of injury* caused by increased imports should be remedied by safeguards.[430] In order to devise a measure that remedies such a portion of injury and not more, the causal effects of the other factors would have to be identified and separated. Such a task can be significantly difficult and complicated, if not completely impossible.[431] Leading scholars, including Grossman, Irwin, and Kelly, have proposed economic methodologies for this,[432] but virtually any methodology to be employed by the national authorities to separate and assess the causal effects of the other factors would be susceptible to chal- **5.49**

---

and Injury Attribution in US Section 201 Cases" (2003) 2(3) *World Trade Review* 297–325; and Kenneth Kelly, "The Analysis of Causality in Escape Clause Cases" (1988) 37 *Journal of Industrial Economics* 187–207.

429 Thus the Panel in *Dominican Republic — Polypropylene Bags and Tubular Fabric* held that the national authority did not provide a reasoned explanation of a causal link between the increased imports and the injury. The Panel also found that the national authority did not provide an analysis as to how it was ensured that the effects of the injury to the domestic industry caused by other factors were not attributed to the increased imports when its investigation reports confined themselves to citing relevant legal provisions. According to the Panel, the national authority only repeated the arguments of the interested parties during the national investigation procedure and merely suggested that there are elements of injury that "'could determine the existence' of a 'direct link' between the increased imports of polypropylene bags and tubular fabric and the commercial situation facing the domestic industry," which was insufficient to establish a causal link. *Dominican Republic — Polypropylene Bags and Tubular Fabric*, *supra* note 70, paras. 7.347–7.354.

430 *See* the relevant discussion in Chapter 7.2 *infra*.

431 A study emphasized an importance of adopting quantitative tests for the determination of causation. Henry K. Horn and Petros C. Mavroidis, "United States – Safeguard Measures on Imports of Fresh, Chilled or Frozen Lamb Meat from New Zealand and Australia: What Should Be Required of a Safeguard Investigation?" (2003) 2 *World Trade Review* 395–430.

432 *Supra* note 429.

lenge. Members will have considerable difficulty in defending their causation determination should panels and the Appellate Body apply a strict scrutiny.

5.50 Finally, it should be noted that the Appellate Body decision requiring the demonstration of "unforeseen developments" under Article XIX seems to have created another layer of causation requirement in addition to the one under Article 4.2(b).[433] As a result of the development in defining legal elements of this ambiguous "unforeseen developments" clause, Members are required to demonstrate *how* unforeseen developments *have led to* the injurious increase in imports.[434] Since neither Panels nor the Appellate Body have adopted an elaborate, multi-layer test for this "demonstration" such as the one adopted for the causation requirement under Article 4.2(b), it appears that Members are not yet required to apply the same analytical rigor (e.g., analysis of other contributing factors) to the demonstration of "unforeseen development" as that required under Article 4.2(b).[435] Nonetheless, an addition of this requirement only imposes an unnecessary analytical burden on Members that was not intended by the participants of the Uruguay Round.[436]

433 *See* Chapter 3.2 *supra* for the relevant discussion.

434 *Supra* notes 197 and 204.

435 Panels and the Appellate Body have not yet devised a "test" for this demonstration, but the adoption of a rigorous test such as the non-attribution test would create a substantial difficulty in the application of a safeguard measure.

436 *See* Chapter 3.2 for a further discussion of the application of "unforeseen developments" clause.

6

PROCEDURAL REQUIREMENTS

6.1 INVESTIGATION

Article 3, one of the new provisions in the SA, regulates the conduct of investigations for safeguard measures. It provides: **6.01**

> A Member may apply a safeguard measure only following an investigation by the competent authorities of that Member pursuant to procedures previously established and made public in consonance with Article X of GATT 1994. This investigation shall include reasonable public notice to all interested parties and public hearings or other appropriate means in which importers, exporters and other interested parties could present evidence and their views, including the opportunity to respond to the presentations of other parties and to submit their views, *inter alia*, as to whether or not the application of a safeguard measure would be in the public interest. The competent authorities shall publish a report setting forth their findings and reasoned conclusions reached on all pertinent issues of fact and law (Article 3.1).

Both transparency and procedural fairness are the key elements. Under this Article, the competent national authorities are obligated to issue public notice to all interested parties and provide opportunity to the interested parties to present their own views concerning the proposed application of a safeguard measure. A fair investigation procedure would enable national authorities not only to examine the facts properly but also to consider the views of the concerned parties and balance their different interests. The national authorities would also have to examine all the facts presented by the interested parties, as the authorities are obligated to examine "all facts" in their possession.[437] **6.02**

437 Refer to the discussion on the standard of review in Chapter 4.1 *supra*.

6.03 *Investigation Period.* The Article does not stipulate the period that the investigation should cover or the duration of the investigation itself. The process of an investigation is left to the competent national authorities.[438] In *Korea – Dairy Products*, the Korean Trade Commission (KTC) initiated an investigation on May 2, 1996, and conducted an investigation of the conditions of the domestic industry during the period from January 1993 to April 1996. Investigation periods should be sufficiently long to evaluate the changing conditions of the domestic industry. Safeguard investigations have normally covered three years or more preceding the investigation. The KTC completed the investigation on October 23, 1996, about six months after the initiation of the investigation. In the United States and the European Union, legislation provides for the maximum duration of an investigation. The US statutory provisions stipulate that the USITC must make the injury determination within 120 days (180 days if the petition alleges that critical circumstances exist) after filing of the petition.[439] The EU rules also provide that the investigation must be completed within nine months after its initiation (the period is extendable by two months in exceptional circumstances).[440]

6.04 *Consideration of Public Interest.* The national authorities not only have to find accurate facts about the imports and the condition of the domestic industry, but also need to ensure that the different interests and positions of all interested parties are considered in determining the application of the measure. After considering the views and positions of all interested parties, the national authorities must make a proper judgment regarding whether or not the application of a safeguard measure would be in the public interest, even if the application of a safeguard measure would be legitimate under the rules.

6.05 *Investigation Report.* Article 3 provides in relevant part, "The Competent authorities shall publish *a report* setting forth their findings and reasoned conclusions reached on all pertinent issues of fact and law" (emphasis added).[441] A question has been raised with respect to the adequacy of the investigation report. The Panel held in *Korea – Dairy Products* that Korea's investigation was not adequate since, *inter alia*, it failed to include all the necessary reasoning for

438 Thus, in *Ukraine – Passenger Cars*, the Panel found "no basis" to find that the national authorities' investigation should have taken less time than it did when the authorities extended the duration of the investigation, but the duration remained below the maximum permitted under the national safeguards law. *Ukraine – Passenger Cars, supra* note 70, para. 7.176.

439 Section 202(b)(2)(A) of Trade Act of 1974. 150 days and 210 days, respectively, if the Commission determines that the investigation is extraordinarily complicated (Section 202(b)(2)(B)).

440 Regulation (EU) No. 2015/478 of 11 March 2015, Article 6.

441 Article 3.1 of the Agreement on Safeguards.

its finding of serious injury in its final investigation report.[442] In the course of the panel proceedings, Korea provided additional explanations for its injury determination and also pointed out that part of its analysis was included in its mid-investigation report, which was also published. The Korean authority did not include in its final report the portion of the injury analysis that had been presented in its mid-investigation report. The Panel refused to accept these additional explanations and analysis since they were not included in the final investigation report.[443]

This Panel decision means that the investigation report should be carefully drafted to include all the reasoning that has been employed by the national authorities in making injury determination. The *Dairy* Panel accepted nothing outside the final investigation report. According to this Panel position, it seems that the completeness of the report should determine the legal justification for the safeguard measure in question, even where the grounds for the action can be found in a source other than the final investigation report that has been published. The wording of Article 3, which requires a comprehensive analysis on all pertinent issues in "*a published report*,"[444] seems to support the Panel decision in one way. Nevertheless, it is somewhat difficult to accept that the legitimacy of a safeguard measure should depend solely upon the technical completeness of the final investigation report.[445] **6.06**

As discussed above, the Panel in *Korea – Dairy Products* refused to accept any explanation outside the final investigation report.[446] Nevertheless, no systematic problem would seem to occur by allowing Members to supplement their reasoning found in the investigation report at a later stage, should their measures be challenged. For instance, it is possible to draw different conclusions from the same set of facts, and the relevant national authorities may not have examined all other possible conclusions and reasoning in the report, perhaps because they were not brought to their attention. The complainant may challenge the national authorities' conclusion with alternative reasoning that leads to a different conclusion later in the panel proceedings. In such a case, the **6.07**

442 *Korea – Dairy Products*, *supra* note 70, paras. 7.58–7.59.

443 *Id.*, para. 7.69.

444 Article 3.1 of the Agreement on Safeguards states that the competent authorities shall "publish *a report* setting forth their findings and reasoned conclusions reached on all pertinent issues of fact and law" (emphasis added).

445 *See* Lee (1999), "Review of the First WTO Panel Case on the Agreement on Safeguards: Korea – Definitive Safeguard Measure on Imports of Certain Dairy Products" *supra* note 1, pp. 39–40.

446 *Korea – Dairy Products*, *supra* note 70, para. 7.76. *See also* Lee (1999), "Review of the First WTO Panel Case on the Agreement on Safeguards: Korea – Definitive Safeguard Measure on Imports of Certain Dairy Products" *supra* note 1, p. 39.

national authorities should be given an opportunity to defend their conclusion with supplementary reasoning and explanations, although they may not have been included in the original report. Likewise, it does not seem to cause any significant problem to allow Members to present evidence of their consideration of the relevant injury factors from official sources other than the final investigation report, provided that the authenticity of the sources is established and those sources have been published and made available to the interested parties in time.

6.08 In addition, previous decisions required that the explanation and reasoning included in the investigation report must be based on sufficient data. Competent national authorities need not justify a particular methodology for data collection or injury assessment, although an inherent bias or other critical problems with the methodology which lead to biased conclusions can subject such methodology to review. The authorities will have to explain *how* their analysis led to the injury determination.[447]

6.09 The issue of the published report was raised once again in *Chile – Agricultural Products*. In its letter to the Panel, Chile confirmed that the Minutes of Sessions Nos 181, 185, 193 and 224 of the Chilean Distortions Commission ("CDC") constitute the "published report" within the meaning of Article 3.1 of the SA. The Minutes of the relevant CDC sessions had not been "published" through any official medium. Rather, they were transmitted to the interested parties and placed at the disposal of "whoever wishes to consult them at the library of the Central Bank of Chile." The Panel found that those Minutes did not constitute the published report under Article 3.1, since it interpreted "publication" in the meaning of the Article as "to make generally available through an appropriate medium" rather than simply "making publicly available."[448]

6.10 The Panel in *United States – Steel Products* considered acceptability of a supplementary report, which came *after* the original report, to address the issue of "unforeseen developments." The complainants argued that this supplementary report should be disregarded as it did not comprise the original USITC report and was an *ex post* attempt to demonstrate the existence of "unforeseen developments."[449] With respect to the multiplicity of the investigation report, the Panel considered that the national authority's report may be produced in parts as long as they form a coherent and integrated explanation providing satisfac-

447 *See* Chapter 4.1 *supra* for a discussion of the standard of review.

448 *Chile – Agricultural Products, supra* note 70, para. 7.128.

449 *United States – Steel Products, supra* note 70, para. 10.47.

tion with the requirements of Article XIX and the Agreement on Safeguards.[450] The Panel, based on this finding, subsequently accepted the supplementary report for its review.[451]

Confidential Information. Article 3.2 protects confidential information. It provides: 6.11

> Any information which is by nature confidential or which is provided on a confidential basis shall, upon cause being shown, be treated as such by the competent authorities. Such information shall not be disclosed without permission of the party submitting it. Parties providing confidential information may be requested to furnish non-confidential summaries thereof or, if such parties indicate that such information cannot be summarized, the reasons why a summary cannot be provided. However, if the competent authorities find that a request for confidentiality is not warranted and if the party concerned is either unwilling to make the information public or to authorize its disclosure in generalized or summary form, the authorities may disregard such information unless it can be demonstrated to their satisfaction from appropriate sources that the information is correct.

The injury determination requires detailed information from the relevant domestic industry. Such information may include sensitive business information (e.g., trade secrets), disclosure of which may undermine the interest of the domestic producers. Thus, the Article protects the confidentiality of such information. The authorities may choose not to use confidential information if they find that a request for confidentiality is not warranted and the party concerned is either unwilling to make the information public or does not authorize its disclosure in a generalized or summary form. 6.12

There is also an important issue with respect to confidential information protected under Article 3.2. In many instances, confidential information has been redacted from the national authorities' investigation reports and was not made available for examination by other parties. Although the need for confidentiality should be recognized, the non-disclosure of such confidential but nevertheless essential information for the injury determination creates certain problems. 6.13

First, the unavailability of key information for the injury determination would render interested parties unable to review whether the condition of the domestic industry would warrant the application of a safeguard measure. In *United States – Wheat Gluten*, certain information used for the USITC's 6.14

450 *Id.*, para. 10.50.
451 *Id.*

injury determination had been redacted from the public version of the USITC Report. The EC complained that the USITC's findings, which were based on undisclosed data, were unreviewable and unverifiable.[452] The Panel upheld the USITC's decision not to disclose confidential information, finding that the provisions of Article 3.2 allowed national authorities a wide discretion on the determination of confidential information and its disclosure.[453]

6.15 Although there is a clear need to protect confidential information, the non-disclosure of crucial information based on confidentiality may also compromise the transparency of the investigation. The lack of confidence in the investigation process caused by the unavailability of crucial information can lead to disagreements and disputes over the application of a safeguard measure. While sensitive business information needs some measure of protection, such a wide discretion, as granted to the national authorities under Article 3.2, should be reduced. The scope of confidential information and its treatment should be more narrowly and clearly provided in Article 3.[454]

6.16 Secondly, another problem involves the availability of confidential information to the panel. In *United States – Wheat Gluten*, the United States failed to meet the Panel's request to provide confidential information. The Panel found that the requested information would facilitate its objective assessment of the facts of the case.[455] To ensure protection of confidentiality, the Panel adopted "Procedures Governing Private Confidential Information."[456] The United States did not agree to the adopted procedure. The parties and the Panel subsequently exchanged several communications on this issue over a significant period of time, but they failed to agree upon a mutually satisfactory procedure.

6.17 The Panel subsequently found that there was sufficient information for its review, even in the absence of requested information, and proceeded with it. However, the failure by the United States to meet the Panel request for confidential information, as the Panel noted, presented a serious systemic problem "as to the relationship between, on the one hand, the confidentiality obligations under Article 3.2 SA of a Member's investigating authorities with respect to confidential information obtained in the course of a domestic safeguards

---

452 *United States – Wheat Gluten*, *supra* note 70, para. 8.13.

453 *Id.*, para. 8.20.

454 In contrast, the EU safeguard rules provide a definition of confidential information. Article 8.4 of Regulation (EU) 2015/478 provides, "Information shall in any case be considered to be confidential if its disclosure is likely to have a significantly adverse effect upon the supplier or the source of such information."

455 *United States – Wheat Gluten*, *supra* note 71, para. 8.7.

456 *Id.*, Attachment 4.

investigation and, on the other hand, the duties of Members when faced with a panel request for such confidential information under Article 13 DSU."[457]

The Panel in *United States – Line Pipe* acknowledged the need to review confidential information in order to "make an objective assessment" of the dispute but also stated that the need for the protection of confidentiality obligates the Panel to show proper restraint in requesting confidential information.[458] At any rate, a Member's failure to provide information would compromise the Panel's ability to conduct an effective review. The Member may also prejudice its own position by failing to produce the requested information. Therefore, a uniform procedure governing submission and review of confidential information should be made to resolve such problems. **6.18**

Another issue concerns a party's request for confidential information during the panel proceedings. In *United States – Line Pipe*, the complainant sought certain confidential information through the Panel. The Panel granted the complaint's requests in part, for only such information that the Panel considered relevant to the objective assessment of the case and to the claim advanced by the complainant.[459] During the panel proceedings, the United States also proposed to provide the Panel with computerized models, one to evaluate the impact of imports on the domestic industry and another to assess the impact of the proposed measure. The United States subsequently failed to provide these models. **6.19**

As mentioned above, there must be a clear working procedure as to the treatment of confidential information. The requirement of confidentiality may force national authorities to refuse disclosure of certain confidential information to the other parties or even to the Panel. In addition, Members may be tempted not to produce sensitive information during the panel proceedings under the umbrella of "confidentiality" because the information in question may not support their position. However, national authorities should be aware that failure to provide crucial information only weakens their position, and therefore, non-disclosure should be limited to the minimal extent necessary to protect the narrowly and clearly defined confidentiality. **6.20**

457 *Id.*, para. 8.11.

458 *United States – Line Pipe, supra* note 70, para. 7.4.

459 Specifically, the Panel granted Korea's requests for an addendum to the dissenting views of an ITC (International Trade Commission) commissioner as well as import data. It did not grant its request for the full confidential record of the investigation. *United States – Line Pipe, supra* note 70, para. 7.4.

6.2 NOTIFICATION

6.21 Article 12 of the SA requires a Member to issue notifications to the Committee on Safeguards prior to the application of a safeguard measure.[460] Those notifications are an essential procedural requirement. As the application of a safeguard measure would affect the interests of various parties, it is necessary to inform those parties on the progress of the investigation process in time so that they are made aware of the development and may also take appropriate steps to prepare for the possible consequences. Therefore, proper notifications are necessary to ensure transparency and fairness of the investigation and application process.

6.22 *Timing of Notification*. The timing of notification is important. The purposes of the notification would not be met, and the interests of other parties would be prejudiced, if they were not notified in time due to delays in notifications. Article 12.1 of the SA provides:

> A Member shall *immediately* notify the Committee on Safeguards upon (a) initiating an investigatory process relating to serious injury or threat thereof and the reasons for it; (b) making a finding of serious injury or threat thereof caused by increased imports; and (c) taking a decision to apply or extend a safeguard measure (emphasis added).

6.23 Under this provision, Members are required to issue notifications at three stages of the process for the application of a safeguard measure (at the timing described in (a), (b), and (c) above). In order to keep interested Members informed about the progress of the investigation and application process, notifications are required at each of these stages. It should be noted that these notifications must be made *immediately*. This timing issue is not always straightforward, since certain delays seem inevitable due to the administrative and logistical issues (e.g., translation).

6.24 The timing of notification has been a recurring issue. The Panel in *Korea – Dairy Products* affirmed that notifications should be made immediately after the relevant action. It rejected Korea's argument that the timing of its notifications should be considered adequate since those notifications were made as soon as practically possible.[461] The Panel did not find that "as soon as prac-

---

460 The Panel in *Polypropylene Bags and Tubular Fabric* held that both GATT Article XIX:2 and SA Article 12.1(c) determines obligations to notify safeguard measures, but Article XIX:2 stipulates no additional obligation applicable independently of the latter SA provision. *Dominican Republic — Polypropylene Bags and Tubular Fabric*, *supra* note 70, paras. 7.415–7.433. For the relationship between GATT Article XIX and the SA, *see* Chapter 3 *supra*.

461 *Korea – Dairy Products*, *supra* note 70, paras. 7.130–7.145.

tically possible" is equated to "immediately" as required in Article 12.1. The Panel subsequently found certain delays in Korea's notifications unacceptable.

Nevertheless, the Panel did not provide any objective standard to determine the immediacy of notifications. Again, in practice, the internal administrative processes and logistical issues would make certain time gaps inevitable in the notification process. The Panel also acknowledged the possibility of this inevitable delay. It observed, "The more detail that is required, the less 'instantly' Members will be able to notify. In this context we are also aware that Members whose official language is not a WTO working language may encounter further delay in preparing their notifications."[462] **6.25**

The timing of notifications was also an issue in *United States – Wheat Gluten*.[463] The Panel in this case also stressed the importance of immediacy. It considered the immediate notifications as a matter of the rights of the other Members. The Panel stated, "A safeguard measure is imposed on imports of a product irrespective of its source and potentially affects all Members. All Members are therefore entitled to be kept informed, without delay, of the various steps of the investigation."[464] **6.26**

On the review of specific notifications by the United States, the Panel considered that the delay of 15 days between the US initiation of the investigation and its notification and that of 26 days between its finding of serious injury and its notification were not acceptable. On the other hand, it found that the five-day lapse between its decision to take a safeguard measure and the final notification under Article 12.1(c) satisfied the immediacy requirement of the notification. Nonetheless, the timing of the Article 12.1(c) notification was still found inconsistent with the requirement of Article 12, since it was made *after* the application of the safeguard measure. The Panel considered that the notification pertaining to the proposed measure must be made *before* the implementation of the measure so that the other affected Members have an opportunity to discuss the proposed measure with the notifying Member in the subsequent consultations and to seek a mutually agreeable settlement.[465] The prior notification also allows the result of such discussions to be reflected in the final implementation of the measure.[466] The Panel in *Dominican Republic – Polypropylene Bags and Tubular Fabric* also affirmed that the notice must be **6.27**

462 *Id.*, para. 7.218.

463 *United States – Wheat Gluten*, *supra* note 70, paras. 8.189–8.207.

464 *Id.*, para. 8.194.

465 *Id.*, paras. 8.205–8.207.

466 *Id.*, paras. 8.205–8.207.

given before the application of a safeguard measure but may be given *after* its adoption (i.e., after the decision to apply the safeguard).[467]

6.28 As discussed above, the timing of notification has been subject to repeated controversy. The absence of a specific time limit in the provision of the SA is a reason for this ambiguity. Although the immediacy of the notification may be considered on a case-by-case basis, a practical solution would be to modify the relevant provision of Article 12.1 and specify a time limit for notifications. The time to prepare notifications would generally depend on the amount of information to be included. While notifications under Article 12.1(a) and (c) would include relatively brief information of a rather technical nature, the notification under Article 12.1(b) would include substantive information as to the injury factors evaluated under Article 4.2(a). Therefore, Article 12.1(b) may require more time than the notifications under Article 12.1(a) and (c).

6.29 *Contents of Notification.* Article 12.2 stipulates the required contents of the notifications. Article 12.2 provides in relevant part:

> [T]he Member proposing to apply or extend a safeguard measure shall provide the Committee on Safeguards with all pertinent information, which shall include evidence of serious injury or threat thereof caused by increased imports, precise description of the product involved and the proposed measure, proposed date of introduction, expected duration and timetable for progressive liberalization. In the case of an extension of a measure, evidence that the industry concerned is adjusting shall be also provided ....

6.30 The adequacy of the contents of the notifications has been an issue. Proper notifications should provide the interested parties with information sufficient to enable them to understand the development of the process and prepare them for the consultations. On the one hand, the interested parties would wish to collect as much information as possible about the on-going process. On the other hand, however, a Member considering a safeguard measure may have an inclination not to disclose all of the information before it completes the investigation process. A requirement for an excessive amount of information would also be a logistical burden and could delay notifications. A balance needs to be found between these conflicting needs among the parties.[468]

---

467 *Dominican Republic — Polypropylene Bags and Tubular Fabric*, *supra* note 70, para. 7.433.

468 The Committee on Safeguards issued guidance on notifications entitled, *Formats for Certain Notifications under the Agreement on Safeguards*, G/SG/1/Rev.3 (May 4, 2021). The Secretariat of the WTO also issued *Technical Cooperation Handbook on Notification Requirements*. Both contain a disclaimer that they do not constitute a legal interpretation of the relevant notification requirements.

Article 12 of the SA provides that in making the second and third notifications referred to above in paragraphs 1(b) and 1(c), the Member proposing to apply or extend a safeguard measure must provide the Committee on Safeguards with *all pertinent information* (Article 12.2). In *Korea – Dairy Products*, the scope of "all pertinent information" was at issue. The contents of the notifications under Article 12.1(a) and 12.1(c) are specifically listed in the provision of Article 12.1, and therefore, the question was the contents of notification under Article 12.1(b) concerning injury determination. **6.31**

The EC contended in *Korea – Dairy Products* that the contents must be as complete as possible: i.e., all the details of the recommendations and reasoning to be found in the investigation report should be included in the notifications.[469] The Panel rejected this argument, as it determined that such information would be overly broad. The Panel ruled that the amount of information notified must be sufficiently useful to Members with a substantial interest in the proposed safeguard measure.[470] The Panel determined that Korea's notification under Article 12.1(b) was sufficient as it contained sufficient information on what Korea considered to be evidence of injury caused by increased imports.[471] The Panel also expressed that it may be desirable for the notification to include a reference to the published report referred to in Articles 3.1 and 4.2, although such a reference is not required by the SA.[472] **6.32**

The Appellate Body concurred with the Panel that the contents of notification need not include all the details of the recommendations and reasoning to be found in the investigation report.[473] However, it disagreed with the Panel that evidence of serious injury in Article 12.2 is determined by what the notifying Member considers to be sufficient information.[474] The Appellate Body ruled that the standard set by Article 12 with respect to the contents of "all pertinent information" is an objective standard independent of the subjective assessment of the notifying Member.[475] It believed that "evidence of serious injury" in Article 12.2 should refer, at a minimum, to the injury factors to be evaluated under Article 4.2(a).[476] Therefore, the Appellate Body found that the minimum contents of notifications, pursuant to paragraphs 1(b) and 1(c) **6.33**

469 *Korea – Dairy Products*, *supra* note 70, paras. 4.693–4.697.
470 *Id.*, para. 7.127.
471 *Id.*, para. 7.136.
472 *Supra* note 470.
473 *Korea – Dairy Products*, *supra* note 71, para. 109.
474 *Id.*, para. 108.
475 *Id.*
476 *Id.*

of Article 12, must include all the items specified in Article 12.2, as well as the injury factors listed in Article 4.2.[477]

6.34 The analysis of the injury factors could be extensive, and it is not sufficiently clear from the Appellate Body decision how much has to be included in the notification. It would seem necessary to include the assessment of each injury factor and the reasoning for the injury determination, so that the affected Members are informed of the basis for the injury determination. The analysis of causation was not mentioned in the Appellate Body decision. Nevertheless, the inclusion of the causal analysis would be helpful for the interested parties to understand the relationship between increased imports and injury.

6.3 CONSULTATION

6.35 Article 12.3 provides for consultations *prior to* the application of a safeguard measure:

> A Member proposing to apply or extend a safeguard measure shall provide adequate opportunity for prior consultations with those Members having a substantial interest as exporters of the product concerned, with a view to, *inter alia*, reviewing the information under paragraph 2, exchanging views on the measure and reaching an understanding on ways to achieve the objective set out in paragraph 1 of Article 8.

6.36 Consultation is also an essential part of the procedural requirements. The objective of the consultation is to provide the opportunity to exchange views between the Member proposing to apply a safeguard measure and the other affected Members, with hopes to reach a mutually satisfactory settlement. The importing country may be persuaded to modify the measure, not to apply it at all, or to agree on compensation during consultations. Consultation would be a proper forum to discuss compensation to maintain the balance of concessions, which would be upset by the application of a safeguard measure.

6.37 *Timing of Consultation*. The timing of consultation would, therefore, be important to achieve this objective. Consultations should be held prior to the final determination and the implementation of the measure so that the exchange of views, as well as any agreement during the consultations, would be properly reflected in the final implementation of the measure.[478] Successful consulta-

477 *Id.*

478 *See also* the relevant Panel rulings in *United States – Wheat Gluten*, *supra* note 70, paras. 8.216–8.217.

tions would lead to mutually agreeable compromises and thereby enable the parties to avoid disputes and retaliations.[479]

In *Korea – Dairy Products*, the timing of the consultations held between Korea and the EC was at issue. The Panel noted the importance of the timing of the consultations. It subsequently found that Korea's modification of its original quota level, in response to the EC's concern raised during the consultations, indicated that the timing of the consultations in fact allowed for a meaningful exchange of views, which subsequently led to the modification of the measure.[480] Members are not required to modify or withdraw their measures after consultations, but a reasonable accommodation of the interests and concerns of affected Members would minimize the potential for disputes. **6.38**

Sufficient Information for Consultation. The adequacy of consultation was also examined in *United States – Wheat Gluten*.[481] The Panel emphasized that consultations are an important means of achieving the aim of Article 8.1 of the SA, which is to maintain the balance of concessions.[482] The Appellate Body also determined that a Member proposing to apply a safeguard measure is required under Article 12.3 to "provide exporting Members with sufficient information and time to allow, through consultations, for a meaningful exchange on the issues identified."[483] **6.39**

In *United States – Wheat Gluten*, consultations were held based on the USITC recommendations to the President and the information contained in the USITC Report. The Report did not have any information on specific quota shares for individual countries. It stated in relevant part that, "within the overall quantitative restriction, the President allocate separate quantitative restrictions for the European Communities, Australia, and 'all other' non-excluded countries, taking into account the disproportional growth and impact of imports **6.40**

---

479 Inadequate consultations, on the other hand, would lead to disputes and potential retaliations as shown in *United States – Steel Products*. Refer to the relevant discussions in Chapter 14 *infra*.

480 *Korea – Dairy Products*, *supra* note 70, para. 7.152. The timing of consultations was reiterated in *United States – Wheat Gluten*, *supra* note 70, paras. 8.215–8.219.

481 *United States – Wheat Gluten*, *supra* note 70, paras. 8.215–8.219.

482 Article 8.1 provides, "A Member proposing to apply a safeguard measure or seeking an extension of a safeguard measure shall endeavour to maintain a substantially equivalent level of concessions and other obligations to that existing under GATT 1994 between it and the exporting Members which would be affected by such a Member .... To achieve this objective, the Members concerned may agree on any adequate means of trade compensation for the adverse effects of the measure on their trade."

483 *United States – Wheat Gluten*, *supra* note 71, para. 136. The Appellate Body also added that the information for consultations should include a precise description of the proposed measure and its proposed date of introduction.

of wheat gluten from the European Communities…."[484] The Appellate Body determined that the information without a specific quota level assigned to the EC did not allow the European Communities to "assess accurately the likely impact of the measure being contemplated, nor to consult adequately on overall equivalent concessions with the United States."[485]

6.41 Consultation was also at issue in *United States – Line Pipe*. The measures recommended by the USITC were the basis for the consultations. Subsequent to the consultations, substantially different measures were announced in the press release and subsequently applied. Both the Panel and the Appellate Body found that the United States failed to provide adequate opportunity for consultations, since it had not provided the information on the measure that was actually to be applied.[486] The Appellate Body considered that the period of 18 days between the announcement of the final US measure and its implementation was insufficient for exporting Members to analyze the effect of the measure and to enter into consultations.[487] This type of inadequacy was also shown in the subsequent *United States – Steel Products* case, where a period of only 15 days was given between the announcement of the measures and their implementation.

6.42 The Appellate Body considered that the fair amount of time necessary to prepare for consultations should be decided on a case-by-case basis.[488] It also believed that the measure considered under consultations does not have to be precisely identical to the one actually applied, since the measure may be modified as the result of consultations.[489] In any case, exporting Members should be allowed the time necessary to analyze the proposed measure and determine its consequences before entering into consultations so that they may have a meaningful exchange of views on the proposed measure. As the Appellate Body emphasized, proper consultations are in the best interests of *both* importing and exporting Members, since a mutual understanding and settlement during

---

484 *Wheat Gluten*, USITC Pub. No. 3423 (May 2001).

485 *United States – Wheat Gluten*, *supra* note 71, para. 141.

486 *United States – Line Pipe*, *supra* note 71, paras. 102–113.

487 *United States – Line Pipe*, *supra* note 71, paras. 107–108. The Panel held that the United States was in violation of Article 12.3 on the ground that the press release was not an adequate means to provide necessary information. *United States – Line Pipe*, *supra* note 70, para. 7.314. The Appellate Body, on the other hand, determined that the press release can be an adequate means and decided that the issue in the case was whether the complainant had received necessary information sufficiently in advance.

488 *United States – Line Pipe*, *supra* note 71, para. 107.

489 *Id.*, para. 104.

consultations will enable them to avoid costly disputes and potential retaliatory action.[490]

490 *Id.*, para. 109.

7

APPLICATION OF SAFEGUARD MEASURE

7.1 NEED FOR A MINIMALIST APPROACH

7.01 The proper application of a safeguard measure requires three considerations. First, the measure has to be taken in the circumstances authorized by the SA – that is, serious injury (or threat thereof) to the domestic industry caused by an increase in imports. Secondly, the measure should comply with all the procedural requirements for its application, notably the requirements concerning investigation, notification, and consultation. Finally, the measure itself should not be excessive, and it must be proportionate to the extent of injury caused by the increased imports. Therefore, due consideration should be given to the appropriateness of the proposed measure prior to its application. Unlike GATT Article XIX, the SA provides rules concerning the duration, extension, re-application, and mid-term review of the measure, and these rules provide a control on the application of safeguards as follows.

7.02 *Durational Limit, Extension, Re-application, Mid-term Review.* The Agreement on Safeguards specifies the maximum period for safeguard measures as not exceeding four years (Article 7.1). If the continuation of the measure is determined necessary to remedy or prevent serious injury and if there is evidence that the industry is adjusting, the measure may be extended once, for up to four years (Article 7.2). The total period of a safeguard measure, including the period of any preceding provisional measure, cannot exceed eight years, including a once-only extension (Article 7.3).[491]

491 However, as discussed in the commentary on Article 9.2 *infra*, developing countries can apply safeguard measures for up to ten years.

An extension of the measure requires another investigation, which should follow the procedures in Articles 2–5. If the duration of a safeguard measure is more than one year, the measure must be liberalized at regular intervals (Article 7.4). An extended measure cannot be more restrictive than it was at the end of the initial period and should continue to be liberalized (Article 7.4). Time equal to the duration of the previous safeguard measure, provided the period of non-application is at least two years, must lapse before the re-application of a safeguard measure with respect to the same product (Article 7.5).[492] If the duration of a safeguard measure exceeds three years, the Member applying the measure must review the situation no later than the mid-term of the measure and, if appropriate, withdraw the measure or increase the pace of liberalization (Article 7.4).[493] **7.03**

The specified duration and the required time interval before the re-introduction of a safeguard measure highlight the temporary nature of safeguards. The liberalization requirement should encourage the domestic industry to make the necessary adjustments. The mid-term review provides an opportunity to place a safeguard measure under examination before its expiry. **7.04**

Proportionality. Article 5.1 of the Agreement provides that the measure must be proportionate. It provides in relevant part, "A Member shall apply measures *only to the extent necessary to prevent or remedy serious injury and to facilitate adjustment.*" This requirement of proportionality is adequate because import restrictions, whether or not justified under the provisions of the SA, inevitably interfere with a normal stream of trade, upsetting the balance of concessions negotiated among Members. Therefore, a measure that is carefully calibrated not to exceed its necessity to remedy or prevent the injury will minimize the distortion of trade. **7.05**

Indeed, a minimalist approach should be taken for safeguard measures in consideration of domestic economic welfare. Import restrictions compromise the economic welfare of domestic consumers for the benefit of selected domestic producers. A study of welfare economics indicates that welfare sacrifice to customers is inevitably greater than the welfare gains by domestic producers from import restrictions, resulting in net loss to the whole economy.[494] Thus, an excessive measure would unfairly compromise consumer interest. Producers **7.06**

492 The period is shorter for developing countries. *See* Article 9.2 *infra*.

493 The SA does not prescribe any procedural guideline for the mid-term review. The procedure for the initial application and the extension can be adopted even though the provision of Article 7.4 does not specifically require Members to observe those provisions for the mid-term review.

494 *Supra* note 30.

tend to be better organized than consumers and therefore more influential in the government decision to apply a trade measure. Therefore, national authorities should carefully balance the interests of consumers and producers in devising a specific measure. The procedural requirements such as a public hearing in Article 3.1, discussed in Chapter 6 above, would provide the authorities with opportunity to hear and consider the views and interests of diverse groups to be affected by the measure.

7.07 Furthermore, in the internationally interdependent economic environment today, excessive safeguard measures may cause unintended effects to the economy of the Member applying these measures. Safeguards may damage not only the interest of the export industry of the Member subject to the measure but also its overall economy. This will be particularly true where a country's economy is heavily dependent upon a few main export products and has become subject to a safeguard measure in its major export markets. Such an economic difficulty in that exporting country may, in turn, reduce demand for products, including imported products from the Member applying the measure. In other words, excessive measures may inadvertently hurt the exports of the Member applying the measure.

7.08 Trouble with exports may also come in a more direct way. The greater the extent of the measure, the larger the compensation needs to be, and therefore, the harder an agreement on compensation would likely be to reach. The failure of compensation may entail retaliation by the exporting Members. The application of retaliatory measures would reduce exports from the Member applying the safeguard.[495] The three-year bar to the retaliation under Article 8.3 has relieved the importing Member of this concern to some extent, but the exporting Members are permitted to apply retaliatory measures where the duration of the measure is greater than three years or the measure is not consistent with the provisions of the SA.[496]

7.09 The issues on the application of a safeguard measure include: determination and demonstration of an appropriate level; settlement of reference periods for quota levels; presentation of adjustment plans; and liberalization of the measure. As mentioned, Article 5.1 of the SA limits the extent of a safeguard measure to that necessary to prevent or remedy serious injury. In addition to this legal requirement, it is also in the long-term economic interest of

495 For a further discussion of retaliatory measures. *See* Chapter 8 *infra*.
496 Article 8.3 of the SA.

Members to take a minimalist approach to safeguard measures to reduce the distortion of trade.

7.2 DETERMINATION OF APPROPRIATE MEASURE

Assessment of Appropriate Level. If a safeguard measure must not exceed the extent of its necessity as discussed above, how then should a Member decide the specific level of its measure? Article 5 is silent about the methodology.[497] The Article stipulates only that the measure should be applied "only to the extent necessary" to prevent or remedy serious injury. This proportionality requirement can only be met after the extent of injury is first measured. In practice, it is done rather crudely: e.g., the extent of injury may be equated to the revenue decrease for the domestic industry. Suppose that a domestic automobile industry claims serious injury, attributing a revenue decrease of 30 percent to increased imports. The 30 percent decrease in revenue may well be taken as the extent of injury. On the other hand, remedying injury may not necessarily mean a full recovery of the lost revenue. It is left to the national authorities to determine how much recovery in terms of the revenue should be made in order to remedy a significant overall impairment in the position of that particular industry. This suggests that the national authorities have discretion in the determination of an appropriate level of the measure. A degree of subjectivity and arbitrariness would be unavoidable since there is no hard-and-fast rule to determine the appropriate level.[498] **7.10**

The existence of other protection, such as anti-dumping and countervailing measures, does not necessarily preclude an application of a safeguard measure or require its adjustment. In *United States – Washers*, the Panel did not accept Korea's argument that the safeguard measure adopted by the United States was excessive because it failed to account for the protection already afforded to the domestic industry by the imposition of anti-dumping and countervailing measures on the product under consideration. The Panel noted that "if the serious injury has been found despite the existing trade remedy measures, **7.11**

497 Thus, in *United States – Washers*, the Panel found that Article 5.1 does not require investigating authorities to set the safeguard measure to match the degree of price underselling. *United States – Washers*, *supra* note 70, para. 7.229.

498 Perhaps a "cap" was established in the *Line Pipe* case in a sense that the national authorities may provide remedies *up to* a portion of the injury that is caused by the increase in imports. *United States – Line Pipe*, *supra* note 71, para. 260.

nothing in the Agreement on Safeguards would require Members to adjust the safeguard measures to account for existing trade remedy measures."[499]

7.12 *Form of Restriction.* Suppose that national authorities decide that the domestic industry should recover at least 50 percent of its lost revenue as a minimal revenue base to remedy serious injury. Then a quota, a tariff increase, or a combination of both can be applied to the extent that the industry is expected to recover 50 percent of its lost revenue.[500] There is a limit to the quota application. Article 5.1 also provides:

> If a quantitative restriction is used, such a measure shall not reduce the quantity of imports below the level of a recent period which shall be the average of imports in the last three representative years for which statistics are available, unless clear justification is given that a different level is necessary to prevent or remedy serious injury. Members should choose measures most suitable for the achievement of these objectives.

7.13 All Members having a substantial interest[501] in supplying the product concerned must agree to the quota allocation. If agreement cannot be reached, the quota may be allocated according to the import share of the Members during a representative period.[502] In the Uruguay Round negotiations, some participants preferred to preserve an ability to apply a safeguard measure selectively according to the origin of the products. Although Members finally decided to adopt the principle of non-selective application, Article 5.2(b) of the SA allows a Member to deviate from the MFN quota allocation if (i) imports from certain Members have increased in a disproportionate percentage in relation to the total increase of imports in the representative period, (ii) the reasons for the deviation are justified, and (iii) the conditions of the deviation are equitable to all suppliers of the product concerned. The non-MFN quota cannot

---

499 *United States – Washers, supra* note 70, para. 7.235.

500 As of June 2023, 37 of the 40 existing safeguard measures were tariff-related measures, including tariff-quotas, and only three quantitative measures existed, indicating clear preference for non-quantitative measures. WTO, *Report (2023) of the Committee on Safeguards, supra* note 26, Annex 3. While quantitative restrictions may be more effective in controlling imports, non-quantitative restrictions have been known to have less trade-distorting effects. Salvatore, *supra* note 30, pp. 222–228, 258–260.

501 It is an imprecise terminology, but such interest can be identified by the market shares taken by the exporter: a ten percent rule has been applied generally as a threshold to determine the substantial interest. *Analytical Index: Guide to GATT Law and Practice, supra* note 85, p. 941, citing TAR/M/16, p. 10.

502 Thus a study concluded that a SG implemented as a quota tends to preserve historical market shares more than a SG implemented as a tariff and that when a SG is implemented as a quota, countries that have recently increased market share face reductions in market share relative to other suppliers. Chad P. Bown and Rachel McCulloch, "The WTO Agreement on Safeguards: An Empirical Analysis of Discriminatory Impact," *in* Michael J. Plummer (ed.), *Empirical Methods in International Trade* (Cheltenham, UK: Edward Elgar Publishing, 2004), pp. 145–169.

be extended beyond the initial four years and is not permitted in the case of a threat of serious injury.[503]

7.14 Concern was raised that the allowance of the MFN deviation in quota allocation might cause discrimination against new entrants to the market. It has been observed that the "flexibility to impose such 'selective' safeguards seems designed to protect against competitive exporters in Asia and Eastern Europe. In particular, it seems to presage a strategy for dealing with potential import surges from China."[504] This observation seems plausible. It should be noted, however, that the *conditional* allowance of a selective measure was a compromise reached among the participants of the Uruguay Round after long and difficult negotiations.[505] Article 5.2(b), imposing conditions on selective quota allocations, should work to curtail rampant applications of selective measures. The vast majority of safeguards applied under the SA have been non-quantitative measures,[506] and there has not been a dispute over a non-MFN quota allocation in previous panel cases.

7.15 The authorization of quantitative restrictions should be reconsidered. Quantitative restrictions are generally known to be more trade-restrictive than non-quantitative measures such as tariffs. Where import restrictions are applied to address "unfair" trade practices such as "dumping" or "subsidy," quantitative restrictions are not authorized. It seems unjustified, therefore, for the innocent exporters to have their exports subject to quantitative restrictions in the absence of any unfair trade practice on their part, whereas those exporters accused of unfair trade practices are not. Ideally, quantitative restrictions should be removed from safeguards. At the minimum, consideration should be given to adding conditions, which would be additional to the minimum quota levels discussed above, for the application of quantitative restrictions.

7.16 A provision can be devised to link the application of quantitative restrictions to the provision of compensation under Article 8: a Member may apply a quantitative restriction only if it agrees on a means of trade compensation with all other Members with a substantial interest in supplying the product concerned. This mandatory compensation is justified in the application of quantitative restrictions since they are the most trade-restrictive protection and are not even authorized in anti-dumping or countervailing measures. As Members have

503 Article 5.2(b) of the SA.

504 Jeffrey J. Schott, *The Uruguay Round, An Assessment* (Washington, DC: Institute for International Economics, 1994), p. 114.

505 *See* the relevant discussions in the history of safeguard negotiations in Chapter 2 *supra*.

506 WTO, *Report (2023) of the Committee on Safeguards*, *supra* note 26, Annex 3.

shown clear preference for non-quantitative restrictions,[507] this new restriction is unlikely to encourage a serious evasion of the SA rules, such as gray-area measures that proliferated in the past.

7.17 The mandatory provision of compensation may not be necessary for non-quantitative measures. In fact, non-quantitative measures have been the most prevalent form of safeguard measures.[508] Article 6 requires a refund of increased duties made in the provisional safeguard measures if the injury determination is negative. The same requirement for a refund should also be considered for definitive safeguard measures where (i) pursuant to the dispute settlement provisions provided under Article 14, the measure is found inconsistent with the provisions of the SA or not based on an absolute increase in imports by a decision from the Dispute Settlement Body, and (ii) no compensation has been made *and* no retaliatory measure has been applied. Under Article 8.3, Members may resort to retaliation where the applied measure does not conform to the provisions of the SA or is not taken as a result of an absolute increase in imports. Members which are entitled to apply the immediate retaliation under Article 8.3 (subject to the procedural requirement under Article 8.2),[509] but have nevertheless refrained from it and instead resorted to the dispute settlement procedure, should be properly reimbursed for increased duties.

7.18 Finally, it is to be noted that under certain circumstances tariff increases below maximum binding rates may be considered safeguard measures under Article XIX and the SA. In *Dominican Republic – Polypropylene Bags and Tubular Fabric*, the Dominican Republic increased duties equivalent to 38 percent *ad valorem* below the level of 40 percent *ad valorem* bound for tubular fabric and polypropylene bags in its schedule of concessions, from the levels of 14 percent *ad valorem* and 20 percent *ad valorem*, respectively.[510] The Panel held that the increased duties are safeguard measures under Article XIX and the SA where they were not applied on an MFN basis (imports originating in Colombia, Indonesia, Mexico, and Panama excluded), and were not found to be "ordinary customs duties" or any of the measures provided for in Article II:2 of the GATT 1994, but were applied and notified in accordance with the procedures laid down by Article XIX and the SA with the objective of remedying a situ-

507 *Id.*
508 *Id.*
509 *See* Chapter 8 *infra* for the relevant discussion.
510 *Dominican Republic — Polypropylene Bags and Tubular Fabric*, *supra* note 70, para. 7.57.

ation of serious injury to the domestic industry brought about by an increase in imports.[511]

Reference Period. Where a quota is applied, its level cannot be lower than the minimum prescribed in the provisions of Article 5.1 above. There is a question with respect to the reference period of "three representative years" for the determination of the minimal quota levels. As Article 5.1 does not designate the beginning and end points of the reference period, the determination of "three representative years" is left to the discretion of the national authority. The choice of the reference period can alter the minimal quota level substantially. For instance, once the investigation for a safeguard measure is decided, the importers may increase the import of the product in question in fear of a possible adoption of the measure. Therefore, the amount of minimal quota can be substantially different depending on whether or not the reference period covers the period after the beginning of the investigation process. This issue was raised in *Korea – Dairy Products*, but the Panel did not address this issue, as it had already found that Korea's measure was inconsistent with the provision of Article 5.1.[512] **7.19**

Clear guidance should be provided with respect to the reference period. For instance, Article 6.8 of the Agreement on Textiles and Clothing (ATC), which is no longer in force,[513] provided a reference period for the determination of quota levels. In contrast to the provision of Article 5.1 SA, Article 6.8 clarified the starting and end points of the period, with a reference to the time of the request for consultation. It provided that the level of a transitional safeguard is fixed at a level not lower than the actual level of exports and imports from the Member concerned during the 12-month period terminating two months preceding the month in which the request for consultation was made. Article 5.1 of the SA needs to be modified to include clear reference points for the "three representative years," such as the ones found in Article 6.8. **7.20**

Justification of Extent. A question was also raised as to whether the provision of Article 5.1 requires Members to prove that the extent of their measure is necessary to prevent or remedy injury and to facilitate adjustment. On the one **7.21**

511 *Id.*, paras. 7.50–7.91. The Panel held that the obligations under GATT Article I (MFN requirement) and GATT Article II:2 are included in the obligations that may be suspended by the application of a safeguard measure under Article XIX and the Agreement on Safeguards. *Id.* The Panel also noted that Dominican Republic justified the exclusion of the four countries on the grounds of SA Article 9.1. *Id.*, para. 7.68.

512 *Korea – Dairy Products*, *supra* note 70, para. 7.111.

513 The Agreement on Textiles and Clothing is a transitional agreement that was terminated on January 1, 2005. The relevant provision of the Agreement is introduced for a reference purpose.

hand, such requirement may help to ensure that Members will not apply an excessive measure; on the other hand, the requirement may also place a burden on Members since it would involve a series of complicated and costly economic analyses. The strength of such proof would also be doubtful even if an economic test is somehow devised and conducted.

7.22 This issue has been raised in *Korea – Dairy Products*. The EC argued that Korea failed to comply with the requirement of Article 5.1 by failing to demonstrate the necessity of the chosen measure. The Panel found that the first sentence of Article 5.1 requires a Member to justify the extent of its safeguard measure and held that Korea was in violation of this requirement.[514] The Appellate Body acknowledged that Article 5.1 creates a general obligation on Members to apply a non-excessive measure. However, it did not believe that the provision obligates Members to justify their measure, unless the applied measure is a quantitative restriction which reduces the quantity of imports below the prescribed minimum set by Article 5.1 – the average of imports in the last three representative years.[515] This Appellate Body decision gave significant relief to the national authorities – those of developing countries in particular – whose available expertise and resources may not allow them to conduct extensive economic analyses to prove the adequacy of their measure.

7.23 In *European Union – Steel Products*, the Panel found that Article 5.1 of the SA does not require the period that the Member uses to set the level of a safeguard measure to be identical to the period of investigation (i.e., "the period during which the Member concerned finds an increase in imports that causes or threatens to cause serious injury").[516] In this case, the complainant argued that the EC determined a threat of serious injury based on import data, which included the first six months of 2018, but did not include the data on imports during those six months when it calculated the size of its tariff-quota measures.[517] The complainant concluded that the EC's measures, therefore, lacked the

514 *Korea – Dairy Products*, *supra* note 70, para. 7.101. The panel stated, "Members are required, in their recommendations or determinations on the application of a safeguard measure, to explain how they considered the facts before them and why they concluded, at the time of the decision, that the measure to be applied was necessary to remedy the serious injury and facilitate the adjustment of the industry."

515 The Appellate Body stated, "we do not see anything in Article 5.1 that establishes such an obligation (i.e., obligation to justify) for a safeguard measure *other* than a quantitative restriction which reduces the quantity of imports below the average of imports in the last three representative years. In particular, a Member is *not* obliged to justify in its recommendations or determinations a measure in the form of a quantitative restriction which is consistent with 'the average of imports in the last three representative years for which statistics are available'" (explanations added). *Korea – Dairy Products*, *supra* note 71, para. 99.

516 *European Union – Steel Products*, *supra* note 70, para. 7.257.

517 *Id.*, para. 7.253.

required rational connection with the objective of preventing serious injury.[518] The Panel disagreed and found that the complainant failed to explain why the measures established based on the data, including those six months, "would be connected to the state of the domestic industry below which the industry will experience serious injury," whereas the measures based on the data excluding that period were not. [519] The Panel concluded that the complainant, therefore, failed to establish the inconsistency of the EC measures with SA Article 5.1.[520]

Portion of Injury Remedied by Safeguard. The justification for the measure and its permissible extent also became an issue in *United States – Line Pipe.* The Appellate Body affirmed its previous decision that national authorities are not required to justify the adequacy of their measures unless the measures are quantitative restrictions below the minimal level set by Article 5.1.[521] The Appellate Body further determined that the measure complying with the obligations under the SA is of an adequate extent. It found, "The Member imposing a safeguard measure must, in any event, meet several obligations under the *Agreement on Safeguards.* And, meeting those obligations should have the effect of clearly explaining and *justifying* the extent of the application of the measure."[522] **7.24**

The Appellate Body linked the compliance with Article 5.1 with the observance of the causation requirement of the SA. It stated, "By separating and distinguishing the injurious effects of factors other than increased imports from those caused by increased imports, as required by Article 4.2(b), and by including this detailed analysis in the report that sets forth the findings and reasoned conclusions, as required by Articles 3.1 and 4.2(c), a Member proposing to apply a safeguard measure should provide sufficient motivation for that measure. Compliance with Articles 3.1, 4.2(b) and 4.2(c) of the *Agreement on Safeguards* should have the incidental effect of providing sufficient 'justification' for a measure and ... should also provide a benchmark against which the permissible extent of the measure should be determined."[523] The Appellate Body ruled that Article 5.1 of the SA requires Members to apply safeguard measures only to the extent that they address serious injury attributed to **7.25**

518 *Id.*, para. 7.259.
519 *Id.*, para. 7.259.
520 *Id.*, para. 7.260.
521 *United States – Line Pipe, supra* note 71, para. 235.
522 *Id.*, para. 236.
523 *Id.*

increased imports:[524] that is, to remedy *a portion of injury* that is attributed to the increase in imports.

7.26 This Appellate Body decision is significant. It would be possible to address a portion of injury attributable to increased imports only after separating and distinguishing the injurious effects of increased imports from those of the other factors under the requirement of Article 4.2(b). Therefore, the failure to comply with this requirement raises a presumption that the measure is not limited to the permissible extent under Article 5.1.[525] However, the Appellate Body also held that a violation of the attribution requirement of Article 4.2(b) does not become an *automatic* violation of Article 5.1. It stated, "even if the USITC failed to separate and distinguish the injurious effects of the increased imports from the injurious effects of the other factors, it is still possible that the safeguard measure may have been applied in such a manner that it addressed only a portion of the identified injurious effects, namely, the portion that is equal to or less than the injurious effects of increased imports."[526] In this case, the Member would have to justify the extent of its measure in order to rebut the presumption of violation.

7.27 In the earlier example, suppose that the revenue of the domestic automobile industry has decreased by 30 percent. The Appellate Body ruling indicates that the national authority would have to determine the portion of that revenue decrease that is attributable to increased imports and then apply a safeguard measure to the extent necessary to address only that portion of the injury. The separation and assessment of the injurious effects of *the other factors* should precede the determination. Otherwise, the national authority will have to find another way to demonstrate that the extent of the measure is sufficient to remedy only the portion of injury caused by increased imports, or less. Such a demonstration would, in fact, be a difficult task without the separation and assessment of the injurious effects of other factors.[527]

---

524 *Id.*, para 260.

525 *Id.*, para. 261. Therefore, the Appellate Body found that by establishing that the United States violated Article 4.2(b) of the Agreement on Safeguards, Korea made a *prima facie* case that the application of the line pipe measure was not limited to the extent permissible under Article 5.1. *See* Chapter 4.1 for a further discussion of *prima facie* case.

526 *Id.*, para. 262.

527 Perhaps such a demonstration may still be possible, without the causation review, in hypothetical cases in which the extent of a safeguard measure is so limited comparing to the perceived injury, and the measure could have not been beyond the permissible extent under Article 5.1. However, applying such a limited safeguard, which may not be sufficient to address injury, would seem unlikely in practice.

The Panel in *Chile – Agricultural Products* brought another test to determine the compliance with the first sentence of Article 5.1. The Panel found that there must be, at a minimum, a *rational connection* between the measure and the objective of preventing or remedying serious injury and facilitating adjustment. In the absence of such a rational connection, a Member could not possibly *ensure* that the measure is applied only to the extent necessary.[528] In *Chile – Agricultural Products*, the Panel determined that Chile was in violation of Article 5.1 since the lower threshold of its Price Band System (PBS), which determined the extent of its safeguard measure, had no rational connection to the state of the domestic industry, as the PBS was calculated on the basis of international prices.[529] **7.28**

Ceiling for Non-Quantitative Measures. The last issue concerning the determination of an appropriate level of the measure concerns a ceiling for non-quantitative measures. As shown above, the Appellate Body ruled that no justification is necessary for non-quantitative measures (provided that the requirement of Article 4.2(b) is observed). Unlike the case of quantitative restrictions, no ceiling is stipulated in the SA for non-quantitative measures. In *Korea – Line Pipe*, Korea argued that the US tariff-quota measure was more restrictive than the minimal quota prescribed in Article 5.1, and therefore, the minimum quota requirement should apply. The Panel rejected this argument, finding that the tariff-quota is not the quantitative restriction subject to the minimum amount requirement of Article 5.1.[530] **7.29**

Non-quantitative measures such as tariffs and tariff quotas are generally known to be less restrictive than quantitative restrictions. Nevertheless, both tariffs and tariff quotas could also be as restrictive as, or even more restrictive than, quantitative restrictions without proper ceilings. Therefore, an appropriate ceiling should also be stipulated for tariff measures. For instance, the US safeguard legislation places a limit on the increase in tariff to 50 percent *ad valorem*.[531] A similar ceiling needs to be added to Article 5 to prevent the abuse of non-quantitative measures. **7.30**

Minimizing Trade Distortion. As discussed above, the minimal approach should be encouraged for the determination of an appropriate measure. The permissible extent provided in Article 5 should be considered the maximum,[532] **7.31**

528 *Chile – Agricultural Products*, *supra* note 70, para. 7.183.

529 *Id.*, para. 7.184.

530 *Korea – Line Pipe*, *supra* note 70, para. 7.69.

531 Section 203(e)(3) of the Trade Act of 1974.

532 *United States – Line Pipe*, *supra* note 71, para. 245.

and Members are not obligated to apply safeguards to the maximum extent. The welfare loss of import restrictions has already been discussed. It is political reality that the producers would want maximum protection, but competent national authorities should endeavor to minimize the trade distortion and welfare loss by trying to reduce the extent of the measure. For instance, a combination of government subsidy and safeguard should be considered to address the injury to reduce the extent of the measure. Preference should also be given to non-quantitative measures such as tariff increases and tariff quotas over quantitative restrictions.[533]

7.3 ADJUSTMENT PLAN AND LIBERALIZATION

7.32 *Need for Adjustment Plan.* Article 5.1 provides, "A Member shall apply safeguard measures only to the extent necessary to … *facilitate adjustment*" (emphasis added). The Preamble of the SA also emphasizes "the importance of structural adjustment." As discussed in Chapter 1, facilitation of economic adjustment is an economic justification for safeguards. Therefore, a safeguard would be of little value should no adjustment be made during the period of protection, since the Member may well face the same problem caused by imports all over again when the temporary protection of the measure expires.

7.33 What constitutes structural adjustment for the purpose of the Safeguards Agreement? The US safeguards legislation offers a description of a positive adjustment. It provides that a positive adjustment to import competition occurs when the domestic industry is able to compete successfully with imports after the safeguard measure is terminated, or the domestic industry experiences an orderly transfer of resources to other productive pursuits, and that dislocated workers in the industry experience an orderly transition to productive pursuits.[534] It also provides that the domestic industry may be considered to have made a positive adjustment to import competition even though the industry is not of the same size and composition as at the time the investigation was initiated.[535]

7.34 The state of a positive adjustment is evidenced by the industry's readiness either to compete with imports once again or to pursue other production, in which case the industry is no longer affected by the imports that caused the injury. Therefore, adjustment plans may include plans to improve competitive-

533 *Supra* note 500.
534 Section 201(b) of the Trade Act of 1974.
535 *Id.*

ness of the domestic industry (e.g., modernization of production, re-training of workers, adoption of new management strategy, or improved marketing) or an "exit plan" (e.g., divestment or re-training of workers for other productive pursuits). After successful adjustments, the domestic industry may be substantially downsized and/or function with different structure/production priorities. The value of adjustment plans will be considerable as they will guide the domestic industry through the potentially complicated and costly adjustment process.

There was controversy as to whether Article 5.1 requires Members proposing a safeguard measure to consider an adjustment plan.[536] The Panel in *Korea – Dairy Products* acknowledged the reference to the adjustment in the SA and believed that the question of adjustment should be a part of the authorities' reasoned explanation of the measure it has chosen to apply.[537] Nevertheless, the Panel found no specific requirement in Article 5.1 or elsewhere in the SA that an adjustment plan must be considered.[538] On the other hand, it noted that examination of an adjustment plan would be "strong evidence that the authorities considered whether the measure was commensurate with the objective of preventing or remedying serious injury and facilitating adjustment."[539] **7.35**

Although an adjustment plan is not specifically required under Article 5.1, consideration should be given to the introduction of such a requirement on the following grounds. Safeguard measures should not be applied as a protectionist response to an increase in imports. Safeguards should be implemented with a clear perspective of economic adjustment. Without the necessary adjustment, safeguards do not achieve anything productive except giving temporary relief to the domestic industry and thereby temporarily appeasing protectionist demand. The existence of an adjustment plan would be necessary to coordinate safeguard measures to the adjustment process. The requirement of an adjustment plan would discourage safeguard applications motivated by industrial protection without any intention to adjust. **7.36**

Liberalization. Article 7.4 of the SA requires that a safeguard measure, with a duration of more than one year, progressively liberalize at regular intervals during the period of application.[540] An extended measure cannot be more **7.37**

536 *Korea – Dairy Products*, *supra* note 70, para. 4.611.

537 *Id.*, para. 7.108.

538 *Id.*

539 *Id.*

540 A question was raised as to whether a Member applying a safeguard measure is required under Article 7.4 to notify a liberalization plan before the application of a safeguard measure. The Panel in *Ukraine – Passenger Cars* found that Article 7.4 does not include such a requirement. The Panel opined that "a Member can, in our view, comply with its obligation in Article 7.4 even if it has not previously provided a timetable for pro-

restrictive than it was at the end of the initial period and should continue to be liberalized (Article 7.4). This requirement of liberalization reduces trade distortion by decreasing import restrictions over the period of a safeguard application and also facilitates adjustment by gradually lifting protection. The pace of liberalization can be coordinated with an adjustment plan and calibrated according to the expected pace of the adjustment. Under the provision of Article 7.4 requiring a mid-term review, the Member is obligated to increase the pace of liberalization where appropriate. In fact, successful adjustment may enable a Member to increase the pace of liberalization, and even withdraw the measure earlier than scheduled.

7.38 The current provisions of the SA do not regulate the pace of liberalization. The Panel in *Ukraine – Passenger Cars* also found that Article 7.4 does not specify the length of liberalization intervals or require liberalization starting at a given point in time, concluding that Ukraine did not act inconsistently with Article 7.4 by not starting the liberalization of the measure by the time the panel was established.[541] Should the minimum pace be regulated in the text of the SA? Where a safeguard measure is applied merely as a protectionist effort, without a sound adjustment plan, the measure would be likely to be applied to the maximum extent with little liberalization taking place. In fact, the Panel in *European Union – Steel Products* found that the Member may *reduce* the rate of liberalization from an announced schedule.[542] The specification of the minimum pace would encourage Members to take positive steps for adjustment. Transitional safeguard provisions in the ATC specified an annual minimum reduction of 6 percent in the restriction level.[543] A similar provision should be adopted in the SA.

gressive liberalization. Article 7.4 is a substantive provision that requires actual liberalization of the measure. The mere fact that a Member has failed to provide a timetable for such liberalization does not preclude that Member from taking the required liberalization steps regardless. We see nothing in Article 7.4 that prohibits a Member from taking liberalization steps pursuant to a decision that post-dates the decision to apply a safeguard measure. Moreover, as we discuss below, our conclusion does not render Article 7.4 inoperative, as it remains possible, even in the absence of a timetable provided in advance, for a complaining party to demonstrate and a panel to determine whether a Member has acted inconsistently with Article 7.4, by failing to actually progressively liberalize its safeguard measure." *Ukraine – Passenger Cars supra* note 70, para. 7.360.

541 *Id.*, paras. 7.362 and 7.364.

542 *European Union – Steel Products, supra* note 70, para. 7.318.

543 Article 13 of the Agreement on Textiles and Clothing (expired on January 1, 2005).

7.4 CONCLUSION

The determination of an appropriate measure is as important as the injury determination and the procedural compliance with the SA. Nevertheless, there is no specific guideline for the determination of an appropriate measure in the SA except the minimum quota level provided in Article 5.1. The choice of an appropriate form and extent of the measure is, therefore, largely left to Members applying the measure. As discussed above, Members should take a minimalist approach to determine the extent of the measure to keep trade distortion and welfare loss to the minimum. **7.39**

Non-quantitative measures such as tariffs and tariff quotas are preferable since they have less distorting effects on trade, and Members have shown a clear preference for them.[544] The SA does not stipulate a ceiling for non-quantitative measures such as tariff quotas, but a Panel decision emphasized the requirement of a rational connection between the basis of the measure (i.e., how a specific tariff increase is calculated) and the objective of preventing or remedying serious injury.[545] This requirement does not obligate Members to justify their non-quantitative measure or quantitative measure taken below the ceiling specified in Article 5.1. Nevertheless, an arbitrary increase of tariffs, which has no rational connection with the state of domestic industry, would probably render the measure in violation of Article 5.1. Members applying a safeguard measure should also be reminded that a violation of the non-attribution requirement in Article 4.2(b) raises a presumption that the applied measure is also inconsistent with Article 5.1, as discussed above. **7.40**

544 *Supra* note 500.
545 *Supra* note 528.

8

COMPENSATION AND RETALIATION

8.1 INTRODUCTION

8.01 A multilateral trading system operates based on mutually agreed concessions among trading nations, and its success depends on their observance of the negotiated concessions. The problem with import restrictions such as safeguard measures is that such restrictions upset the balance of concessions between the importing and exporting Members.[546] Thus, it is reasonable to allow Members to obtain compensation for the loss of their trade caused by the application of a safeguard measure.

8.02 Thus, where compensation is not offered, the affected Members should, arguably, be allowed to suspend or withdraw their own concessions. Such a responsive measure is often described as retaliation. However, despite the negative connotation of the term, retaliation in the context of safeguards is not necessarily punitive in nature, as it attempts to restore the balance between the importing and exporting Members of concessions that have already been upset by the application of a safeguard measure.

8.03 Nevertheless, retaliatory action is applied unilaterally to the trade of a Member applying a safeguard measure, often accompanying political and diplomatic feuds between the importing and exporting Members over the justification

546 The counter-measures against dumping or illegal subsidy are not included in the category of the import restrictions such as safeguards, as anti-dumping measures and countervailing duties do not upset the balance of concessions but rather attempt to remedy damage caused by "unfair trade practices" such as dumping and illegal subsidy.

of the action.[547] The trade relations of those Members may well deteriorate as a result of retaliation and the subsequent disputes. The Member whose trade is affected by retaliation may also apply yet another responsive measure, and in the worst scenario, the downward spiral of sequential retaliations is a possibility, and this type of trade war would cause a grave disruption to the multilateral trading system. Therefore, serious efforts must be made for the settlement of compensation before any attempt at retaliation.[548]

Article XIX provided for both compensation and retaliation in the form of suspension of substantially equivalent concessions or other obligations under GATT 1994. The Article required Contracting Parties to proceed with a negotiation for compensation before they may resort to retaliation (Article XIX:3(a)). In the GATT era, a report indicated that Members had been more inclined to favor compensation over retaliation: there were almost twice as many compensation offers/agreements as retaliation implementations/proposals (20 cases and 11 cases, respectively).[549] As gray-area measures proliferated, the number of compensations was also reduced substantially (there were 18 cases of compensation offer/agreement between 1950 and 1969; 2 cases since 1970).[550] **8.04**

Suspension of Retaliation. The Agreement on Safeguards modifies the GATT provisions for compensation and retaliation. The major modification is the conditional suspension of the right to retaliation "for the first three years that a safeguard measure is in effect, provided that the safeguard measure has been taken as a result of an absolute increase in imports and that such a measure conforms to the provisions of this Agreement" (Article 8.3). As Members had prevalently sought import restrictions outside the GATT,[551] it was felt **8.05**

547 In the US *Steel Safeguard* case, the United States never conceded that its measure did not conform to the provisions of the SA. However, several Members including the EC and Japan proposed retaliatory measures which are not permitted where a safeguard measure is based on an absolute increase in imports and conforms to the provisions of the SA (Article 7.3). *See* Chapter 13 for a discussion of the US *Steel Safeguard* case.

548 The Report in 1984 by the Chairman of the Council to the Fortieth Session on "Safeguards" made a similar observation: "There is a convergence of views that contracting parties should retain the right given to them in the General Agreement to re-establish the balance of rights and obligations under the Agreement if this is significantly modified. At the same time, it is recognized that the right to retaliation can, in practice, be used more effectively by some contracting parties than others. There is furthermore a convergence of views that the threat of retaliation could also promote agreement on compensation. There is, at the same time, a recognition that retaliatory action has trade disruptive effects. The conclusion that many participants draw is that, wherever possible, constructive settlements should be reached involving compensation rather than the retaliatory withdrawal of benefits ...." MDF/4, 31S/136, 137 para. 8, *cited in* WTO, *Analytical Index: Guide to GATT Law and Practice*, *supra* note 85, p. 524.

549 WTO, *Analytical Index: Guide to GATT Law and Practice*, *supra* note 85, pp. 539–559.

550 *Id.*

551 *See* the discussions of gray-area measures provided in Chapter 2.3 *supra* and 9.1 *infra*.

necessary to provide some incentives for the Members to adhere to the new rules on safeguards.[552] The requirement of compensation and the possibility of retaliation was an important reason for the Members to avoid Article XIX and to resort to gray-area measures. The purpose of this suspension is to provide Members with an incentive to channel all emergency import restrictions to the authorized safeguard mechanism and to apply a measure for a shorter term. Also, this suspension may prevent further distortion of trade resulting from the application of retaliatory measures.[553]

8.06 Although a Member is not subject to retaliation for failure to agree on compensation, at least for the first three years, compensation is still an important element. Article 8.1 requires Members to "endeavour to maintain a substantially equivalent level of concessions and other obligations to that existing between it and the exporting Members."[554] It further provides, "To achieve this objective, the Members concerned may agree on an adequate means of trade compensation for the adverse effects of the measure on their trade." Nevertheless, Members applying a safeguard measure are significantly less inclined to offer compensation voluntarily where the three-year suspension is applicable. As of April 2024, there have been only a few compensation agreements.[555]

8.07 Critics argue that the offer of compensation has become politically difficult under the new rules. Since retaliation is now barred for the first three years of an application of a safeguard where the measure conforms to the provisions of the SA and is based on an absolute increase in imports, a Member proposing to apply a safeguard measure need not make an offer of compensation to avoid retaliation. Therefore, a compensation offer may even appear as an admission of the inconsistency of the measure with the provisions of the SA (provided that there was an absolute increase in imports). The government of the importing Member may have considerable difficulty in persuading its domestic constituencies to accept its offer of compensation as a measure of

---

552 *See* Chapter 2.4 *supra* for the negotiation of the SA.

553 Bhala and Kennedy, *supra* note 87, p. 928.

554 The Appellate Body found that this requirement under Article 8.1 is linked to the Member's consultation obligation under Article 12.3 and opined that a Member cannot "endeavor to maintain" an adequate balance of concessions unless it has provided an adequate opportunity for prior consultations on a proposed measure. *United States – Wheat Gluten, supra* note 71, paras. 145–146. *See also United States – Line Pipe, supra* note 71, paras. 108 and 119 and *Ukraine – Passenger Cars, supra* note 70, paras. 7.552–7.553. Failure to comply with the Article 12 notification requirement may also constitute a violation of Article 8.1 as this omission leads to the consideration that no endeavor is being made to maintain the required balance. *Id.*

555 WTO docs. G/L/1108 (March 5, 2015), G/L/1112 (March 31, 2015), G/L/1400 (September 13, 2021), and G/L/1480 (March 3, 2023).

good will to "maintain" the balance of concessions for the exporting Members. On the other hand, should the legality of the measure become an issue, the government of the importing Member proposing to apply a safeguard may be able to justify its compensation offer by indicating the possibility of retaliation.

8.2 ADEQUATE COMPENSATION

Timing. Article 8.2 sets time limits for reaching agreement on compensation (within 30 days of the consultation). If the importing and exporting countries fail to reach agreement on compensation, Article 8 allows exporting Members to suspend their concessions and other obligations to recover their loss (Article 8.2). Due to the 30-day time limit, a Member applying a safeguard that delays negotiations on compensation would be subject to retaliation. Any form of compensation and proposed suspension under Article 8.2 must be notified immediately to the Council for Trade in Goods (Article 12.5). **8.08**

Form of Compensation. If compensation is offered, the form and the extent of proper compensation would be an issue. Article 8 of the SA does not specify the proper form of compensation. The first sentence of Article 8.1 provides: **8.09**

> A Member proposing to apply a safeguard measure or seeking an extension of a safeguard measure shall endeavour to maintain a substantially equivalent level of concessions and other obligations to that existing under GATT 1994 between it and the exporting Members which would be affected by such a measure ….

If compensation is provided in an effort to "maintain a substantially equivalent level of concessions," as provided in Article 8.1, it can be made by increasing concessions to the imports from the Members affected by the safeguard measure. In such cases, compensation can be offered by way of tariff reductions.[556] **8.10**

Suppose that country A increases by 10 percent a tariff on product X imported from country B as a safeguard measure. Due to this safeguard measure, country B's export of product X to country A decreases by $100 million. As compensation, country A can offer a tariff reduction to the other imports from country B, which would yield a $100 million increase in the imports from country B. **8.11**

---

556 Commentators suggested that Members may also agree to a tariff increase on the export of a Member applying a safeguard measure. Bhala and Kennedy, *supra* note 87, p. 932. It is doubtful that this type of arrangement is desirable, as it further restricts trade and creates trade distortion. In addition, as it includes an agreement on restraining trade between Members, such an arrangement is arguably a violation of Article 11:1(b) of the SA, which prohibits gray-area measures.

Such an arrangement would restore the balance of concessions between A and B. Tariff reductions were offered as compensation for the application of safeguard measures in the previous GATT era.[557]

8.12 *Extent of Compensation.* The determination of an adequate level of compensation involves certain issues. The first concerns the basis of determining the adequate extent of compensation. An application of a safeguard measure may drive less competitive exporters out of the protected market or substantially reduce their exports. The actual loss of their trade during the period of the measure should be included in the compensation. In addition, those exporters who are driven out of the market may also find it impossible or substantially difficult to re-enter it even after the expiry of the measure because of the loss of sales networks, brand power, and/or customers' goodwill. Would that exporting Member be able to recover the loss occurring due to the future exclusion from the market? The importing Member would probably not consider that this type of loss can be compensated. Any compensation offer is likely to cover trade loss that actually occurs during the period of protection and not more. Even the calculation of this "actual" loss can be significantly different depending upon the methodology adopted.

8.13 *Compensation Affecting Trade of Third Countries.* The next question arises from the essentially selective nature of a compensatory measure. In other words, if the importing Member agrees to reduce tariffs as compensation, would such tariff reductions not affect the exports of a third country? Suppose that the United States agrees to offer a 5 percent tariff reduction to its imports of ships from China as compensation for its safeguard measure to its imports of steel products from China. This tariff reduction, if agreed to, would give a competitive edge to Chinese exporters not only over the US domestic producers (as intended) but also against the exporters of third countries, for instance, Japan (as presumably not intended).

8.14 If Japanese exporters sustain losses because of this compensatory measure in favor of Chinese exporters, what can be done? Do those Japanese exporters have any recourse? Compensation is essentially made only to the Members affected by the safeguard measure, and a third country does not seem to have specific recourse under the SA. The third country may be able to invoke Article XXIII for nullification or impairment of the benefit accruing under the

557 WTO, *Analytical Index: Guide to GATT Law and Practice*, *supra* note 85, pp. 539–559. A tariff quota is another possible form of compensation. See WTO doc. G/L/1108 (March 5, 2015), G/L/1112 (March 31, 2015), G/L/1400 (September 13, 2021), and G/L/1480 (March 3, 2023).

GATT. Should the remedy be provided under this Article, the effect would then be that the compensation would not be limited to the Members directly affected by the safeguard measure.

Other Problems with Compensatory Tariff Reductions. Another issue concerns the sufficiency of compensation in the form of tariff reduction. As the result of a series of multilateral trade negotiations, tariff rates for most non-primary products have been substantially reduced. The average tariff rate on non-primary products of industrial countries has become a mere 3.9 percent after the Uruguay Round negotiations.[558] As such, further tariff reductions may not be an adequate compensation with respect to non-primary products. **8.15**

Lowering tariffs for primary products instead of non-primary products as a way of compensation may also prove difficult because of the political sensitivity attached to the relevant sector.[559] Also, the importing Member may simply be unable to find suitable products imported from the affected Member on which to apply a compensatory tariff reduction: e.g., the exporting country may have no other suitable major product exported to the importing Member; the competing domestic producers may not accept lowering tariff rates on the product chosen for compensation; the exporting Member may have political and economic preferences for a set of products to which the importing Member is not willing to offer tariff reductions. Should this be the case, are there any alternative forms of compensation? **8.16**

Possibility of Monetary Compensation. Where suitable products are not found for tariff reductions as discussed above, the payment of a monetary sum, although it has not yet been done, should be considered as an alternative form of compensation. Again, the provision of Article 8.1 seems to be predicated on the compensatory measure being in the form of trade concessions,[560] and therefore, it is debatable whether monetary compensation can be included in the notion of "trade compensation" under it. Nevertheless, a settlement of another form of compensation, even involving monetary payment, is still preferential to retaliatory action. Where an increased tariff is applied as a form of a safeguard measure, some portion of the tariff revenue may be used for compensation. It **8.17**

558 Jackson, *supra* note 78, p. 74.

559 The special protection of the agricultural sector, reflected in the provisions of the Agreement on Agriculture, indicates the political sensitivity of the agricultural sector throughout the world.

560 Article 8.1 provides in relevant part: "To achieve this objective (maintaining a substantially equivalent level of concessions and other obligations to that existing under GATT 1994), the Members concerned may agree on any adequate means of trade compensation for the adverse effects of the measure on the trade."

would also be possible to consider a combination of a monetary sum and tariff reductions as a compensation package.

8.3 RETALIATION

8.18 Where no agreement is reached on compensation, retaliation is an alternative remedy for the exporting Members. The authorized form of retaliation is the suspension of substantially equivalent concessions or other obligations under GATT 1994 (Article 8.2). As mentioned above, the right to retaliation is suspended for the first three years that a safeguard measure is in effect unless either the applied measure does not conform to the provisions of the SA or it is not based on an absolute increase in imports (Article 8.3).

8.19 Article 8.2 also sets a time limit on retaliation (no later than 90 days after the application of the measure). Such time limit would be necessary to settle the rights and obligations of the parties early, thereby preventing further disruptions in trade by a series of cross-retaliations. Proposed suspension under Article 8.2 must be notified immediately to the Council for Trade in Goods (Article 12.5). The proposed retaliation is applicable upon the expiration of 30 days from the receipt of such notice by the Council as long as the Council does not "disapprove" the proposed measure.[561] At the request of the Member applying a safeguard measure, the Committee on Safeguards reviews whether retaliatory proposals to suspend concessions and other obligations are "substantially equivalent" and reports as appropriate to the Council for Trade in Goods (Article 13.1(e)). It should also be noted that Article 8 does not authorize the immediate suspension of its concessions or other obligations provided in paragraph 3(b) of Article XIX, where delay would cause irreparable damage to the domestic producers of the exporting country. The immediate retaliation is not compatible with the policy of suspension of retaliation under Article 8.3.[562]

8.20 The extent of a proposed retaliatory measure is an issue. The retaliatory measure should not exceed the extent of the injury to the export caused by the safeguard measure, as the authorization of the retaliatory measure under Article 8.2 is limited to the suspension of *substantially equivalent* concessions

561 The Report of the Review Session Working Party on "Quantitative Restrictions" stated that the affected parties are not obliged to obtain prior approval for the proposed measure and that the phrase in Article XIX, requiring the absence of "disapproval," merely indicates that the Contracting Parties have a right to require adjustments in the action taken if they consider that the action goes beyond what is necessary to restore the balance of benefits. GATT doc. L/332/Rev.1 and Addenda, adopted in March 1955, 3S/170, 182, para. 39.

562 *See also* the discussion of the applicability of immediate retaliation in Chapter 3.3 *supra*.

and other obligations under GATT 1994. On the other hand, Article 8 does not pose a limitation on the range of products to which a retaliatory measure can be applied. Article 8.2 provides that the retaliatory suspension is applied "to the trade of" the Member applying the safeguard measure. Thus, retaliatory action is applied to any product that is imported from the Member applying the measure[563] and not from a third country. A retaliatory measure is therefore inherently selective, as it should be.

Measure of Equivalent Suspension. As discussed above, the retaliatory suspension should not exceed the extent of injury caused by the safeguard. What is the measure of equivalent suspension in practice?[564] Suppose that Member A applies a safeguard measure and increases a tariff to a set of products imported from Member B. To determine an appropriate retaliatory measure, Member B may identify the amount of trade affected by the increase in tariffs as well as the amount collectable by increased tariffs. It can then select the products imported from Member A and increase tariffs to those products by the extent which the affected export and the amount collectable by increased tariffs would be equivalent to those resulting from the original safeguard measure. Some Members have calculated the amount of retaliatory tariff increases this way.[565] Where a safeguard measure places quantitative restrictions on imports, the decrease in revenue could be used as the reference for the retaliatory measure. The Members proposing retaliation should note that retaliation not only has import-limiting effects but also reduces the economic welfare of their own consumers. As discussed earlier, a net loss to the economy would occur as a result of applying import restrictions,[566] and therefore the retaliatory measure should be implemented with caution, even where it is justified under the provisions of the SA. **8.21**

Retaliation in Retrospect. The temporal basis of retaliatory suspension has been subject to controversy. In the 1982 Council discussion of proposed EEC measures under Article XIX:3 with respect to imports from Australia, the Australian representative stated that "although a contracting party was entitled to re-establish the balance of concessions, it was not entitled to calculate ret- **8.22**

563 The EC's proposed retaliation in response to the US safeguard measures applied to its imports of steel products in March 2002 presented a product list, including various fruits, vegetables, and clothes as well as steel products from the United States. WTO doc. G/SG/43 (May 15, 2002).

564 For a further discussion of proportionality of countermeasures, *see* Thomas M. Franck, "On Proportionality of Countermeasures in International Law" (2008) 102(4) *The American Journal of International Law* 742–752.

565 For instance, the EC adopted this method in calculating its retaliatory tariff increase in response to the US steel safeguard measures. WTO doc. G/SG/43 (May 15, 2002).

566 *Supra* note 30.

rospectively and to take retaliatory action on alleged trade losses over a subsequent period of years beyond the original ninety-day period."[567]

8.23 No retrospective retaliation seems justified under Article 8, as its provisions require Members to "maintain" the balance of concessions. A retaliatory measure to recover past as well as present losses would inevitably make its extent exceed that of the safeguard measure currently applied. Consequently, the balance of concessions would not be "maintained" but instead be shifted in favor of the retaliating Member. It is, therefore, doubtful that retaliation for past loss would be consistent with the requirement of Article 8.

8.24 Where the three-year bar to retaliation is applied, retaliatory action may be taken in the fourth year and beyond if the measure is still in effect. The procedural requirements under Article 8.2 still apply, and the exporting Member would not be able to apply the measure in the fourth year, unless it has already met those requirements (e.g., entered into negotiations for compensation and failed to reach agreement within the 30 days, as specified under Article 8.2). This means that if the exporting Member has never negotiated compensation during the consultations under Article 12.3, it cannot apply the retaliatory measure in the fourth year. Should the measure be extended, the affected Member would have the opportunity to negotiate compensation in the consultations held for the extension of the measure under Article 12.3.

8.25 If the exporting Member is authorized to apply a retaliatory measure, can the extent of such measure include the loss of trade during the first three years? The three-year bar operates as an exception to the balance of concessions between exporting and importing Members, for the purpose of encouraging Members to apply safeguard measures for a shorter period. Therefore, the author previously concluded that the incentive should cease to apply for a safeguard measure exceeding three years, and that the balance of concessions should be restored by compensation or a retaliatory measure that covers the exporting Member's losses since the beginning of the measure.[568] On the other hand, the author considers equally persuasive the argument that the inclusion of the losses of trade during the first three years is in effect retaliation in retrospect, and therefore, should not be allowed. It may well be the case that the provisions of Article 8.3 not only suspend the retaliation for the first three years but also limit the extent of the trade losses recoverable by retaliation

567 GATT doc. L/4099/Add.25, L/4526/Add.23; discussions at C/M/155, pp. 1–11, *cited in* WTO, *Analytical Index: Guide to GATT Law and Practice*, *supra* note 85, p. 528.

568 Lee (2000), *supra* note 2, p. 146.

to those only accruing after those three years, as an incentive to encourage Members not to deviate from the requirements of the new safeguard rules. To avoid any confusion, Article 8.3 can be amended to specify the prevention of any retrospective retaliation.

Procedure of Retaliation. There has been some confusion concerning the actual procedure of retaliation where the three-year bar to retaliation is not applied, either because a safeguard measure is inconsistent with the provisions of the SA, or because no absolute increase in imports is found (Article 8.3). The provisions of Article 8.2 should be understood in conjunction with the provisions of Article 12.3. First, consultations on compensation should be held pursuant to the provision of Article 12.3. Retaliation is authorized if agreement on compensation is not reached within 30 days from the beginning of the consultations. **8.26**

When the affected Members decide to suspend concessions or other GATT obligations, they would need to notify the Council for Trade in Goods of the proposed suspension. The Members may apply retaliatory measures, which the Council for Trade in Goods does not disapprove of. Proposed retaliatory measures have never been disapproved of since the GATT era. The 1955 Report of the Review Session Working Party on "Quantitative Restrictions" stated, with respect to the phrase of Article XIX:3(a), "the suspension of which the CONTRACTING PARTIES do not disapprove," that "it is clear, both from the text itself and from the practice followed so far by the CONTRACTING PARTIES, that the object of this phrase quoted is merely to indicate that the CONTRACTING PARTIES have a right to require adjustments in the action taken if they consider that the action goes beyond what is necessary to restore the balance of benefits."[569] Only in one instance, involving a Turkish Article XIX:3 action against the United States, did the Contracting Parties take a formal decision *not* to disapprove the proposed retaliatory action.[570] **8.27**

The reading of the provision of Article 8.2 indicates that there is a 90-day time limit for the initiation of the retaliation: "Members shall be free, *not later than* 90 days after the measure is applied, to suspend…" (emphasis added). Should Members be prohibited under any circumstance from applying a retaliatory measure after those 90 days? The 90-day limit was extended by the decisions **8.28**

569 WTO, *Analytical Index: Guide to GATT Law and Practice*, *supra* note 85, p. 528.
570 *Id.*

of the Contracting Parties where two parties agreed to do so.[571] This practice has also continued after the WTO entered into force.[572]

8.29 The next question is, in the absence of such agreement for extension, may the exporting Member unilaterally choose to apply retaliatory measures after the 90 days? The proposed retaliations against the US steel safeguard measures[573] did not limit their implementation date within those 90 days after the application of the measure.[574] The time limit on the decision to apply a retaliatory measure is necessary for the following reason: the retaliatory suspension of concessions further interferes with trade, which is already affected by the application of a safeguard measure. Therefore, the possibility of retaliation creates uncertainty, which may lead to further disruption of trade. For instance, the importers of the exporting Member that is contemplating retaliation may increase imports from the Member applying a safeguard measure in fear of future retaliation. The exporters of the importing Member, on the contrary, may seek to export to other Members so that their exports will not be restrained by retaliation. The 90-day requirement limits the period of this uncertainty.

8.30 On the other hand, the later implementation of retaliatory measures may be favorable and reduces trade distortion, as the duration of retaliation may become shorter by its later application, as long as those measures are not

571 WTO, *Analytical Index: Guide to GATT Law and Practice*, *supra* note 85, pp. 525–526. In a request for such an extension in 1984, concerning a US safeguard measure, the Director-General of the GATT stated that if the two parties agree on the extension, the period can be extended. He also continued that, however, if one party is in disagreement on such extension, the Council could not postpone the entry into force of a retaliatory measure. *Id.*

572 For instance, in April 2000, the EC agreed with Argentina to extend the 90-day limit with respect to Argentina's safeguard measure and made an Article 12.5 notification to the Council for Trade in Goods. WTO doc. G/SG/N/12/EEC/3 (April 19, 2000). *See also* the subsequent agreements on the extension of the 90-day period between the United States and various other Members with respect to the US steel safeguard measures applied in March 2002. WTO docs. G/SG/N/12/USA/6 (May 16, 2002), G/SG/N/12/USA/7 (May 16, 2002), G/SG/N/12/USA/8 (May 17, 2002), G/SG/N/12/USA/9 (May 17, 2002), G/SG/N/12/USA/10 (June 14, 2002).

573 For the proposed retaliatory measures, *see* the WTO docs. G/SG/43 (May 15, 2002), G/SG/44 (May 21, 2002), G/SG/45 (May 21, 2002), G/SG/46 (May 21, 2002), G/SG/47 (May 22, 2002).

574 The EC's proposed retaliation stated with respect to the implementation of its retaliatory measure, "Without prejudice to the effective exercise of its right to suspend substantially equivalent concessions or other obligations referred to in Article 8.2, the EC hereby reserves its right to apply the proposed suspension not earlier than 18 June 2002 and until Annex II applies as regards Annex I and from 20 March 2005 or from the fifth day following the date of a decision from the WTO Dispute Settlement Body that the safeguard measure imposed by the United States is incompatible with the WTO Agreements, if that is earlier, and until the United States' safeguard measure is lifted as regards Annex II": WTO doc. G/SG/43 (May 15, 2002). It is interesting to note that the adoption of either the Panel report (if there is no appeal) or the Appellate Body report by the WTO Dispute Settlement Body automatically triggers the application of additional tariffs on the long list of products comprised in Annex II. It is to encourage the United States to withdraw its measure immediately on a decision from the WTO Dispute Settlement Body. Commission of the European Communities, *Report from the Commission to the Council on Steel re-balancing action* (September 24, 2002).

cumulative and retrospective. The uncertainty created by pending retaliation can be reduced by the announcement of the proposed retaliatory measure and its expected implementation date. Such an announcement needs to be made within the 90-day period unless the period is extended by mutual agreement between exporting and importing Members. The delay of the implementation may also open a possibility that the exporting and importing Members may subsequently agree on compensation. The current provision of Article 8.2 should be modified to clarify the authorization of the delayed implementation of retaliatory measures as long as the proposed retaliation is announced within the 90-day period and the measures to be applied later in time are neither cumulative nor retrospective.

Retaliation: Feasible Remedy? Finally, the feasibility of retaliation as a remedy to the affected Members is an issue. Retaliatory measures will be effective only if the retaliating Member also provides a significant export market for the products of the Member applying a safeguard measure. For instance, the United States made a series of announcements to exclude a total of 727 products from its steel safeguard measures[575] after extensive retaliations had been proposed by powerful economies such as the EC and Japan. Members of smaller economies taking in a relatively insignificant portion of exports from the Member applying a safeguard measure do not have an effective means of retaliation. Thus, smaller trading partners of the United States opted for the extension of negotiations with the latter[576] while Members with large markets such as China, Japan, and the EC proposed retaliatory measures in response to the US steel safeguard measures. This disparity is an inherent limitation in the consideration of retaliation as an effective means of remedy. **8.31**

Notifications of retaliation remained relatively small until 2017 (10 notifications),[577] but there has been a sharp increase since 2018 (25 notifications).[578] **8.32**

---

575 US Department of Commerce, "Department of Commerce and USTR Announce Final Set of Products to Be Excluded From Safeguard on Steel Products," *Commerce News*, August 22, 2002. In terms of tonnage, the excluded products accounted for around 25 percent of the original list (320 million tons out of 1,310 million tons). Although this press release stated that the exclusion was based on the US consumer need and on the determination that the exclusion would not undermine the effectiveness of the safeguard measure, it was widely considered that the purpose of the exclusion is to avoid serious trade conflict with the major trading partners of the United States. "Tariff Exemptions Expanded," *Washington Post*, August 23, 2002, p. E02.

576 *See supra* notes 572 and 573.

577 WTO docs. G/L/251, G/SG/N/12/TUR/1, G/L/625, G/L/626, G/L/738, G/SG/N/12/TUR/1, G/L/1032, G/L/1076, G/L/1117, G/L/1183 (excluding corrigendum).

578 WTO docs. G/L/1221, G/L/1220, G/L/1226, G/L/1224, G/L/1223, G/L/1239, G/L/1237, G/L/1242, G/L/1241, G/L/1240, G/L/1296, G/L/1306, G/L/1304, G/L/1076, G/L/1350, G/L/1353, G/L/1357, G/L/1356, G/L/1359, G/L/1364, G/L/1395, G/L/1396, G/L/1422, G/L/1485, G/L/1528 (excluding corrigendum, supplements, and revisions). *See also* Hiromi Yano, "Rebalancing the Trading Scale? Recent

The increasing trend coincides with the period in which the United States has been blocking appointments to the Appellate Body, incapacitating it and thereby disabling the DSB from rendering final decisions once panel decisions are appealed to the non-functional Appellate Body, which a majority of losing Members tend to do.[579] Without the prospect of final decisions from the DSB, Members affected by trade measures would be more inclined to resort to immediate retaliation.

Trends in the Implementation of Article 8 of the Safeguards Agreement" (2024) 19(2) *Global Trade and Customs Journal* 110–113.

579 A group of 47 WTO Members created a new Multi-Party Interim Appeal Arbitration Arrangement (MPIA) in 2020 under Article 25 of the DSU as an alternative appeal mechanism open to Members, but this process is not binding on the non-participating Members such as the United States and, thus, does not replace the Appellate Body. Geneva Trade Platform, *Multi-Party Interim Appeal Arbitration Arrangement (MPIA)* (2024), https://wtoplurilaterals.info/plural_initiative/the-mpia/ (accessed May 14, 2024).

9

REMAINING ISSUES

9.1 PROHIBITION OF "GRAY-AREA MEASURES"

Article 11 clarifies one of the most important objectives of the Agreement on Safeguards: the prohibition of gray-area measures. The definition of gray-area measures, their historical background, their economic inefficiency, their inconsistencies with the GATT provisions, and their inherent unfairness have already been discussed in Chapter 2.3 above. This chapter provides a discussion of the current status of the prohibition of gray-area measures and presents cases of suspect gray-area measures. 9.01

Current Status. Article 11.1 of the SA prohibits all forms of gray-area measures. Under this provision, Members may not "seek, take or maintain any voluntary export restraints, orderly marketing arrangements or any other similar measures on the export or the import side"[580] (Article 11.1(b)). Article 11.3 goes beyond the prohibition of all gray-area measures agreed between governments and requires Members not to "encourage or support the adoption or maintenance by public and private enterprises of non-government measures equivalent to those referred to in paragraph 1." The economic effect of any private market arrangement among large industries worldwide could be tantamount to the inter-governmental arrangements prohibited in Article 11.2. 9.02

580 The footnote of Article 11.1 describes examples of these similar measures, including "export moderation, export-price or import-price monitoring systems, export or import surveillance, compulsory import cartels and discretionary export or import licensing schemes, any of which afford protection."

The provisions of Article 11 cannot directly prohibit the conduct of private parties.[581] [582]

9.03 After the implementation of the SA, the proliferation of gray-area measures seems finally to have been inhibited. Article 11.2 of the Agreement provides that all pre-existing gray-area measures shall be terminated within four years after the date of entry into force of the WTO Agreement. The Committee of Safeguards reported that all notified pre-existing measures, covered by Articles 10 and 11 of the Agreement, were phased out by January 1, 2000.[583] However, there have been suspect gray-area measures since the implementation of the WTO,[584] and some of the suspect measures are discussed below.

9.04 *Softwood Lumber Agreement.* Despite the Committee Report indicating the non-existence of a gray-area measure, it is still possible that gray-area measures are taken without any notification to the Committee, and a question has been raised with respect to the provisions of a bilateral trade agreement, the "Softwood Lumber Agreement between the Government of the United States and the Government of Canada" (hereinafter, "SLA").[585] The five-year agreement, entered into in 1996, required the Canadian government to levy fees on exports of softwood lumber to the United States when the export quantity is above a pre-fixed level. Article II.1 of the SLA provided in its relevant part:

---

581 Although private market arrangements may escape the regulation in Article 11, such arrangements may be subject to domestic legal disciplines against anti-competition practices.

582 Since private arrangements of this kind would also violate the anti-monopoly laws of many countries, the question arises whether the failure of a Member to enforce those laws against such an arrangement would violate Article 11.3. Given that the WTO does not yet regulate competition policy, it is doubtful that the mere lack of or insufficient enforcement of anti-monopoly laws would be considered government support or endorsement of trade-restricting private arrangements. In *Japan – Measures Affecting Consumer Photographic Film and Paper*, the Panel did not find that the alleged "business restrictive practices and measures" of Japan impaired or nullified benefits accruing to the United States within the meaning of GATT Article XXIII:1(b) nor accorded less favorable treatment to imported photographic film and paper within the meaning of GATT Article III:4. *Japan – Measures Affecting Consumer Photographic Film and Paper*, Report of the Panel, WT/DS44/R (March 20, 1998), paras. 10.402–10.404.

583 WTO, Report (2000) of the Committee on Safeguards, G/L/209 (November 23, 2000), para. 23.

584 *See also* Roman Grynberg *et al.*, "Bilateral Commodity Agreements – New Generation Grey Area Measures?: A Scoping Study," *in* Veniana Qalo (ed.), *Bilateralism and Development: Emerging Trade Patterns* (Cameron May, 2008). The study presents cases of suspect violations of SA Article 11, including the US–Canada Softwood Lumber Agreement, as well as a new breed of gray-area measures which may not directly violate the Article but creates similar trade restrictive effects through technical regulations (i.e., various wine agreements by EU) or discriminatory trade arrangements (textile agreements applicable to imports from China under TSM). *Id.*

585 *See* the author's work on the issue of the revival of gray-area measures. "Revival of Gray-Area Measures? – The US-Canada Softwood Lumber Agreement: Conflict with the WTO Agreement on Safeguards" (2002), *supra* note 1.

> Canada shall place softwood lumber on the Export Control List under the Export and Import Permit Act, as amended, and require a federal export permit for each exportation to the United States of softwood lumber first manufactured in the province of Ontario, Quebec, British Columbia or Alberta ....[586]

Article II.2 also provided: **9.05**

> Canada shall collect a fee on issuance of a permit for export to the United States of softwood lumber first manufactured in the province of Ontario, Quebec, British Columbia or Alberta for quantities above the established base in a given year. The fee shall be determined in accordance with the following schedule:

Exports (yearly)	Fee
(a) 14.7 billion board feet (the established base) or less	Free
(b) More than 14.7 and less than or equal to 15.35 billion	US$50 per thousand board feet (the lower fee base)
(c) Amounts in excess of 15.35 billion board feet	US$100 per thousand board feet (the upper fee base)

9.06 In return for this export restraint by way of export fees, the United States was committed not to initiate any trade action against the import of Canadian softwood lumber (Articles I and II of the SLA). This agreement was a voluntary export restraint and a violation of Article 11. However, the agreement was never challenged in the WTO, as no third party seemed to have its interest affected by this arrangement. The Committee on Safeguards was not notified of the measure.[587]

9.07 The original SLA expired on March 31, 2001. However, efforts were made to renew the SLA, and a new SLA (the 2006 SLA) came into effect on October 12, 2006.[588] The 2006 SLA was more trade restrictive than the original SLA due to the introduction of optional quotas.[589] Article VII of the 2006 SLA required each Region in Canada to elect either export charges or export charges with volume restraints (quotas) in the following schedule.[590]

9.08

586 For the text of the agreement, refer to the website of the Department of Foreign Affairs and International Trade of Canada, available at: https://gac.canadiana.ca/view/ooe.b3000485/4 [https://perma.cc/N4SU-BFPH].

587 The SLA was not notified as an existing gray-area measure and therefore did not qualify under the exception provided by Article 11.2. In any event, it continued until 2001, past the deadline of 1999 by which all existing gray-area measures must expire.

588 The SLA 2006 came into effect on October 12, 2006 and was to remain effective for seven to nine years by terms of the Agreement. *See* the SLA text, available at: http://www.treaty-accord.gc.ca/text-texte.aspx?id=105072&lang=eng (accessed September 29, 2013).

589 SLA (2006), Article VII.

590 *Id.*

Prevailing Monthly Price	Option A – Export Charge (Expressed as a % of Export Price)	Option B – Export Charge (Expressed as a % of Export Price) with Volume Restraint
Over US$ 355	No Export Charge	No Export Charge and no volume restraint
US$ 336-355	5%	2.5% Export Charge + maximum volume that can be exported to the United States cannot exceed the Region's share of 34% of Expected US Consumption for the month
US$ 316-335	10%	3% Export Charge + maximum volume that can be exported to the United States cannot exceed the Region's share of 32% of Expected US Consumption for the month
US$ 315 or under	15%	5% Export Charge + maximum volume that can be exported to the United States cannot exceed the Region's share of 30% of Expected US Consumption for the month

The 2006 SLA expired in 2015, but a recurrence of this sort of bilateral arrangement would undermine one of the most important objectives of the Agreement on Safeguards – the prohibition of gray-area measures. As previously shown in the proliferation of gray-area measures during the 1980s, the difficulty in restraining such measures is that there is unlikely to be any complainant to invoke Article 11 except in limited cases where the export is diverted to a third country as a result of this measure.[591] Given the clear and unequivocal prohibition of gray-area measures under the SA, Members may find it difficult to disregard the requirement of Article 11 altogether and enter into such an arrangement. Nevertheless, the surveillance role of the Committee of Safeguards would be vital in preserving the disciplines of Article 11. The Committee should closely monitor the implementation of the Agreement – the requirements of Article 11 in particular – and report to the Council for Trade in Goods any suspect violation so that the Council may take proper action as necessary.

9.09 *Transitional Product-Specific Safeguard Mechanism and Textile-Specific Safeguard Clause.* The concern about the revival of gray-area measures is also justified in light of the Transitional Product-Specific Safeguard Mechanism (the "TSM"[592]) and the Textile-Specific Safeguard Clause ("TSSC"). China's entry into the WTO in 2001 and the expiration of the Agreement on Textiles and Clothing in 2005 raised concern about "the flooding of cheap Chinese exports."[593] In response to this concern, the Protocol on China's entry into the WTO ("the Protocol")[594] lowers the threshold for the application of

591 *Supra* note 123.

592 Both the Transitional Product-Specific Safeguard Mechanism and an individual measure are abbreviated as "TSM," with the former to be denoted with a definite article. The "TSM" may also refer to a specific measure as appropriate in the context.

593 *Infra* note 793.

594 WTO doc. WT/L/432.

a safeguard measure against imports from China with the introduction of the TSM, applicable to all products imported from China, and TSSC, applicable to the textile and clothing products from China covered by the ATC.[595] Both the TSM and TSSC require China to take action to prevent or remedy market disruption, albeit for limited transitional periods, where its exports cause such "disruption" in the market of another Member.[596] Although this requirement is not a gray-area measure *per se*, as it was agreed under the WTO framework and therefore technically not in violation of the rules, it nevertheless has an element of a gray-area measure, as discussed below.

The TSSC, which lasted until the end of 2008,[597] provided in relevant part: **9.10**

> (a) In the event that a WTO Member believed that imports of Chinese origin of textiles and apparel products covered by the ATC as of the date the WTO Agreement entered into force, were, due to market disruption, threatening to impede the orderly development of trade in these products, such Member could request consultations with China with a view to easing or avoiding such market disruption
>
> ...
>
> (c) Upon receipt of the request for consultations, China agreed to hold its shipments to the requesting Member of textile or textile products in the category or categories subject to these consultations to a level no greater than 7.5 per cent (6 per cent for wool product categories) above the amount entered during the first 12 months of the most recent 14 months preceding the month in which the request for consultations was made;
>
> (d) If no mutually satisfactory solution were reached during the 90-day consultation period, consultations would continue and the Member requesting consultations could continue the limits under subparagraph (c) for textiles or textile products in the category or categories subject to these consultations....

The relevant provision required China to take action to remedy or prevent "market disruption" and to hold its export shipments of textile and clothing products. It also allowed the exporting Member to limit the imports from China. **9.11**

595 As a result of the introduction of the TSM and the TSSC, an analysis suggested that prospects for China's textile and clothing exports after WTO accession may not be as optimistic as was generally assumed. Huan Liu and Laixiang Sun, "Beyond the Phaseout of Quotas in the Textile and Clothing Trade: WTO-Plus Rules and the Case of US Safeguards Against Chinese Exports in 2003" (2004) 11(1) *Asia-Pacific Development Journal* 49–71.

596 Paragraph 16 of the Protocol provides conditions for the application of TSMs.

597 The Report of the Working Party on the Accession of China to the WTO (WT/MIN(01)3 of 10 November 2001) attached to the Protocol of Accession of China to the WTO (WT/L/432 of 23 November 2001) introduced in its paragraph 242 a provision that would enable WTO Members to introduce safeguard measures against imports of textile and clothing products from China.

9.12 Paragraph 16.2 of the Protocol (the TSM), which was to remain until November 2013,[598] also requires China to take action to remedy or prevent "market disruption" to importing countries. It provides:

> If, in the course of these bilateral consultations, it is agreed that imports of Chinese origin are such a cause and that action is necessary, China shall take such action as to prevent or remedy the market disruption. Any such action shall be notified immediately to the Committee on Safeguards.

9.13 The Protocol requires China to control its exports and not to cause "market disruption" to another Member. The requirement under the TSSC and the TSM apparently contains an element of export restraints, which is mentioned in Article 11.1(b) of the SA.[599] In fact, it could be called another type of gray-area measure imposed multilaterally against imports from China. Two agreements – the US–China Textile Agreement and EC–China Textile Agreement – which purport to limit the growth of China's textile exports were adopted in 2005 under the TSSC.[600]

9.14 It might be argued that the measures under paragraph 16.2 and the TSSC were justified because they were approved by the Members as a condition for China's entry to the WTO. Nevertheless, these measures are not consistent with the general policy under Article 11.1(a), against all import restrictions other than the safeguards regulated under the SA. It should be remembered that this new policy was finally adopted after decades of difficult negotiations, and therefore should not be readily compromised.

9.15 Significant political pressure within certain Members, primarily from their domestic producers demanding to keep inexpensive Chinese imports in check, may have led to the adoption of specific safeguard measures, but such political pressure is not a valid reason for deviating from the important principles of the

598 Paragraph 16.9 of the Protocol stipulates that the application of the TSM provisions shall be terminated after 12 years from the date of China's accession to the WTO. Lee (2002), *infra* note 790. *See also* Chapter 11.4 *infra* for a discussion of specific safeguard measures.

599 Article 11.1(b) provides in relevant part, "a Member shall not seek, take or maintain any voluntary export restraints, orderly marketing arrangements or any other similar measures on the export or the import side ...." A footnote of the Article enlists examples of similar measures, which include: "export moderation, export-price or import-price monitoring systems, export or import surveillance, compulsory import cartels and discretionary export import licensing schemes, any of which afford protection."

600 The US–China Textile Agreement limited the growth of certain Chinese textile and clothing exports to the United States to between 8 percent and 10 percent in 2006, by 12.5 percent in 2007, and by 15 percent to 16 percent in 2008. For the EU–China, the corresponding numbers were between 8 and 12.5 percent per year for 2005, 2006, and 2007 in accordance with the pre-set criteria. EU, Press Release, Brussels, June 12, 2005, MEMO/05/201, text available at: http://europa.eu/rapid/press-release_MEMO-05-201_en.htm?locale=en (accessed April 21, 2024) and "US and China sign textiles deal," *BBC News*, November 8, 2005, text available at: http://news.bbc.co.uk/1/hi/business/4416858.stm [https://perma.cc/QH44-9EAF].

multilateral agreement such as the prohibition against gray-area measures. On the contrary, making an exceptional arrangement as a concession to domestic political pressure sets an undesirable precedent for compromising the multilateral disciplines on international trade and creates a danger of destabilizing the world trading system.[601]

The Steel and Aluminum Quota Agreements. In March 2018, the United States announced the imposition of a 25 percent *ad valorem* tariff increase on steel products and a 10 percent increase in tariffs on aluminum products under Section 232 of the Trade Expansion Act of 1962.[602] While making this announcement, the United States also sought to negotiate alternative arrangements with its trading partners in return for an exemption from the tariffs.[603] The outcome was import quota agreements with South Korea, Brazil, and Argentina that were gray-area measures prohibited under Article 11 of the SA.[604] Despite the inconsistency with the SA, South Korea agreed to an annual export quota for steel products and was exempted from the steel tariffs.[605] Brazil also agreed to an annual quota for steel products and obtained tariff exemption.[606] Argentina agreed to annual quotas for both steel and aluminum products.[607] **9.16**

South Korea is one of the major exporters of steel products to the United States, accounting for 10 percent of all US steel imports in the first half of 2018.[608] South Korea sought a waiver from the tariffs and agreed to an annual quota for 54 categories of iron or steel products, setting the maximum exportable amounts to 2.68 million metric tons.[609] This quota agreement would reduce around 30 percent of its steel exports to the United States from the 2015-17 **9.17**

601 This concern was shared by the representative of China in his statement to the Committee on Safeguards. He considered that "some members imposed upon China what are exactly prohibited by Article 11 of the Safeguard Agreement, by inserting paragraph 16 into China's Protocol of Accession to WTO. With that paragraph, voluntary export restraints on the part of China were provided for as an alternative to product-specific safeguard measures." *Infra* note 806.

602 Proclamation 9705 of March 8, 2018 "Adjusting Imports of Steel Into the United States," 83 *Federal Register* 11625 (March 15, 2018); and Proclamation 9704 of March 8, 2018 "Adjusting Imports of Aluminum Into the United States," 83 *Federal Register* 11619 (March 15, 2018).

603 Congressional Research Service, *Section 232 Investigations: Overview and Issues for Congress* (updated November 21, 2018), at 7.

604 For further discussion, *see* Lee, "The Steel and Aluminum Quota Agreements: A Question of Compatibility with WTO Disciplines and Their Impact on the World Trading System," *supra* note 1.

605 Proclamation 9740 of April 30, 2018, 83 *Federal Register* 20683 (May 7, 2018).

606 Proclamation 9759 of May 31, 2018, 83 *Federal Register* 25857 (June 5, 2018).

607 Proclamation 9758 of May 31, 2018, 83 *Federal Register* 25849 (June 5, 2018).

608 US International Trade Administration, "Steel Imports Report: United States," *Global Steel Trade Monitor* (September 2018), at 3.

609 Proclamation 9740, *supra* note 605.

average in return for a permanent exemption from the steel tariffs.[610] Korea did not negotiate on a quota agreement for aluminum, and tariffs were applied to its aluminum exports as of May 1, 2018.

9.18 As for Brazil, the country supplied 12 percent of all US steel imports for the first half of 2018, being the second largest steel exporter to the United States. Brazilian steel exporters negotiated with the United States and agreed on a quota agreement. The annual steel quota was assigned to 54 iron or steel product categories.[611] The agreement would limit Brazilian steel exports to 70 percent of the 2015–17 average for finished steel products and 100 percent of the three-year average for semi-finished steel products, setting the maximum export limits to 3.5 million tons of semi-finished steel goods and around 687,000 tons of finished steel.[612] Brazil also did not negotiate a quota agreement for aluminum, and tariffs were applied to its aluminum exports.

9.19 Argentina agreed on both steel and aluminum quotas with the United States. The steel quota assigned to Argentina's steel exports exceeded its three-year average in 2015–17 by 35 percent, with a total amount of 180,000 metric tons in 54 product categories.[613] The aluminum quota was agreed at 100 percent of its average annual exports in 2015–17, and this quota was set on only two product categories (9903.85.05 and 9903.85.06). The quotas assigned to Argentina were less restrictive than those assigned to South Korea and Brazil because Argentina is not a major steel or aluminum exporter to the United States, taking up only 0.6 percent of US steel imports and 2.3 percent of its aluminum imports.

9.20 These quota agreements are gray-area measures prohibited under Article 11.1(b) of the SA. They qualify as "any voluntary export restraints, orderly marketing arrangements or any other similar measures on the export or the import side," including "actions taken by a single Member as well as actions

---

610 *Id.* The quota schedule is accessible online at: https://www.federalregister.gov/documents/2018/05/07/2018-09841/adjusting-imports-of-steel-into-the-united-states (accessed January 4, 2019). The quota schedule might also be adjusted, as the Proclamations authorize the Secretary of Commerce to grant exclusions from the duties upon request of affected parties if the steel or aluminum articles are determined not to be produced in the United States in a sufficient and reasonably available amount or of a satisfactory quality or based upon specific national security considerations. *Supra* note 602. The Department of Commerce published an interim final rule for how parties located in the United States may request exclusions. Department of Commerce, Bureau of Industry and Security, "Requirements for Submissions Requesting Exclusions From the Remedies Instituted in Presidential Proclamations Adjusting Imports of Steel Into the United States and Adjusting Imports of Aluminum into the United States," 83 *Federal Register* 12106 (March 19, 2018).

611 Proclamation 9759, *supra* note 606.

612 *Id.*

613 *Id.*

under agreements, arrangements and understandings entered into by two or more Members" that "a Member shall not seek, take or maintain" under Article 11.1(b) of the SA.[614] The quota agreements demonstrate the key elements of gray-area measures by (i) limiting steel and aluminum trade (ii) in the form of an agreement, of which existence is confirmed by the Proclamations.[615] The United States invoked the national security exception under GATT Article XXI to justify its steel and aluminum tariff measures, but the Panel determined that the US measures were not justified under the exception.[616] Accordingly, the quota agreements would not have any justification under this exception.

Caution Against Rule Evasion. The gray-area measures that the United States sought and adopted in the form of the steel and aluminum quota agreements are concerning as they undermine one of the most important objectives of the SA, which is the elimination of the trade-distorting gray-area measures. The Biden administration, which succeeded the Trump administration that adopted these measures, did not lift them, citing that it was under no obligation to rescind the tariffs because there was no "final decision" from the DSB.[617] The US approach raises concerns for the integrity of the rule-based international trading system as the US administration appealed the Panel decision to the non-functional Appellate Body that has lost a quorum due to its block of all appointments to the latter.[618] **9.21**

Another concern is the possibility of rule evasion by private enterprises. As global competition among a number of industries has increased trade disputes over the years, major producers have approached one another to seek ways to avoid these disputes and cooperate in support of mutual interests. For instance, the representatives from the chemical industries and governments of China and Japan are known to have met in Beijing and Tokyo in March 2002 and **9.22**

614 SA, art. 11.1(b).

615 Proclamation 9740, *supra* note 605 and Proclamation 9759, *supra* note 606.

616 *United States –Steel and Aluminum Products*, *supra* note 70, para. 7.164.

617 Nina M. Hart and Brandon J. Murrill, *Section 301 Tariffs on Goods from China: International and Domestic Legal Challenges*, Congressional Research Service, LSB10553 3–4 (July 22, 2021).

618 The United States raised ambiguous systemic issues, such as the alleged judicial overreach of the Appellate Body, as the justification for its block, but commentators consider that successful challenges to a number of anti-dumping measures, countervailing measures, and safeguards applied by the United States are more likely a reason. For further discussion, *see* Kenneth A. Reinert, "Steel, Security and the WTO Dispute Settlement Mechanism: A Trade Catastrophe in the Making," *The World Economy* (February 28, 2024), available at: https://onlinelibrary.wiley.com/doi/abs/10.1111/twec.13556 (accessed April 21, 2024). *See also* Chad P. Bown, "Trump Ended WTO Dispute Settlement. Trade Remedies Are Needed to Fix It" (2022) 21(3) *World Trade Review* 312–329.

August 2003, respectively, to have a dialogue on, *inter alia*, production, prices, import and export of chemical products, and certain anti-dumping issues.[619]

9.23 While the exchanges of information and views would not *per se* affect trade adversely, a settlement of any agreement, formal or informal, on the control of trade in such consultations may do so. Yet an agreement between non-governmental entities such as exporters and domestic producers is not subject to the WTO disciplines, although this sort of arrangement is inherently anti-competitive. Nonetheless, the Members will violate the provisions of Article 11 if their governments encourage or support the adoption of such an agreement. Article 11.3 clarifies that "Members shall not encourage or support the adoption or maintenance by public and private enterprises of non-government measures equivalent to those referred to in paragraph 1."

9.24 Therefore, governments should not induce or involve themselves in any gray-area measure-type agreements between exporters and the competing domestic producers and should also apply their own competition laws where these agreements violate them.[620] Given the clear prohibition of gray-area measures under Article 11, such government inducement or involvement, if any, is likely to remain unofficial, and therefore, this type of violation would be increasingly difficult to prove. In this regard, the role of the Committee on Safeguards is essential, and it should vigilantly monitor government involvements in private consultations and any agreement made between exporters and domestic producers as a result of such consultations. Efforts should be made, particularly by powerful trading economies such as the US and EU, to ensure that one of the most important objectives set by the SA, the complete prohibition of gray-area measures, would not be further circumvented and undermined.

9.2 PROVISIONAL MEASURE, DIFFERENTIAL TREATMENT, SURVEILLANCE

9.25 The SA also provides for provisional measures, special and differential treatment for developing countries, and surveillance. The remainder of this chapter

619 Japan Chemical Industry Association, News Release, August 28, 2003. Another study concluded that VERs can still be used without formal intergovernmental agreements where exporters fear an application of a safeguard measure under certain circumstances including a large drop in export prices. Koichi Kagitani and Kozo Harimaya, "Safeguards and Voluntary Export Restraints under the World Trade Organization: The Case of Japan's Vegetable Trade" (2015) 36 *Japan and the World Economy* 29–41.

620 Nonetheless, the failure of applying competition law would not seem a violation of Article 11. *Supra* note 582.

examines relevant provisions, followed by a discussion of the determinants of safeguard measures and the overall assessment of the SA.

Provisional Safeguard Measure. Article 6 authorizes provisional safeguard measures applicable upon a preliminary determination that increased imports have caused, or are threatening to cause, serious injury to a domestic industry *in critical circumstances* where delay in remedy would cause irreparable damage to the industry. Article XIX also provided for provisional safeguard measures. However, unlike its predecessor, the SA limits the duration of the provisional measures to 200 days.[621] If a definitive measure is applied, the period of a provisional measure is counted as part of the initial period of the safeguard measure.[622] **9.26**

The normal investigation process must follow the application of a provisional measure. The form of the provisional measure is limited to tariff increases to be promptly refunded if the subsequent investigation does not determine that increased imports have caused or threatened to cause serious injury to a domestic industry.[623] Article 12.4 also requires notification of a provisional safeguard measure to the Committee on Safeguards *prior to* its application, as well as an initiation of consultations *immediately after* the measure is taken. **9.27**

A provisional measure, applicable without *prior* consultations, is a device to prevent or remedy irreparable damage to a domestic industry in critical circumstances where the Member cannot afford to wait until the investigation is completed due to the risk of irreparable damage caused by delay. The urgency of the situation is the key to determining the validity of a provisional measure.[624] A provisional measure should not be applied as a protectionist response to a safeguard measure adopted by another Member where the existence of critical circumstances justifying the provisional measure is not clear. The issue of whether such circumstances existed was questioned in the EC provisional measure on steel products taken shortly after the implementation of controversial US steel safeguard measures.[625] **9.28**

621 Article 6 of the SA.

622 *Id.*

623 *Id.*

624 The previous US request for the establishment of a panel to review the EC provisional measure on steel products challenged the justification for the provisional measure applied in response to the preceding US safeguards. WTO doc. WT/DS260/4 (August 19, 2002).

625 The controversy surrounding the application of the US safeguard measures on steel products and the subsequent EC provisional measure is discussed in Chapter 14 *infra*.

9.29 *Preferential Treatment for Developing Members.* The SA provides for differential and preferential treatment for developing countries in consideration of their economic needs. Under Article 9.1 of the SA, safeguard measures shall not be applied against a product originating in a developing country Member as long as its share of imports of the product concerned in the importing Member does not exceed 3 percent, provided that those developing country Members with less than three percent import share collectively account for not more than nine percent of total imports of the product concerned.[626] Developing countries may also extend the period of a safeguard measure by up to two years beyond the maximum period of the eight years authorized by Article 7.3. They may also re-introduce a safeguard measure for the same product after a period equal to half of the duration of the previous measure, provided that the period of non-application is at least two years (Article 9.2).[627]

9.30 This *de minimis* rule attempts to balance the need for preferential treatment for developing countries and the need to protect domestic industries. The former is reflected in the exemption of imports originating from developing country Members. The latter is shown in the limitation of the 3 and 9 percent ceilings. It is not certain from the text of the Article whether these percentages are in terms of import volume or the value of the imports, though in practice they have been measured by volume. It has also been noted that a developing country Member may not benefit from the *de minimis* exemption depending

626 Developing Members have been exempted from the application of safeguard measures under this provision. For instance, the US safeguard measures on steel products exempted imports from the following Members (except products that account for more than 3 percent of the imported product): Albania, Angola, Antigua and Barbuda, Argentina, Bahrain, Bangladesh, Barbados, Belize, Benin, Bolivia, Botswana, Brazil, Bulgaria, Burkina Faso, Burundi, Cameroon, Central African Republic, Chad, Chile, Colombia, Congo (Brazzaville), Congo (Kinshasa), Costa Rica, Cote d'Ivoire, Croatia, Czech Republic, Djibouti, Dominica, Dominican Republic, Ecuador, Egypt, El Salvador, Estonia, Fiji, Gabon, the Gambia, Georgia, Ghana, Grenada, Guatemala, Guinea, Guinea Bissau, Guyana, Haiti, Honduras, Hungary, India, Indonesia, Jamaica, Jordan, Kenya, Kyrgyzstan, Latvia, Lesotho, Lithuania, Madagascar, Malawi, Mali, Mauritania, Mauritius, Moldova, Mongolia, Morocco, Mozambique, Namibia, Niger, Nigeria, Oman, Pakistan, Panama, Papua New Guinea, Paraguay, Peru, Philippines, Poland, Romania, Rwanda, Saint Kitts and Nevis, Saint Lucia, Saint Vincent and the Grenadines, Senegal, Sierra Leone, Slovakia, Solomon Islands, South Africa, Sri Lanka, Suriname, Swaziland, Tanzania, Thailand, Togo, Trinidad and Tobago, Tunisia, Turkey, Uganda, Uruguay, Venezuela, Zambia, and Zimbabwe. United States, *Notifications Pursuant to Article 12.1 (c) and Article 9, Footnote 2, of the Agreement on Safeguards on Taking a Decision to Apply a Safeguard Measure*, G/SG/N/11/USA/5 (March 14, 2002).

627 Critics argued that the three percent ceiling as provided in Article 9 of the SA is too limiting and inadequate. In addition, the two-year additional extension of a safeguard measure and the shortened interval before the re-introduction of a measure are also considered not particularly helpful for developing countries. *See* Jai S. Mah, "Injury and Causation in the Agreement on Safeguards" (2001) 4 *Journal of World Intellectual Property* 380–382.

upon how strict the applicable rule of origin is in a Member applying a safeguard measure.[628]

It is to be noted that Members are not allowed to exclude qualifying developing country Members selectively from the application of the *de minimis* rule under Article 9.1. In *Dominican Republic – Polypropylene Bags and Tubular Fabric*, Dominican Republic failed to include Thailand in application of the rule, which accounted for 0.32 percent of the Dominican Republic's total imports during the period investigated.[629] The Panel held that the Member imposing a safeguard measure must ensure that products from origins that fall within the provision in Article 9.1 are exempted and that Dominican Republic did not comply with Article 9.1 by having failed to include Thailand in the list of countries excluded from the measure's coverage while it included some other developing country Members.[630] The Appellate Body also reiterated the importing Member's duty to ensure that *de minimis* imports from developing countries are excluded from the application of the measures,[631] although the Member is not required to provide a specific list of the Members excluded from the safeguard measure.[632] **9.31**

Surveillance. Finally, the SA provides a monitoring mechanism for the application of its provisions. The surveillance mechanism was strongly voiced during the negotiations of the SA.[633] Article 13 establishes a Committee on Safeguards for surveillance of the implementation of the SA. Various notifications required under the SA are made to the Committee, and the Committee monitors the implementation of the Agreement. Article 13.2 also requires the publication of annual reports regarding the implementation of the SA. **9.32**

628 Bhala and Kennedy, *supra* note 87, p. 902. Also, the present ceilings seem too limiting and may need to be modified. *See* Chapter 15.1 *infra* for a further discussion of the modification.

629 *Dominican Republic - Polypropylene Bags and Tubular Fabric, supra* note 70, para. 7.394.

630 *Id.*, paras. 7.396–7.402. Dominican Republic argued that Thailand was excluded because there had been no imports from this origin in 2009 and that it would be prepared to grant exemption if Thailand began exporting to the Dominican Republic. However, the Panel found that it would be insufficient to comply with Article 9.1 since four other developing country Members, from three of which there had been no imports in 2009, were explicitly included in the list. *Id.*, paras. 7.399–7.400. The Panel emphasized that the Member applying a safeguard measure must "take all *reasonable measures* available to it to exclude from application of the measures contested all developing countries which export less than the *de minimis* levels indicated in Article 9.1 of the Agreement on Safeguards." *Id.*, para. 7.402.

631 *United States – Line Pipe, supra* note 71, paras. 129 and 132.

632 *Id.*, paras. 127–128.

633 Refer to the relevant discussions in Chapter 2 *supra.*

9.3 WHAT DETERMINES SAFEGUARD MEASURES?

9.33 Identifying WTO safeguards would be straightforward in most cases. A Member that applies a safeguard measure is likely to do so under the safeguards legislation reported to the Committee on Safeguards, with clarification that its measure is applied under GATT Article XIX and the SA. The applying Member will also send the required notifications to the Committee on Safeguards, creating little doubt as to whether the applied measure is indeed a safeguard under WTO law (subject to the possibility of a dispute over its consistency with the WTO safeguard rules). However, recent cases have raised a question as to whether a measure that the applying Member does not pronounce as a safeguard under Article XIX and the SA may nevertheless constitute a safeguard measure or *vice versa* when the parties do not dispute the applicability of the SA. In *Indonesia – Safeguard on Certain Iron or Steel Products*, the Panel found that Indonesia's measures did not constitute a safeguard measure under the provisions of the SA where the parties did not dispute their applicability.[634] The Appellate Body subsequently affirmed the Panel decision, clarifying that such determination is within the Panel's mandate.[635] In a subsequent case, *United States – Steel and Aluminum Products*, the complaint argued that the SA applies where the respondent denied that its measures were safeguard measures. This section examines this case and discusses the determinants of safeguard measures under the SA.[636]

9.34 *2018 US Steel and Aluminum Tariffs*. In March 2018, the United States increased tariffs on all imported iron or steel products by 25 percent and on all categories of aluminum imports by 10 percent.[637] The United States justified the tariffs on national security grounds under GATT Article XXI. The investigations performed by the US Department of Commerce under Section 232 of the Trade Expansion Act concluded that steel and aluminum products were imported into the United States "in such quantities and under such circumstances as to threaten to impair the national security of the United States."[638] The Department, thus, recommended actions to adjust the imports of steel articles and aluminum, such as tariffs and quotas, as necessary to ensure that

---

634 *Indonesia – Safeguard on Certain Iron or Steel Products*, *supra* note 71, para. 5.24.

635 *Id.*, para. 5.31.

636 This section draws from the author's previous work, "Identifying WTO Safeguards," *supra* note 1 and "Are Retaliatory Trade Measures Justified under the Agreement on Safeguards?" *supra* note 1. For further discussion of the determinants of a safeguard measure, *see also* Thomas J. Prusa and Edwin A. Vermulst, "Indonesia – Safeguard on Certain Iron or Steel Products: If it looks like a duck, swims like a duck, and quacks like a duck, then it is not a duck" (2020) 19 *World Trade Review* 152–163.

637 Proclamation 9705, *supra* note 602 and Proclamation 9704, *supra* note 602.

638 *Supra* note 634.

such imports will not threaten to impair the national security of the United States.[639]

Retaliations. Several exporting Members affected by the US tariffs, including the EU, China, Mexico, Canada, India, Russia, and Turkey, adopted retaliatory measures in the form of their own tariff increases (from 5 percent to 50 percent) on a variety of imports from the United States, including agricultural, industrial, and steel and aluminum products.[640] **9.35**

Several retaliating countries, including the EU, India, Russia, China, and Turkey, justified their own measures under the provision of the SA and made due notifications to the Committee on Safeguards.[641] For example, the EU argued that the US tariffs are safeguard measures in the form of a tariff increase on imports of certain steel and aluminum products with an unlimited duration.[642] The retaliating Members did not accept the US view that these measures are justifiable under GATT Article XXI. The key point of the controversy was whether the US tariffs are a safeguard measure under the SA or whether they are tariffs applied to protect the security interests of the United States. **9.36**

Are the US Tariffs Safeguards? The complainants contended that the US tariffs are safeguards that are not compliant with the SA.[643] The EU argued that the United States violated Article 2.1 of the SA by applying safeguard measures "without first having determined, pursuant to the subsequent provisions of the Agreement on Safeguards, that such products are being imported into its territory in such increased quantities, absolute or relative to domestic production, and under such conditions as to cause or threaten to cause serious injury to the domestic industry that produces like or directly competitive products."[644] Concurring, China also argued that the US tariffs are safeguards because the **9.37**

---

639 *Id.*

640 WTO docs. G/SG/N/12/EU/1 (May 18, 2018); G/SG/N/12/RUS/2 (May 22, 2018); G/SG/N/12/CHN/1 (April 3, 2018); G/SG/N/12/TUR/6 (May 22, 2018); G/SG/N/12/IND/1/Rev.1 (June 14, 2018), *Customs Notice 18-08: Surtaxes Imposed on Certain Products Originating in the United States* (June 29, 2018, revised July 11, 2018) (Canada); *Decree Modifying the Tariff Schedule of the Law of General Import and Export Taxes, the Decree establishing the General Import Tax Rate applicable during 2003 for goods originating in North America, and the Decree establishing Various Sectoral Promotion Programs* (enacted June 5, 2018; effective June 5, 2018) (Mexico).

641 WTO docs. G/SG/N/12/EU/1 (May 18, 2018); G/SG/N/12/RUS/2 (May 22, 2018); G/SG/N/12/CHN/1 (April 3, 2018); G/SG/N/12/TUR/6 (May 22, 2018); G/SG/N/12/IND/1/Rev.1 (June 14, 2018).

642 WTO doc. G/SG/N/12/EU/1 (May 18, 2018).

643 *United States – Certain Measures on U.S. Steel and Aluminum Products,* DS550, DS563, DS548, DS547, DS551, DS552, DS554, DS556, DS564.

644 *United States – Certain Measures on Steel and Aluminum Products – Request for consultations by the European Union*, WT/DS548/1 (June 6, 2018). In addition, the EU also claimed that United States had breached GATT Article XIX:1(a), XIX:2, SA Articles 2.1, 2.2, 3.1, 4.1, 4.1, 5.1, 7, 9, 11.1(a), 12.1, 12.2, 12.3. *Id.*

tariffs are based on the conclusion of the US investigation reports that the steel and aluminum imports injured the domestic industry (albeit without a specific reference to injury).[645] The United States maintained that the SA is not applicable to the US tariffs at all because they were applied to redress national security concerns.[646]

9.38 The Appellate Body provided a guide that can be applied to determine whether the US tariffs are safeguards. In *Indonesia – Iron or Steel Products*, the EU argued that the suspension of an obligation and/or the withdrawal or modification of a concession is the defining feature of safeguard measures.[647] According to the Appellate Body ruling, the measure must "suspend, in whole or in part, a GATT obligation or withdraw or modify a GATT concession" (which is in line with the EU argument), but, additionally, the measure "must be designed to prevent or remedy serious injury to the Member's domestic industry caused or threatened by increased imports of the subject product."[648]

9.39 Applying this guide to the US tariffs, the US measure is consistent with the requirement of the first prong – suspension of a GATT obligation or withdrawal or modification of a GATT concession – because the US measure, by imposing the additional tariffs on steel and aluminum products, suspends its obligation under the concession.[649] The second prong – whether the measure is designed to prevent serious injury to the domestic industry – requires further analysis of the procedural (i.e., the manner in which the measure is characterized under the domestic law and procedure of the Member concerned) and the substantive elements of the measure.[650]

9.40 Procedurally, the US government invoked Section 232 of the Trade Act covering national security grounds for trade measures instead of Section 201, which applies to the imposition of a safeguard measure. As a result, the US government followed the procedures under Section 232 and not Section 201, which requires the injury assessment as mandated by the SA.[651] The United States did not make a notification to the WTO Committee on Safeguards at any stage of its investigation process or upon adoption of the tariffs. Thus, relevant factors, such as the manner in which the US measures are characterized

---

645 WTO Committee on Safeguards, *Minutes of the Regular Meeting Held on 23 April 2018*, G/SG/M/53 (July 25, 2018), at 11.

646 *Communication from the United States*, WT/DS548/13 (July 6, 2018).

647 *Indonesia – Iron or Steel Products*, *supra* note 71, para. 5.49.

648 *Id.*

649 Lee, "Are Retaliatory Trade Measures Justified under the Agreement on Safeguards?" *supra* note 1, p. 450.

650 *Id.*

651 Proclamations 9705 and 9704, *supra* note 602.

under US domestic law (Section 232), the domestic procedures that led to the adoption of the measure, and the absence of any relevant notifications to the WTO Committee on Safeguards, indicate that the US measures were not applied as safeguards under the SA.[652]

On the substantive point, the core element of a safeguard under the Appellate Body decision is a remedy of injury. None of the official investigation documents made any reference to injury or injury analysis, but the absence of these terms is not determinative, and further examination of the investigation reports is necessary to discern the design and purpose of the measure. To determine the effect of imports of steel and aluminum on national security, the reports examined the following factors: the importance of steel and aluminum on national security; the adverse impact of imports on the welfare of the domestic steel and aluminum industries; and the adverse impact of the displacement of domestic steel industries and of global excess capacity on the welfare of domestic economy.[653] **9.41**

Without specifically mentioning "injury," the report's impact analysis displays certain overlaps with the injury assessment required by the SA. For example, the steel investigation report analyzes factors such as increases in imports, prices, employment, financial distress, and capital expenditure.[654] These are analogous to the assessment requirement in Article 4.2 of the SA, which provides: **9.42**

> In the investigation to determine whether increased imports have caused or are threatening to cause serious injury to a domestic industry under the terms of this Agreement, the competent authorities shall evaluate all relevant factors of an objective and quantifiable nature having a bearing on the situation of that industry, in particular, *the rate and amount of the increase in imports of the product concerned in absolute and relative terms, the share of the domestic market taken by increased imports, changes in the level of sales, production, productivity, capacity utilization, profits and losses, and employment* (emphasis added).

The steel and aluminum reports seem to perform a similar analysis, discussing increases in imports in conjunction with negative developments in factors such as production capacity, domestic production, employment, financial status, capital expenditure, and prices.[655] **9.43**

652 Lee, "Are Retaliatory Trade Measures Justified under the Agreement on Safeguards?" *supra* note 1, p. 450.

653 US Department of Commerce, *The Effect of Imports of Steel on the National Security*, An Investigation Conducted under Section 232 of the Trade Expansion Act of 1962, as amended January 11, 2018 ("Steel Report") and *The Effect of Imports of Aluminum on the National Security*, An Investigation Conducted under Section 232 of the Trade Expansion Act of 1962, as amended January 17, 2018 ("Aluminum Report").

654 Steel Report, *id.*, pp. 27–40.

655 Steel Report, *supra* note 653, pp. 27–41 and Aluminum Report, *supra* note 653, pp. 89–103.

9.44 The overlaps between the investigation reports and the injury assessment required by the SA, however, do not necessarily render the investigation reports equivalent to the report required by the SA. First, the focus of the investigation reports is not the injury assessment as required under the SA; the investigation reports examine the importance of steel and aluminum to US national security (national defense and critical infrastructure), which is outside the scope of an injury analysis required by the SA.[656] The reports analyze the impact of imports on the welfare of the overall domestic economy, while the scope of assessments under the SA is limited to injury to a particular domestic industry. Moreover, the analytical focus of the reports is the effect on national security, so the analytical scope is broader than one for the investigation report required under the SA.[657]

9.45 Secondly, the reports do not conduct the type of injury analysis as required by the SA. The Appellate Body in *Indonesia – Iron or Steel Products* concluded that a measure must be designed to prevent or remedy serious injury to the Member's domestic industry caused or threatened by increased imports of the subject product to qualify as a safeguard.[658] The US reports do not reveal such a design: they do not examine whether the alleged effect amounts to "a significant overall impairment in the position of a domestic industry" or if it is a "serious injury that is clearly imminent," as defined by the SA.[659] None of the official documents, the investigation reports, the Secretary's recommendation, and the Proclamations makes a single reference to the existence of an injury or the necessity to remedy the injury to the domestic industries, instead consistently advocating the necessity of protecting the allegedly weakened domestic industries for the protection of national security.[660]

9.46 It is arguable that the analysis of the weakened state of the domestic industry is not substantively different from the injury assessment, but both the SA and the Appellate Body decisions require that the measure should be designed to address "serious injury," which is distinguishable from mere "injury" under WTO jurisprudence, and the reports do not perform the required injury assessment.[661] The examination of the investigation reports indicates that the US tariffs are not designed to prevent or remedy serious injury to the Member's domestic industry and, thus, are not safeguards under the SA. The retaliatory

656 Lee, "Are Retaliatory Trade Measures Justified under the Agreement on Safeguards?" *supra* note 1, p. 455.
657 *Id.*
658 *Indonesia—Iron or Steel Products, supra* note 70, para 5.49.
659 SA, Article 4.1(a) and (b).
660 Steel and Aluminum Reports, *supra* note 653.
661 Lee, "Are Retaliatory Trade Measures Justified under the Agreement on Safeguards?" *supra* note 1, p. 455.

measures, which are predicated on the US tariffs being safeguards, are accordingly not justified under the SA.

The Panel decision in *United States – Steel and Aluminum Products* is consistent with this conclusion.[662] The Panel opined that the domestic legal status or statements by a Member to official WTO bodies are not determinative of the legal characterization of measures under the covered agreements in dispute settlement, but the Panel considered such evidence to be relevant, particularly where "there is evidence contemporaneous with the adoption of the measures that is confirmed by other relevant evidence of the measures' design and application."[663] The Panel concluded that the US measure is not a safeguard because "a central aspect of the design and application of the measures at issue" is their relations to the US determination of a threat to its national security under the relevant domestic laws (Section 232), rather than safeguards.[664] The outcome of this case is illustrative of the determinants of a safeguard measure under the SA. **9.47**

9.4 IS THE SAFEGUARDS AGREEMENT WORKING?

The preceding chapters have provided elaborate discussions of the rules under the current safeguard regime, and based on this discussion, this final section concludes Part II of the book with a brief assessment and observation of the implementation of the Safeguards Agreement. As noted above, the decades of debates and negotiations finally came to a close at the end of the Uruguay Round, and the negotiation results were embodied in the new Agreement on Safeguards. The new Agreement has brought enhanced clarity and objectivity to the system,[665] and there has been a substantial increase in resort to safeguard measures compared to the previous GATT era.[666] **9.48**

Perhaps the most important achievement of the new regime is the prohibition of gray-area measures. The Committee on Safeguards reported that all notified **9.49**

662 *United States – Steel and Aluminum Products*, *supra* note 70, para. 7.100.

663 *Id.*, para. 7.96.

664 *Id.*

665 John Jackson commented that the Agreement on Safeguards is "a substantial achievement and a heroic statement of principle" and that it sets forth "reasonably specific and explicit rules" on many aspects of safeguards. Jackson, *supra* note 78, p. 210.

666 While 150 measures were reported during the five decades of the GATT era, as many as 213 safeguard measures were imposed for less than three decades (between January 1, 1995 and December 31, 2023) since the beginning of the WTO. WTO, *Safeguard Measures by Reporting Member*, *supra* note 21.

pre-existing measures were phased out by January 1, 2000.[667] Despite suspect cases discussed earlier in this chapter, including the steel and aluminum quota agreements still in force,[668] there seems to be no indication that gray-area measures will proliferate again in the near future, as had been prior to the settlement of the SA. As the negotiators in the Uruguay Round intended, emergency import restrictions have been channeled to the safeguard measures. This success should be largely attributed to the improved effectiveness of the WTO system as a whole, as well as to the prohibition of gray-area measures stipulated in the Agreement on Safeguards, although a continuing US block of appointments to the Appellate Body, which has incapacitated the Appellate Body, is concerning.[669]

9.50 Does the Safeguards Agreement provide effective and coherent disciplines on safeguards? Despite the overall enhancement of clarity in comparison to the Article XIX regime, there are some ambiguities in the provisions of the SA.[670] Some of the Panel and Appellate Body decisions, instead of clarifying, have added ambiguities and confusion to the interpretation and implementation of the rules on safeguards, as discussed in the preceding chapters.[671] One of the most notable examples is the Appellate Body decision that affirmed the applicability of outdated Article XIX provisions, such as the "unforeseen developments" clause.[672]

9.51 The relatively high rate of disputes over the applied safeguard measures,[673] and the decisions of previous Panels and the Appellate Body affirming the inconsistency of the disputed safeguard measures with the current rules, suggest that the ambiguities with the current disciplines may have led to the controversies regarding the interpretation and application of the SA and contributed to the failure of Members to comply with the rules.[674] Certain modification of these

---

667 *Supra* note 583.

668 *See* Chapter 9.1 *supra.*

669 *See* Reinert, *supra* note 618.

670 Discussions in the preceding chapters have revealed these ambiguities and proposed modifications of the existing rules.

671 *See also* Sykes, *infra* note 674.

672 *See* Chapter 3.2 *supra.*

673 About 29.1 percent of all safeguard measures applied since 1995 were brought to the WTO dispute settlement procedure (i.e., request for consultation) in comparison to about 3.2 percent of anti-dumping measures. Calculated from relevant data excerpted from WTO, *Safeguard Measures by Reporting Member, supra* note 21; WTO, *Anti-dumping Measures by Reporting Member 01/01/1995 - 30/06/2023*, available at: https://www.wto.org/english/tratop_e/adp_e/AD_MeasuresByRepMem.pdf [https://perma.cc/ECL3-6SD3]; WTO, *Disputes by agreement*, available at: https://www.wto.org/english/tratop_e/dispu_e/dispu_agreements_index_e.htm [https://perma.cc/44R4-2M2P].

674 A commentator observed that incoherent textual preconditions for the application of safeguards and a series of dubious Appellate Body rulings has made it almost impossible for Members to apply safeguard measures

provisions is deemed necessary to resolve the inherent ambiguities and to ensure the proper application of safeguard measures. The modified text of the proposed modification of the SA is reproduced in Appendix 4, pursuant to the discussions in Part II. The Agreement on Safeguards was not included in the Doha Round agenda, and the modification may not be discussed in the near future. What then is the current state of affairs with safeguard applications and what needs to be done pending such modification?

Call for Caution. A pessimistic view asserts that Members cannot apply a safeguard measure without a near certainty that it will be found invalid.[675] That all the disputed safeguards to date but one[676] have been found inconsistent with the rules creates an impression that this has been the case. However, it should also be noted that these disputed safeguard cases have exhibited apparent oversights of the rules, some repeatedly, and did not provide reasoned explanations for the national authorities' determinations on the contested issues.[677] Also, nearly half of panel disputes to date concerned safeguards applied by a particular country (United States) that showed repeated violations of the same rules.[678] **9.52**

Concern has been raised that Panels and the Appellate Body have failed to provide clear guidance of the interpretation and application of the rules.[679] While it is true that some of Panel and the Appellate Body decisions lacked clear guidance or even added ambiguities – as, for instance, shown in the Appellate Body decision pertaining to the "unforeseen developments" clause – one should nevertheless not readily dismiss the guidance that Panel and the Appellate Body decisions provide simply because it lacks a specific quantitative benchmark. **9.53**

It is easy to question the value of qualitative, not quantitative, guidance for lacking "specificity," but one should note that general quantitative guidelines might not be feasible and appropriate in cases where particulars of each case may have to be considered. In addition, an international organization such as **9.54**

---

without a near certainty that they will be found invalid. Alan O. Sykes, "The Safeguard Mess: A Critique of WTO Jurisprudence" (2003) 2 World Trade Review 261–295. Another commentator believed that the perceived difficulties in the safeguard regime are purposeful and deliberate, as a result of political compromise among the Uruguay Round negotiators and not to make safeguard measures readily available. Kent Jones, "The Safeguards Mess Revisited: The Fundamental Problem" (2004) 3 *World Trade Review* 83–91.

675 Sykes, *supra* note 674.

676 *United States — Photovoltaic Products*, *supra* note 70. The complainant (China) appealed the Panel decision in September 2021, but the Appellate Body has been unable to review the case due to the lack of quorum caused by a US block of appointments to the Appellate Body.

677 Article 3.1 of the SA requires that competent national authorities do so.

678 SA, Article 2.

679 Sykes, *supra* note 674.

the WTO operates based on the consensus of Members. Therefore, dispute settlement panels and the Appellate Body, unlike national judiciaries backed by sovereign powers, may well be reluctant to set forth precise quantitative guidelines, which may be seen as "rule-making" beyond the interpretation of the existing rules,[680] without a clear mandate from Members.[681]

9.55 Qualitative guidance is not without value. For example, the Appellate Body made a decision that increased imports should be "recent enough, sudden enough, sharp enough, and significant enough, both qualitatively and quantitatively,"[682] and this decision gives us a good idea of what kind of increase in imports is required, although it does not exactly provide a specific time frame or the amount of increase required. It would certainly be feasible for Members to follow the guidelines relating to increased imports cited above and apply them to test whether a specific increase in imports fits this category. Of course, absent quantitative (numeric) benchmarks, the determination will be inherently subjective. Nonetheless, Panels and the Appellate Body have allowed this subjectivity by clarifying that they would not engage in a *de novo* review of the national authorities' investigations but instead inquire into the manner in which the national authorities arrive at their determination: e.g., the scope of the facts considered and the reasoned explanation.[683] The common feature of all the disputed safeguard measures subsequently found invalid is the failure by national authorities to provide such explanation. Panels and the Appellate Body have acknowledged compliance with the rule where a reasoned explanation is given, including in the areas of increased imports, injury, and causation,[684] where particular difficulties with compliance have been perceived.[685]

9.56 Again, this does not mean that there is no ambiguity in the text of the rules and Panel and Appellate Body decisions. Clarifications should be made, and Panels and the Appellate Body have an important role in providing as much guidance as possible as to what a Member is required to do to comply with the rules within, of course, the mandate provided by Members.[686] Noting this

680 Also, many Members do not share the "common law tradition" originating from England in which the judiciary is more active in the development of law and recognized of certain "rule-making" authority.

681 Jones, *supra* note 674.

682 *Argentina – Footwear*, *supra* note 71, para. 313. *See* Chapter 4 *supra* for the relevant discussion of increased imports.

683 *See* Chapter 4.1 *supra* for a discussion of the standard of review.

684 For instance, in safeguard cases, including *United States – Steel Products*, the national authority's determination of increased imports and of causation was validated where an adequate explanation was given. *See* Chapter 4.2 and 5.2 *supra* for the relevant discussions. *See also infra* notes 991 and 992.

685 Sykes, *supra* note 674.

686 Despite certain ambiguities, Panel and Appellate Body decisions have provided useful guidance of the interpretation and application of the SA, and based on this guidance, the first edition of this book could identify

role of Panels and the Appellate Body, one should also understand that this guidance might not necessarily be numerical benchmarks but often qualitative in nature, which is to be interpreted and applied in the context of individual cases.[687]

What causes a greater concern for the implementation of the Agreement on Safeguards and other WTO agreements is a US block of appointments to the Appellate Body, which has continued since the first Trump administration.[688] The United States has raised rather ambiguous "systemic issues," but it is believed that a number of successful challenges to its anti-dumping and countervailing measures, as well as safeguard measures, are likely the primary reason for its block.[689] By incapacitating the Appellate Body, Panel recommendations against US positions once appealed to the non-functioning Appellate Body would be deemed not "final," and the United States may maintain its measures regardless of any adverse panel decision. The United States has indeed appealed such Panel decisions to the Appellate Body that it incapacitated via its own veto and maintained its measures, which the Panels found inconsistent with WTO law.[690] The US block raises significant concern not only for the implementation of the SA but also for the preservation of the rule-based international trading system.[691] 9.57

the inconsistencies of the US steel safeguards with the relevant rules before the Panel and the Appellate Body decisions came out. Yong-Shik Lee, *Safeguard Measures in World Trade* (The Hague: Kluwer Law International, 1st ed., 2003), pp. 166–168. The subsequent Panel and Appellate Body decisions affirmed these inconsistencies, except those not raised by the complainants. *See* Chapter 14 *infra.*

687 Qualitative guidance is not unique in WTO jurisprudence. In every jurisdiction, one must rely on various qualitative languages, such as "reasonable" and "foreseeable," as constituting core legal standards. Surely, it is far from absolute clarity: what may be reasonable to someone may very well be not so to another. Nonetheless, national governments apply the legal standard of qualitative nature to a specific case interpreting qualitative legal elements. The same applies to the qualitative guidance given by Panel and Appellate Body decisions: Panels and the Appellate Body cannot be demanded to overcome these inherent linguistic limitations and come up with the standards that are absolutely clear to everyone. It is simply not feasible, and again, general numerical guidelines cannot be provided for every case.

688 WTO, *Appellate Body*, available at: https:// www .wto .org/ english/ tratop _e/ dispu _e/ appellate _body _e .htm #: ~: text = Currently %2C %20the %20Appellate %20Body %20is ,expired %20on %2030 %20November %202020 [https://perma.cc/8UQK-228U]. *See also* Reinert, *supra* note 618.

689 Reindert, *supra* note 618.

690 For example, the United States has maintained the increased tariffs against China since the Panel found them to be inconsistent with WTO law. *See United States – Tariff Measures on Certain Goods from China*, DS543 (2018), available at: https://www.wto.org/english/tratop_e/dispu_e/cases_e/ds543_e.htm [https://perma.cc/KF2N-EQCV].

691 The incapacitation of the Appellate Body by the United States would also be counterproductive to US interests. Panel decisions favoring US positions, as well as those against them, will not be "finalized" once they are appealed to the non-functioning Appellate Body. Without a fully functioning dispute settlement system, trade disputes may return to power politics, which the United States sought to avoid by contributing to the establishment of the WTO dispute settlement system in the Uruguay Round. *See* Reinert, *supra* note 618.

PART III

OTHER SAFEGUARD PROVISIONS

10

DISCUSSIONS ON SAFEGUARD MEASURES IN THE SERVICE TRADE: GATS ARTICLE X

10.1 INTRODUCTION[692]

Since the Uruguay Round negotiations brought the service trade into the multilateral trading system in the framework of the General Agreement on Trade in Services (GATS), Members have discussed the introduction of a safeguard measure in the context of trade in services (an emergency safeguard measure: an ESM[693]) as a built-in agendum in the new agreement on service trade. Article X of the GATS requires the holding of multilateral negotiations on the question of emergency safeguard measures. It provides that "the results of such negotiations … enter into effect on a date not later than three years from the date of entry into force of the WTO Agreement." **10.01**

Members failed to meet the three-year time limit stipulated in Article X.1. The negotiating mandate was extended,[694] but the discussion of the emergency **10.02**

692 Discussions of this chapter draw from the author's previous work, "Emergency Safeguard Measures under Article X in GATS – Applicability of the Concept in the WTO Agreement on Safeguards" (1999) 33(4) *Journal of World Trade* 47–59.

693 The previous versions of this book abbreviated "Emergency Safeguard Measure" as "ESG" and "Emergency Safeguard Mechanism" as "ESM," but "ESM" also refers to the former in WTO documents. To follow the WTO usage, both terms are abbreviated as "ESM" in this edition, with the latter to be denoted with a definite article.

694 The Council for Trade in Services decided to extend the negotiating mandate under Article X until March 15, 2004, on the recommendation of the Chairman of the Working Party on GATS rules. WTO doc. S/L/102 (March 27, 2002). The negotiating mandate was extended until the conclusion of the current Doha

safeguard mechanism in the service trade (the ESM[695]) has been discontinued since 2016 following the closure of the Doha Round.[696] The group of proponents of the ESM (the "Friends of ESM") reaffirmed their continued interest in pursuing work on the ESM in 2016, but given the long lapse of negotiations since then, it is unclear whether Members would reach an agreement on the ESM. The fundamental issues about the ESM, such as its desirability,[697] have not been resolved.[698] Three decades after the settlement of the GATS, the rules for trade in services are still incomplete, and the discussion of the ESM is analogous to the introduction of the escape clause to the GATT more than seven decades ago when the international rules for goods trade were being formed. An ironic difference is that, whereas the United States was then the driving force for the adoption of Article XIX based on its own escape clause legislation,[699] it has remained cautious about the adoption of the ESM.[700]

10.03 The complexity of the service area has made it difficult to construct a uniform set of rules on trade in services.[701] There are more than 100 distinct sectors in

---

Round. "The results of such negotiations shall enter into effect on a date not later than the date of entry into force of the results of the current round of services negotiations." WTO doc. S/L/159 (March 17, 2004).

695 *Id.*

696 WTO, *Annual Report of the Working Party on GATS Rules to the Counsel for Trade in Services (2017)*, WTO doc. S/WTGR/28 (November 16, 2017). *See also* WTO, *Annual Report of the Working Party on GATS Rules to the Counsel for Trade in Services (2016)*, WTO doc. S/WTGR/27 (November 23, 2016).

697 *See Working Party on GATS Rules – Communication from the United States – Desirability of a Safeguard Mechanism for Services: Promoting Liberalization of Trade in Services*, WTO doc. S/WPGR/W/37 (October 2, 2001). A view was raised that the complexity of the service trade leaves little scope for GATT-type safeguards in services, and a transitory arrangement, which allows for suspensions of new commitments during an implementation phase, might encourage more ambitious liberalization under the GATS. *See* Rudolf Adlung, "Negotiations on Safeguards and Subsidies in Services: A Never-Ending Story?" (2007) 10(2) *Journal of International Economic Law* 235–265. A waiver to temporarily withdraw services commitments was also supported by Clogstoun *et al. See* Roy Clogstoun, Ray Trewin, and Malcolm Bosworth, "Would Emergency Safeguard Measures Work for Services?" (2006) 20(2) *Asian-Pacific Economic Literature* 56–69. Another study advocated a sectoral approach. Shin-Yi Peng, "Emergency safeguard measures for trade in services: a case study of intradisciplinary fragmentation," *in* C.L. Lim and Brian Mercurio (eds.), *International Economic Law After The Global Crisis: A Tale of Fragmented Disciplines* (Cambridge University Press, 2015), pp. 237–261.

698 Debates included the definition of "domestic industry" as applicable to the ESM, issues associated with the collection and use of statistics on service trade, and review of various concepts and options applicable for a possible safeguard mechanism. WTO docs. S/WPGR/20 (November 8, 2010), S/WPGR/22 (November 10, 2011), and S/WPGR/23 (November 29, 2012).

699 *See* the relevant discussion of the US role in the adoption of Article XIX in Chapter 2.1 *supra*.

700 *Supra* note 697. The US reluctance about the introduction of the ESM seems largely due to its interest as a primary service provider in international trade. In contrast, the United States was concerned about the "flooding" of cheaper foreign products into the US market in the beginning of the GATT and therefore actively advocated the adoption of the escape clause. Apparently, the United States is not so concerned about such a possibility with regards to foreign services. On the other hand, other Members concerned about the domination of foreign services in their markets have been more willing to consider the adoption of the ESM.

701 The prolonged and complicated negotiation history for the GATS is described in Stewart, *supra* note 114, pp. 2335–2663.

services,[702] and the intangible nature of service transactions adds much complexity to the regulation of service trade. Further compounding the problem is a lack of reliable statistics for many service sectors. Even the concept of "trade" is not straightforward in the service context; while trade in goods concerns cross-border transactions of goods, different modes exist in the service trade. Article 1 of the GATS defines four modes of trade in services as the following: "the supply of a service: (a) from the territory of one Member into the territory of any other Member (cross-border service transactions analogous to trade in goods, mode 1); (b) in the territory of one Member to the service consumer of any other Member (movement of consumer, mode 2); (c) by a service supplier of one Member, through commercial presence in the territory (flow of capital, mode 3); (d) by a service supplier of one Member, through presence of natural persons of a Member in the territory of any other Member (movement of natural person, mode 4)."

Questions arose as to whether uniform rules on emergency safeguards applicable to all service sectors are feasible and desirable, despite the extraordinary complexity and diversity in service trade.[703] Critics doubted the necessity of the ESM, citing the wide leeway allowed to Members in making specific commitments under the GATS and in changing their commitments *ex post*.[704] Even if the necessity of safeguard measures in the service trade was accepted, there would still be the question of whether there should be a general safeguard mechanism applied to all modes of the service trade or if a mode-by-mode approach would be more appropriate. This chapter examines the necessity of the ESM, considers its possible structure, and also discusses the applicability **10.04**

702 GATT doc. MTN.GNS/W/120 (July 10, 1991).

703 WTO doc. S/WPGR/M/18 (November 13, 1998). A communication from the European Communities to the Working Party highlighted the complexity of modal application of an emergency safeguard measure. WTO doc. S/WPGR/W/38 (January 21, 2002). *See also* WTO docs. S/WPGR/M/54 (February 22, 2006), S/WPGR/M/56 (July 4, 2006), and S/WPGR/M/57 (May 9, 2007). A study also explained the difficulty in adopting the GATT-type safeguard measures to digital services. *See* Nayung Kim, "Trade Remedy Rules for Digital Services: Inapplicability of GATT-type Safeguard Rules" (2020) 54(5) *Journal of World Trade* 813–829.

704 *Note by the Secretariat of the Working Party on GATS Rules*, illustrates the flexible structure of the GATS. WTO doc. S/WPGR/W/1 (July 6, 1995). It states, "The GATS permits signatories to circumscribe their commitments in several ways. First, the GATS contains relatively few general obligations that apply in the absence of specific commitments. Moreover, the single most important general obligation – the most-favored-nation (MFN) rule of Article II – will not apply if a Member exempts certain measures from MFN at the time of entry into force of the agreement. Secondly, specific commitments only apply if a sector has been scheduled, and all Members have omitted sectors from their positive lists of commitments. Even where a sector has been scheduled, particular modes of delivery may be excluded from any commitment, and the precise terms of commitments undertaken can be conditioned through market access limitations (Article XVI) and national treatment limitations (Article XVII)."

of concepts of the general safeguards provided in the SA regardless of the prospects of its adoption in the near future.

10.2 NECESSITY OF EMERGENCY SAFEGUARD MEASURES UNDER THE GATS

10.05 The GATS provides the mandate for the multilateral negotiations on the ESM. The first part of GATS Article X.1 reads: "There shall be multilateral negotiations on the question of emergency safeguard measures based on the principle of non-discrimination." However, this mandate does not obligate Members to introduce the ESM. The negotiating history of Article X and the use of the phrase "negotiation *on the question* of emergency safeguard measures" (emphasis added) in the Article indicate that the necessity of the ESM should be considered by Members, but they are *not* obligated to adopt the ESM in the end.[705] The necessity and feasibility of the ESM was an on-going discussion point through the negotiation process.[706] The objections to the introduction of the ESM were as follows.

10.06 An argument was raised that the ESM is not necessary because of the flexibility built into the GATS.[707] According to this position, the GATS allows Members considerable flexibility in their commitments. Unlike GATT 1994, the GATS allows Members to permit market access only to the extent of their specific commitments in their schedules (Article XVI). They may exclude certain sectors and modes from their commitments. Exceptions to the MFN rule are allowed (Article II), and the principle of national treatment can also be subject to qualifications (Article XVII). In addition, Article XXI allows Members to re-negotiate scheduled commitments. The flexibility built into the structure of the GATS provides the Members with ample latitude to shape their commitments *ex ante* and enables them to modify their commitments *ex post*. In this view, the necessity of the ESM is subject to doubt.

10.07 However, the aforementioned provisions in the GATS are not designed to protect a domestic industry against a radical increase in imports, as the ESM would. A timely response is difficult under the framework of the existing

705 WTO doc. S/WPGR/W/1 (July 6, 1995).

706 WTO doc. S/WPGR/M/47 (April 22, 2004). The ASEAN group (excluding Singapore) indicated that they had fundamental economic and political interests in the issue of emergency safeguards. Those countries were the primary driving force in the negotiation meetings in proposing ESM-related topics and solutions. *See* WTO docs. S/WPGR/M/55 (May 4, 2006), S/WPGR/M/79 (October 16, 2012) and S/WPGR/M/85 (November 5, 2014).

707 WTO doc. S/WPGR/W/1 (July 6, 1995).

provisions of GATS. For instance, Article XXI.1(a) reads: "A Member may modify or withdraw any commitment in its Schedule, at any time after three years have elapsed from the date on which that commitment entered into force ...." Three years must pass before any scheduled modification can be made. Subsequent provisions of Article XXI also require that there be consultations with Members potentially affected by the modifications. Those consultations, whose purpose would be to set acceptable compensation, are likely to be protracted, thus making it difficult for Members to react in a timely manner to emergencies. Even if emergencies could be dealt with adequately by the current GATS provisions, the use of those provisions for emergency import restrictions could lead to a destabilization of the system. Problems caused by emergencies are often of a temporary nature, and therefore, call for temporary measures. The modification of specific commitments contemplated under Article XXI is not intended to be a temporary measure. Resorting to Article XXI in response to emergencies means re-negotiations of already-scheduled commitments, which would make the existing schedules of Members unstable.

In addition, if the time-consuming and cumbersome modification process of Article XXI is the only recourse available to them in times of emergency, Members are likely to be conservative when scheduling specific commitments in order to preserve their ability to respond to emergencies. Members seem to have taken a minimalist approach in scheduling their commitments. Most Members have bound below the *status quo* for many services with restrictive measures in their schedules that do not even exist.[708] **10.08**

The new round of trade negotiations began in November 2001, with an objective of increasing market access to more service sectors.[709] The Members have relatively little information on the effect of increasing market access in many service sectors. As a result, the Members may well be reluctant to increase market access in those sectors for which they do not know the effect of an increase in such access. The introduction of the ESM would offer Members recourse against risks not presently perceived and thereby induce them to make higher commitments.[710] **10.09**

708 *See* Malcolm Bosworth, "GATS Emergency Safeguard Measures," *in Report on the Implementation of Safeguards in the Area of Trade and Distribution Services* (Korea Institute for Industrial Economics and Trade (KIET, 1998), p. 243.

709 The Doha Round, launched in Doha, Qatar, in November 2001, was discontinued in 2015 without much progress on many of its negotiation agendas. *See* WTO docs. WT/MIN(01)/DEC/1 (November 14, 2001) and WT/MIN(15)/DEC (December 19, 2015).

710 The United States argued that the "trade liberalization" effect of the ESM cannot be assured unless Members present specific evidence that the ESM would in fact increase market access in service trade. Hence, the United States invited "Members favoring a safeguard to provide examples of the additional commitments

10.10 Another objection to the introduction of the ESM is based on economic analysis. It is the argument which also applies to the discussion of general safeguard measures under the SA.[711] Proponents of temporary assistance measures such as safeguards argue that the temporary protection (short-term assistance) may facilitate structural adjustment. Detractors of temporary assistance measures, on the other hand, point out that an industry that truly has long-run competitiveness would always be able to have access to industry-specific resources; that is, the capital market would be able to recognize the long-term potential and render short-term assistance. If the problem lay with the imperfection of the capital market, then the appropriate action would be to correct that imperfection and not to restrict imports.[712]

10.11 As already discussed in Chapter 1 above, it is not always feasible to cure the imperfection of the capital market. The critics also argue that short-term assistance actually slows down transition by inefficiently keeping resources in "dying" industries. They say that other contingency plans, such as re-education subsidy programs and insurance, are more adequate measures than short-term trade restriction.[713] Again, it is not certain that government subsidy is always more efficient than safeguards, and it may be politically and economically difficult to provide adequate subsidy.[714]

10.12 The economic efficiency of emergency safeguard measures is subject to debate, as seen during the discussion of general safeguards. However, just as in the case of general safeguards, political and social justifications for the ESM should not be overlooked. For instance, economic and political problems, such as unemployment caused by the sudden downfall of an industry, can significantly hamper efforts to increase market access. The introduction of the ESM would serve as a necessary political compromise and enable Members to continue

they would be prepared to undertake were a safeguard made available." *Supra* note 697. It does not appear that most Members would be able to respond to such invitation, as the ESM is not the only factor for Members to consider in the determination of a specific additional commitment. In addition, they would not be able to figure out the additional commitment that they can make, where the final form of the ESM is not even determined. Even if they do know the additional commitments that they can provide, they may well choose not to disclose their positions while the negotiations for market access are still in progress. The United States itself did not present the additional commitments that they would provide should a safeguard mechanism be in place when it advocated the introduction of Article XIX or the more elaborate Agreement on Safeguards during the subsequent Uruguay Round negotiations. It would be difficult to accept that the absence of unobtainable specific evidence based on a hypothetical introduction of the ESM is an impediment to acknowledging the trade liberalization effect of the ESM.

711 *See* the relevant discussions on the controversy over economic justification for safeguards in Chapter 1 *supra*.

712 *See supra* note 45.

713 *See* Bosworth, *supra* note 708, p. 246.

714 *See* the relevant discussion in Chapter 1 *supra*.

with a market opening. As in the case of SGs, the application of an emergency safeguard will cause loss of economic welfare.[715] Competent national authorities should consider the loss of economic welfare as an important factor for the application of an ESM and decide whether the need for the measure justifies such loss.

If political and economic necessities for the ESM justify its introduction, it should also be determined whether a general safeguard mechanism applicable to all service sectors would be preferable to a mechanism applicable only to individual sectors. As to the latter a suggestion was made for the inclusion of safeguard-type provisions for specific sectors in a Member's schedule of commitments.[716] While a sector-specific approach might be able to craft instruments designed for the unique requirements of individual service sectors, such an approach could lead to a fragmentation of the system, and the functioning of the GATS would be complicated by sector-specific rules.[717] There is also a concern that small economies without strong bargaining power might have problems securing their inclusion in negotiations.[718] On balance, a general safeguard mechanism applying to all service sectors is preferable.[719] **10.13**

The remaining question concerns the modal application of an emergency safeguard. As outlined above, four modes of supply exist in the service trade and the difficulty with modal applications has been discussed.[720] Should there be a safeguard mechanism applicable to all modes of service supply, or to individual modes only? The separation of modes is in many cases difficult (e.g., service provided through the Internet), and one mode is intrinsically linked to different modes.[721] Therefore, a mode-by-mode approach would complicate the system and might also distort trade by encouraging the supplying Members to switch to another mode, should the ESM be limited to a particular mode. Therefore, a general safeguard mechanism applicable to multiple modes of service supply is more desirable. **10.14**

---

715 *See* the relevant discussion on the welfare loss associated with the application of a safeguard measure in Chapters 1 and 7.

716 *See Communication from the United States*, *supra* note 697.

717 *See* WTO doc. S/WPGR/M/19 (January 21, 1999).

718 *See* WTO doc. S/WPGR/M/20 (March 17, 1999).

719 Most Members within the Working Group showed support for this approach. WTO docs. S/WPGR/M/19 (January 21, 1999), S/WPGR/M/20 (March 17, 1999). The availability of sector-specific data for potential safeguard investigation was also under discussion. WTO doc. S/WPGR/21 (April 14, 2011).

720 *See Communication from the European Communities*, *supra* note 703. *See also* WTO doc. S/WPGR/M/49 (October 27, 2004).

721 *Id. See also* M. Marconini, *Emergency Safeguard Measures in the GATS: Beyond Feasible and Desirable*, UNCTAD Working Paper (2005), UNCTAD/DITC/TNCD/2005/4.

10.3 APPLICABILITY OF CONCEPTS IN THE AGREEMENT ON SAFEGUARDS

10.15 Although trade in services is set apart from trade in goods by important differences such as the diversity of the more than 100 distinctive service sectors, the multiple modes of supply, and the lack of reliable statistics, it does not preclude consideration of the applicability of safeguard mechanisms applicable to trade in goods. The following WTO agreements have provided for emergency import restraints: the Agreement on Safeguards; the Agreement on Agriculture; the Agreement on Textiles and Clothing; and the Understanding on the Balance-of-Payments Provisions of the GATT 1994. Which among those would be the most appropriate model for the ESM?

10.16 Article 5 of the Agreement on Agriculture, providing special safeguard measures (SSGs) for certain agricultural products, has been advocated as a useful model for the ESM.[722] Members may apply an SSG for either certain import volume increases or import price reductions.[723] Unlike SGs, there is no injury requirement for the application of an SSG. The application of an SSG requires accurate information of import volume, price and domestic consumption. This type of specific data requirement would be difficult to obtain in the service area. Even if such data were obtainable, it would be improper to make an ESM applicable solely on a simple criterion such as import increase or price reduction without any evidence of injury to the domestic industry. An SSG does not require an injury test for its application so as to enable Members to invoke protection for agricultural products more easily due to the political and economic sensitivity attached to the agricultural sector. The same need to lower a threshold for protection may not be found in the area of the service trade.

10.17 Some Members have upheld Article 6 of the Agreement on Textiles and Clothing (ATC) as a potential model for the ESM.[724] Prior to its expiration in 2005, Article 6 of the ATC provided transitional safeguard measures (TSGs) on certain textile and clothing products. While Article 6 required an injury assessment similar to that provided in the SA, a TSG was applied selectively to imports from a particular Member/Members, conforming to the existing

---

722 WTO doc. S/WPGR/W/27 (November 20, 1998). *See also Communication from the United States*, *supra* note 697.

723 *See* Articles 1, 4, 5 of the Agreement on Agriculture for the detailed conditions for the application of SSGs. *See also* the relevant discussions in Chapter 11 *infra*.

724 WTO doc. S/WPGR/W/27 (November 20, 1998).

arrangements in textile and clothing trade.[725] Article X of the GATS requires the consideration of the ESM based on the MFN principle, and the adoption of a selective safeguard mechanism such as transitional safeguards would not be compatible with this requirement.

The Understanding on the Balance-of-Payments Provisions of the GATT 1994 also provides import restrictions to remedy the balance-of-payment (BOP) problems. The adoption of the BOP measures would also be improper since they are not designed for the protection of a specific domestic industry facing short-term difficulties but for the improvement of the BOP situation during a BOP crisis.[726] The ESM does not involve a BOP situation, and there is a separate provision in the GATS (Article XII) to address BOP problems. This mechanism is therefore not suitable for the ESM. **10.18**

The Agreement on Safeguards, providing disciplines for general safeguards for trade in goods, would be a proper model for the ESM.[727] The SA is marked for detailed procedural requirements and specific guidelines for the application of a safeguard measure.[728] The SA offers by far the best model for the ESM, as it provides a complete set of procedural and substantive requirements for a safeguard measure based on the MFN application. The remainder of this chapter examines the applicability of the concepts in the SA in the service context. **10.19**

The Concept of Safeguards. Article 2.1(a) of the SA provides the concept and the general conditions for the application of a safeguard measure. It provides: **10.20**

> A Member[1] may apply a safeguard measure to a product only if that Member has determined, pursuant to the provisions set out below, that such product is being imported into its territory in such increased quantities, absolute or relative to domestic production, and under such conditions as to cause or threaten to cause serious injury to the domestic industry that produces like or directly competitive products.
>
> (Footnote 1, Article 2.1(a)) A customs union may apply a safeguard measure as a single unit or on behalf of a member State. When a customs union applies a safeguard measure as a single unit, all the requirements for the determination of serious injury or threat thereof under this Agreement shall be based on the conditions existing in the customs

725 The Agreement on Textiles and Clothing expired on January 1, 2005. The relevant provision of the Agreement is discussed for a reference purpose.

726 For details, *see* Jai S. Mah, "Reflections on the Balance-of-Payment Provisions in the WTO" (1998) 21(5) *World Competition* 139–148.

727 More Members in the Working Party seemed to consider the Agreement on Safeguards to be a proper model for the ESM. For instance, the draft agreement on emergency safeguards formulated by the ASEAN Members follows the model in the Agreement on Safeguards (Job No. 6830, October 31, 2000).

728 Y.S. Lee and Jai S. Mah, "Reflections on the Agreement on Safeguards in the WTO" (1999) 21(6) *World Competition* 26–28.

union as a whole. When a safeguard measure is applied on behalf of a member State, all the requirements for the determination of serious injury or threat thereof shall be based on the conditions existing in that member State and the measure shall be limited to that member State. Nothing in this Agreement prejudges the interpretation of the relationship between Article XIX and paragraph 8 of Article XXIV of GATT 1994.

10.21 As discussed in Chapter 4, Article 2.1(a) of the SA provides conditions for the application of a safeguard measure: (i) an increase in imports; (ii) causing or threatening to cause; (iii) serious injury to the domestic industry that produces like or directly competitive products. Those conditions are also applicable to the ESM, as the ESM should be applied only to the injurious imports of services. As to the increase in imports, invoking an ESM in the absence of increased service imports would be difficult to justify. The injury test should also be required, as the ESM is applicable to legitimate trade in the absence of any unfair trade practices. The causal link between increased imports and injury should also be established since the application of an emergency safeguard to non-injurious service imports would not remedy injury claimed by domestic service providers. The ESM may adopt the general conditions in the SA, but certain terms used for the general safeguards require clarification in the service context.

10.22 First, while the concept of import is straightforward in trade of goods, this is not the case for trade in services due to the multiple modes of supply (Article 1.2 of GATS). The concept of import is more easily captured in the goods trade as the importation of goods necessarily involves physical movement of goods through borders. The intangible nature of the service trade makes it difficult to identify how services are "imported." The concept of import needs to be re-defined for the purpose of the ESM. Specifically, the scope of applicable import should be determined along the lines of the four modes of service supply. The participants in the Working Party expressed diverse views on the scope of imports that should be subject to the ESM. In applying safeguards to services, most Members support the protection of "acquired" rights of foreign investment already established within their territories.[729] Over 3,300 international investment agreements (2,835 bilateral investment treaties and 466 treaties with investment provisions)[730] currently protect foreign investment.

---

729 WTO docs. S/WPGR/M/19 (January 21, 1999) and S/WPGR/M/20 (March 17, 1999).

730 *See* UNCTAD, *International Investment Agreements Navigator*, available at: https://investmentpolicy.unctad.org/international-investment-agreements [https://perma.cc/LM3G-HKPA]. *See also* Rudolf Dolzer and Christoph Schreuer, *Principles of International Investment Law* (Oxford University Press, 2008) for further discussion of BIT.

It would make little sense to apply the ESM to services offered by locally established firms only because of their foreign ownership; in the goods area, safeguards are not applied to the products of locally established foreign firms. It is also doubtful that a clear distinction can be made between "national" firms and locally established "foreign" firms. In addition, it would be in the economic interests of many Members that the implementation of the ESM should not lead to forced divestment. The application of emergency safeguards to services provided by locally established firms may discourage foreign investors from making investments, which would run counter to vital economic interests of Members seeking to attract and retain foreign investments.[731] **10.23**

On the other hand, some Members have also been concerned that the MFN principle may be violated if the rights of locally established foreign firms are protected.[732] This issue could be resolved by including locally established foreign firms in the notion of "domestic" suppliers entitled to protection, as in the SA. This inclusion would limit the scope of imports to the other three modes of supply and resolve the potential problem of MFN violation because services supplied by locally established foreign firms are, under this definition, not regarded as imports. **10.24**

The next issue concerns the notion of increased imports as a condition for the application of a safeguard measure (Article 2 of the Agreement on Safeguards). While the measure of quantitative increase in the goods trade is straightforward, there is no uniform measure for the quantity of services rendered. The measure of quantity should be determined on a case-by-case basis, with the characteristics of the particular service transactions taken into account. For instance, for full-time school education, the number of student enrollments could be taken as a measure of the quantity of education service. Given the complexity of service transactions, it is important that Members are allowed sufficient latitude in determining the measure of increase in imports on a case-by-case basis. **10.25**

Finally, the notion of "like or directly competitive services" in the SA should also be introduced in the ESM. There would be no justification for restricting imports of service for the protection of an unrelated domestic service industry. **10.26**

---

731 Regarding this issue, the US delegation in the Working Party on GATS Rules opined, "it was imperative that these (acquired rights) be protected, should there be agreement to negotiate provisions on emergency safeguards. Introducing restrictions not contemplated by services suppliers at the time of establishment would result in a poor investment climate, provide an unstable basis for business decisions, and could have a negative effect on employment in the country imposing the safeguard." WTO doc. S/WPGR/M/47 (April 22, 2004).

732 WTO docs. S/WPGR/M/19 (January 21, 1999) and S/WPGR/M/20 (March 17, 1999).

In the absence of the universally accepted categorization of services, like or directly competitive services should also be determined on a case-by-case basis. For SGs, criteria such as physical characteristics and commercial usage are used to determine like or directly competitive products. The invisibility of services makes the physical variables inapplicable to the service trade. On the other hand, commercial usage may be considered. Criteria such as purpose, category of users, and normal duration of services could be used to determine the similarities in commercial usage between imports and domestic services. The measure of substitutability[733] between foreign and domestic services in question will also be useful to determine "like or directly competitive services."

10.27 *Investigation.* Article 3 of the SA sets forth detailed requirements for an investigation. Following the SA provision, competent national authorities, rather than private entities, should be made responsible for the investigation since it is a Member and not a private entity that is ultimately responsible for upholding the WTO rules. The procedural requirements in Article 3 – reasonable public notice to all interested parties, public hearings, publication of a report of the findings and reasoned conclusions on all pertinent issues of fact and law, and protection of confidentiality – should also be applied to maximize transparency.

10.28 *Injury Determination.* It was contended in the Working Party that serious data problems preclude the possibility of an injury test.[734] Again, safeguards are invoked regardless of any unfair trade practice on the part of exporters. Therefore, there should be a clear justification for taking a safeguard action, because a safeguard measure restricts the trade of innocent exporters. The justification for taking such a measure would be either serious injury or its threat to a domestic industry that is caused by increased imports. If a Member proposing to apply a safeguard cannot demonstrate the injury for lack of reliable data or for any other reason, the alleged injury may not exist in the first place, and therefore, the Member should not be allowed to take a safeguard measure.

10.29 Article 4 of the Agreement on Safeguards defines "serious injury" and "threat of serious injury." Article 4.1 provides in relevant part, "(a) serious injury shall be understood to mean a significant overall impairment in the position of a domestic industry; (b) threat of serious injury shall be understood to mean serious injury that is clearly imminent, in accordance with the provisions of paragraph 2...." Both of these definitions are appropriate in the service context as well.

---

733 *Supra* note 310.
734 WTO doc. S/WPGR/M/20 (March 17, 1999).

Article 4.2 of the SA specifies eight factors to be considered for the injury determination: "the rate and amount of the increase in imports of the product concerned in absolute and relative terms, the share of the domestic market taken by increased imports, and changes in the level of sales, production, productivity, capacity utilization, profits and losses, and employment." The identification of appropriate injury criteria applicable to diverse service sectors would be a difficult task. In fact, it would be virtually impossible to develop criteria that are applicable to all services, due to the extraordinary complexity and diversity of services. Even in the goods area, it has been shown that not all of the eight factors listed in Article 4.2 are always relevant in determining injury. For instance, in the dairy sector where employment decreases as a result of an increase in imports, production does not tend to decrease for a few years. The decrease in employment, therefore, leads to an increase in productivity. In this case, increase in productivity is not a relevant factor in determining injury.[735] **10.30**

Therefore, a practical solution would be to list in the text of the ESM certain factors that are considered relevant to determine injury in many service sectors as examples, and to allow consideration of additional factors where necessary. Those relevant factors may include: the rate and amount of the increase in imports of the service concerned in absolute and relative terms; the share of the domestic market taken by increased imports; revenue from value-added taxes; offer/sales statistics; the number of suppliers in the market; changes in prices and the price structure; capital flows; profits and losses; and employment. **10.31**

Another important issue concerns causation. The use of the ESM would only be justified where the injury is caused by increase in imports. Article 4.2(b) of the SA provides: **10.32**

> The determination referred to in subparagraph (a) shall not be made unless this investigation demonstrates, on the basis of objective evidence, the existence of the causal link between increased imports of the product concerned and serious injury or threat thereof. When factors other than increased imports are causing injury to the domestic industry at the same time, such injury shall not be attributed to increased imports.

While the concept of causation in Article 4.2(b) above is generally applicable to the ESM, there is some ambiguity in the application of the latter part of the Article. In actual cases, an injury to a domestic industry is rarely attributed to the increase in imports alone. There are almost always other contributing factors, whether significant or not, to the alleged injury. For instance, Country A maintains a relatively restrictive taxation system for the telecommunication **10.33**

735 Lee and Mah, *supra* note 728, p. 28.

service. Suppose that a sudden increase in imports of telecommunication services causes injury to the domestic telecommunication service industry, but it is also found that the restrictive tax system is a contributing factor. In this case, is the required causation not established because of the existence of this contributing factor even if the increase in imports is the major cause? The language of Article 4.2(b) is not very clear on this point.[736] In the service context, the second part of Article 4.2(b) should be revised to specify that the imports must be a *major* cause of the injury.

10.34 *Application of Safeguards.* Article 5.1 of the SA provides that "[a] Member shall apply measures only to the extent necessary to prevent or remedy serious injury and to facilitate adjustment." As discussed in Chapter 7 above, inappropriate use of an ESM would fall into two categories. The first is where an ESM is applied in a case where the conditions for its application do not exist (e.g., no injury). The second is where those conditions exist, but the measure goes beyond what is necessary to prevent or remedy serious injury and to facilitate adjustment. The first type would be an outright violation of the rules. The second type also constitutes an abuse. In order to prevent the second type of violation, an investigation should reasonably determine the extent of injury or threat thereof and prescribe a measure that corresponds to the extent of injury. There should be proportionality between the injury and the measure. In an SG case, the Appellate Body decision ruled that the extent of the measure should not exceed the amount of injury caused by increased imports.[737]

10.35 Once the justification for the application of an ESM is made, a Member should be able to choose a measure adequate to the unique circumstances of the service in question. In goods trade, safeguard measures take the forms of tariffs and quotas. More latitude should be allowed to Members in prescribing a measure for the service trade, given the diverse nature of service transactions. A withdrawal of national treatment would be one example, and it would be impractical to list all possible forms of emergency safeguard measures in the text. Members should also be allowed to apply an effective measure whether it affects one or more modes of service supply. For instance, a restriction on advertisement of the foreign tourism industry could be contemplated to remedy injury caused by the industry engaging in aggressive advertising campaigns. In any case, an ESM must be applied to imports from all sources. The selective

---

736 Chapter 5.3 *supra* provides a discussion of inherent problems with the causation requirement under Article 4.2(b).

737 *United States – Line Pipe*, *supra* note 71, paras. 241–260. *See also* the relevant discussions in Chapter 7 *supra.*

application of an ESM on a Member-to-Member basis would contravene the MFN principle.

Difficulties with restricting service transactions have been discussed.[738] The intangible nature of service transactions is a primary reason for this difficulty. For instance, if a service is provided through the Internet, how can it be effectively restricted? Is it feasible to prohibit access to the Internet? Should the government go ahead and block the relevant site(s) in question? The restriction of service transactions may also involve restriction of related activities, which may be considered basic rights. For instance, can government prevent people from traveling out of the country to restrict the use of medical services abroad? **10.36**

Many service transactions may also involve other services and/or transaction of goods as well, and therefore, by restricting a particular service, those other services or transactions of goods that the government has no intention to restrict may be also inhibited. For instance, the government may decide to restrict passenger air transportation service provided by foreign airliners. With this restriction, not only may the intended air transportation service be reduced, but domestic support business for foreign air transportation services, such as catering services for in-flight meals, may also be affected. In addition, service restriction focused on one mode of supply may drive consumers to another mode of supply. If government decides to restrict English education service by foreign nationals within their territory, domestic consumers may elect to go abroad to receive English education there. If the ESM does not apply to mode 3 as many Members prefer, applications of the emergency safeguards would actually encourage Members to establish service-providing firms in the importing country. **10.37**

All those complexities indicate that the application of the ESM and its impact would not be straightforward. The effects of the ESM could also be limited, as it may prove difficult to restrict *all* modes of supply.[739] Nevertheless, the ESM could still affect the consumption of a service in question, and some relief to the domestic industry would be possible through carefully devised measures. For instance, the government can implement surcharges on Internet transactions from a foreign source, although complete enforcement may be difficult. (The potential penalty of tax evasion should at least encourage large service **10.38**

738 *See Communication from the European Communities*, *supra* note 703.

739 For those who are concerned about the disruptive effect of the ESM to service trade, its potentially limited impact, due to the inherent problem in the control of multiple modes of supply, should provide some relief. The potentially limited effects of the ESM may also reduce its adverse impact on service trade and henceforth reduce the risk of its inclusion in the GATS.

providers to comply.) Also, it may be difficult to prevent people from traveling abroad, but it would be possible to limit aggressive advertisement campaigns of foreign service suppliers within its own territory.

10.39 *Provisional Safeguard Measures.* The concept of provisional safeguard measures in Article 6 of the SA is also applicable in the service trade. As in the goods context, the application of such a provisional measure would be justified in critical circumstances where delay would cause irreparable damage. The maximum duration of such a provisional measure should be set. The normal investigation process should also follow the application of a provisional measure. Article 6 limits the form of provisional measures to tariff increases, but such restraint would not be proper in the service trade given the diversity of service transactions.

10.40 *Duration, Mid-term Review, Extension.* As provided in Article 7 of the SA, a limit should also be set for the duration of an ESM as a temporary measure. Article 7 also provides for the extension of safeguard measures. A one-time extension can also be applicable to an emergency safeguard provided that there is evidence for structural adjustment on the part of the domestic industry.[740] Article 7 also provides for a mid-term review where the duration of a safeguard exceeds three years. This concept of a mid-term review is also applicable. The investigation and publication of findings should also be required for the mid-term review to ensure transparency of the review. The requirement for a progressive liberalization of safeguard measures over one year is also desirable in the service trade. To prevent abuse of emergency safeguards, there should also be a time interval during which an ESM cannot be invoked again on the same service.

10.41 *Level of Concessions, Developing Country Members.* The success of the WTO system will depend on its ability to maintain the balance of concessions negotiated among Members. Therefore, the principle advocating the balance of concessions in Article 8 of the SA should be adopted: both exporting and importing countries should endeavor to maintain the balance of concessions in the service trade. The application of an emergency safeguard should therefore entail compensation by the Member applying the measure. Upon failing to

740 The author was initially opposed to the extension of an emergency safeguard measure, as it was believed that the need for an extension indicates the necessity of a more permanent modification. If so, resort to Article XXI of the GATS would have been a more proper remedy. Lee (1999), *supra* note 692, p. 57. However, the author revises his initial opinion on the basis that the time required for structural adjustment for a service industry may be longer than the initial period of an emergency safeguard, as in the goods trade. In such cases, an extension should be allowed provided that structural adjustment is taking place.

reach agreement on compensation, the exporting Members should be allowed to suspend substantially equivalent concessions.

Article 8.3 of the SA provides that the right of suspension shall not be exercised for the first three years that a safeguard measure is in effect, provided that the safeguard measure has been applied as a result of an absolute increase in imports and that such a measure conforms to the provisions of the Agreement on Safeguards. This provision offers Members an incentive to comply with the safeguard rules and to apply a shorter duration safeguard measure. The underlying motive of this incentive is to discourage Members from resorting to gray-area measures. Unlike in the goods trade, the proliferation of gray-area measures is doubtful since major providers of services are Members with powerful economies and considerable bargaining power and are unlikely to accept any agreement for voluntary trade restrictions. On the other hand, the incentive may still be valid in order to encourage Members to apply a measure with a shorter duration. **10.42**

Preferential treatment for developing countries whose exports are *de minimis* (Article 9.1 of the SA) is also applicable since such a preference would aid developing countries to meet their development needs. The relaxed requirements on the re-introduction of safeguard measures to the same product are an acceptable preference for developing countries (Article 9.2). The longer extension of the measure would also be appropriate with regard to developing countries. The proposed reform in the context of the general safeguard with respect to the special and deferential treatment for developing countries is also applied to the ESM.[741] **10.43**

Notification and Consultation, Surveillance, Dispute Settlement. Article 12 of the Agreement on Safeguards lays down detailed requirements for notifications and consultations. The Article requires separate notifications (i) at the initiation of the investigation, (ii) at making a finding of injury, and (iii) at making a decision to apply or extend a measure. These provisions in Article 12.1 should be adopted in the ESM to promote the transparency of the process. The consultation requirements in Article 12 should also be adopted. These prior consultations with the exporting Members would facilitate exchange of information and views, which could lead to a mutually agreeable settlement. **10.44**

741 *See* Chapter 9.2 for the relevant discussion.

10.45 It will be necessary to monitor implementations of emergency safeguards.[742] Consideration should be given to the establishment of the Committee on Safeguards under the Council for Trade in Services to conduct surveillance and monitor application of emergency safeguards and assess their impact on service trade. The efforts of the Committee would be essential for the stabilization of the system since confusion and difficulty may arise in the early stages of the implementation of the ESM.[743] With respect to the process of dispute settlement, the DSU should govern pursuant to Article XXIII of the GATS.

10.4 CONCLUSION

10.46 Are safeguard measures necessary for trade in services? While a growing number of Members and observers perceived that a safeguard mechanism would encourage Members to open up their markets for the service trade, the fear of the potential abuse of safeguards in this relatively new type of trade has also existed. As a result, Members in the Working Party on GATS Rules did not reach agreement on fundamental issues, such as the necessity of a safeguard mechanism for the service area. The prospect for agreeing on the ESM is anything but clear since the Working Party on GATS Rules has held no meeting, neither formal nor informal, since November 2016.[744]

10.47 Despite the unclear prospect and the complex and diverse nature of service transactions, a uniform safeguard mechanism applying to all sectors of services and all modes of service supply is feasible and desirable (except, perhaps mode 3 for the reasons discussed in the previous section).[745] The well-structured Agreement on Safeguards offers a good model for the ESM. The concepts in the SA are applicable, although certain modifications are necessary to accommodate the unique features of services and the service trade. This applicability

742 Article 13 of the SA provides for the establishment of the Committee on Safeguards and designates its functions, including surveillance.

743 Some Members were concerned about serious data problems in the service trade. WTO doc. S/WPGR/M/20 (March 17, 1999). Perhaps guidance on statistical sources and indicators to be used in services safeguard investigation could also be developed. *See also* WTO doc. S/WPGR/27 (November 23, 2016).

744 WTO docs. S/WPGR/28 (November 16, 2017), S/WPGR/29 (November 27, 2018), S/WPGR/30 (November 21, 2019), S/WPGR/31 (November 27, 2020), S/WPGR/32 (October 18, 2021), S/WTGR/22 (December 6, 2022), S/WTGR/34 (November 27, 2023).

745 Marconini also opined that "[w]ith appropriate S&D, an ESM is a useful instrument to encourage progressive liberalization, including through successive bindings of evolving regulatory situations, while respecting national policy objectives. An ESM could achieve this in two ways: it would help members to 'sell' the logic of GATS liberalization at home; and, it would do much to improve the overall functioning of the Agreement." Marconini, *supra* note 721, p. 28.

does not mean that the application of those concepts will offer a complete solution to all the problems expected of the application of the ESM.

Nonetheless, the ESM is necessary since the same political, economic, and even psychological needs for the general safeguard in the goods trade[746] also exist in the service trade. Thus, the introduction of a reasonably appropriate services safeguard, although not necessarily perfect, would meet those needs. In the negotiations, Members (including both ESM proponents and ESM opponents) focused on discussing technical aspects of the ESM, including definition of "domestic industry" and availability of data and statistics in the service sectors that could potentially be used for safeguard investigation.[747] The discussion of the ESM has halted since November of 2016 when the Working Party on GATS Rules ceased its activities, but nevertheless the need for the ESM has not expired,[748] as indicated by the proliferation of ESM-type provisions in regional trade agreements.[749] **10.48**

It took 50 years after the birth of the GATT for a relatively complete agreement on safeguards to be introduced. Still, the SA is not without deficiencies and in need of certain modifications.[750] Therefore, it will also take some time to develop a reasonably complete safeguard mechanism for the service trade. If Members agree on the ESM, further modifications could also be made after its initial implementation to resolve problems that may emerge with the application of the system. The rapid evolution of the service area will make such **10.49**

---

746 *See* Chapter 1 for a discussion of political and economic grounds for a safeguard.

747 The representatives from the US, the EC, and Canada, the countries that had not been convinced on the necessity of ESM, also agreed that a focused discussion on technical issues was a productive way forward. WTO doc. S/WPGR/M/54 (February 22, 2006).

748 The Working Party noted the need expressed by the proponents of the ESM, who were "encouraged by recent developments in statistics suggesting that elements present in goods safeguards were also, in principle, possible for safeguards in services." WTO doc. S/WPGR/M/86 (May 22, 2015).

749 The WTO secretariat issued a note on ESM-type provisions in 32 instances of regional trade agreements. WTO doc. S/WPGR/W/64 (September 4, 2014). The note classified the ESM-type provisions into the following three types: "(a) measures providing for the possibility to take a safeguard action in case of a substantial adverse impact to a service sector; (b) a mere commitment by the parties to develop mutually acceptable procedures for the application of emergency safeguard measures in the future; or (c) a commitment by the parties to conduct a review, upon conclusion of the multilateral negotiations pursuant to Article X of the GATS, for the purpose of discussing appropriate amendments to the RTA so as to incorporate those results." *Id. See also* Yanning Yu, "China's Adopting Emergency Safeguard Measures for Services: A Political Economy Analysis" (2011) 6 *Asian Journal of WTO and International Health Law and Policy* 429–453. Article 9 of the China–ASEAN Free Trade Agreement provides, "The Parties note the multilateral negotiations pursuant to Article X of the GATS on the question of emergency safeguard measures based on the principle of non-discrimination. Upon the conclusion of such multilateral negotiations, the Parties shall conduct a review for the purpose of discussing appropriate amendments to this Agreement so as to incorporate the results of such multilateral negotiations."

750 Refer to the Chapters in Part II *supra* pertaining to the provisions of the SA.

modifications inevitable. Based on discussions in this chapter, in Appendix 5 the author proposes a text of the ESM with explanatory notes.

11

OTHER EMERGENCY IMPORT RESTRICTIONS IN THE WTO

11.1 INTRODUCTION

The WTO system also provides emergency import restrictions other than the general safeguard provided under the SA. Those measures share certain common features with SGs: they also allow Members to apply unilateral import restrictions of a non-permanent nature, and they are also distinguished from the other measures of administered protection, namely countervailing measures and anti-dumping actions, in that they do not require any unfair trade practice on the part of exporters, such as dumping or subsidization. Those other import restrictions are provided under Article XII, Article XVIII, the Understanding on Balance of Payments of the GATT 1994, the GATS, and the Agreement on Agriculture. The Agreement on Textiles and Clothing (ATC), which expired on January 1, 2005, had also provided transitional safeguard measures (TSGs), which are no longer applicable. TSGs applied to the textile and clothing products that were listed under the ATC and had not been integrated into the GATT 1994.[751] **11.01**

There are distinctions between those measures and SGs: while SGs apply to any product integrated into the GATT 1994, the other measures apply to a limited range of products covered by the specific agreements or their objective is to meet more general economic needs of the importing Members, such **11.02**

751 A previous version of this book included a section on TSGs, but the section has been removed as TSGs have no longer been applicable since 2005. A section on "Transitional Product-Specific Safeguard Measures" (TSMs), which were applicable until November 2013, is provided as a historical reference.

as securing a balance of payments, rather than protecting a specific domestic industry. TSGs formerly provided under the ATC and special safeguard measures (SSGs) under the Agreement on Agriculture fall under the former category and import-restrictive measures to improve the balance-of-payments (BOP) measures belong to the latter.

11.03 The use and the future prospects of those special measures are somewhat limited. TSGs ceased to exist when all the listed textile and clothing products were integrated into the GATT 1994 by January 1, 2005. There was also discussion of replacing SSGs with a new special safeguard mechanism (SSM), which is available only for developing countries, but Members have not agreed on the SSM for more than two decades, and SSGs are still in place.[752] Members cannot readily apply BOP measures, as these measures may also affect their own export industries (e.g., may cause difficulty in obtaining imported parts needed for export products), which would limit the intended improvement on the balance of payments. The import restrictions imposed by BOP measures may also have adverse impacts on the economic development by cutting off the import of foreign resources needed for development. Those special measures, therefore, have only limited applications under limited circumstances. This chapter discusses the WTO provisions for SSGs, BOP measures, as well as "Transitional Product-Specific Safeguard Measures" (TSMs) temporarily introduced under the Protocol on the Accession of China to the WTO as a historical reference.

11.2 SPECIAL SAFEGUARD MEASURES

11.04 *Background.* SSG provisions are part of the Agreement on Agriculture and comprise new disciplines on agricultural trade agreed in the Uruguay Round negotiations. Article 6 of the Agreement on Agriculture provides that SSGs are applicable to certain agricultural products. As the reform process for agricultural trade is in progress,[753] the SSG provisions are considered temporary in nature, but has remained in force for three decades, perhaps much longer

752 WTO, *Market Access: Special Agricultural Safeguards (SSGs)*, available at: https:// www .wto .org/ english/ tratop_e/agric_e/negs_bkgrnd11_ssg_e.htm [https://perma.cc/B4PM-XG32]. Major exporters of agricultural products, such as Australia, New Zealand and Argentina, had also voiced for the repeal of the SSG provisions. Chang B. Lee, "The Results of the Fifth WTO Committee on Agriculture" (March 1998) 57 *International Agricultural Reporter* 6–7.

753 Article 20 of the Agreement on Agriculture acknowledges that the long-term objective of making substantial, gradual reduction in support and protection—ultimately leading to fundamental reform—is an ongoing process.

than the initially anticipated duration of the reform process as provided under Article 20 of the Agreement on Agriculture (Article 5.9).

The political sensitivity of the agricultural sector has delayed the full integration of agricultural products into the world trading system. The GATT rules on the trade in goods did not apply to agricultural trade. The Committee on Trade in Agriculture was established pursuant to the Ministerial Declaration of November 1982 with an objective of greater liberalization in agricultural trade. As the result of continued effort, the Uruguay Round settled the Agreement on Agriculture, providing a basis for the liberalization of trade in agricultural products.[754] Whereas the ATC expired on the full integration of textile and clothing products into GATT 1994 by 2005, such integration has not been scheduled for agricultural products. **11.05**

SSGs allow Members to restrict imports of certain agricultural products based on either increased import volume or decreased product price. The threshold for the application of an SSG is considered lower than SGs as it does not require an injury test. The SSG mechanism is designed to insulate the domestic agricultural sector from any "disruptive" effect that may be caused by imports of agricultural products during the reform process. **11.06**

General Conditions. SSGs are applied to an agricultural product of which the import measure has been converted into an ordinary customs duty and also designated with the symbol "SSG" in the Member's Schedule (Article 5.1).[755] Either an increase in the import volume over a specified trigger level (for "volume-based" SSGs) or a certain trigger gap between the import- and domestic- prices (for "price-based" SSGs) is required to invoke an SSG. Again, injury analysis is not part of the application process of an SSG. They are applied in the form of additional duties, pursuant to the provisions of Article 5. No quantitative restriction is allowed. **11.07**

Volume-Based SSG. For volume-based SSGs, Article 5.4 provides that the trigger level is set according to market access opportunities defined as percentages of the corresponding domestic consumption taken by imports during **11.08**

---

754 For further discussions on the Agreement on Agriculture, *see* GATT, *The Results of the Uruguay Round of Multilateral Trade Negotiations* (1994) and Joseph F. Francois, Bradley McDonald, and Hakan Nordstrom, *Assessing the Uruguay Round* (Geneva: WTO, 1995). *See also* J. MacMahon, *The WTO Agreement on Agriculture, A Commentary: Oxford Commentaries on WTO Agreements* (Oxford University Press, 2006).

755 39 WTO Members reserved the right to use a combined total of 6,156 special safeguards on agricultural products. Most developing countries did not reserve this right to apply SSGs. WTO doc. G/AG/NG/S/9/Rev.1 (February 19, 2002).

the three preceding years for which data are available: (a) where such market access opportunities for a product are less than or equal to 10 percent, the base trigger level is 125 percent (i.e., 25 percent increase in the volume); (b) where such market access opportunities for a product are greater than 10 percent but less than or equal to 30 percent, the base trigger level is 110 percent; (c) where such market access opportunities for a product are greater than 30 percent the base trigger level is equal to 105 percent. Any additional duty imposed by a volume-based SSG may be maintained until the end of the year in which it has been imposed and may only be levied at a level which does not exceed one-third of the level of the ordinary customs duty in effect in the year in which the action was taken (Article 5.4). There is no restriction on the repetition of a volume-based SSG after its expiry; therefore, the measure can be applied consecutively so long as the conditions for invoking an SSG are met. The additional duty cannot exceed one-third of the original customs duty level.

11.09 *Price-Based SSG.* For price-based SSGs, Article 5.5 provides that the additional duty is set under the following schedule: (a) if the difference between the import price and the trigger price, which is equal to the average 1986–1988 reference price for the product concerned, is less than or equal to 10 percent of the trigger price, no additional duty can be imposed; (b) if such difference is greater than 10 percent but less than or equal to 40 percent of the trigger price, the additional duty is 30 percent of the amount by which the difference exceeds 10 percent; (c) if the difference is greater than 40 percent but less than or equal to 60 percent of the trigger price, the additional duty is 50 percent of the amount by which the difference exceeds 40 percent, plus the additional duty allowed under (b); (d) if the difference is greater than 60 percent but less than or equal to 75 percent, the additional duty is 70 percent of the amount by which the difference exceeds 60 percent of the trigger price, plus the additional duties allowed under (b) and (c); (e) if the difference is greater than 75 percent of the trigger price, the additional duty is 90 percent of the amount by which the difference exceeds 75 percent, plus the additional duties allowed under (b), (c), and (d).

11.10 *Application of SSG.* With respect to perishable and seasonal products, Article 5.6 allows shorter base periods for the application of volume-based SSGs and different reference prices for different periods for price-based SSGs. The Article does not specify those shorter periods and different prices, and therefore they are left to the discretion of the authorities applying SSGs. Transparency in the application of an SSG is emphasized. Members applying an SSG are obligated to give notice to the Committee on Agriculture and provide interested Members with an opportunity for consultations with respect to the proposed measure. Members also undertake, as far as practicable, not to apply a price-based SSG where the volume of imports of the products concerned are declining (Article 5.7). Article 5.8 prohibits Members from applying an SG and an SSG to the same product simultaneously.

Future Prospects. As discussed above, SSGs are not intended as a permanent part of the WTO disciplines and rather are a temporary device to relieve Members of the political pressure that can be created in the process of the liberalization of the sensitive agricultural sector, although this process has taken more than three decades. At the end of the Uruguay Round, 38 Members designated SSG products in their Schedules. Although the majority of those Members have not invoked the SSG provisions, SSGs have been applied to a number of products by some major trading nations. For instance, during the first year in which the SSG provisions were operational, the United States invoked price-based SSGs for 24 products.[756] For the EC, price-based SSGs were made operational for 14 products and volume-based SSGs for 47 products during 1996–1997.[757] Developed country Members retain a variety of highly protected products with SSG status.[758] The US remains an active SSG user, invoking price-based SSGs for 34 products in 2022.[759] **11.11**

As the reform process for agricultural trade is expected to continue with no clear end date in sight, the SSG provisions will also be likely to remain in place despite some Members' preference for their total repeal.[760] As an alternative to complete repeal, modifications of the current SSG provisions have been suggested. For instance, under the current provision, a mere 1 percent increase in import volume can invoke an SSG if the market access opportunity is, for instance, as small as 4 percent, because, in this case, this small increase meets the trigger level that is equal to 125 percent. It has therefore been suggested that the trigger level should be raised so that a minuscule increase in imports does not provide a basis to invoke an SSG.[761] It has also been argued that **11.12**

---

756 WTO, *Committee on Agriculture – Notification – United States – Special Safeguard Provisions*, G/AG/N/USA/4 (March 28, 1996).

757 WTO, *Committee on Agriculture – Notification – European Communities – Special Safeguard Provisions*, G/AG/N/EEC/10 (April 2, 1998).

758 *See* WTO, *Market Access: Special Agricultural Safeguards (SSGs)*, available at: https://www.wto.org/english/tratop_e/agric_e/negs_bkgrnd11_ssg_e.htm [https://perma.cc/B4PM-XG32].

759 WTO doc. G/AG/N/USA/172 (September 28, 2023).

760 *See supra* note 752.

761 *See* Jai S. Mah, "Reflections on the Special Safeguard Provision in the Agreement on Agriculture of the WTO" (1999) 33(5) *Journal of World Trade* 197–204, at 201; David Harris, *Special Safeguards and Agricultural Trade Liberalization*, Rural Industries Research and Development Corporation, 08/125 (2008); Tarun Jain, "Special Safeguard Measures under the Agreement of Agriculture: A Jurisprudential Analysis" (2008) VII(3) *The Icfai University Journal of International Business Law* 7–26.

Members should be allowed to designate a few additional SSG products of critical importance to their agricultural sector, which were made subject to tariffs after the conclusion of the Uruguay Round, and therefore, could not have been declared SSG products.[762] Other suggestions include: clear definition of perishable and seasonal products; definite criteria for the reference periods and for reference prices in relation to these products; and provision of preferential treatment for developing countries.[763] Other commentators have opined that the SSG provisions should be modified to better address the problem of the extended periods of low prices for the competing agricultural sectors of food-importing developing countries after market liberalization.[764] A study also revealed that the quantity-based safeguard increases domestic price volatility rather than insulating developing countries in those regions from price volatility, largely by restricting imports when domestic output is low and prices are high.[765]

11.13 *Special Safeguard Mechanism.* The Doha trade negotiations have involved a number of discussions on SSG. Considering the negative trade impact on agricultural exports from developing countries,[766] a proposal was made that developed countries should no longer be allowed to invoke SSGs or should be subject to more stringent conditions for the application of an SSG (e.g., reduce the number of tariff lines eligible for the SSG).[767] Developing countries are concerned that further tariff cuts would increase the vulnerability of their agriculture industries, especially where there is a call for SSG to be lifted gradually. Therefore, the "Special Safeguard Mechanism" (SSM), which is similar to the

762 Mah, *id.*, p. 204.

763 Mah, *id.*, pp. 197–204.

764 Alberto Valdés and William Foster, "Special Safeguards for Developing Country Agriculture: a Proposal for WTO Negotiations" (2003) 2(1) *World Trade Review* 5–31. *See also* J. Grant and K. Meilke, *Triggers, Remedies and Tariff Cuts: Assessing the Impact of a Special Safeguard Mechanism for Developing Countries*, Canadian Agricultural Trade Policy Research Network Working Paper 2008-09 (2008).

765 Thomas W. Hertel, Will Martin, and Amanda M. Leister, "Potential Implications of a Special Safeguard Mechanism in the World Trade Organization: The Case of Wheat" (2010) 24(2) *The World Bank Economic Review* 330–359.

766 For example, the price-based safeguard discriminates against lower price exporters and contributes to producer price instability. *Id.*

767 WTO, Chairperson's Working Documents November 2007 to January 2008, No. 14, *Special Agricultural Safeguard (SSG)*, text available at: http://www.wto.org/english/tratop_e/agric_e/workdoc_14sag_e.pdf [https://perma.cc/A8G5-BFKS].

SSG (i.e., applicable on a price decrease or an import volume increase)[768] but only available for developing countries, was proposed.[769]

However, the negotiations on the SSM met considerable challenges. While a coalition of developing countries (G-33) advocating flexibilities in open markets argued for a simple and accessible SSM as a trade remedy tool to mitigate price volatility risks and to balance distortions in agricultural trade, others had a preference for greater discipline in the SSM so that efforts toward market access reform or Members' existing commitments to agricultural tariffs would not be compromised.[770] Negotiations continued,[771] but Members could not bridge gaps in their positions, leading to an impasse in 2008. The 2015 Ministerial Decision confirmed that developing country Members will have the right to have recourse to a special safeguard mechanism, with a stipulation that there will be dedicated sessions of the Committee on Agriculture in Special Session to pursue negotiations on the SSM for developing country Members.[772] However, progress has been slow and no agreement on the SSM has been reached since then.[773] **11.14**

768 Finger criticized this "formula" approach for lacking the necessary flexibility in the application of a special safeguard. J. Michael Finger, "A Special Safeguard Mechanism for Agricultural Imports: What Experience with Other WTO Safeguards Tells Us about What Might Work" (2010) 9(2) *World Trade Review* 289–318.

769 WTO, *An Unofficial Guide to Agricultural Safeguards: Special Safeguard Mechanism (SSM) and Special Agriculture Safeguard (SSG)*, text available at: http://www.wto.org/english/tratop_e/agric_e/guide_agric_safeg_e.htm#problem [https://perma.cc/99WJ-JB37] and WTO, *Revised Draft Modalities for Agriculture Special Safeguard Mechanism*, TN/AG/W/7 (December 6, 2008). *See also* Raul Montemayer, *Implications of the Proposed Modalities for the Special Safeguard Mechanism: A Simulation Exercise*, ICTSD Issue Paper No. 10 (November 2007). The SSM proposal is coupled with the designation of "Special Products" ("based on criteria of food security, livelihood security and rural development needs"). *See* Christopher Stevens, *The Need for Special Products and Special Safeguard Mechanisms for Agriculture in the WTO: A Situational Analysis*, IDS Working Paper (September 30, 2004). The SSM can assist developing countries by shielding their domestic agriculture from low import prices by giving them flexibility to increase tariffs. Amanda M. Countryman and Badri G. Narayanan, "Price Volatility, Tariff Structure and the Special Safeguard Mechanism" (2017) 64 *Economic Modeling* 399–408. Another commentator was less optimistic and opined that the proposed SSM is expected to deliver only a small fraction of the loss-averting benefits. Jayanthi Thennakoon and Kym Anderson, "Could the Proposed WTO Special Safeguard Mechanism Protect Farmers from Low International Prices?" (2015) 50 *Food Policy* 106–113.

770 WTO, *id.*

771 The issues that have been negotiated include price and volume cross-check, seasonality, price-based SSM, flexibilities for Small, Vulnerable Economies (SVEs), and pro-rating. WTO, *Negotiation Group on Agriculture*, TN/AG/25 (March 22, 2010), paras. 31–36. *See also*, Grant and Meilke, *supra* note 764.

772 WTO, *Ministerial Decision of 19 December 2015, Special Safeguard Mechanism for Developing Country Members*, WT/MIN(15)/43 (December 21, 2015).

773 WTO doc. WT/MIN(24)/W/13. For a further discussion of the SSM, *see* Abhijit Das, Sachin Kumar Sharma, Raihan Akhter, and Teesta Lahiri, "Special Safeguard Mechanism for Agriculture: Implications for Developing Members at the World Trade Organization" (2021) 22 *Journal of World Investment and Trade* 835–859.

11.3 BALANCE-OF-PAYMENTS MEASURES

11.15 *Introduction.* GATT Article XII authorizes Members to apply unilateral import restrictions to secure the appropriate level of balance of payments (BOP measures). Among all emergency import-restrictive measures, BOP measures share fewer common characteristics with SGs than SSGs, as BOP measures do not concern protection of a specific domestic industry. The Understanding on the Balance-of-Payments Provisions of the GATT 1994 augments the provisions of GATT Article XII, which provides measures to address the balance-of-payments problems. Article XVIII:B also provides for the balance-of-payments difficulties associated with economic development. GATS Article XII provides BOP measures for trade in services.

11.16 The objective of BOP measures is to resolve serious balance-of-payments problems through temporary import restrictions. The International Monetary Fund (IMF) is a primary international institution in charge of the international reserve problem. Cooperation between the WTO and the IMF is emphasized in the GATT Article XV. Article XV obligates Members to consult with the IMF with respect to international reserves, balance of payments, or foreign exchange arrangements (Article XV:2). The IMF also participates in Members' consultations with the Committee on Balance-of-Payments Restrictions, provides documentation, and makes formal statements. Nevertheless, BOP measures operate under separate jurisdiction from that of the IMF. Members are not obligated to seek any review or approval from the IMF to apply a BOP measure.

11.17 *Provisions of GATT Article XII.* Article XII authorizes the application of a BOP measure[774] in each of two situations: (i) to forestall the imminent threat of, or to stop, a serious decline in the Member's monetary reserves, or (ii) to achieve a reasonable rate of increase in its reserves (where it is very low) (Article XII:2(a)). Paragraph 2(b) of the Article requires Members to relax a BOP measure progressively after its application and to maintain it only to the extent and for the duration necessary. Paragraph 3(d) also allows Members to apply and maintain a BOP measure where their monetary reserve is threatened by high demand for imports as the result of expansionary economic policy.

774 Under the provision of Article XII:1, BOP measures may restrict the quantity or value of merchandise permitted to be imported.

Article XII:4 requires a BOP measure reviewed by the Committee on Balance-of-Payments Restrictions (the Committee)[775] immediately following its application and annually thereafter. After such review, if the Committee finds that the measure is not consistent with the provisions of Article XII, it will indicate the nature of the inconsistency and may advise suitable modification of the measure (paragraph 4(c)(i)). If the Committee determines that the BOP measure seriously violates the requirements of Article XII or those of Article XIII[776] and that the measure causes or threatens to cause damage to the trade of any Member, it makes recommendations to secure conformity within the specified period of time. Failure to comply with such recommendations may lead to the authorization of retaliatory measures to be adopted by Members whose trade is adversely affected (paragraph 4(c)(ii)). Paragraph 4(d) also provides that such review can be initiated at the request of an individual Member that can establish a *prima facie* case that a BOP measure is inconsistent with the rules, provided that the injured Member was unsuccessful to resolve the issue in direct discussions with the Member applying the measure. **11.18**

Provisions of Article XVIII. GATT Article XVIII, which concerns general assistance with economic development, also provides for BOP measures with respect to a Member in the early stages of development and whose economy can only support low standards of living. Section B provides for BOP measures. The threshold for the application of a BOP measure appears somewhat relaxed under Article XVIII:B. As mentioned above, the Article XII measure requires either an "imminent threat" of a serious monetary decline or "very low monetary reserve." The term "imminent" is omitted from the corresponding provision of Article XVIII, and the term "very low" is replaced with "inadequate," which is understood as "inadequate" to implement its program of economic development. **11.19**

Another difference in the BOP provisions under Article XVIII:B is that the Member applying a BOP measure is subject to review every two years instead of every year under the provision of Article XII. In December 1972, the GATT Council approved the modified "Procedure for Regular Consultations on Balance-of-Payments Restrictions with Developing Countries" to allow for a simplified consultation process for periodic consultations with developing countries.[777] **11.20**

---

775 The Committee replaces the Contracting Parties under the GATT with respect to the discipline of BOP measures.

776 Article XIII requires non-discriminatory administration of quantitative restrictions, subject to certain exceptions prescribed under Article XIV.

777 BISD 20S/47-49.

11.21 *The 1979 Declaration.* The 1979 Declaration on Trade Measures Taken for Balance-of-Payments Purposes extended the application of Article XII to all trade measures, either quantitative or non-quantitative, imposed for balance-of-payments reasons.[778] The 1979 Declaration also introduced three new conditions for the application of balance-of-payments measures: (i) preference for the measures which have "the least disruptive effect on trade"; (ii) no simultaneous application of more than one trade measure for balance-of-payments purposes; and (iii) public announcement of a time schedule for the removal of the measures whenever possible. It was further specified that BOP measures should not be taken "for the purpose of protecting a particular industry or sector."

11.22 *UBOP.* The Understanding on the Balance-of-Payments Provisions of the GATT 1994 (UBOP) was settled in the Uruguay Round negotiations. The UBOP clarifies the provisions of Article XII and XVIII:B, mostly relating to procedural matters.[779] The UBOP requires Members to make a public announcement to set the time schedules for the removal of a BOP measure (paragraph 1), affirming the temporary and emergency nature of BOP measures. In addition, under the UBOP, quantitative restrictions are not prohibited, but Members are required to provide justification as to why price-based measures are not adequate instruments to deal with the BOP situation (paragraph 3). Not more than one type of BOP measure may be applied to the same product (paragraph 3).

11.23 BOP measures should only be applied to control the general level of imports (i.e., should not protect a specific domestic industry) and may not exceed what is necessary to address the BOP situation (paragraph 4). Nonetheless, BOP measures may limit or exclude surcharges to admit "essential products" (i.e., products to meet basic consumption need or improve the balance-of-payment situation: e.g., capital goods or inputs needed for production) (paragraph 4).

11.24 Consultations with the Committee on Balance-of-Payments Restrictions are required for a new adoption or substantial intensification of a BOP measure within four months of its adoption (paragraph 6).[780] BOP measures are also subject to periodic review by the Committee under the relevant provisions of

---

778 BISD 26S/205.

779 The footnote of the preamble of the UBOP stipulates that nothing in the UBOP is intended to modify the rights and obligations of Members under Articles XII or XVIII:B of GATT 1994.

780 *See* WTO, *Analytical Index: Guide to GATT Law and Practice*, *supra* note 85, pp. 386–391 for more discussions on BOP consultations. *See also* WTO, *Analytical Index: Guide to WTO Law and Practice* (Geneva: WTO, 3rd. ed. 2012), pp. 252–254, 292–294.

Article XII or Article XVIII, subject to the possibility of altering the periodicity of consultations in agreement with the consulting Member or pursuant to any specific review procedure that may be recommended by the General Council (paragraph 7). The 1970 full consultation procedures[781] are applied with the participation of the IMF,[782] except where simplified procedures are applicable for the least-developed country Members or for developing country Members pursuing liberalization efforts in conformity with the schedule presented to the Committee in previous consultations. The IMF still participates in consultations under the simplified procedures and provides documentation but does not address the Committee. No more than two successive consultations may be held under the simplified procedures except for the least-developed country Members (paragraph 8).

An introduction of a BOP measure or any changes to an announced BOP **11.25** measure must be notified to the General Council (paragraph 9). Any Member may bring to the attention of the Committee any restrictive import measure suspected to have been taken for a BOP purpose (paragraph 10). The basic documentation for consultation is also specified (paragraph 11). The report on consultations must be made to the General Council with the Committee's conclusions accompanied with the facts and reasons to support them. The Committee should endeavor to include specific recommendations in its report. The General Council's adoption of the report gives effect to those recommendations (paragraph 13).

GATS Article XII. Article XII of the GATS provides for BOP measures **11.26** for trade in services. Article XII:2 requires that the measure must be (i) non-discriminatory; (ii) consistent with the Articles of Agreement of the IMF; (iii) not unnecessarily damaging to the commercial, economic, and financial interests of any other Member; (iv) not excessive; and (v) temporary and phased out progressively. Members may give priority to the supply of services which are more essential to their economic or development programs. Members must notify a BOP measure or its change to the General Council and consult promptly with the Committee on Balance-of-Payments Restrictions. As in the goods trade, the IMF carries out an important role in consultations. The IMF participates in consultations and provides documentation. Paragraph 5(e) provides that the Committee conclusions shall be based on the IMF's assessment of the Member's balance of payments and its external financial situation.

781 BISD 18S/50-51.

782 The IMF provides documentation concerning the monetary situation of the Member concerned and makes a formal statement to the Committee.

BOP measures in the service area will gain more importance as market access increases in that area.

11.27 *Evaluation*. In the GATT era, as many as 13 countries were reported to have consultations for the application of BOP measures.[783] It was argued that the resort to BOP measures impeded the liberalization of trade and undermined the integrity of the world trading system.[784] In response to this criticism, the UBOP attempts to minimize the negative impact of BOP measures on international trade through elaborate notification and consultation procedures. The BOP measures have been in use since the establishment of the WTO,[785] but it is notable that neither South Korea nor Indonesia resorted to BOP measures during their financial crises in 1997. It has been observed that the IMF bailout package for those two countries achieved policy changes in the direction of further trade liberalization rather than restriction.[786]

11.28 It was pointed out that there is a potential conflict between the recommendations of the IMF during the financial crisis and the provisions of the WTO limiting import restrictions.[787] To resolve this conflict and to enhance the clarity of the current BOP provisions, modifications of the UBOP were proposed.[788] The proposal includes that the UBOP should provide specific procedures to avoid any conflict between IMF recommendations and WTO disciplines, recognize the need for quantitative restrictions as more effective means to address BOP problems, limit the duration of BOP measures, and define the terms used for the conditions of invoking a BOP measure.[789]

783 WTO, *Analytical Index: Guide to GATT Law and Practice*, *supra* note 85, p. 383.

784 Isaiah Frank, "Imports Quotas, the Balance of Payments and the GATT" (1987) 10 *The World Economy* 307–317.

785 By June 2017, 84 notifications had been made to the WTO General Council concerning the introduction of or any changes in BOP measures. WTO docs. WT/BOP/N/1~84.

786 *Inside US Trade* (February 27, 1998), p. 4.

787 *See Argentina – Measures Affecting Imports of Footwear, Textiles, Apparel and Other Items*, Report of the Appellate Body, WT/DS56/AB/R (March 27, 1998). In this case, the Memorandum of Understanding between Argentina and the IMF was not recognized as a legally binding agreement. The Appellate Body stated, "there is nothing in the Agreement Between the IMF and the WTO, the Declaration on the Relationship of the WTO with the IMF or the Declaration on Coherence which justifies a conclusion that a Member's commitments to the IMF shall prevail over its obligations under … the GATT 1994." *Id.*, para. 70.

788 Jai S. Mah, "Reflections on the Balance of Payments Provisions in the WTO" (1999) 21(5) *World Competition* 139–148.

789 *Id.*

11.4 TRANSITIONAL PRODUCT-SPECIFIC SAFEGUARD MEASURES: HISTORICAL REFERENCE[790]

Background. By the year 2000, WTO membership had expanded to include more than 140 countries,[791] with China and Russia the only major economies left out of this world trade club. In the Doha Ministerial Conference in November 2001, after long negotiations, finally came approval of China's entry to the WTO.[792] Through this act, this nation with around one-fifth of the world's population finally became a part of the global trading system, expecting to take both benefits and responsibilities that come with membership of the WTO. **11.29**

With the country's rapid economic growth since the 1980s,[793] China's entry into the WTO brought Members of the WTO not only expectations and hopes for increased market access to this potentially largest market in the world, but also some concerns.[794] Some Members feared that China's membership of the WTO, which would also provide it with market access to the other Members, may lead to "flooding" of cheaper imports from China. This concern led to the inclusion of the "Transitional Product-Specific Safeguard Mechanism" in the Protocol on the Accession of China to the WTO (here- **11.30**

790 The contents of Chapter 11.4 are drawn from the author's previous articles, "The Specific Safeguard Mechanism in the Protocol on China's Accession to the WTO" (2002) 5 *The Journal of World Intellectual Property* 219–231 and "First WTO Case on Transitional Product-Safeguard Measure under Section 16 of the Protocol of China's Accession to the WTO: Affirming Discriminatory Safeguard Measure by WTO?" (2012) 44 *Journal of World Trade* 913–936. *See also,* Scott Andersen and Christian Lau, "Hedging Hopes with Fears in China's Accession to the World Trade Organization" (2005) 5(3) *The Journal of World Intellectual Property* 405–476 and Jing Ma, "Product-Specific Safeguard in China's WTO Accession Agreement: An Analysis of Its Terms and Its Initial Application in Section 421 Investigations" (2004) 22 *Boston University International Law Journal* 189–217.

791 The WTO membership has further increased to 166 countries. For the list of WTO Members, *see* WTO, *Members and Observers*, http://www.wto.org/english/thewto_e/whatis_e/tif_e/org6_e.htm [https://perma.cc/QQ92-8ZRC].

792 The People's Republic of China originally made an application for accession to the WTO dated December 7, 1995. After a series of lengthy negotiations, the Ministerial Conference finally approved the accession of the People's Republic of China to the WTO on November 10, 2001. WTO doc. WT/L/432 (November 23, 2001).

793 The implications of China's entry to the WTO were highly significant. Although China was still considered a developing country, it had already become a major trading nation by the time of its entry to the WTO: by 2001, China had become the 7th largest exporter of merchandise trade (249.2 billion US dollars, 3.9 percent of the world market share) and the 8th largest importer (225.1 billion dollars, 3.4 percent share). China also had become the 12th largest exporter of commercial services (29.7 billion dollars, 2.1 percent share) and the 10th largest importer (34.8 billion dollars, 2.5 percent share). WTO, *2001 Press Releases*, Press/243 (September 17, 2001).

794 *See* Ramesh Adhikari and Yongzheng Yang, "What Will WTO Membership Mean for China and Its Trading Partners?" (2002) 39(3) *Finance and Development* 1–9. The authors opined that the opening of an economy as large as China's can be disruptive to some developing countries in the short run, but, in the long run, it should benefit not only China but also its trading partners.

inafter, "the Protocol").[795] Paragraph 16 of the Protocol allows Members to restrict imports from China by adopting a transitional product-specific safeguard measure ("TSM"[796]) under more relaxed conditions than those required for the general safeguards.[797] This special safeguard measure, applicable solely to imports from China, was intended to be a temporary device lasting for 12 years after the date of China's accession to the WTO.[798] At the writing of this book, the TSM had already expired; thus, discussion of its detailed provisions may no longer be necessary, but its historical implications and the systemic risks that it presented call for an evaluation.

11.31 *Evaluation.* The TSM provisions exhibited several problems that were not compatible with the underlying objectives and policies of the general safeguards as well as those of the WTO in general. First, the inherent unfairness in the selective and discriminatory application of a TSM solely to imports from one Member is an issue. As discussed above, the threshold for the application of a TSM was lower than that of an SG, and it was not compatible with the MFN principle underlying the application of SGs.[799] The MFN treatment is the core principle of the WTO system as a whole.[800] The danger of "flooding of imports from China," if it ever materialized, could be and should be dealt with by SGs just as qualified increases in imports from any other country would have been, and there is no justification for creating a separate safeguard system applicable to the imports from a single Member.

11.32 In addition, there is inherent ambiguity in the concept of "market disruption" that was used as a threshold for the application of a TSM. Paragraph 16.4 of

---

795 The conditions for China's accession to the WTO are stipulated in the "Protocol on the Accession of the People's Republic of China," WTO doc. WT/L/432 (November 23, 2001).

796 *Supra* note 592.

797 WTO doc. WT/L/432, pp. 8–9. A separate safeguard machanism, the Textile-Specific Safeguard Clause (TSSC), which contained similar requirements for invocation based on "market disruption" and was applicable to the textile and clothing products from China covered by the ATC, was also approved by the Protocol and lasted until the end of 2008. For a discussion of the TSSC, *see* Xingzheng Hou and Rongming Ren, "Cooperate or Antagonize: The EU's Dilemma on Anti-dumping and Safeguard Measures against China" (2006) 14(6) *China and World Economy* 76–78.

798 Paragraph 16.9 of the Protocol stipulated that the application of TSM provisions shall be terminated after 12 years from the date of China's accession to the WTO.

799 The TSM seems to have defeated the important objective of the SG – channeling all emergency actions on imports through a single, well-defined mechanism.

800 The TSM also conflicted with the idea of the uniform application of rights and obligations under the WTO concerning all its Members without discrimination. The WTO is known as a "one package deal," meaning that all Members share the equal rights and obligations under indiscriminate rules. The rights of an individual Member should not be single-handedly hampered. The TSM provisions discriminated against the imports from China by subjecting them to import restraints with a lower threshold. China, on the other hand, did not seem to have a corresponding right. Lee (2002), *supra* note 790, p. 226.

the Protocol used "material injury"[801] or its threat for the determination of market disruption. However, the relevant provisions of the Protocol did not provide any definition for material injury.[802] Material injury is generally considered a lesser injury than the serious injury used for SGs, but this comparison alone does not eliminate the ambiguity associated with the concept of market disruption. Paragraph 16.4 of the Protocol specified certain factors for the determination of market disruption, such as the volume of imports, the effect of imports on prices for like or directly competitive articles, and the effect of such imports on the domestic industry producing like or directly competitive products. Those enlisted factors were few and less precise than the eight injury factors enumerated in Article 4.2(a) of the SA.[803] The TSM provisions did not provide clear guidelines for the determination of the existence of market disruption. This ambiguity created ample room for arbitrary decision and abuse by importing Members.

The lack of clear rules and definitions for the application of a TSM was a significant problem. For instance, the TSM provisions, unlike those of the SA, did not have a definition of key terms, such as domestic industry. They did not provide any guidelines to determine causation between the increase in imports and market disruption. The absence of a non-attribution requirement as found in Article 4.2(b) of the SA led to the Panel decision that the importing country applying a TSM had no obligation to quantify the injury caused by increasing imports, or separate and distinguish that injury from injury caused by other factors, which was apparently a different standard from that applied for SGs.[804] The TSM rules were also silent about the allocation of quotas where quantitative restrictions are applied, the maximum period for a TSM, compensation, and the timing and contents of notifications concerning the application of **11.33**

801 "Material injury" is used in the injury analysis in Paragraph 6(a) of Article VI of the GATT, Article 3 of the Agreement on Implementation of Article VI of the General Agreement on Tariffs and Trade 1994, and Article 15 of the Agreement on Subsidies and Countervailing Duties.

802 In contrast, Article 4.1(a) of the Agreement defines "serious injury" as "a significant overall impairment in the position of a domestic industry."

803 Article 4.2 of the Agreement provides: "In the investigation to determine whether increased imports have caused or are threatening to cause serious injury to a domestic industry under the terms of this Agreement, the competent authorities shall evaluate all relevant factors of an objective and quantifiable nature having a bearing on the situation of that industry, in particular, *the rate and amount of the increase in imports of the product concerned in absolute or relative terms, the share of the domestic market taken by increased imports, changes in the level of sales, production, productivity, capacity utilization, profits and losses, and employment*" (emphasis added).

804 WTO, *United States – Measures Affecting Imports of Certain Passenger Vehicle and Light Truck Tyres from China* ("*United States – Certain Tyres*"), Report of the Panel, WT/DS399/R (December 13, 2010), para. 7.414. For a discussion of the non-attribution requirement, *see* Chapter 5.2 *supra*.

a safeguard measure.[805] Some of the rules for the application of a TSM were closely proximate to those of the SA, but it was not clear whether the missing definitions and requirements were to be inferred from the provisions of the SA. A degree of arbitrariness and ambiguity remained in the application of a TSM under the Protocol.

11.34 China expressed concern about the TSM with regard to its discriminatory nature.[806] In response to this concern, there was an understanding among Members of the Working Party on China's Accession that the utmost restraint would be exercised in having recourse to the TSM and that it would only be applied under very special circumstances where other trade remedy measures were not effective.[807] However, it is doubtful that the TSM in *United States – Certain Tyres* was applied in these circumstances: the alleged injury to the domestic industry appeared to have been caused by the voluntary reduction of domestic production by domestic producers as part of their own global business strategy, and China's exports merely filled "a supply gap" in the domestic market as a result of this voluntary reduction.[808] Interestingly, the petition for the TSM was not supported by the tire producers in this case, but was initiated by the unions, and certain domestic producers denied that they were materially injured.[809]

11.35 The TSM, by the terms of the Protocol, had a finite life of 12 years from China's accession into the WTO, but the temporary nature of TSM did not justify its derogation from the core principle of the SA, that is, the MFN application of potentially the most protective import restraining measures of all.

---

805 The SA requires notifications in the three stages during the investigations: when initiating an investigatory process; when making a finding of serious injury or threat thereof caused by increased imports, and finally, when making a decision to apply or extend a safeguard measure (Article 12.1). The purpose of detailed notification requirements is to ensure transparency of the process by informing all interested parties of the progress of the investigation in each of the key stages.

806 China reiterated that this selective safeguard mechanism "was discriminatory in nature, and contrary to the basic principles of the WTO. Experience over the years had revealed the fact that injury suffered by domestic industries was attributable in most cases to imports from several exporting Members, rather than a single one. Thus, invoking the product-specific safeguard mechanism – which targeted solely imports originating in China – was not only discriminatory, but also failed to counteract the injury suffered by domestic industries. In that spirit, it was China's belief that trade remedies within a framework of the WTO should always be the resort of priority in the case of domestic injuries. China sincerely hoped that all Members would abide by the fundamental principles of the WTO and exercise maximum caution in considering the application of the transitional product-specific safeguard mechanism." Committee on Safeguards, *Chairman's Report to the Council for Trade in Goods on Transitional Review of China*, G/SG/66 (November 17, 2003).

807 Committee on Safeguards, *Statement by Head of the Chinese Delegation on the Transitional Review of China to the Committee on Safeguards*, G/SG/W/192 (November 4, 2002).

808 Lee (2012), *supra* note 790, p. 929.

809 *Id.* For a further discussion of the case, *see* Steve Charnovitz and Bernard Hoekman, "US–Tyres: Upholding a WTO Accession Contract – Imposing Pain for Little Gain" (2013) 12(2) *World Trade Review* 273–296.

The TSM is for this reason a rather undesirable precedent which represented "a serious systematic risk to the WTO regime."[810]

810 Patrick A. Messerlin, "Economic Effects of China's Accession to the World Trade Organization" (2004) 18(1) *The World Bank Economic Review* 127–128. A study also observed that the impact of the TSM on employment is limited, and a total employment and average wages in the tire industry was unaffected by the safeguard as imports from China were completely diverted to other exporting countries partly due to the strong presence of multilateral corporations in the world tire market. Sunghoon Chung, Joonhyung Lee, and Thomas Osang, "Did China Tire Safeguard Save U.S. Workers?" (2016) 85 *European Economic Review* 22–38.

12

NATIONAL/REGIONAL RULES ON SAFEGUARDS

12.1 INTRODUCTION

12.01 This chapter discusses selected national and regional rules on safeguards. The US provisions on safeguards, as well as the EU provisions, are considered.[811] Under the provisions of Article XVI:4 of the Marrakesh Agreement Establishing the World Trading Organization (the WTO Agreement), Members must ensure conformity of their laws, regulations, and administrative procedures, including their national safeguard rules, with the WTO rules. Article 12.6 of the Safeguards Agreement requires Members to notify the Committee on Safeguards of their laws, regulations, and administrative procedures relating to safeguard measures as well as any modifications made to them.

12.02 The texts of national and regional rules on safeguards display notable differences among themselves and from the provisions of the SA. The national provisions need not be identical to the text of the SA to be consistent with the WTO requirements. Nevertheless, the application of a safeguard measure pursuant to the relevant national safeguard rules should also ensure conformity with the provisions of the SA. There has been a question whether safeguard measures applied under the national rules are consistent with the requirements of the WTO rules, as discussed later in this chapter. This chapter also reviews

811 For the US rules on safeguards, *see* Sections 201–204 of the Trade Act of 1974, as amended (19 U.S.C. §§ 2251–2254). WTO doc. G/SG/N/1/USA/1 (April 6, 1995). For the EU rules, *see* Regulation (EU) 2015/478 of the European Parliament and of the Council of 11 March 2015 G/SG/N/1/EU/2 (June 12, 2015).

the provisions of national and regional safeguard rules in conjunction with the corresponding WTO provisions.

12.2 US PROVISIONS ON SAFEGUARDS – SECTIONS 201–204 OF THE TRADE ACT OF 1974[812]

History of US Safeguard Provisions. As discussed in Chapter 1, the escape clause of the United States–Mexico Trade Agreement in the 1930s and the subsequent executive orders setting forth procedures and criteria for escape-clause relief were the first safeguard provisions in modern trade history. The concept of safeguards was fostered in the United States as the US Congress addressed concerns about possible injury to domestic industries from concessions granted in trade treaties. In February 1947, President Truman issued an Executive Order requiring inclusion of an escape clause in every subsequent trade agreement negotiated under the 1934 Trade Act.[813] The provisions of Article XIX are modeled after the language of the 1947 Executive Order. The escape clause became a permanent part of US trade provisions by its adoption in Section 7 of the Trade Agreement Extension Act of 1951. **12.03**

The threshold for the application of a safeguard measure was high during the early period of the US safeguard regime. A four-point test was used by the US Tariff Commission for the application of a safeguard measure: that (1) there was an increase in imports; (2) the increase resulted from unforeseen conditions; (3) the increase was a result of trade concessions; and (4) the increased imports are causing or threatening to cause serious injury.[814] The difficulty in obtaining relief under such conditions caused legislative changes in the early 1950s, including elimination of "unforeseen conditions" from the conditions required for the application of a safeguard measure.[815] Another legislative change in 1958 was made in the Trade Agreements Extension Act, **12.04**

812 The contents of Chapter 12.2 are based on the author's article, "Reflections on U.S. International Trade Law and Practice – Compatibility with the WTO Rules and Call for Modification" (2003) 13(2) *Currents: International Trade Law Journal* 31–43.

813 Exec. Order No. 10004, 3 C.F.R. §§ 819–22 (October 9, 1948). The Order was amended by subsequent Executive Orders. For a further discussion of Section 201 US safeguards, *see* Joshua E. Kurland, "Dusting-Off Section 201: Re-Examining A Previously Dormant Trade Remedy" (2018) 49(2) *Georgetown Journal of International Law* 609–674. *See also* David Ryan, "The Effects of Section 201 Safeguards on U.S. Industries" (2012) 44(1) *Georgetown Journal of International Law* 249–310. This study examines the performance of three domestic industries that received safeguard protection. The study finds that none of the three industries were restored to sustained competitiveness and proposes reforming Section 201 to enhance its effectiveness. *Id.*

814 Trade Agreements Extension Act of 1951: Hearings on H.R. 1612 Before the Senate Comm. on Finance, 82d Cong., 1st Sess. 1322 (1951), pp. 1323–1324, *cited in* Stewart, *supra* note 114, p. 1731, n. 65.

815 Stewart, *supra* note 114, p. 1733.

giving Congress power to override any change by the President of relief recommended by the Tariff Commission with a two-thirds vote by each House.[816]

12.05 A new change was made to the US regime of safeguards in the early 1960s. The Trade Expansion Act of 1962 was an effort to expand trade. Present in this legislation was a new, higher threshold for an application of a safeguard measure, which provided: (1) that there was an actual increase in imports; (2) that the increase in imports was in major part the result of tariff concessions; and (3) that the increase in imports was the major factor in creating or threatening to create serious injury to the domestic industry.[817] This change also strengthened causation requirements.[818] The tougher standard resulted in only 3 positive injury determinations out of 28 cases between 1962 and 1964.[819]

12.06 The changing economic environment of the 1970s caused Congress to relax the conditions for safeguards. Congress promulgated Section 201 of the Trade Act of 1974, which became the primary US safeguard provision. (US safeguard action is therefore commonly referred to as "Section 201 action.") The seemingly insurmountable requirement of a "major" cause (a cause greater than all other causes combined) was replaced in the Act with a requirement of "substantial" cause, defined as "cause which is important and not less than any other." Congress also reduced the requirements for the Congressional override to a simple majority vote of each House. On the other hand, the legislative change also enabled the President to refuse relief for national economic interests.[820]

12.07 As the US economy faced growing economic competition from abroad in the 1980s, new legislative action was demanded to face this challenge. The Omnibus Trade and Competitiveness Act of 1988 was the response that followed. A widely publicized negative determination on the automobile safeguard petition caused public outcry and brought subsequent changes to safeguard provisions. In the safeguard petition against imports of Japanese automobiles, the USITC made a negative injury determination after finding that the impact of a recession outweighed the impact of imports causing the

816 *Id.*

817 Applebaum, "Section 201 of the Trade Act of 1974" *in The New Trade Law: Omnibus Trade and Competitiveness Act of 1988*, 179, 187 (Public Law Institute, 1988), *cited in* Stewart, *supra* note 114, p. 1735.

818 "In major part" cited in the conditions was understood as being "a cause greater than all other causes combined." S. Rep. No. 1298, 93rd Cong., 2d Sess. 120 (1974).

819 Stewart, *supra* note 114, p. 1735.

820 *Id.*, p. 1736.

injury.[821] In response to this determination, Congress once again relaxed a causation requirement and enacted a provision against aggregating the causes of declining demand associated with a recession (such as unemployment, reduced business expenditure, etc.).

The history of the US safeguard provisions reveals a series of changes in response to different economic environments. At times of economic expansion, the conditions for a safeguard measure were tightened to make the grant of import restraint more difficult. When the economy experienced intense foreign competition and a downturn recession, changes were made to ease conditions for the application of safeguards. The United States became concerned that some issues clarified in Section 201 still remained unresolved in Article XIX and subsequently persuaded the Uruguay Round participants to incorporate many of the Section 201 concepts into the Agreement on Safeguards, including injury criteria, procedures to ensure transparency, a durational limit on a safeguard measure, and the liberalization requirement for a measure enduring for more than one year.[822] **12.08**

Despite a series of legislative changes, the safeguard measures were difficult to obtain, for both legal and political reasons.[823] As a result, gray-area measures were favored as an alternative to safeguards.[824] The importance of safeguard provisions has been revived as gray-area measures are now prohibited under the SA.[825] Between 1995 and 2023, the President ordered relief in eight cases out of 13 investigated,[826] a substantial increase in relief in relative terms over previous periods.[827] It is interesting to note that six out of those eight cases were formerly disputed at the WTO, and in all of those disputed cases, except one currently on appeal, US safeguard measures were found inconsistent with the WTO rules.[828] This may signify systematic problems with the US meas- **12.09**

821 *Certain Motor Vehicles and Certain Chassis and Bodies Therefore*, Inv. No. TA-201-44, Pub. No. 1110, 2 ITRD 5241 (1980).

822 Bhala and Kennedy, supra note 87, p. 899. *Statement of Administrative Action for the Uruguay Round Agreement on Safeguards*, supra note 151, pp. 1577–1585.

823 Reflecting this sentiment, Senator Ernest F. Hollings once stated that "going the [Section] 201 route is for suckers." *Cited in* Patrick Low, *Trading Free* (1993), p. 57.

824 In 1989, the United States was in 69 out of 189 voluntary export restraint agreements. Dominick Salvatore, *International Economics* (Prentice Hall, 5th ed., 1995), p. 261, table 9-1. *See* Chapter 2.3 *supra* for a discussion of gray-area measures.

825 *See* Chapter 9.1 for the relevant discussion.

826 *See* Appendix 1 *infra*.

827 For example, between 1975 and 1990, the USITC found that the statutory requirements for the application of a safeguard measure were satisfied in 30 of the 62 cases filed. The President ordered relief in only 10 out of the 30 affirmative determinations. I.M. Destler, *American Trade Politics* (3rd ed., 1995), pp. 145–146.

828 In *United States — Photovoltaic Products*, the Panel found that the complainant (China) failed to demonstrate the inconsistency of the US safeguard measure with the provisions of the SA and Article

ures applied under its national safeguard provisions, as discussed later in this chapter.

12.10 *Overview of US Safeguard Measure.* Chapter 1 of Title II (Sections 201–204) of the Trade Act of 1974, as amended by Section 1401 of the Omnibus Trade and Competition Act of 1988 and by Sections 301–304 of the Uruguay Round Agreements Act, sets forth the authority and procedures for imposing a safeguard measure. The aim of the US safeguard is consistent with the objective of the Agreement on Safeguards. According to the US Senate Committee on Finance, "[i]t [a safeguard measure] is aimed at providing temporary relief for an industry suffering from serious injury, or the threat thereof, so that the industry will have sufficient time to adjust to the freer international competition."[829]

12.11 The application of a US safeguard measure involves two stages. First, the USITC makes a factual determination whether increased imports cause or threaten to cause serious injury to a domestic industry.[830] If the USITC makes a positive injury determination by a majority vote of the commissioners, it then reports its relief recommendations to the President.[831] In the second stage, the President makes a political decision whether to apply a safeguard measure. The President also has discretion to apply a remedy, which may differ from the one that is recommended by the USITC, subject to a possible Congressional override. Between 1975 and 1990, the USITC found that the statutory requirements for the application of a safeguard measure were satisfied in 30 of the 62 cases filed. The President ordered relief in only 10 out of the 30 affirmative determinations.[832] The practice has changed since the establishment of the WTO. Between 1995 and 2023, the President ordered relief in all six affirmative determinations.[833] The unavailability of alternative import restrictions such as gray-area measures could be the reason for this change.

12.12 *General Conditions.* Section 201 prescribes the conditions for the application of a safeguard measure to facilitate a positive adjustment. Under Section 201(a), a safeguard measure is applicable where "an article is being imported into the

---

XIX. *United States — Photovoltaic Products, supra* note 70, paras. 8.1 and 8.2. China appealed the Panel decision to the Appellate Body in June 2021, but the Appellate Body is unable to review this appeal due to lack of the quorum, which has been caused by a US veto of all appointments to the Appellate Body. *See* Reinert, *supra* note 618 (discussing US veto).

829 Senate Committee on Finance, S. Rep. No. 93-1298, 93rd Cong., 2nd Sess. 195.

830 Trade Act of 1974, Sections 202(a)~202(d).

831 Trade Act of 1974, Sections 202(e)~202(f).

832 Destler, *supra* note 827.

833 *Id.*

United States in such increased quantities as to be a substantial cause of serious injury, or the threat thereof, to the domestic industry producing an article like or directly competitive with the imported article."[834] The wording of this provision closely approximates that of Article 2.1 of the SA except that Section 201 requires a "substantial cause" instead of "cause" under the SA.[835] Under Section 202 of the Trade Act, imports have increased when the increase is "either actual or relative to domestic production."[836] The USITC ruled that an increase in imports was found where the absolute amount of imports actually declined, albeit less than that of the reduction in domestic production.[837]

Injury Determination. Section 202(c) lists specific factors for injury assessment. The factors specified for the assessment of serious injury and threat of serious injury are not identical to those listed in Article 4.2(a) of the SA. For serious injury, the listed injury factors are capacity utilization, profit, and employment (Section 202(c)(1)(A)). The consideration of injury is not limited to the assessment of those factors (i.e., additional factors, such as those listed in SA Article 4.2(a), may be considered), and the presence or absence of injury in any of those factors is not necessarily conclusive for the injury determination (Section 202(c)(3)).[838] With respect to threat of serious injury, the factors include sales, market share, inventory, production, profits, wages, productivity, employment, ability to generate capital to finance modernization of their domestic plants and equipment, inability to maintain existing levels of expenditures for **12.13**

834 The USITC discussed the concept of "like or directly competitive articles." It defined "like articles" as "those which are substantially identical in inherent or intrinsic characteristics (i.e., materials from which made, appearance, quality, texture, etc.)" and "directly competitive articles" as "those which, although not substantially identical in their inherent or intrinsic characteristics, are substantially equivalent for commercial purposes, that is, are adapted to the same uses and are essentially interchangeable." *Certain Canned Tuna Fish*, 6 I.T.R.D. (B.N.A) 2466 (1984).

835 The United States Senate Committee on Finance stated that "substantial cause" means "an important cause and no less important than any other single cause." US Senate Committee on Finance, S. Rep. No. 93-1298, 93rd Cong., 2nd sess. p. 195. In contrast, the WTO Appellate Body did not consider that the causation requirement under the SA requires that the increase in imports be the most important cause. *See* the relevant discussions of causation in Chapter 5.2.

836 Section 202(d)(1)(C)(ii) of Trade Act of 1974 (19 U.S.C. § 2252(c)(1)(C)). USITC, *Fresh, Chilled, or Frozen Blueberries*, Investigation No. TA-201-77, Publication 5164 (March 2021), p. 22.

837 *Steel Products*, 5 I.T.R.D. (B.N.A.) 2246–2251 (1984).

838 In *Electric Shavers*, the USITC made a negative injury determination where most injury factors, including profits and growth, had declined in the first three quarters of 1985. The overall trend was emphasized: prior to the decline, the industry had shown substantial improvement from 1979 to 1984, and that most indicators became stabilized by the fourth quarter of 1985. *Electric Shavers*, 8 I.T.R.D. (B.N.A.), p. 1830 (1986) *cited in* Leslie Alan Glick, *Guide to the United States Customs and Trade Laws after the Customs Modernization Act* (The Hague: Kluwer Law International, 2nd ed., 1997), p. 144. In *Fresh, Chilled, or Frozen Blueberries*, the USITC also made a negative injury determination when it found that the domestic industry "remained reasonably profitable throughout the period of investigation and experienced increases in acreage, production, employment (workers and wages), productivity, and shipments," although the domestic industry's profitability showed a decrease in profitability in certain years. USITC, *supra* note 836, p. 35.

research and development, and the extent to which the US market is the focal point for the diversion of exports of the article concerned by reason of restraints on exports/imports into third country markets (Section 202(c)(1)(B)).

12.14 Some of the injury factors specified in SA Article 4.2(a) are not listed: increases in imports, market share, sales, production, and productivity are not specified with respect to serious injury. In the case of a threat of serious injury, the increase in imports and capital utilization are not listed. On the other hand, factors such as inventory, wages, financial capacity to modernize, ability to maintain the current expenditure for R&D, and diversion of exports are additional to those listed in the SA. The presence of additional factors does not render national safeguard rules inconsistent with the WTO disciplines, as Members may choose to raise a threshold for the application of a safeguard measure. However, the absence of some of the factors specified in the SA is a potential problem if such absence leads to a lack of consideration of those factors that require mandatory consideration under WTO jurisprudence.[839] In the US steel safeguard case, not all of the factors listed in the SA were considered.[840]

12.15 *Causation.* The standard for the requisite causation is a "substantial cause." Substantial cause is defined as "a cause which is important and not less than any other cause" (Section 202(b)(1)(B)). The existence of a substantial cause is determined by an increase in imports (either actual or relative to domestic production) and a decline in the proportion of the domestic market supplied by domestic producers (Section 202(c)(1)(C)). It is prohibited to aggregate the causes of declining demand associated with a recession or economic downturn in the US economy into a single cause (Section 202(c)(2)(A)). As discussed above, this provision is to make it easier for the USITC to establish a requisite causation at the times of recession. The USITC is also required to examine factors other than imports which may be a cause (Section 202(c)(2)(B)). The definitions of domestic industry, serious injury, and threat of serious injury are provided in Section 201(c)(6), and they are identical to those provided in the SA.[841]

12.16 On the other hand, Section 202 does not include the non-attribution requirement as found in SA Article 4.2(b), which provides in relevant part, "When

839 *See* Chapter 5.1 *supra* for the relevant discussion.

840 *See* the relevant discussion of the consistency of the US steel safeguard measures with the SA in Chapter 14 *infra*.

841 Article 4.1 of the SA provides the identical definitions of those terms. *See* Chapters 4 and 5 *supra* for the relevant discussion.

factors other than increased imports are causing injury to the domestic industry at the same time, such injury shall not be attributed to increased imports."[842]

12.17 *Procedural Requirements: Petition, Adjustment Plan, and Investigation.* A petition requesting a safeguard measure may be filed by "an entity, including a trade association, firm, certified or recognized union, or group of workers, which is representative of an industry" (Section 202(a)(1)). The petition must also specify the purpose for which a safeguard measure is sought. Those purposes may include "facilitating the orderly transfer of resources to more productive pursuits, enhancing competitiveness, or other means of adjustment to new conditions of competition" (Section 202(a)(2)(A)). The petitioner may also request provisional relief (Section 202(a)(2)(B)). The USITC promulgated detailed safeguard investigation rules, which include the petition process.[843]

12.18 Section 202(a)(4)–(7) provides for the submission of an adjustment plan by the petitioner. Although the submission of an adjustment plan is not required, the petitioner may submit a plan to facilitate adjustment to competition with imports. Before its submission, the petitioner may request a consultation with the United States Trade Representative ("USTR") on the adequacy of the plan.[844] The existence of an adequate adjustment plan would apparently support the position of the petitioner.

12.19 Section 202(b)(1)(A) provides that the USITC may also initiate a safeguard investigation at the request of the President or the USTR, by the resolution of either the Committee on Ways and Means of the House of Representatives or the Committee on Finance of the Senate, or on its own motion. The USITC is required to make its determination within 120 days from the petition or request as stated above (150 days for an extraordinarily complicated case). An additional 60 days are added in each of those cases, if the petition alleges that critical circumstances exist. Public hearings are also required during the investigation (Section 202(b)(3)).

12.20 Section 202(a)(8) regulates handling of confidential information, which was added by Section 301(a) of the Uruguay Round Agreements Act to implement the results of the Uruguay Round negotiations. It provides in relevant part:

842 A commentator observed that the non-attribution requirement has been a persistent source of difficulty for the United States and proposed an economic method that attributes injury to various factors as a way to comply with the SA requirement. Irwin, *supra* note 428.

843 19 CFR Part 206.

844 Trade Act of 1974, Section 202(a)(5).

> The Commission may request that parties providing confidential business information furnish non-confidential summaries thereof or, if such parties indicate that the information in the submission cannot be summarized, the reasons why a summary cannot be provided. If the Commission finds that a request for confidentiality is not warranted and if the party concerned is either unwilling to make the information public or to authorize its disclosure in generalized or summarized form, the Commission may disregard the submission.[845]

12.21 The SA also adopts this provision verbatim and authorizes national authorities to request parties providing confidential information to furnish non-confidential summaries and to disregard the information if the authorities find that a request for confidentiality is not warranted and if the party concerned is either unwilling to make the information public or to authorize its disclosure in generalized or summary form.[846]

12.22 *Provisional Measure*. Provisional relief is available with respect to imports of perishable agricultural products or citrus products provided that the product was subject to monitoring by the USITC for not less than 90 days (Section 202(d)(1)). Such monitoring may be requested with respect to a perishable agricultural product or citrus product. Provisional measures are also available for any other product in critical circumstances where delay in taking action would cause irreparable damage to a domestic industry (Section 202(d)(2)).

12.23 The USITC determines whether the application of a provisional measure is warranted within 21 days of receiving the request for perishable agricultural products or citrus products, 60 days for any other product in critical circumstances. The President makes the final determination on the application of a provisional measure within 7 days of receiving a report from the USITC for perishable agricultural products or citrus products and 30 days for any other product in critical circumstances. The period of a provisional relief cannot exceed 200 days where it is applied to critical circumstances (Section 202(d)(2)(D)) but no time limit is specified for provisional measures applied with respect to perishable and citrus products. The USITC is obliged to give preference to tariff measures as opposed to quantitative restrictions (Sections 202(d)(1)(E), 202(d)(2)(D)).

12.24 The SA authorizes provisional safeguard measures for critical circumstances, whether or not the product is perishable or citrus. These special provisions for agricultural products seem unnecessary since the Agreement on Agriculture

845 Trade Act of 1974, Section 202(a)(8).

846 Article 3.2 of the SA. *See* discussion *supra* Section 6.1 for relevant discussion.

provides special safeguard measures which may be invoked based on either import increase or import price reduction without an injury test.[847] In fact, the United States has not invoked this provision since the implementation of the special safeguards under the Agreement on Agriculture, and instead has actively used the special safeguard measures under the Agreement on Agriculture. The provisions for provisional measures invoked on the basis of critical circumstances seem consistent with the provisions of Article 6 of the SA, except that the SA authorizes only tariff increases and not quantitative restrictions for the application of a provisional measure. Section 202(d)(2)(D) does not expressly prohibit quantitative restrictions.

USITC Recommendation. The USITC is obligated to make a recommendation for relief if it makes an affirmative injury determination (Section 202(e)). The recommendation may include the application of increased tariffs, the imposition of quantitative restrictions, or a combination of both. A public hearing is also required prior to its recommendation (Section 202(e)(5)(A)). The recommendation is decided by a majority vote of the Commissioners, and only those USITC Commissioners who have agreed to the affirmative determination of injury may vote on the proposed recommendation. The USITC is also required to submit a report to the President on its investigation (Section 202(f)). The report includes the injury determination and recommendation and the basis on which they are founded. The short- and long-term effects of the implementation *vs.* non-implementation of the recommended action must be described in the report (Section 202(f)(2)(G)). **12.25**

Application of Safeguard. Section 203(a) provides for the application of a safeguard measure. The President has the final authority on the application of a safeguard. Section 203(a)(1)(A) provides: **12.26**

> After receiving a report under Section 202(f) containing an affirmative finding regarding serious injury, or the threat thereof, to a domestic industry, the President shall take all appropriate and feasible action within his power which the President determines will facilitate efforts by the domestic industry to make a positive adjustment to import competition and provide greater economic and social benefits than costs.

The President must decide on the application of a safeguard measure within 60 days from receiving the USITC report. Section 203(a)(2) lists various economic and political factors to be considered for the President's decision. **12.27**

847 *See* the discussion of SSG in the preceding chapter.

12.28 The President is not bound by the USITC recommendations and may decide to apply a different measure from the action recommended or may even decide not to apply a safeguard measure at all. Section 203(b) obligates the President to report to Congress the reasons for applying a measure that differs from the USITC recommendation or for not applying the measure at all. In such a case, Congress may adopt a joint resolution of disapproval within 90 legislative days.[848]

12.29 Section 203(e) provides limitations on the safeguard measure. The duration of a safeguard cannot exceed four years, extendable only once if the President determines that the measure continues to be necessary to prevent or remedy serious injury; and where there is evidence that the domestic industry is making a positive adjustment to import competition (Section 203(e)(1)(B)).[849] The measure should be taken only to the extent that the cumulative impact of such measure does not exceed the amount necessary to prevent or remedy the serious injury (Section 203(e)(2)).

12.30 Specific limits are imposed on the tariff increases and quantitative restrictions. As to the tariff measures, no more than a 50 percent *ad valorem* tariff increase is permitted. In the case of quantitative restrictions, the quota should be no less than the average quantity or value of such product entering the United States in the most recent three representative years for which data are available, unless there is a clear justification otherwise (Sections 203(e)(3), 202(e)(4)). This limit on the quantitative restrictions is identical to that imposed in the SA. The cap on tariff increases is not found in the SA provision, but the restriction is reasonable since, although tariff increases are generally considered less trade-restrictive than quantitative measures, the prohibitively high tariff rates are still no less restrictive than quantitative measures.

12.31 Section 203(e)(5) requires that if the duration of the measure exceeds one year, it should be gradually phased out at regular intervals. Section 203(e)(7) also requires a certain lapse of time before re-applying a safeguard measure to the same product (i.e., the period equal to the duration of the previous measure or two years after the termination of the measure, whichever is greater; if the previous measure was 180 days or less, one year after the termination of the measure would be acceptable, provided that the measure was not applied more than twice in the previous five-year period). The requirement of liberalization

848 Trade Act of 1974, Section 152.

849 Section 201(b) sets out the criteria for what constitutes a positive adjustment.

as well as the period of non-application is consistent with the relevant provisions of the SA (Articles 7.5 and 7.6).

The Trade Act of 1974 authorizes the President to conduct negotiations with the exporting country concerning the application of safeguard measures. Section 203(a)(3)(E) allows the President to negotiate, conclude, and carry out agreements to limit the export from foreign countries and the import into the United States. This provision is inconsistent with Article 11 of the SA, which prohibits entering into any kind of gray-area measures. Under Article 11.1(b), a Member is not allowed to make an agreement with another Member to limit the export or import of a product. Section 203(f) authorizes the President to suspend or terminate a safeguard action, in whole or in part, in accordance with the agreement with a foreign nation to limit its export to the United States. The President has not entered into such agreements with foreign nations concerning the application of a general safeguard since the implementation of the Agreement on Safeguards, which would have been a gray-area measure prohibited under Article 11 of the SA.[850] **12.32**

Monitoring, Modification and Termination. Section 204 governs monitoring, modification and termination of a safeguard measure. The USITC is obligated to monitor developments after the implementation of a safeguard measure, including the progress and specific efforts to make economic adjustment (Section 204(a)(1)). The USITC must issue a mid-term report for all safeguard measures that exceed three years. The President may reduce, modify, and terminate a safeguard measure under certain conditions in which the domestic industry fails to make economic adjustment or the economic circumstances change so as to impair the effectiveness of the safeguard action (Section 204(b)). The President exempted a number of products from the steel safeguard measures after reviews.[851] **12.33**

Section 204 also authorizes an extension of a safeguard measure following the USITC's determination of its necessity. The evidence of a positive adjustment is required for the extension (Section 204(a)). A positive adjustment is defined under Section 201(b)(1), which states that there is a positive adjustment where (i) the domestic industry is able to compete with imports or (ii) resources are transferred to other productive pursuits. Section 201(b)(2) also provides **12.34**

850 The measures cited in Chapter 9.1, the 1996 and 2006 United States – Canada Softwood Lumber Agreements, the 2005 United States – China Textile Agreement, and the 2018 Steel and Aluminum Quota Agreements, were not made in the context of the application of a general safeguard. *See* discussion Chapter 9.1 *supra*.

851 *See* Chapter 14 *infra* for the relevant discussion.

that under a positive adjustment, dislocated workers in the troubled domestic industry experience an orderly transition to productive pursuits. Section 201(2) envisages that the size and the composition of the domestic industry may change after the adjustment process. The USITC is also required to evaluate the effectiveness of the applied measure (Section 204(d)).

12.35 *USMCA Implementation Provisions.* Imports from the members of the United States–Mexico–Canada Agreement (USMCA), which replaced the NAFTA since July 2020, may be exempted from the application of a safeguard measure by operation of certain USMCA provisions. Under Section 301(a) of the USMCA Implementation Act, the USITC is obligated to determine whether (1) imports from a USMCA country, considered individually, account for a substantial share of total imports, and (2) those imports contribute importantly to the serious injury or threat thereof caused by imports. Under Section 302 of the Act, the President is required to exclude the imports from a USMCA country from a safeguard measure if the President determines that those imports do not account for a substantial share of total imports or that they do not contribute importantly to serious injury or threat thereof.

12.36 What are the criteria for the exemption conditions, "substantial share" and "important contribution to injury"? Section 301(b) of the Act provides that imports from a USMCA country do not account for a substantial share of total imports if that country is not among the top five suppliers of the imported product, measured in terms of import share during the most recent three-year period. The Section also provides that the imports from a USMCA country are not considered to contribute importantly to serious injury or its threat if the growth rate of those imports is apparently lower than that of total imports for the same period. This exemption provision, which also existed in its predecessor NAFTA, has raised a question about the consistency of US safeguard measures with the WTO rules.

12.37 *Consistency of the US Safeguards with the WTO Rules.* As noted above, the concept of safeguards in the world trading system today originates from the US "escape clause." The US safeguard provisions have influenced the provisions of both Article XIX and the Agreement on Safeguards substantially. The current US safeguard provisions precede the Agreement on Safeguards, except to the extent modified by the Uruguay Round Agreement Act. Since the implementation of the WTO, six out of the eight US safeguard measures applied to date have been disputed at the WTO, and all of these disputed measures but one have been found inconsistent with the WTO rules.[852]

Those inconsistencies included, *inter alia*, failure to demonstrate "unforeseen developments," inadequate demonstration of serious injury and causation, improper exclusion of imports from the other NAFTA members, and inadequate notice and consultations. Chapters 3 to 9 above provide a detailed discussion of the Panel and Appellate Body findings on those issues. Some of those problems have been caused by the inconsistencies in the US statutory provisions with the WTO requirements. **12.38**

For instance, the USMCA implementation provisions obligate the US President to exclude imports from other USMCA members if certain conditions are met. Previous Panels and the Appellate Body found that the exclusion of the NAFTA members from the application of a safeguard measure, after considering imports from all sources for the injury determination including those from the other NAFTA countries, was not consistent with the MFN requirement of Article 2.1.[853] The relevant NAFTA provisions (Sections 311 and 322), which caused inconsistency with the requirement under the SA, have not been revised to remove this inconsistency but instead replicated in Sections 301 and 302 of USMCA verbatim, likely due to the treaty obligations of the United States under the USMCA.[854] As another example, the notifications and consultations offered by the United States in the application of safeguards were also found inadequate to meet the requirements of the SA.[855] Unlike the SA, which includes elaborate provisions on notifications and consultations, the **12.39**

852 *United States – Wheat Gluten, United States – Lamb Meat, United States – Line Pipe, United States – Steel products, supra* notes 70, 71, and *United States – Washers, supra* note 70.

853 Chapter 4.4 provides a discussion of the MFN application and the customs union. A question was raised as to whether a Member may exclude imports from another member of the customs union even if it considers imports only from non-member countries for its injury determination. The Panel in Line Pipe found that GATT Article XXIV provides a legal ground for such exclusion. The Appellate Body did not rule on this question, but it seems to have approved the exemption provided that the requirement of parallelism is met: it found that any gap between the scope of injury assessment and the scope of safeguard measure is justified if the Member establishes explicitly that imports from sources covered by the measure satisfy the conditions for the application of a safeguard measure as set out in Article 2.1. *United States – Line Pipe, supra* note 71, para. 181, quoting its previous decision in *United States – Wheat Gluten, supra* note 71, para. 98.

854 Article 10.1 of the USMCA provides in relevant part: "Any Party taking an emergency action under Article XIX and the Safeguards Agreement shall exclude imports of a good from each other Party from the action unless: (a) imports from a Party, considered individually, account for a substantial share of total imports; and (b) imports from a Party considered individually, or in exceptional circumstances imports from Parties considered collectively, contribute importantly to the serious injury, or threat thereof, caused by imports."

855 For instance, the timing of the US notifications and consultations has been considered to be a problem. *See* the relevant discussion of notifications and consultations in Chapter 6 *supra*.

US statutory provisions do not include any requirement pertaining to notification and consultation.

12.40 The provision of Section 203(a)(3)(E) of the Trade Act, which allows the President to negotiate, conclude, and carry out agreements with foreign countries to affect the exports from foreign countries to the United States, is also a potential problem. Although this provision has not been invoked in the context of a general safeguard, it nonetheless contravenes the prohibition of gray-area measures provided under Article 11 of the SA, as discussed above. A comprehensive review of the US safeguard provisions and their modification would seem necessary to ensure compliance of the US measures with the WTO rules.[856]

12.3 EU RULES ON SAFEGUARDS – REGULATION (EU) NO. 2015/478

12.41 The EU safeguard rules are provided in Regulation (EU) No. 2015/478 (hereinafter, "Regulation").[857] The Regulation replaces the old EC rules on safeguards (Council Regulation 260/2009, Council Regulation 3285/94, and Regulation 288/82). The Regulation provides Union-wide safeguard measures as well as surveillance action taken on behalf of its Member States against imports from third countries. The Commission undertakes an investigation for a safeguard measure. The Regulation consists of 27 articles in six chapters: General Principles (Chapter I); Union Information and Consultation Procedure (Chapter II); Union Investigation Procedure (Chapter III); Surveillance (Chapter IV); Safeguard Measures (Chapter V); Final Provisions (Chapter VI). The remainder of this chapter examines EU safeguard provisions.

12.42 *General Coverage*. Article 1 sets forth the general coverage of the Regulation. The Regulation applies to imports of all products, except some textile products

856 A commentator, however, observed that there was, at best, a questionable level of political motivation to amend US domestic law to bring it into line with Appellate Body safeguard decisions. Daniel B. Pickard and Tina Potuto Kimble, "Can U.S. Safeguard Actions Survive WTO Review? Section 201 Investigations in International Trade Law" (2007) 29 *Loyola L.A. International Law and Comparative Law Review* 43–59. As of April 2025, the US safeguard legislation has not been amended.

857 The previous version of this book discussed Council Regulation No. 260/2009, which was then the EU rules on safeguards. The EU has since then amended the rules and enacted Regulation (EU) No. 2015/478, which is the current EU rules on safeguard measures. Edwin Vermulst and Folkert Graafsma offer an overview of EU safeguard law and practice up to 2018. Edwin Vermulst and Folkert Graafsma, "EU Safeguard Law and Practice: 1995–2018" (2018) 13(9) *Global Trade and Customs Journal* 355–375.

covered by Regulation (EC) 517/94 and the products from certain countries listed in Regulation (EC) 625/2009. The Regulation specifies that no quantitative restriction other than safeguards may be imposed on imports (Article 1.2) and is therefore the only European authority on the general quantitative import restrictions.

Consultation. Member States of the EU (hereinafter, "Member States") are obligated to inform the EU Commission (hereinafter, "Commission") should the trend in imports call for surveillance or safeguard measures (Article 2). The new consultation procedure, required for the application of a safeguard measure, specifies that the Commission is to be assisted by a Committee on Safeguards—a committee within the meaning of Regulation (EU) No. 182/2011—composed of representatives of the Member States (Article 3.1). The consultation process follows the procedures set out in Regulation 182/2011, which establishes how the European Union adopts acts requiring uniform implementation conditions, particularly when such acts are subject to oversight by the Member States.[858] **12.43**

Investigation. Articles 4–9 provide for the investigation procedure for the application of a safeguard measure. The investigation determines whether imports of the product in question are causing or threatening to cause serious injury to the Union producers. Article 4.3 provides the definitions of "serious injury," "threat of serious injury," and "Union producers." Those definitions are consistent with the SA definitions under Article 4.1.[859] **12.44**

The Commission determines the initiation of the investigation within one month of receipt of information from a Member State and publishes a notice in the Official Journal of the European Union (Article 5.1). The interested parties are given an opportunity to present their views and opinions (Article 5.1). These parties may also inspect all relevant, non-confidential information used in connection to the investigation and may also communicate their views on the information to the Commission (Article 5.4). If the Commission considers that the Union surveillance or safeguard measures are necessary, the decision has to be made within nine months from the initiation of the investi- **12.45**

858 Regulation (EC) No. 182/2011, Article 1.

859 Article 4.3 of the Regulation provides, "The following definitions shall apply: (a) 'serious injury' means a significant overall impairment in the position of Union producers; (b) 'threat of serious injury' means serious injury that is clearly imminent; (c) 'Union producers' means the producers as a whole of like or directly competing products operating within the territory of the Union, or those whose collective output of like or directly competing products constitutes a major proportion of the total Union production of those products."

gation. This nine-month limit may be extended by a maximum of two months in exceptional circumstances (Article 6.3).

12.46 *Provisional Safeguard Measures.* Article 7 provides for provisional safeguard measures. Provisional safeguard measures may be applied where two conditions are met: (i) critical circumstances exist where delay would cause damage which would be difficult to repair, making immediate action necessary; and (ii) a preliminary determination provides clear evidence that increased imports have caused or are threatening to cause serious injury (Article 7.1). The maximum duration is 200 days and the provisional measures can only be applied in the form of tariff increases. Those requirements are in line with the provisions of Article 6 of the SA regulating provisional measures.

12.47 *Confidentiality.* Article 8 requires protection of confidential information submitted for the investigation. While the Commission is required to meet a request for confidentiality, it may disregard any information if such request for confidentiality is not justified. Article 8 also includes the definition of confidential information. It provides, "Information shall in any case be considered to be confidential if its disclosure is likely to have a significantly adverse effect upon the supplier or the source of such information" (Article 8.4). The SA also regulates handling of confidential information (Article 3.2), but it does not provide a definition of confidential information.

12.48 *Injury Determination.* Article 9 specifies factors to consider for the injury assessment: volume of imports (including increases in either absolute or relative terms), price of imports, production, capacity utilization, stocks, sales, market share, prices (i.e., depression of prices or prevention of price increases which would normally have occurred), profits, return on capital employed, cash flow, and employment. The Regulation includes all of the injury factors listed in the SA and more. The factors such as price, return on capital, and cash flow are not specified in Article 4.2(a) of the SA. In *Korea – Dairy Products*, the EU argued that price analysis is required under the provision of the SA, which was not subsequently accepted by the Panel.[860] This EU argument appears to have been influenced by its own requirement for price analysis.

12.49 Where a threat of serious injury is alleged, the Commission also examines whether it is clearly foreseeable that a particular situation is likely to develop into actual injury (Article 9.2). The following elements are considered: rate of

860 *Korea – Dairy Products, supra* note 70, paras. 7.51–7.52.

increase of the exports to the Union, export capacity of the exporting country, and likelihood that capacity will be used to export to the Union (Article 9.2).

Surveillance. Surveillance is a monitoring system, which may be adopted where an increase in imports threatens to cause injury to Union producers (Article 10). The Regulation provides for both retrospective and prior surveillance (Article 10.1). The period of surveillance expires at the end of the second six-month period following the six months in which the surveillance measure was introduced unless stipulated otherwise in the decision to conduct surveillance (Article 10.3). A surveillance document is required for imports subject to surveillance. The document is for the purpose of monitoring imports and cannot be used to curtail imports. Competent national authorities are obligated to issue a surveillance document free of charge within five working days from receiving a declaration by any Union importer (Article 11.1). The Regulation includes a model form of the surveillance document in Annex I and also limits the extent of information required for the importer's application for surveillance documents except where the decision to impose surveillance provides otherwise (Article 11.2). Member States are obligated to communicate to the Commission on a monthly basis the details of imports and, in the case of prior surveillance, the total value (calculated on the basis of cif prices) and the quantities of imports (Article 14.1). **12.50**

Application of Safeguard. If the Commission, acting at the request of a Member State or on its own initiative, determines that a product is imported into the Union in such greatly increased quantities and/or on such terms or conditions as to cause, or threaten to cause, serious injury to Union producers, the Commission may (a) limit the period of the validity of surveillance documents; (b) require an import authorization, the granting of which shall be governed by such provisions and subject to such limits as the Commission shall lay down (Article 15.1). These measures are to be taken immediately. The Commission may exceptionally authorize the application of surveillance or safeguard measures limited to one or more regions of the Union where the injury or its threat is found in those regions (Article 16). **12.51**

Where a quota is imposed, its level should not be set lower than the average level of imports over the last three representative years for which statistics are available unless a different level is necessary to prevent or remedy serious injury (Article 15.3). The provision is consistent with the minimum quota requirement under Article 5.1 of the SA. The quota allocation is in principle decided by agreement among the suppliers with substantial interests. Should no agreement be reached, the quota is determined in proportion to the share **12.52** of imports subject to consideration of any specific factors which may have affected or may be affecting the trade in the product (Article 15.4). The Union may depart from this method of allocation if imports originating in one or more supplier countries have increased in a disproportionate percentage in relation to the total increase of imports (Article 15.4). As discussed in Chapter 2, the departure from the MFN quota allocation was demanded by the EU during the Uruguay Round in return for its compromise to accept the MFN principle in the application of a safeguard measure.

12.53 *Preferential Treatment.* The EU rules also provide for preferential treatment for developing countries. A safeguard measure is not applied to a developing country Member of the WTO so long as that Member's import share does not exceed 3 percent, provided that developing country Members with an import share of less than 3 percent collectively account for not more than 9 percent of the total imports (Article 18). The provision is identical to the relevant provisions of the SA (Article 9).

12.54 *Duration.* The duration of a safeguard measure, as well as the conditions for its extension, is also consistent with the provisions of the SA. The maximum period of a safeguard is four years, extendable once, and the total period cannot exceed eight years (Article 19). The measure needs to be liberalized progressively if its duration exceeds one year. The evidence of adjustment, as well as the continued necessity of the measure, should be demonstrated for its extension. The required lapse of time before a re-application of a safeguard measure to the same product is also identical to that provided in the SA (Article 22): that is, the period equal to the duration of the previous measure, no less than two years, must lapse.

12.55 *Examination of the Measure.* Once a safeguard measure is applied or surveillance is imposed, the Commission may, either at the request of a Member State or on the initiative of the Commission, (a) examine the effects of the measure; (b) determine whether and in what manner it is appropriate to accelerate the pace of liberalization; and (c) ascertain whether its application is still necessary (Article 20.1). This examination should be conducted no later than the mid-point of the measure if its duration exceeds three years. Where the Commission considers that the measure should be revoked or amended, it shall revoke or amend the measure (Article 20.2).

12.56 *Evaluation.* No apparent inconsistency is found between the current provisions of the Regulation and those of the SA. However, the Regulation lacks some key provisions of the SA, including those pertaining to notifications and consultations. The causal link between increased imports and injury is not elaborated in the Regulation: that is, the non-attribution requirement provided in Article 4.2(b) of the SA is absent. The Regulation does not specifically prohibit gray-area measures as provided in Article 11 of the SA. The Final Provisions of the Regulation sets out that the Regulation is not to preclude the fulfillment of obligations arising from agreements between the Union and third countries (Article 24.1). Obviously, such obligations cannot include those arising from an agreement amounting to gray-area measures prohibited under Article 11 of the SA.

After its accession to the WTO, the EU (formerly EC) had not applied a safeguard measure until 2002[861] and had remained vigilant against the application of safeguard measures. The EC challenged the safeguard measure applied by Korea on the imports of dairy products, although exports did not even fill the quota levels assigned by Korea.[862] The EC brought five of the nine safeguard disputes to dispute settlement panels until March 2013, but the number decreased to two challenges for the next ten years. The initial practice against the application of safeguard measures changed since its own application of a provisional safeguard measure and a subsequent definitive measure on steel products,[863] which were taken in response to the controversial US steel safeguard measures in 2002. The EU since then adopted three additional definitive safeguard measures as of April 2024.[864] Chapter 14 provides a discussion of the controversial EC and the US steel safeguard measures and examines their consistency with the WTO rules. **12.57**

861 *See* Vermulst, Pernaute, and Lucenti, *supra* note 111.

862 For the background of the case, *see Korea – Dairy Products*, *supra* note 70.

863 WTO docs. G/SG/N/7/EEC/1 (April 2, 2002), G/SG/N/10/EEC/1 (September 11, 2002). Commission Regulation (EC) No 560/2002 of March 27, 2002, as amended by Commission Regulation (EC) No 950/2002 of June 3, 2002, and Commission Regulation (EC) No 1287/2002 of July 15, 2002. The EC has applied three additional safeguard measures since then. WTO docs. G/SG/N/10/EEC/2 (November 6, 2003), G/SG/N/10/EEC/3 (August 16, 2004), G/SG/N/10/EU/1 (January 4, 2019). For a further discussion of the application of safeguards by EC, *see* Vermulst, Pernaute, and Lucenti, *supra* note 111. The EC's analysis of causation was considered insufficient to justify its safeguards. *Id.*

864 *Id.*

13

REGIONAL TRADE AGREEMENTS AND SAFEGUARD MEASURES

13.1 INTRODUCTION: PROLIFERATION OF RTAS

13.01 Alongside the multilateral trade agreements under the auspices of the WTO, which provide legal disciplines on international trade for 166 countries,[865] there also exist a number of regional trade agreements (RTAs)[866] agreed between two or more countries as reciprocal trade agreements on preferential terms.[867] As of January 22, 2025, 615 RTAs were notified to the WTO.[868] Of these, 373 were in force. RTAs today not only set forth trade liberalization for the signatory countries, but also provide rules on trade in various areas, including trade remedy measures such as safeguard measures, rules of origin, trade-related intellectual property rights, investment, and government procurement. Since virtually all of the WTO Members have joined one or more RTAs, the rules provided by RTAs comprise an important part of the global legal disciplines applicable to international trade, along with the WTO legal disciplines.[869]

865 As of April 2025, *see* WTO, *supra* note 791.

866 Most RTAs are also free trade agreements (FTAs), so the terms "RTA" and "FTA" are used interchangeably in this chapter.

867 GATT Article XXIV authorizes RTAs under certain conditions. *See* Mitsuo Matsushita and Y.S. Lee, "Proliferation of Free Trade Agreements and Some Systemic Issues – In Relation to the WTO Disciplines and Development Perspectives" (2008) 1(1) *The Law and Development Review* 29–34. *See also* Yong-Shik Lee, "Reconciling RTAs with the WTO Multilateral Trading System: Case for a New Sunset Requirement on RTAs and Development Facilitation" (2011) 45 *Journal of World Trade* 625–647.

868 For more information on statistics on RTAs, *see* WTO, *Regional Trade Agreements*, available at: http://www.wto.org/english/tratop_e/region_e/region_e.htm [https://perma.cc/C78W-EP6M].

869 *See* Matsushita and Lee (2008), *supra* note 867, pp. 23–25 and Lee (2011), *supra* note 867, pp. 629–631.

Many of these rules, set by hundreds of RTAs, are not identical and also show significant differences from the WTO legal disciplines.[870] This creates potential conflicts between the WTO disciplines and RTAs, as well as among different RTAs.[871] For a WTO Member which is also a signatory of RTAs, a formidable amount of administrative tasks will create a dilemma where it has to deal with, for instance, multiple rules of origin among the RTAs. The Member may also have to face the forum selection issue where a trade issue with its trading partner can be addressed by different forums applying different substantive and procedural rules, which might therefore lead to a different outcome.[872] The multiplicity of trade rules created by hundreds of RTAs may also undermine the regulatory stability of international trade and erode the position of WTO disciplines as a global legal framework for international trade.[873] **13.02**

Many RTAs include provisions on safeguards. This chapter reviews safeguard provisions in major RTAs in comparison with SA rules. It also examines whether the co-existence of the safeguard provisions in WTO disciplines and those in RTAs creates any conflict. **13.03**

13.2 SAFEGUARD PROVISIONS IN RTAS

Origin. The first safeguard provision in RTA traces back to the "escape clause" of the United States Reciprocal Trade Agreement of 1942 with Mexico. The relevant clause provided: **13.04**

> If, as a result of unforeseen development and of the concession granted on any article enumerated and described in the Schedules annexed to this Agreement, such article is being imported in such increased quantities and under such conditions as to cause or threaten serious injury to domestic producers of like or similar articles, the Government of either country shall be free to withdraw the concession, in whole or in part, or to modify it to the extent and for such time as may be necessary to prevent such injury."[874]
> This clause, which enables the importing member country of the Agreement to adopt a safeguard measure against injurious imports from the other, was a model for GATT Article XIX, which provided the first multilateral rules on safeguards.[875]

---

870 Lee (2011), *supra* note 867, pp. 631–635.

871 *Id.*

872 *Id.*

873 *Id.*

874 Agreement on Reciprocal Trade, December 23, 1942, US–Mexico, Article XI, 57 Stat. 833, 845–866. The use of the term "escape clause," referring to a provision for safeguard measures, seems justifiable since the provision allows parties to the trade agreement to "escape" from their commitments made in their import concessions.

875 For the relevant discussion, *see* Chapter 2.1 *supra*.

13.05 Many subsequent RTAs have also adopted safeguard provisions, as discussed below.

13.06 *Rationale.* The rationale of adopting safeguard provisions in RTAs is analogous to that applied for SGs, discussed in Chapter 1. Trade liberalization by RTAs may cause injurious import surges which may lead to serious problems such as substantial unemployment in the affected domestic industry. Thus, it stands to reason that RTAs provide for a temporary import restraining measure to address the problems ("regional safeguard measures" or "RSGs"[876]), buying the affected industry some time to make necessary adjustments. Thus, the rationale for RSGs is to address serious problems associated with import surges caused by the trade liberalization afforded by RTAs, additional to that agreed on a multilateral basis.[877] For example, if an RTA between two countries removes a 10 percent tariff *ad valorem* on automobiles which has been applied on a MFN basis, then either signatory country may subsequently adopt an RSG against the imports of automobiles from the other signatory country, but only for the injury of the domestic industry caused by the removal of the 10 percent tariff *ad valorem*. As such, RSGs are distinguished from SGs in that they are inherently selective, to address the problems associated with the additional trade liberalization afforded by the relevant RTAs only. The remainder of this section examines safeguard provisions of select RTAs[878] in comparison with the corresponding SA provisions.

---

876 RSGs include safeguard measures provided in bilateral trade agreements (bilateral safeguard measures) as well as in other types of regional trade agreements with more than two member countries.

877 Thus RSGs may be considered mechanisms for adjusting the pace of further liberalization once FTA parties implement the tariff elimination plan. Won-Mog Choi, "FTAs and Safeguard Norms: Their Variation and Compatibility" (2011) 6 *Asian Journal of WTO and International Health Law and Policy* 81–108, at 105.

878 The 17 referenced RTAs include: Regional Comprehensive Economic Partnership (enacted in 2022, "RCEP"); United States–Mexico–Canada Agreement (replacing NAFTA in 2020, "USMCA"); Comprehensive and Progressive Agreement for Trans-Pacific Partnership (2018, "CPTPP"); Free Trade Agreement the United States of America and the Republic of Korea (enacted in 2012, hereinafter "US–Korea"); Free Trade Agreement between the European Community and its Member States, of the one part, and the Republic of Korea, of the other part (2011, "EU–Korea"); Convention Establishing the European Free Trade Association (1960, amended 2001, "EFTA"); Agreement on the Common Effective Preferential Tariff Scheme For the ASEAN Free Trade Area (1993, "AFTA"); Economic Partnership, Political Coordination and Cooperation Agreement between the European Community and its Member States, of the one part, and the United Mexican States, of the other part (2000, "EU–Mexico," safeguard provisions included in the Interim Agreement); Free Trade Agreement the United States of America and Australia (2005, "US–Australia"); Australia–New Zealand Closer Economic Relations Trade Agreement (1983, "Australia–New Zealand"); Free Trade Agreement the United States of America and the Republic of Singapore (2004, "US–Singapore"); Agreement Between Japan and the United Mexican States for the Strengthening of the Economic Partnership (2005, "Japan–Mexico"); Agreement between Japan and Republic of Singapore for a New-Age Economic Partnership (2002, "Japan–Singapore"); Free Trade Agreement between the Government of the Republic of Korea and the Government of the Republic of Chile (2004, "Korea–Chile"); Free Trade Agreement between the Government of the Republic of Korea and the Government of the Republic of Singapore (2005, "Korea–Singapore"); Framework Agreement on Comprehensive Economic Cooperation

Conditions of Invocation. Safeguard provisions in RTAs set conditions for the invocation of an RSG. US–Korea provides that an RSG is applicable "[i]f, as a result of the reduction or elimination of a customs duty under this Agreement, an originating good of the other Party is being imported into the territory of a Party in such increased quantities, in absolute terms or relative to domestic production, and under such conditions that the imports of such originating good from the other Party constitute a substantial cause of serious injury, or threat thereof, to a domestic industry producing a like or directly competitive good."[879] **13.07**

US–Korea sets out three conditions for the application of a safeguard measure: (1) an increase in imports; (2) serious injury or threat thereof to domestic producers of like or similar articles; and (3) the causal relationship between increased imports and injury. This is consistent with the SA, which sets out identical requirements for the invocation of a SG.[880] **13.08**

It bears mentioning that, unlike in the early US escape clause,[881] the phrase "as a result of unforeseen developments"[882] is omitted from the RSG provisions in US–Korea. This phrase was adopted in GATT Article XIX, and there has been a substantial controversy as to whether the phrase should impose an affirmative legal obligation on the importing country applying a safeguard measure.[883] Its explicit omission removes this ambiguity. **13.09**

Most of the referenced RTAs[884] set out identical requirements, except Korea–Chile and USMCA, which do not have separate RSG provisions, and EFTA, which allows a member state to adopt a unilateral measure on a broader basis **13.10**

Between ASEAN and the People's Republic of China (2003, "China–ASEAN"); The Dominican Republic–Central America–United States Free Trade Agreement (2006, "CAFTA–DR"). RSGs in some of the cited RTAs, including Japan–Singapore, China–ASEAN, and CAFTA–DR, have expired, and their provisions are referenced for a comparative purpose. RSGs in some other cited RTAs, such as US–Korea, EU–Korea, US–Australia, and US–Singapore, can be adopted only with the consent of the other party since the transition periods have expired.

879 Article 10.1, US–Korea.

880 Article 2.1 of the SA provides: "A Member may apply a safeguard measure to a product only if that Member has determined, pursuant to the provisions set out below, that such product is being imported into its territory in such increased quantities, absolute or relative to domestic production, and under such conditions as to cause or threaten to cause serious injury to the domestic industry that produces like or directly competitive products."

881 *Supra* note 874.

882 *Id.*

883 For further discussion of the "unforeseen development" clause, *see* Chapter 3.2 *supra*.

884 *Supra* note 878.

on societal, economical, and environmental grounds, without any reference to an increased import, injury, or causal link.[885]

13.11 As to the requisite increase in imports, two of the referenced RTAs, Japan–Mexico and Japan–Singapore, allow only an increase in imports in absolute terms as a basis of invoking an RSG.[886] The other referenced RTAs either specifically allow an increase in imports in both absolute and relative terms, as in the SA,[887] or do not regulate at all.

13.12 On the injury criteria, most of the referenced RTAs – except Korea–Chile and EFTA, as discussed above – require "serious injury" or "threat of serious injury" as the SA.[888] "Serious injury" is defined as "a significant overall impairment in the position of a domestic industry,"[889] and it is considered a higher level of injury than that required for anti-dumping measures or countervailing measures.[890] On specific injury factors, Article 4.2(a) of the SA lists eight injury factors, including the rate and amount of the increase in imports of the product concerned in the absolute and relative terms, the share of the domestic market taken by increased imports, changes in the level of sales, production, productivity, capacity utilization, profits and losses, and employment. All of the referenced RTAs entered into after 1995, except EU–Mexico, incorporate the SA provision specifying these injury factors. Others, including EFTA, AFTA, EU–Mexico, and Australia–New Zealand, do not regulate on the injury factors.

13.13 On the causal link, US–Korea requires "a substantial cause," which is defined as "a cause that is important and not less than any other cause."[891] The SA does not provide any definition for the required cause, but Article 4.2(b) sets out the non-attribution requirement that "[w]hen factors other than increased imports are causing injury to the domestic industry at the same time, such injury shall

885 EFTA provides in relevant part, "If serious economic, societal or environmental difficulties of a sectorial or regional nature liable to persist are arising, a Member State may unilaterally take appropriate measures," *cited in* Akira Kotera and Tomofumi Kitamura, *On the Comparison of Safeguard Measures of Free Trade Agreements*, RIETI Discussion Paper Series 07-E-017 (March 2007), Table 2: Actual Regulations of the Selected Bilateral Safeguard Clauses.

886 Kotera and Kitamura, *supra* note 885, Table 2.

887 Article 2.1 of the SA provides in relevant part, "that such product is being imported into its territory in such increased quantities, absolute or relative to domestic production…."

888 Australia–New Zealand uses the term "severe material injury" and "an imminent and demonstrable threat" which does not appear to be distinguished from "serious injury" and "threat of serious injury."

889 SA Article 4.1, US–Korea, Article 10.6.

890 "Material injury" is required for the invocation of anti-dumping measures and countervailing measures, which is considered a lower level of injury than "serious injury" required for a safeguard. *See also supra* note 801.

891 US–Korea, Article 10.6.

not be attributed to increased imports." Of the other referenced RTAs, US–Australia, US–Singapore, Japan–Mexico, Japan–Singapore, Korea–Singapore, US–Korea, and CAFTA–DR require a "substantial cause," and others do not have a definition for the requisite cause. Also, US–Singapore, Japan–Mexico, Japan–Singapore, Korea–Singapore, and China–ASEAN provide a non-attribution requirement such as the SA.[892]

Procedural Requirements. All of the referenced RTAs – except USMCA and Korea–Chile, which have no separate RSG provisions – have some provisions on relevant procedural requirements for the application of an RSG. **13.14**

The majority of the referenced RTAs regulate domestic investigation for the application of an RSG. In particular, RCEP, CPTPP, US–Australia, US–Singapore, Korea–Singapore, China–ASEAN, US–Korea, and EU–Korea adopt relevant SA provisions such as Articles 3 and 4.2(c).[893] Japan–Mexico and CAFTA–DR include more detailed investigation provisions than the relevant SA provisions.[894] Australia–New Zealand requires national investigation authority to provide an opportunity for evidence to be presented from the other party.[895] The other referenced RTAs do not regulate the investigation procedure. **13.15**

---

892 Kotera and Kitamura, *supra* note 885, Table 2.

893 Article 3 of the SA provides:

> 1. A Member may apply a safeguard measure only following an investigation by the competent authorities of that Member pursuant to procedures previously established and made public in consonance with Article X of GATT 1994. This investigation shall include reasonable public notice to all interested parties and public hearings or other appropriate means in which importers, exporters and other interested parties could present evidence and their views, including the opportunity to respond to the presentations of other parties and to submit their views, inter alia, as to whether or not the application of a safeguard measure would be in the public interest. The competent authorities shall publish a report setting forth their findings and reasoned conclusions reached on all pertinent issues of fact and law.
> 2. Any information which is by nature confidential or which is provided on a confidential basis shall, upon cause being shown, be treated as such by the competent authorities. Such information shall not be disclosed without permission of the party submitting it. Parties providing confidential information may be requested to furnish non confidential summaries thereof or, if such parties indicate that such information cannot be summarized, the reasons why a summary cannot be provided. However, if the competent authorities find that a request for confidentiality is not warranted and if the party concerned is either unwilling to make the information public or to authorize its disclosure in generalized or summary form, the authorities may disregard such information unless it can be demonstrated to their satisfaction from appropriate sources that the information is correct.

Article 4.2(c) provides, "The competent authorities shall publish promptly, in accordance with the provisions of Article 3, a detailed analysis of the case under investigation as well as a demonstration of the relevance of the factors examined." For further discussion of the procedural requirements of the SA, *see* Chapter 6 *supra*.

894 *See* Kotera and Kitamura, *supra* note 885, Table 2.

895 *Id.*

13.16 On notification and consultation, US–Korea provides in relevant part, "A Party shall notify the other Party in writing on initiation of an investigation … and shall consult with the other Party as far in advance of applying a safeguard measure as practicable, with a view to reviewing the information arising from the investigation and exchanging views on the measure."[896] Compared to the relevant provision of the SA which requires notification at the beginning of the investigation, at the finding of serious injury, and at the adoption of a safeguard measure,[897] the provision of US–Korea is not as detailed, but as the SA, it also requires a consultation opportunity prior to the application of the measure.[898]

13.17 All the referenced RTAs, again except Korea–Chile, have provisions on notification and consultation. Among them, RCEP, CPTPP, China–ASEAN, and CAFTA–DR incorporate the detailed, three-staged notification provision in the SA.[899]

13.18 *Application of the Measure.* RTAs regulate the form and the extent of the measure, maximum duration, adjustment of the domestic industry, and re-application. On the form and the extent, since RSGs attempt to remedy injury associated with additional trade liberalization, the applicable measure should be increased tariffs, rather than quota, to a level not exceeding the rate of duty applicable to non-RTA member countries on an MFN basis.[900] The SA authorizes both tariff and quota under certain conditions, and it does not stipulate an applicable maximum tariff rate.[901]

13.19 Most of the referenced RTAs, except Korea–Chile, EFTA, and AFTA, stipulate the maximum period of initial application and the extension, ranging from one to three years and from one year to the total maximum period of four years (including initial application), respectively, which are in comparison shorter than the maximum of four years for initial application and another period of

---

896 US–Korea, Article 10.2, para. 1.

897 SA Article 12.1.

898 Article 12.3 of the SA provides, "A Member proposing to apply or extend a safeguard measure shall provide adequate opportunity for prior consultations with those Members having a substantial interest as exporters of the product concerned, with a view to, *inter alia*, reviewing the information provided under paragraph 2, exchanging views on the measure and reaching an understanding on ways to achieve the objective set out in paragraph 1 of Article 8."

899 *Supra* note 897.

900 Most of the referenced RTAs prescribe tariffs as the form of the measure. EFTA and AFTA do not prescribe a form of the measure.

901 However, the SA does subscribe the minimal quota level. Article 7.1 provides in relevant part, "If a quantitative restriction is used, such a measure shall not reduce the quantity of imports below the level of a recent period which shall be the average of imports in the last three representative years for which statistics are available, unless clear justification is given that a different level is necessary to prevent or remedy serious injury."

four years for extension under the SA.[902] Several referenced RTAs, including RCEP, CPTPP, EU–Mexico, US–Australia, US–Singapore, Japan–Mexico, Japan–Singapore, Korea–Singapore, China–ASEAN, US–Korea, and CAFTA–DR, require progressive liberalization of the measure at regular intervals where the expected duration of the measure is over a certain period, mostly over one year, as also applicable in the SA.[903]

On the question of adjustment of the domestic industry, the majority of the referenced RTAs require some evidence of adjustment, as a condition for an extension.[904] The SA also makes references to "adjustment" in relation to the determination of the period of initial application (Article 7.1), as a condition of the extension (Article 7.2), and as for the purpose of the progressive liberalization of the initial measures (Article 7.4).[905] **13.20**

As for re-application of the measure, several referenced RTAs, including CPTPP, US–Korea, NAFTA, US–Australia, US–Singapore, Japan–Singapore, and CAFTA–DR, do not allow re-application of an RSG to the same product. Japan–Mexico requires a period of time equal to the duration of the previous measure or one year for re-application. RCEP requires a period of one year, and EU–Mexico requires a period of three years. China–ASEAN adopts the requirement of the SA, which is a period of time equal to that during which such measure had been previously applied, provided that the period of non-application is at least two years (Article 7.5). [906] **13.21**

---

902 SA Articles 7.1 and 7.2.

903 SA Article 7.4.

904 Those RTAs include US–Australia, US–Singapore, Japan–Mexico, Japan–Singapore, China–ASEAN, EU–Korea, US–Korea, and CAFTA–DR.

905 Article 7 of the SA provides:

1. A Member shall apply safeguard measures only for such period of time as may be necessary to prevent or remedy serious injury and to facilitate *adjustment*. The period shall not exceed four years, unless it is extended under paragraph 2.

2. The period mentioned in paragraph 1 may be extended provided that the competent authorities of the importing Member have determined, in conformity with the procedures set out in Articles 2, 3, 4 and 5, that the safeguard measure continues to be necessary to prevent or remedy serious injury and that there is evidence that the industry is *adjusting*, and provided that the pertinent provisions of Articles 8 and 12 are observed.

…

4. In order to facilitate *adjustment* in a situation where the expected duration of a safeguard measure as notified under the provisions of paragraph 1 of Article 12 is over one year, the Member applying the measure shall progressively liberalize it at regular intervals during the period of application. If the duration of the measure exceeds three years, the Member applying such a measure shall review the situation not later than the mid-term of the measure and, if appropriate, withdraw it or increase the pace of liberalization. A measure extended under paragraph 2 shall not be more restrictive than it was at the end of the initial period, and should continue to be liberalized (emphasis added).

906 Kotera and Kitamura, *supra* note 885, Table 2.

13.22 *Expiration of the Measure, Provisional Measure, Compensation, Dispute Settlement.* Under certain RTAs, all RSGs expire at the end of a transition period. For example, US–Korea disallows application of an RSG beyond the ten-year transition period, except with the consent of the other party.[907] Several other referenced RTAs, including RCEP, CPTPP, EU–Korea, US–Australia, US–Singapore, Japan–Singapore, China–ASEAN, and CAFTA–DR, also include similar provisions stipulating a transition period for the expiration of all RSGs.[908] In contrast, the SA does not provide for a transition period at the end of which safeguard measures expire. The RSGs subject to expiration at the end of a transition period operate as a transitional measure such as TSMs and TSGs in WTO disciplines.[909]

13.23 Some RTAs also provide for provisional measures. US–Korea allows a provisional measure "in critical circumstances where delay would cause damage that would be difficult to repair … pursuant to a preliminary determination by its competent authorities that there is clear evidence that imports of an originating good from the other Party have increased as the result of the reduction or elimination of a customs duty under this Agreement, and such imports constitute a substantial cause of serious injury, or threat thereof, to the domestic industry."[910] The maximum duration of a provisional measure is 200 days.[911] Other referenced RTAs such as RCEP, EU–Korea, EFTA, EU–Mexico, US–Singapore, Japan–Mexico, Korea–Singapore, CAFTA–DR, and US–Australia also allow provisional measures on similar terms. The SA also provides for provisional measures applicable "[i]n critical circumstances where delay would cause damage which it would be difficult to repair … pursuant to a preliminary determination that there is clear evidence that increased imports have caused or are threatening to cause serious injury,"[912] with the maximum duration of 200 days.[913]

13.24 Compensation is another important element of RSGs. US–Korea requires as a condition for the application of a safeguard measure to "afford an opportunity

907 US–Korea, Article 10.2, para. 5.

908 RTAs such as AFTA and Japan–Mexico do not have a transition period and allow member countries to adopt an RSG on a permanent basis subject to any durational and re-application requirement. In EU–Korea, US–Australia, and US–Singapore, RSGs can be applied with the consent of the author party, after the expiry of the transition period.

909 All Transitional Safeguard Measures (TSGs) provided in the Agreement on Textiles and Clothing ceased to exist when the ATC expired on January 1, 2005, and Transitional Product-Specific Safeguard Measures (TSMs) applicable to imports from China only expired on December 11, 2013.

910 US–Korea, Article 10.3, para. 1.

911 *Id.*, para. 3.

912 SA Article 6.

913 *Id.*

for the other Party to consult with it regarding appropriate trade liberalizing compensation in the form of concessions having substantially equivalent trade effects or equivalent to the value of the additional duties expected to result from the measure."[914] If no agreement is made on compensation within 30 days after consultations begin, a retaliatory measure may be applied by suspending the application of concessions that have trade effects substantially equivalent to the safeguard measure,[915] which is to be terminated on the date that the safeguard measure also terminates.[916] It is to be noted that unlike the SA, US–Korea does not provide for suspension of retaliation for a certain period of time in which the safeguard measure is in effect.[917] Most of the other referenced RTAs, including CPTPP and EU–Korea, have similar compensation provisions, but RCEP suspends the retaliation for the first three years during which the RSG is in effect, provided that the measure has been applied as a result of an absolute increase in imports and that it conforms to the terms of RCEP.[918]

On the availability of a dispute settlement procedure, most of the referenced RTAs provide for the built-in dispute settlement procedure for disputes arising from RTAs, including those on RSGs.[919] Disputes on SGs may be referred to the WTO dispute settlement procedure under the DSU.[920] **13.25**

Special Agricultural and Textile Safeguards. Some RTAs have special safeguard provisions applicable to certain agricultural and textile products, reflecting the sensitivity of these products. US–Korea provides special safeguard provisions for certain agricultural products and for certain textiles and apparel. The special agricultural safeguard is applicable where the aggregate volume of imports of a listed good in any year exceeds a predetermined trigger level.[921] The special textile safeguard is applicable on the occurrence of serious damage measured by examination of economic indicators such as output, productivity, utilization of capacity, inventories, market share, exports, wages, employment, domestic prices, profits, and investment.[922] Unlike RSGs, these special safeguards do not require compensation for invocation. In addition to US–Korea, EU–Korea, **13.26**

914 US–Korea, Article 10.4, para. 1.
915 *Id.*, Article 10.4, para. 2.
916 *Id.*, Article 10.4, para. 3.
917 Article 8.3 of the SA provides, "the right of suspension … shall not be exercised for the first three years that a safeguard measure is in effect, provided that the safeguard measure has been taken as a result of an absolute increase in imports and that such a measure conforms to the provisions of this Agreement." For further discussion of compensation and retaliation, *see* Chapter 8 *supra*.
918 RCEP, Article 7.7, para. 5.
919 Kotera and Kitamura, *supra* note 885, Table 2.
920 SA Article 14.
921 US–Korea, Article 3.3.
922 *Id.*, Article 4.1.

AFTA, US–Australia, and CAFTA–DR provide for special agricultural safeguards, and CPTPP, US–Australia, US–Singapore, and CAFTA–DR for textile safeguards. The roles of special agricultural and textile safeguards in RTAs are analogous to those of SSGs and TSMs in WTO disciplines.[923]

13.3 RTAS AND WTO REGIME ON SAFEGUARDS: POTENTIAL CONFLICTS?

13.27 According to one view, RSGs and SGs may be considered two different institutions.[924] The two safeguards operate in different fields – one in the context of RTAs only and the other in the general multilateral trade relations outside RTAs – and a study concluded that there is no scope for conflict between them.[925]

13.28 Two scenarios, however, present potential conflicts between RSGs and SGs.[926] One is where the extent of an RSG is to a level exceeding the rate of duty applicable to non-RTA members on an MFN basis. The measure then suspends "the obligation in whole and in part or to withdraw or modify the concession" under Article XIX(a),[927] invoking the Article and the SA, and all the procedural and substantive requirements for the application of a SG would apply. Such RSGs would also violate the terms of RTAs which prohibit suspension of concessions beyond the MFN rates, but regardless of the RTA violation,[928] the affected Members would have rights to demand modification or withdrawal of the offending measure as inconsistent with the requirements of the general safeguard. Where an RTA does not prescribe the maximum applicable RSG

---

923 For the relevant discussion, *see* Chapter 11 *supra*. As noted, the Agreement on Textiles and Clothing, which provided for TSM, expired on January 1, 2005.

924 Kotera and Kitamura, *supra* note 885, p. 8.

925 *Id.*

926 A study suggested that RSG invocations would be rather rare, in which case the chances for actual conflict might be low. Jo-Ann Crawford, Jo McKeagg, and Julia Tolstova, *Mapping of Safeguard Provisions in Regional Trade Agreements*, WTO Staff Working Paper ERSD-2013-10 (October 21, 2013), p. 39. Commentators also analyzed implications that arise from the interplay of RTAs, safeguards, and dispute settlement. Chad P. Bown and Mark Wu, "Safeguards and the perils of preferential trade agreements: Dominican Republic–Safeguard Measures" (2014) 13(2) *World Trade Review* 179–227. Another study examined a case where RSGs may not be consistent with the terms of SGs such as one that grants special and differential treatment to developing countries. Jia Xu, "One Step Forward and Two Steps Back? Evolution of Bilateral Safeguard Provisions in Preferential Trade Agreements" (2021) 55(3) *Journal of World Trade* 433–452.

927 The "obligation" and "concession" denote the obligation and concession arising from the multilateral negotiations under the WTO regime.

928 Some RTAs such as EFTA and AFTA do not prescribe the permissible tariff rate of an RSG.

rate,[929] RSGs permissible under the RTA may not be consistent with the SA if the applied tariff rate of the RSG is higher than the MFN rate.

Another scenario is where the terms of an RTA require exemption of imports from the application of SGs.[930] Article 10.2 of USMCA provides in relevant part, "Any Party taking an emergency action under Article XIX and the Safeguards Agreement shall exclude imports of a good from each other Party from the action unless: (a) imports from a Party, considered individually, account for a substantial share of total imports; and (b) imports from a Party considered individually, or in exceptional circumstances imports from Parties considered collectively, contribute importantly to the serious injury, or threat thereof, caused by imports."[931] **13.29**

WTO Panels and the Appellate Body repeatedly held that exemption of imports on the cited grounds (then stipulated under NAFTA), as had been done by the United States, is not consistent with the SA provision which requires that the scope of measure must be parallel to the scope of injury examination:[932] i.e., the exemption is justifiable under the SA only if the injury to a domestic industry caused by the imports from non-RTA members alone is serious, and the imports from the RTA members must not be excluded,[933] even if they do not contribute importantly to the injury, once they have been included in the injury assessment.[934] **13.30**

There is also another fundamental regulatory issue arising from the different conditions for the invocation of RSGs and SGs. Nearly all of the WTO Members are members of RTAs, and they may adopt RSGs by the terms of the RTA and SGs by those of the SA.[935] Although RTAs normally prohibit a simultaneous application of both safeguards to the same product,[936] RSGs **13.31**

---

929 *Id.*

930 According to a study, a couple of RTAs definitively exclude imports from the RTA partner in a global safeguard action, and roughly a quarter of RTAs provide for the possible exclusion of the RTA partner, subject to certain criteria, thus discriminating against non-parties. Crawford, McKeagg, and Tolstova, *supra* note 926, pp. 4, 38.

931 USMCA, Article 10.2, para. 1 (formerly NAFTA, Article 802, para. 1).

932 SA Article 2.2.

933 A commentator also pointed out that the exclusion also leads to economically inferior trade diversion in favor of RTA member countries. Dukgeun Ahn, "Foe or Friend of GATT Article XXIV: Diversity in Trade Remedy Rules" (2008) 11(1) *Journal of International Economic Law* 107–133.

934 It is because the imports from the RTA members and the non-RTA members may have *collectively* caused serious injury to the domestic industry. For further discussion, *see* Chapter 4.4 *supra.*

935 RTAs specifically allow member countries to adopt both RSGs and SGs. *See* US–Korea, Article 10.5, para. 1 and EU–Korea, Article 3.7, para. 1.

936 US–Korea, Article 10.5, para. 2 and EU–Korea, Article 3.7, para. 4.

may still be applied under different conditions from those applicable for SGs[937] and the importing country faces varying conditions for the application of a safeguard, depending upon which safeguard rules are invoked.[938]

13.32 It is arguable on the one hand that this difference should not be an issue because the exclusive nature of RTA, whose benefits and obligations apply to the RTA members only, may justify different conditions for the application of an RSG. On the other hand, it is questionable whether a safeguard should be applied under different conditions, even in the context of RTAs, where the rationale for applying a safeguard would not be different: i.e., to afford the domestic industry seriously injured by competition with imports temporary protection to make necessary adjustment.[939] The SA, after long negotiations, has settled on the elaborate procedural and substantive requirements for the application of a safeguard measure, and it may be questioned whether a deviation from this accord, even in the context of RTAs, would be a good policy.

13.33 As discussed in the preceding section, many RTAs adopt corresponding SA provisions, closing the potential regulatory gap between RSGs and SGs.[940] It will be indeed preferable to adopt the SG rules for RSGs, rather than creating different rules which may deviate from the procedural and substantive requirements set by the SA. Otherwise, WTO Members joining multiple RTAs will face a different set of conditions and rules for the application of an RSG, which has a danger of causing regulatory complications and confusion in the system, particularly for developing countries with limited resources and expertise to administer complex trade remedy measures.

13.34 Thus efforts should be made to survey various RSG provisions in existence,[941] to exchange information on different RTAs, and to coordinate different RSG

---

937 *See* the relevant discussion in the preceding section for the various procedural and substantive conditions for the invocation of an RSG among different RTAs.

938 RSGs will be applicable on a selective basis, to imports from the other RTA members only, while SGs must be applied to imports on an MFN basis. SA Article 2.1.

939 *See* Chapter 1.2 *supra* for the relevant discussion of economic justification for safeguards.

940 *See* the relevant discussion in the preceding section.

941 A study by Jo-Ann Crawford, Jo McKeagg, and Julia Tolstova surveyed safeguard provisions on trade in goods in 232 regional trade agreements notified to the WTO up to December 2012. Crawford, McKeagg, and Tolstova, *Mapping of Safeguard Provisions in Regional Trade Agreements*, *supra* note 926. An earlier study also examined twelve RTAs and classified RSGs into 1) no General Safeguard Type (Korea–Chile), 2) Quasi Global Safeguard Type (subdivided into WTO Type: Japan–Singapore, China–ASEAN, Japan–Mexico, US–Australia, US–Singapore, Korea–Singapore; GATT Type: AFTA, Australia–New Zealand; and NAFTA Type: NAFTA), and 3) European Type (EFTA, EU–Mexico). Kotera and Kitamura, *supra* note 885, pp. 26–30. Another study offered a comparison between RSG provisions in ASEAN–Korea Free Trade Agreement with WTO rules. Eva Johan, "Safeguard Measures in the Framework of ASEAN-Korea Free

rules to avoid potential conflict and confusion.[942] Consideration should be given to revising the RSG rules that are not consistent with the SA provisions by adopting relevant SA provisions.[943] Convergence of the various RSG rules to those for SGs (SA provisions) would be a preferable development to achieve regulatory consistency between SGs and RSGs.

Trade Agreement (AKFTA) on Trade in Goods Compare to GATT/WTO" (2015) 12(2) *Indonesian Journal of International Law* 208–221.

942 *See* Matsushita and Lee (2008), *supra* note 867, p. 49.

943 Such revisions might not be necessary where RSG rules provide clearer disciplines. For example, US–Korea clarifies that the cause for the increase in imports must be a "substantial cause," which is defined as a cause that is important and not less than any other cause. US–Korea, Articles 10.1 and 10.6. The SA does not provide a definition for cause.

PART IV

SAFEGUARD REGIME: PRESENT AND FUTURE

14

LESSONS TO REMEMBER

14.1 *US STEEL SAFEGUARD* CASE[944]

14.01 Safeguard measures have been subject to a wide range of views: from one considering them the most protectionist device of all,[945] to one advocating them as an inevitable safety arrangement to maintain and further free trade.[946] Perhaps many also understand both of these aspects about safeguards.[947] As discussed at the beginning of this book, there are controversies about safeguard measures from the economic and political perspectives.[948] At any rate, it is clear that the abuse of safeguard measures would lead to the destabilization of the world trading system and cause serious disruption to trade. The widely publicized steel safeguards, which were adopted by the United States more than two decades ago, illustrate this danger.

14.02 *Application of US Steel Safeguard Measures*. On March 20, 2002, despite widespread international opposition, the United States finally applied controversial safeguard measures, comprising increased tariffs up to 30 percent and a tariff quota, to its imports of a wide range of steel products amounting to 1,310

944 Much of the discussion about the US and the EC safeguard measures is cited from section IV of the author's previous work, "Safeguard Measures: Why Are They Not Applied Consistently with the Rules? – Lessons for Competent National Authorities and Proposal for the Modification of the Rules on Safeguards" (2002) 36 *Journal of World Trade* 666–671. *See also* Y.S. Lee, "Test of Multilateralism in International Trade: U.S. Steel Safeguards" (2004) 25 *Northwestern Journal of International Law and Business* 69–98; Youngjin Jung and Ellen Jooyeon Kang, "Toward an Ideal WTO Safeguards Regime–Lessons from *U.S.-Steel*" (2004) 38(4) *The International Lawyer* 919–944.

945 Bhala and Kennedy, *supra* note 87, p. 897.

946 Dam, *supra* note 63, p. 106.

947 *See* Chapter 1 *supra*.

948 *Id.*

million tons per year.[949] These measures have been remembered as among the most controversial and the most significant trade measures. Until then, a typical safeguard measure had been applied to protect a relatively limited number of domestic products, causing only limited impacts on world trade.[950] The implication of those US measures was felt completely differently from the previous safeguards, as these US safeguards were applied for the protection of a major industry by the largest economy in the world, affecting a massive volume of trade.[951] The magnitude of the US measures was sufficient to alarm a number of trading nations around the world. The worldwide concern about the US measures was amplified as the legal basis for these measures did not appear strong under the SA and their application seemed motivated primarily by political reasons. Many were concerned that it could be a signal of a new protectionism[952] by the Bush Administration, which had already shown signs of unilateralism on a number of international issues.[953]

14.03 Strong opposition was raised against the US safeguards in dozens of capitals across the world, from Brussels to Brasilia and from Seoul to Sydney. Major

---

949 The products subject to the US safeguard measures included slabs, flat steel, hot-rolled bar, cold-finished bar, rebar, certain welded tubular products, carbon and alloy fittings, stainless steel bar, stainless steel rod, tin mill products and stainless steel wire. For the details of the measure, refer to "Proclamation 7529 of March 5, 2002 – To Facilitate Positive Adjustment to Competition from Imports of Certain Steel Products" ("Proclamation") and the "Memorandum of March 5, 2002 – Action Under Section 203 of the Trade Act of 1974 Concerning Certain Steel Products by the President of the US" ("Memorandum"), *Federal Register* Vol. 67, No. 45 (March 7, 2002). Facing major retaliation threats from its major trading partners such as the EC and Japan, the US government subsequently removed a number of products from its safeguards. *Supra* note 575.

950 *See* WTO, *Report (2000) of the Committee on Safeguards to the Council for Trade in Goods*, annex 2, G/L/409 (November 23, 2000) and *Report (2001) of the Committee on Safeguards to the Council for Trade in Goods*, annex 2, G/L/494 (October 31, 2001).

951 The announced US steel safeguards were expected to affect as much as 1.31 billion tons of steel trade per year. Lee (2004), *supra* note 944, p. 71. Also, the steel and aluminum tariffs adopted subsequently by the United States in 2018, considered to be among the largest trade measures, were challenged by some Members as safeguard measures inconsistent with Article XIX and the SA. However, the Panel held that the US measures were not safeguards under Article XIX and the SA. *United States – Steel and Aluminum Products*, *supra* note 70. The United States had invoked Section 232 (authorizing the government to adopt trade measures on national security grounds), rather than Section 201, of the Trade Act of 1972. *See* Yong-Shik Lee, "Three Wrongs Do Not Make a Right: The Conundrum of the U.S. Steel and Aluminum Tariffs" (2019) 18(3) *World Trade Review* 481–501.

952 The EC Commission Reports noted that in the medium term, free trade in the steel sector could be "seriously compromised." Commission of the European Communities, *Report to the Council from the Commission on Steel re-balancing action* (September 24, 2002).

953 Non-participation in the Kyoto Protocol on the environment front, opposition to the International Crime Tribunal, as well as the unilateral repeal of the Missile Treaty with Russia were a few of these examples. Such unilateralism was replicated by the subsequent Trump administration that also adopted unilateral, rule-breaching international trade measures including the cited steel and aluminum tariffs and withdrew unilaterally from the Paris Agreement and the Trans Pacific Partnership Agreement that the preceding US administrations had endeavored to conclude.

steel-producing Members rushed to consultations with the United States and failed to resolve the dispute. Several Members, including the EC, China, Korea, Japan, New Zealand, Switzerland, Norway, and Brazil, requested the establishment of a panel to review the consistency of the US measures with the WTO rules. The panel was subsequently established, and reviewed the biggest panel case up to that date in terms of the number of participants and the volume of trade affected.[954] In addition, several Members, including the EC, Japan, China, Switzerland, and Norway, proposed retaliation against the US measures.[955]

Proliferation of Protection. These controversial US safeguard measures also triggered protectionism in other countries. Fearing diversion of steel products from the protected US market, Members, including the EC, China, Hungary, and Poland, applied provisional safeguard measures while initiating investigations for definitive measures.[956] The EC subsequently made an affirmative injury determination and also decided to apply a definitive safeguard measure on imports of seven steel products.[957] Hungary, China, and Poland also applied definitive safeguards.[958] Canada, whose steel exports were not even subject to the US steel safeguards as a member of the NAFTA, also initiated an investigation for the application of a safeguard measure and subsequently made a positive injury determination.[959] Several other Members, including Chile, the Czech Republic, Mexico, Poland, and Bulgaria, followed their lead and also initiated safeguard investigations. The worst-case scenario, which would have led to a downward spiral of protections one after another, was in sight. This dangerous sign of protectionism created a significant concern for preserving free trade and multilateralism in the world trading system. **14.04**

What caused the US government to apply the controversial safeguard measures, despite significant criticism and resistance both from within the country[960] **14.05**

954 WTO docs. WT/DS248/15, WT/DS249/9, WT/DS251/10, WT/DS252/8, WT/DS253/8, WT/DS254/8, WT/DS258/12, WT/DS259/11 (August 12, 2002).

955 *Supra* note 573.

956 WTO docs. G/SG/N/7/EEC/1 (April 2, 2002); G/SG/N/7/CHN/1 (May 23, 2002); G/SG/N/7/HUN/1 (May 23, 2002).

957 Commission Regulation (EC) No 1694/2002 of September 27, 2002 (imposing definitive safeguard measures against imports of certain steel products). *See also* the EC notification to the Committee on Safeguards, G/SG/N/8/EEC/1, G/SG/N/10/EEC/1 (September 11, 2002).

958 WTO docs. G/SG/N/10/HUN/1 (April 7, 2003), G/SG/N/CHN/1 (November 5, 2002).

959 WTO docs. G.SG/N/6/CAN/1 (April 2, 2002), G/SG/N/8/CAN/1 (July 19, 2002).

960 It was reported that the US Treasury Secretary Paul H. O'Neill stated in off-the-record comments after a dinner speech at the Council on Foreign Relations that he disagreed with the Bush administration's decision to impose tariffs on imported steel and that it would cost more jobs in the United States than it would save. *New York Times*, March 16, 2002, p. A1.

and from the rest of the world? In addition, there seemed no strong economic rationale that the import restrictions would improve the condition of the US steel industry, as the problem with the industry was widely perceived as a long-term structural issue which could not be attributed to increased imports.[961] Did the conditions of the US steel industry in any way warrant the application of emergency import restrictions such as safeguards?

14.06 *Background of US Steel Industry*. The US steel industry, once a glorious workhorse of the United States and of the world economy, has been described as "an industry in crisis." A number of cost factors, including pension burden, inefficient facilities, and outdated production techniques, particularly at old and smaller mills, have been pointed to as reasons for the declining state of the industry. A 2001 report found that prices were then at their lowest level in 20 years.[962] Leading US producers sustained significant losses and no fewer than 18 American steel companies filed for bankruptcy between January 1998 and June 2001. Significant job losses were reported, averaging as many as 5,000 a year since 1990 and increasing.[963]

14.07 Job losses and downward pressure on prices were not unique to the US steel industry. Steel industries throughout the world experienced job losses due mainly to the substantial increase in productivity and the resulting over-capacity. Smaller mills became unprofitable and merged into more sizable ones to improve the scale of economy. Production capacity in the steel industry had been known to exceed production by as much as 20 percent.[964] The existence of over-capacity caused a long-term downward trend in prices and made the condition of the steel industry particularly vulnerable to decreases in demand during general economic recessions.

14.08 The US government has for decades been responsive to calls for assistance from the steel industry. Trade protection and financial subsidies have been generously provided to the industry: for instance, according to 2002 statistics, about one half of the existing 264 anti-dumping actions had been taken on the imports of steel products, although steel accounted for only 2 percent of

---

961 A prominent economist considered that the US measure would not improve the condition of the US steel industry. *See* Robert J. Barro, "Big Steel Doesn't Need Any More Propping Up," *Business Week*, April 1, 2001, p. 24. In fact, the US steel industry remained vulnerable for decades afterwards, necessitating the steel and aluminum tariffs despite a number of protective measures including anti-dumping and countervailing measures. *See* Lee (2019), *supra* note 951.

962 "A tricky business," *Economist*, June 28, 2001, available at: https://www.economist.com/business/2001/06/28/a-tricky-business [https://perma.cc/FE29-LTF5].

963 *Id.*

964 *Id.*

total imports – an additional 35 countervailing measures were also applied to steel products.[965] A study revealed that the steel lobby won at least $16 billion ($21.8 billion in constant 1999 dollars) in federal subsidies for domestic steel makers from US taxpayers with additional billions received from State and local governments.[966]

The subsidies included pension bailouts, tax refunds, environmental regulation exemption subsidies, "Buy America" requirements, and emergency loan guarantee schemes.[967] According to the Commission Report of the European Communities, at least six US steel firms received federal and/or State assistance in the year 2002, including a $250 million federal loan guarantee, a grant of $30 million from State governments, a variety of tax breaks, as well as a State guarantee to a local utility company to ensure that it would recover the costs of providing the power supply for a proposed new electric furnace.[968] **14.09**

Impact of US Steel Safeguards. The extensive protections and subsidies have been referred to as reasons for the delay in the necessary structural change in the steel industry.[969] Given the situation, was there any economic justification to apply import restrictions? It was widely believed that the major problem facing the US steel industry was not imports, which had declined in most categories prior to the application of the US steel safeguards,[970] but the high production cost and the heavy pension obligations faced by the industry. Substantial increases in prices of steel products were observed subsequent to the application of the US safeguard measures: more than 20 percent up for hot rolled coil prices for delivery in the third quarter of 2002, compared to prices in the first quarter.[971] The US steel mills were known to be in the process of increasing production, encouraged by this "hike" in steel price, instead of going through structural adjustment. It was forecast that such production increases **14.10**

965 US International Trade Administration, *Antidumping and Countervailing Duty Statistics, Antidumping and Countervailing Duty Orders in effect as of July 26, 2002* (2002).

966 William H. Barringer and Kenneth J. Pierce, *Paying the Price for Big Steel* (American Institute for International Steel, 2000).

967 *Id.*

968 Commission of the European Communities, *Report to the Council from the Commission on Steel re-balancing action* (July 17, 2002).

969 *See* Dan Ikenson, *Steel Trap: How Subsidies and Protectionism Weaken the U.S. Steel Industry*, Trade Briefing Paper, Center for Trade Policy Studies (March 1, 2002), text available at: http://www.cato.org/sites/cato.org/files/pubs/pdf/tbp-014.pdf [https://perma.cc/CY9D-YGEE].

970 According to the US Census Bureau, US imports of steel products decreased substantially from 34,433,707 metric tons in 2000 to 27,350,808 metric tons in 2001. US Census Bureau, US Imports for Consumption of Steel Products, Exhibit 1: All Steel Products (released February 21, 2002).

971 *Supra* note 968.

would cause the "price bubble" to burst and to further collapse, worsening the situation.[972]

14.11 *Political Consideration*. Many believe that political needs, rather than the clear economic justification for import restrictions, prompted the US safeguard measures. The US steel industry has been known for decades to have a powerful lobby in Washington, DC. The steel industry has a substantial influence on the constituencies of the US administration and exercised pressure on the administration to give an immediate response to its demands for protection.[973] It was widely believed that the measures were imposed in order to bolster support for the Republican Party in a number of key states and districts in the November 2002 mid-term Congressional elections. Another political justification was that the measures were necessary to secure the votes of representatives from a number of steel-making districts in support of the bill giving the President trade negotiating ("Fast-Track") authority.[974]

14.12 Although the decision to apply the safeguard measures may have been prompted by political needs, the integrity of the world trading system would still be preserved as long as Members comply with the relevant trade rules. In fact, in the real world, where the economic rationale does not always prevail, politics will not cease to be an important factor in the decision to apply a trade measure. The question is whether the US safeguard measures, regardless of their underlying political motive, were consistent with the WTO rules on safeguards.

14.13 The EC alleged in its request for the establishment of a panel that the US measures violated Articles 2, 3, 4, 5, and 9 of the Agreement on Safeguards as well as Articles I:1, XIII, and XIX:1 of the GATT 1994.[975] The issues in the application of a safeguard measure and the relevant panel and Appellate Body decisions have been discussed extensively in the preceding chapters. Some of the inconsistencies in the requirements of the SA, already observed

---

972 *Id.* An EC Commission Report also stated, "As a result, some time in the second half of next year we are likely to see yet another repetition of the 'steel industry crisis' that has occurred every three to five years. No doubt, as in the past, such a crisis will lead to calls for yet more protectionism, including WTO illegal use of anti-dumping and countervailing duty measures. However, the cycle will only be broken if the US authorities and industry are willing to address the underlying issues, notably the problem of uneconomic capacity and market distortions." Commission of the European Communities, *Report to the Council from the Commission on Re-balancing Action on Steel* (September 24, 2002).

973 An immediate, comprehensive import relief was demanded by the steel industry. *Recommended Action to Solve the Steel Import Crisis*, May 9, 2001, Proposal by the Steel Manufacturers Association.

974 This view seems to be supported by the fact that after the Congressional vote on the trade promotion authority legislation, the Administration granted a large number of exemptions from the safeguard measure.

975 WTO doc. WT/DS248/12 (May 8, 2002).

and discussed in the previous US safeguard measures,[976] recurred in the *US Steel Safeguard* case. The initial edition of this book provided an observation of some evident inconsistencies in the application of the US steel safeguards,[977] which were subsequently affirmed by the Panel and Appellate Body decisions as the following.[978]

First, under the rulings of the Appellate Body, national investigating authorities are obligated to demonstrate in their investigation report the existence of "unforeseen developments" that led to increases in imports causing or threatening to cause injury to the domestic industry.[979] As discussed in Chapter 3.2 above, there is doubt as to whether this old phrase in Article XIX should be given any legal effect. Nevertheless, as the Appellate Body's decision stands unchanged, competent national authorities are required to demonstrate the existence of "unforeseen developments." The USITC Report[980] did not include such a demonstration. The Panel and the Appellate Body found that the United States had failed to demonstrate the "unforeseen developments."[981] **14.14**

Second, the United States had exempted imports from certain countries, including its NAFTA partners, from its application of the steel safeguards.[982] Article 2.2 of the Agreement on Safeguards prohibits a selective application of a safeguard measure according to the product's origin. Previous Panels and the Appellate Body ruled that Members are not allowed to apply safeguard measures selectively where they have considered imports from all sources, including the other RTA members, in their injury determination.[983] **14.15**

In the USITC Report, the injury assessment was based on the analysis of imports of steel products from all sources, including those exempted countries. The Report provided a separate analysis on the injurious effects of the imports from the other NAFTA countries with respect to each steel product. In *United States – Wheat Gluten*, the United States also conducted a separate analysis of **14.16**

976 *See* discussions concerning previous US safeguard cases: *United States – Wheat Gluten*; *United States – Lamb Meat*; *United States – Line Pipe* in Chapters 3 through 9.

977 Yong-Shik Lee, *Safeguard Measures in World Trade: The Legal Analysis* (The Hague: Kluwer Law International, 1st ed., 2003), pp. 166–168.

978 The complainants did not challenge some of those inconsistencies, and therefore, no Panel and Appellate Body decision was made on all of them.

979 Refer to the relevant discussion in Chapter 3.2 *supra*.

980 Steel, USITC Pub. No. 3479 (December 2001).

981 *United States – Steel Products*, Report of the Panel, *supra* note 70, paras. 10.145–10.150, and Report of the Appellate Body, *supra* note 71, para. 330. *See also* the relevant discussions in Chapters 3.2 *supra*.

982 Imports of steel products from Canada, Israel, Jordan, and Mexico were excluded from the US safeguard measures.

983 *See* Chapter 4.4 *supra* for the relevant discussion.

the imports from Canada and subsequently determined that they did not reach the "substantial share" and therefore did not "contribute importantly" to the injury.[984] The Panel found that once the injury determination is made based on the imports from all sources, a safeguard measure must be applied to the imports from all sources regardless of the result from such an analysis, because imports from different sources may have *collectively* caused the injury.[985] The rationale of this decision was also applicable to the US measures, and the US exemption of certain imports from its steel safeguard measures was not consistent with the requirement under Article 2.2 as confirmed by both Panel and the Appellate Body.[986]

14.17 *Third*, another inconsistency was found in the injury assessment by the USITC. As discussed in Chapter 5 above, Article 4.2 of the Agreement on Safeguards requires Members to consider specific injury factors. Previous Panels and the Appellate Body also found that Members are obliged to consider *all* injury factors listed under Article 4.2(a). The USITC Report did not provide an analysis of all mandatory injury factors. For instance, productivity, which is one of those listed injury factors, was not analyzed.[987]

14.18 An analysis of productivity is important particularly where a claim for injury is based on an increase in unemployment. An increase in unemployment is an important motivation for applying a safeguard measure as it often causes serious social and political problems.[988] However, such increase in unemployment may not necessarily be indicative of serious injury in the domestic industry when unemployment is a result of increased productivity. For instance, an adoption of labor-saving production and management technology may result in a corresponding decrease in the amount of labor force necessary for the same production.[989]

---

984 Under Section 312 of the NAFTA Implementation Act (the predecessor of the current USMCA Implementation Act), the President was required to exclude imports from a NAFTA country from a safeguard measure if the President determined that if those imports did not account for a substantial share of total imports or they did not contribute importantly to serious injury or threat thereof. This particular requirement, which has been replicated in the current USMCA Implementation Act, presents a conflict with the requirement under the SA. *See* Chapter 12.2 *supra* for the relevant discussion.

985 *United States – Wheat Gluten*, *supra* note 70, para. 8.176. The Appellate Body also upheld the Panel findings. *United States – Wheat Gluten*, *supra* note 71, paras. 98–100.

986 *United States – Steel Products*, Report of the Panel, *supra* note 70, paras. 10.609, 10.623, 10.633, 10.643, 10.653, 10.660, 10.670, 10.680, 10.692, 10.699, and Report of the Appellate Body, *supra* note 71, para. 474.

987 *Supra* note 980.

988 *See* Chapter 1 *supra*.

989 The Panel and the Appellate Body did not address the absence of productivity consideration and inadequate consultation, and rendered no decisions on these issues.

Fourth, there is also a significant procedural inconsistency found in the application of the US steel safeguards. Article 12.3 of the Agreement on Safeguards provides, "A Member proposing to apply or extend a safeguard measure shall provide adequate opportunity for prior consultations with those Members having a substantial interest as exporters of the product concerned, with a view to, *inter alia*, reviewing the information provided under paragraph 2, exchanging views on the measure and reaching an understanding on ways to achieve the objective set out in paragraph 1 of Article 8." **14.19**

As discussed in Chapter 6, consultation is an essential procedural requirement in the application of a safeguard measure since they provide all parties with opportunity to discuss the proposed measure and to reach a mutually satisfactory settlement. Indeed, the requirement of consultation is a manifestation of multilateralism in international trade, obliging Members to consider the interests of the other affected Members and encouraging them to accommodate those interests if possible *before* applying a trade measure. Successful consultations would allow Members to avoid further disputes and potential retaliations. **14.20**

Thus, the affected Members should be allowed necessary time to analyze the proposed measure and determine its impact before entering into consultations so that they can have a meaningful exchange of views on the proposed measure in the consultations. The United States announced its decision to apply a safeguard measure on March 5 and implemented the measure only 15 days after its decision. Although several affected Members rushed to consultations with the United States, no settlement could be reached. As discussed above, the Appellate Body in *United States – Line Pipe* considered that the period of 18 days between the announcement of the US measure and its implementation was insufficient for the exporting Members to analyze the effect of the measure and enter into consultation.[990] Therefore, the period of 15 days – even less than the period given in *United States – Line Pipe* – is unlikely to be justifiable. **14.21**

The Panel subsequently held the US safeguard measures in violation of GATT Article XIX and the SA. In addition to the unforeseen developments and parallelism issues already discussed, the United States was found to have shown neither a causal link between the increased imports and any actual or threatened injury to the domestic industry for most products,[991] nor an increase in imports **14.22**

990 *United States – Line Pipe*, WT/DS202/AB/R, para. 107.

991 The Panel determined that the causation requirement was not met with respect to CCFRS, tin mill products, hot-rolled bar, cold-finished bar, rebar, welded-pipe, FFTJ, stainless steel bar, stainless steel wire. *United States – Steel Products*, *supra* note 70, paras. 10.419, 10.422, 10.445, 10.469, 10.487, 10.503, 10.536, 10.569,

for certain products.[992] The United States appealed the panel decision but the Appellate Body upheld the decision, albeit with some modifications.[993] The United States subsequently accepted the decision and withdrew the measures.[994]

14.23 Having faced proposals for significant retaliation by its major trading partners such as the EC and Japan, the United States had already reduced a number of products by as much as 25 percent in terms of tonnage, prior to the Panel decision, from its safeguard list.[995] The EC and Japan did not implement their retaliatory measures in light of the US concessions, followed by the subsequent withdrawal of the safeguards in compliance with the Panel and Appellate Body decisions.[996] A trade war was finally averted.[997] In the meantime, major trading Members, including the EC and China, had applied provisional safeguard measures to prevent a possible "diversion" of foreign steel products from the US market protected by the steel safeguards to their markets.[998]

14.2 ARE "SAFEGUARDS-IN-RESPONSE" JUSTIFIABLE?

14.24 *EC Provisional Measure.* This section considers the justification of an EC provisional measure on steel products applied in response to the US steel safeguard measures.[999] The EC claimed that its measure was necessary to prevent a large

---

10.573. For stainless steel rod, the Panel considered that the USITC's causation analysis was consistent with the requirement under Article 4.2(b). *Id*, para. 10.586.

992 The Panel ruled that no adequate and reasoned explanation was offered to prove an increase in imports for certain carbon flat-rolled steel products (CCFRS), hot-rolled bar, and stainless steel rods, and that the claimed increases in imports were not sufficiently recent. The Panel found that the USITC had provided an adequate and reasoned explanation of increased imports with respect to cold-finished bar, rebar, welded pipe, fittings, flanges and tool joints (FFTJ) and stainless steel bar. *Id.*, paras. 10.419, 10.422, 10.445, 10.469, 10.487, 10.503, 10.536, 10.569, 10.573, 10.586.

993 *United States – Steel Products*, *supra* note 71, paras. 513 and 514. *See also* Lee (2004), *supra* note 944.

994 WTO doc. G/SG/N/10/USA/6/Suppl.8 (December 12, 2003).

995 *Supra* note 575.

996 The EC Commission "welcomed" the US exemption of certain steel products from its safeguard measures. Press release, Brussels, August 23, 2002. In a subsequent Report, the Commission stated that it did not propose the application of the first phase retaliatory measures (Annex I of Regulation 1031/2002) to be implemented before a decision from the DSB. *See* Commission of the European Communities, *Report to the Council from the Commission on Steel Re-balancing Action* (September 24, 2002).

997 In contrast, the United States showed a different attitude concerning some of the later disputes: it did not lift the steel and aluminum tariffs or its extensive tariffs against China (WT/DS543), both adopted in 2018, when the WTO Dispute Settlement Panels found these measures inconsistent with WTO law, citing that those Panel decisions were not "final." The United States appealed the Panel decisions in both cases to the Appellate Body that it incapacitated by vetoing all of its appointments since 2017, with knowledge that it cannot render any decision due to its own conduct. *See* Reinert, *supra* note 618.

998 *Supra* note 956.

999 Commission Regulation (EC) No 560/2002 of March 27, 2002, as amended by Commission Regulation (EC) No 950/2002 of June 3, 2002 and Commission Regulation (EC) No 1287/2002 of July 15, 2002

volume of steel exports from being diverted to its own market due to the higher tariffs imposed by the United States (the steel safeguards).[1000] Nevertheless, this sort of "preventive" safeguard measure is not consistent with the rules on safeguards.[1001] The United States made a request for the establishment of a panel to review the consistency of this provisional measure.[1002]

Article 6 of the Agreement on Safeguards authorizes provisional measures. It provides: **14.25**

> In critical circumstances where delay would cause damage which it would be difficult to repair, a Member may take a provisional safeguard measure pursuant to a preliminary determination that there is clear evidence that increased imports have caused or are threatening to cause serious injury. The duration of the provisional measure shall not exceed 200 days, during which period the measures should take the form of tariff increases to be promptly refunded if the subsequent investigation referred to in paragraph 2 of Article 4 does not determine the increased imports have caused or threatened to cause serious injury to a domestic industry. The duration of any such provisional measure shall be counted as a part of the initial period and any extension referred to in paragraphs 1, 2 and 3, of Article 7.

It is doubtful that the circumstances prescribed in the above provision of Article 6 apply to this case. As the basis for the EC's proposed measure is the threat posed by the possible diversion of steel exports to its own market rather than the existence of current injury,[1003] the questions are whether the EC made a preliminary determination that there were (i) *clear evidence* and (ii) *critical circumstances* as prescribed under the provision of Article 6 cited above. Article 4.1(b) of the Agreement on Safeguards also requires that a determination of the existence of a threat of serious injury shall be based on *facts* and not merely on allegation, conjecture, or remote possibility. **14.26**

Lack of Clear Evidence. With respect to the first question, the relevant Commission Regulation and the notification[1004] pointed out certain changes of the injury factors under Article 4.2(a) in support of its preliminary determina- **14.27**

(hereinafter, "Commission Regulation"). *See also* the EC notification to the Committee on Safeguards, G/SG/N/7/EEC/1 (April 2, 2002). Those documents set out the legal basis for the EC provisional measure.

1000 *Id.*

1001 Hahn discussed unilateral responses to safeguard measures and observed that the introduction of compensation for damages would eliminate the justification for unilateral action against safeguards. Michael J. Hahn, "Balancing or Bending? Unilateral Reactions to Safeguards Measures" (2005) 39(2) *Journal of World Trade* 301–326.

1002 WTO doc. WT/DS260/4 (August 19, 2002). The United States alleged in its request that the EC's provisional measure violated Articles 2.1, 4.1(b), 4.2(a), 4.2(b), 4.2(c), 6, 3, 5.1, 12.1, 12.4, 2.2 and XIX:1(a).

1003 *Supra* note 999.

1004 *Id.*

tion. However, the EC did not provide an explanation as to how each of those factors supported or detracted from its preliminary determination of a threat of serious injury, nor did it explain *how* those changes, considered in aggregate, led to its preliminary determination of a threat of serious injury, both of which the relevant panel and Appellate Body decisions required for injury determination in previous cases.[1005]

14.28 Although the decisions of the previous Panels and Appellate Body requiring competent national authorities to provide reasoned explanations for their injury determination concern definitive safeguard measures, the same rationale should apply to the determination of a preliminary measure: i.e., the preliminary nature of determination may excuse national authorities from making a complete injury analysis based on *all* relevant facts but not from the obligation to provide a reasoned explanation for their preliminary determination based on the facts that they have considered. The difference in the national authorities' obligation between the preliminary and the final injury determination lies in the extent of facts that they gather and consider. Waiver of the reasoned explanation would allow national authorities to apply provisional measures arbitrarily.

14.29 Article 6 requires a Member to apply a provisional measure pursuant to a preliminary determination that there is "clear evidence" of injury. Such a determination cannot possibly be made without adequate demonstration, although preliminary, of *how* those observed changes in the injury factors led to serious injury or the threat of such. The EC did not even present specific figures concerning its analysis of half of the injury factors, while claiming declines in those factors. The lack of reasoned explanation suggests that the EC did not make a proper preliminary determination that there was a threat of serious injury.

14.30 *Lack of Critical Circumstances.* The next question is whether there were critical circumstances that justified the application of a provisional measure. As the EC seems to have failed to provide clear evidence of a threat of serious injury, such critical circumstances could not have been established. The EC contended that the expected diversion of foreign steel exports from the US market to the

1005 *Korea – Dairy Products, supra* note 70, para. 7.58 and *Argentina – Footwear, supra* note 71, paras. 138 and 139. The Appellate Body in *United States – Lamb Meat* also affirmed this point. It stated, "Under Article 4.2(a), competent authorities must conduct a substantive evaluation of the *bearing*, or the *influence* or *effect* or *impact* that the relevant factors have on the 'situation of [the] domestic industry'. (emphasis added) By conducting such a substantive evaluation of the relevant factors, competent authorities are able to make a proper overall determination, *inter alia*, as to whether the domestic industry is seriously injured or is threatened with such injury as defined in the Agreement." *United States – Lamb Meat, supra* note 71, para. 104.

EC market necessitated the application of a provisional measure. According to the EC, the Union market constituted the only viable export markets and the diversion would seem inevitable.[1006] On the contrary, it was subsequently observed that in Korea, one of the major steel exporters, the increased domestic demand offset the decrease in its export to the US market.[1007] The EC analysis also lacked explanations as to *why* expected damage would be irreparable.

The provisional safeguard measures are applicable where there is a true emergency in which Members cannot afford to wait until the conclusion of a full investigation. The EC's provisional measures would be difficult to justify, since the measure appears to be based merely on a precaution of "possible" diversion of the steel exports and not on clear facts or evidence of injury or its threat, violating Article 6 of the SA.[1008] Thus, the safeguard measure applied by the EC would not escape the criticism that it was merely a protectionist response to the US steel safeguards.[1009] **14.31**

14.3 IMPORTANCE OF MULTILATERALISM IN INTERNATIONAL TRADE

The success of the WTO system and the future of free trade depends on maintaining and respecting multilateralism in the international trading system. Without multilateralism in place, the trading system could be vulnerable to protectionist demands and would be endangered by a series of disputes and retaliations down the road. Observing binding concessions that have been agreed in multilateral trade negotiations is essential for the preservation of the free trading system. Therefore, safeguard measures, definitive or provisional, should be taken as an exceptional device of last resort, only to remedy or prevent serious injury caused by increased imports. Those measures should not **14.32**

1006 *Supra* note 999.

1007 *Chosun Ilbo* (Korean newspaper), April 23, 2002.

1008 The Panel in *Argentina – Preserved Peaches* once again emphasized that that the competent authorities' determination of threat of serious injury must be based on facts and not on remote possibility. *Argentina – Preserved Peaches, supra* note 70, paras. 7.83–7.134.

1009 A study also indicated that the EC Commission Regulation (560/2002) violated European Community laws as well as WTO rules and provided ample room for judicial review. Christoph Hoelscher, "A Comment on Commission Regulation (EC) No. 560/2002, Imposing Provisional Safeguard Measures Against Certain Steel Products" (2002) 36(6) *Journal of World Trade* 1081–1087. The EC subsequently adopted a definitive safeguard measure on the steel products, which remained until terminated in December 2004. WTO docs. G/SG/N/10/EEC/1 (November 9, 2002), G/SG/N/10/EEC/1, Suppl.1 (October 23, 2002), and G/SG/N/10/EEC/1, Suppl.2 (December 19, 2003). *See also* WTO, *Report (2004) of the Committee on Safeguards to the Council for Trade in Goods*, G/L/703, Annex 2 (November 1, 2004).

be misunderstood and misused as a political device to appease protectionist demands.[1010]

14.33 The application process of the US steel safeguard measures and the subsequent provisional measures applied by other Members revealed the lack of careful reflection on the importance of multilateralism. The rushed implementation of the steel safeguards, without offering a proper consultation opportunity, as well as the application of provisional measures in the absence of critical circumstance indicated the lack of such reflection. As a result, the application of safeguard measures, lacking compliance with both substantive and procedural requirements, only invited disputes and retaliation proposals, causing a substantial danger of beginning a worldwide trade war.

14.34 This catastrophe was avoided by a series of concessions made by the United States subsequent to the application of the measures[1011] and ultimately by its withdrawal of the safeguard measures in compliance with the WTO Panel and the Appellate Body decisions. The affected exporting Members also showed restraint in undertaking retaliatory measures and adhered to the WTO Dispute Settlement Procedure. The initial disregard of multilateralism, as shown in the improper application of the US steel safeguards and the subsequent provisional measures by the EC, brought a significant danger to trade relations among major economies in the world, and such danger was later averted by the subsequent effort to comply with the multilateral framework of international trade.

14.35 In retrospect, had the United States not rushed to implement the measures and instead taken sufficient time to consult with the other Members, this risky confrontation, which could have started a trade war, may have been avoided from the beginning.[1012] Again, the development of the *US Steel Safeguard* case demonstrated the crucial importance of multilateralism in international trade, with the lessons of possible consequences when this multilateralism is not respected.[1013]

1010 A study discussed the provisions of the SA susceptible to potential misuse and suggested a policy reform. Julien Chaisse, Debashis Chakraborty, and Animesh Kumar, "Mastering a Two-Edged Sword: Lessons from the Rules and Litigation on Safeguards in the World Trade Organization" (2015) 13(4) *Richmond Journal of Global Law and Business* 563–592.

1011 *Supra* note 575.

1012 *See* the preceding discussion of the inconsistency of the US measures with the procedural requirements under Article 12.3.

1013 This lesson was obviously not remembered when the US administration adopted the WTO-inconsistent steel and aluminum tariffs and a series of tariffs against imports from China in 2018, which caused a chain of retaliations and disputes. The lesson was also forgotten when the US administration vetoed all appointments to the Appellate Body thereby incapacitating the latter, and when it also failed to comply with the Panel decisions, citing its appeals to the Appellate Body that it had incapacitated. WTO docs. WT/DS543/10 (October 27, 2020) and WT/DS544/14 (January 30, 2023).

15

FUTURE PERSPECTIVE AND CONCLUSION

15.1 ECONOMIC DEVELOPMENT AND SAFEGUARDS[1014]

This final chapter concludes the book with some thoughts about the future perspective of safeguards. The first section of the chapter provides a discussion of the relations between the current safeguard mechanism and the economic development of developing countries and the need for modification to serve development interests. The second section addresses problems of anti-dumping measures in world trade and presents the case for the replacement of the archaic anti-dumping mechanism with safeguards. Conclusions are provided at the end of the chapter. 15.01

Despite unprecedented economic and technological developments, a majority of the world population has not received the benefit of this prosperity and still lives in poverty.[1015] Thus, many would agree that the improvement of the economic conditions of developing countries is an important task of our time.[1016] This improvement is possible through economic development,[1017] and international trade plays a crucial role in the economic development of developing 15.02

1014 The contents of Chapters 15.1 and 15.2 are cited from the author's book, *Reclaiming Development in the World Trading System*, *supra* note 1, Chapters 1.4, 4.3, and 9.

1015 According to the World Bank report, around 700 million people remain below the extreme poverty line with an income of US $2.15 or less a day. World Bank, *Poverty*, available at: http://www.worldbank.org/en/topic/poverty/overview [https://perma.cc/WC7U-4X5N].

1016 Lee, *Reclaiming Development in World Trading System*, *supra* note 1, Chapter 1.4.

1017 Economic development is the process of the structural transformation of an economy from one primarily based on the production of primary products (i.e., a product consumed in its primary [unprocessed] state) generating low levels of income to another based on modern industries that provides higher levels of income.

countries. In particular, the economic effect of trade measures has long been a subject of substantial academic discussion.[1018] To assist with the economic development of developing countries as proclaimed in WTO disciplines described below, it is important to evaluate the current legal framework of international trade to determine whether it enables developing countries to adopt effective development policies to improve their economy.

15.03 The WTO expresses its support for the economic development of developing countries through expansion of their share in international trade. GATT Articles XXXVI–XXXVIII lay out the commitment of developed countries to assist with the economic development of developing countries. In addition, the Preamble of the WTO Agreement recognizes, in relevant part, that "there is need for positive efforts designed to ensure that developing countries, and especially the least developed among them, secure a share in the growth in international trade commensurate with the needs of their economic development."[1019] In particular, the GATT endorses the promotion of "infant" industries of developing countries for their economic development.[1020] In fact, developing countries have often promoted export as part of their development strategies, with some notable success.[1021]

15.04 For developing countries that depend on exports for their economic development, safeguards, particularly those applied in their major export markets, may significantly hamper their exports and development. As discussed in Chapter 9.2 above, the SA requires exemption of the imports originating from developing countries from safeguards where their market shares in the importing country, both collectively and individually, are insignificant.[1022] Nonetheless,

---

1018 Bernard Hoekman, Aaditya Mattoo, and Philip English (eds.), *Development, Trade and the WTO* (Washington, DC: World Bank, 2002) provides good coverage of the discussions on development and trade. *See also* J. Trachtman and C. Thomas (eds.), *Developing Countries in the WTO Legal System* (Oxford University Press, 2009); M. Janow, V. Donaldson, and A. Yanovich (eds.), *The WTO: Governance, Dispute Settlement and Developing Countries* (Huntington, NY: Juris Publishing Inc., 2008); Carolyn Deere-Birkbeck (ed.), *Making Global Trade Governance Work for Development* (Cambridge University Press, 2011); Yong-Shik Lee, "The Long and Winding Road – Path Towards Facilitation of Development in the WTO: Reflections on the Doha Round and Beyond" (2016) 9(2) *Law and Development Review* 437–465; Yong-Shik Lee, "International Trade Law Post Neoliberalism" (2020) 68(2) *Buffalo Law Review* 413–478.

1019 WTO, *The Legal Texts: The Results of the Uruguay Round of Multilateral Trade Negotiations*, *supra* note 32, p. 4.

1020 "Infant" industries refer to industries at the early stages of development. German economist Friedrich List (1789–1846) argued in his famous work *The National System of Political Economy* (1841) that promotion of infant industries is necessary for economic development of developing countries. GATT Article XVIII authorizes developing countries to adopt trade to establish and promote infant industries for the purpose of economic development.

1021 Lee, *Reclaiming Development in the World Trading System*, *supra* note 1, Chapter 1.4.

1022 Article 9.1 of the SA.

there has been criticism that those ceilings imposed on the total and individual market shares taken by developing countries for the exemption (9 percent and 3 percent, respectively) are too limiting.[1023]

Perhaps these ceilings should be raised, and the total exemption of the imports from the least-developed countries ("LDCs") should also be considered in light of their particularly pressing economic needs. While export can improve the economic condition of LDCs substantially, as it did for some Asian countries,[1024] its impact on the domestic markets of the importing countries tends to be limited due to their insignificant market share.[1025] This means that the exemption of the imports from LDCs would not likely undermine the protective effect of safeguards to any considerable degree. The total exemption of imports from LDCs was discussed during the Uruguay Round but never implemented.[1026] **15.05**

The particularly dire economic conditions as well as their insignificant share in world trade can make an argument for the total exemption of imports from LDCs plausible. May the same argument be made with respect to the safeguard measures applied to imports from non-LDC developing countries? It would indeed be difficult to promote the total exemption of imports from non-LDC countries whose exports may have a significant economic impact on the economy of the importing countries and the world economy as a whole.[1027] **15.06**

If the total exemption of imports from all developing countries is not feasible for this reason, an alternative treatment, other than the current preference, should be considered in order to reduce the adverse impact of safeguards on the exports and, ultimately, the economic development of developing countries.[1028] Under the current rule, a safeguard measure can be applied for the maximum of four years and may be extended once, for up to the same period.[1029] Import **15.07**

1023 *Supra* note 627.

1024 Notably, some Eastern Asian countries, such as South Korea, Taiwan, Singapore, Hong Kong, and later China, have overcome poverty through economic development, and export has been an engine for their rapid development. *Supra* note 1021.

1025 In 2022, the portion of the merchandise exports by LDCs was around 1.1 percent of world exports. WTO, *World Trade Statistical Review 2023*, p. 108. available at: https://www.wto.org/english/res_e/booksp_e/wtsr_2023_e.pdf [https://perma.cc/YC96-X8BM].

1026 Refer to the relevant discussion in Chapter 2 *supra*.

1027 Some non-LDC developing countries have considerable industrial capacities. The implementation of the transitional product-specific safeguard provisions against imports solely from China represents the widespread concern about the import increases from some developing countries, although these seems little justification for such discriminatory provisions. See the relevant discussion in Chapter 11.4 *supra*.

1028 *See also* Lee, *Reclaiming Development in the World Trading System, supra* note 1, Chapter 4.3.

1029 SA Article 7.

restrictions of as long as eight years, particularly in major export markets, would be significantly damaging to developing countries that rely on export for economic development. The length of protection should be balanced against the development need for export promotion on the part of developing countries. This balance can be achieved, for instance, by limiting the extension of a safeguard where a substantial majority (e.g., two-thirds or above) of imports subject to safeguards originate in developing countries.[1030]

15.08 Selective introduction of immediate compensation may also be considered with regard to the application of a safeguard to imports from developing countries. As safeguard measures are applied in the absence of any unfair trade practices on the part of exporters, their application would inevitably upset the balance of concessions previously agreed among Members. Article 8 of the Agreement on Safeguards requires Members to endeavor to maintain a substantially equivalent level of concessions, and this balance can be maintained by providing compensation for the application of a safeguard measure.[1031] A failure to reach agreement on compensation may entitle the exporting Member to suspend the application of substantially equivalent concessions or other obligations under GATT 1994 to the trade of the importing Member,[1032] but the Agreement on Safeguards suspends this right of the exporting Member to apply retaliatory measures for three years where the safeguard conforms to its provisions and is based on an absolute increase in imports.[1033]

15.09 This suspension of retaliation is provided as an incentive for Members conforming to the strengthened rule on safeguards and applying a safeguard for a shorter duration.[1034] Nonetheless, such suspension has been criticized as having nullified the need for compensation. The absence of compensation can be a significant burden on developing countries whose exports are restrained by safeguards. In order to relieve this burden on developing countries and to promote their trade, a developed country adopting a safeguard measure should be required to offer compensation to affected developing countries *prior to* applying the safeguard measure.[1035] Where the required compensation

---

1030 As this limitation is to promote exports of developing countries for their economic development, perhaps the proposed limitation should not be imposed on a developing country Member.

1031 *See* Chapter 8.1 *supra* for the relevant discussion.

1032 SA Article 8.2.

1033 SA Article 8.3.

1034 The prevalence of "gray-area measures" in the 1970s and 1980s and the effort to eliminate them in the trading system was the primary motivator for this suspension. For discussion of gray-area measures and their impact on the negotiation of the SA, *see* Chapters 2.3 and 9.1 *supra.*

1035 *See also* Lee, *Reclaiming Development in the World Trading System, supra* note 1, Chapter 4.3.

is not made, the current suspension of retaliation should not be applied to the affected developing countries.

On the import side, safeguard measures also have an important impact on economic development by preventing, albeit temporarily, infant industries of developing countries from sustaining serious injury from competition with imports. The promotion of infant industries would require securing the positions of these industries in their domestic markets as well as promoting the export of their products.[1036] They may require protection in the domestic markets *until* they have developed enough to compete with imports. In this regard, safeguards can provide the necessary protection for infant industries from the surges of imports that may endanger their positions in their domestic markets. Safeguards are measures of a temporary nature, but the duration of protection can be used to promote infant industries in developing countries.[1037] Currently, the SA authorizes developing countries to apply a safeguard for a longer period of time (two additional years) and to apply it again to an identical product within a shorter interval from the expiry of the previous measure, although this preference is considered somewhat insufficient.[1038] **15.10**

15.2 SHOULD SAFEGUARDS REPLACE ANTI-DUMPING MEASURES?

The current WTO rules allow Members to take anti-dumping (AD) measures in the form of increased tariffs against "dumped" imports to offset the trade impact of dumping, which is presumably unfair.[1039] The WTO Agreement on Implementation of Article VI of the General Agreement on Tariffs and Trade 1994 ("the Anti-Dumping Practices Agreement" or "the ADP Agreement") sets out the concept for "dumping." Dumping is defined as sale at less than "normal value" (e.g., home price). Article 2.1 of the ADP Agreement provides in relevant part: **15.11**

1036 Lee, *Reclaiming Development in the World Trading System, supra* note 1, Chapter 2.3.

1037 Economists hold different views on the effectiveness of infant industry promotion. A Cambridge economist, Dr. Ha-Joon Chang revisited this issue in his work, *Kicking Away the Ladder: Development Strategy in Historical Perspective* (London: Anthem Press, 2002), and accounted that almost every developed country today employed state-led industrial promotion, including trade measures, during their own development process in the past. The US government currently grants large amounts of subsidies to promote semiconductor and electric vehicle manufacture in the United States. The GATT provisions cited above authorize infant industry promotion. Given the law and practices, there seems to be no reason that the safeguard regime should not be used to serve the promotion of infant industries in developing countries as long as the legal conditions prescribed under the SA are met.

1038 *Supra* note 627.

1039 *See* Jackson, *supra* note 78, pp. 247–248 for a discussion of "unfair" trade and "level playing field."

> [A] product is to be considered as being dumped, i.e., introduced into the commerce of another country at less than its normal value, if the export price of the product exported from one country to another is less than the comparable price, in the ordinary course of trade, for the like product when destined for consumption in the exporting country.[1040]

15.12 AD measures are the most frequently applied import measures today. As of June 2023, as many as 2,000 AD actions were reported to be in force.[1041] Developed countries, notably the United States and the European Union, have traditionally been the primary users of AD measures,[1042] but developing countries increasingly also use this device to curtail imports, and current statistics show that some developing countries apply more AD measures than those developed countries other than the United States.[1043] More exports from developing countries than from developed countries have been the target for AD actions: between July 2022 and June 2023, more than 85 percent of the 117 AD investigations targeted imports from developing countries,[1044] whereas exports from developing countries are only about 42 percent.[1045]

15.13 As "dumping" is subject to AD actions for "unfair" trade practices, it would be necessary to consider why exporters "dump" their products in the first place.[1046] Dumping practices are classified into different types, and these classifications are helpful to understand the nature of dumping practices.[1047] First, "persistent dumping," also called international price discrimination, represents the persistent tendency of domestic monopolists to maximize profit by selling their product at a higher price in the domestic market, where it is insulated by transportation costs and possibly trade barriers, than in a foreign market, where they have to compete with foreign producers.[1048] Secondly, "sporadic dumping" is the occasional sale of a product at a lower price abroad than domestically in order to unload an unforeseen and temporary surplus of the product without

---

1040 Article 2.1 of the ADP Agreement. For the specific determination of dumping margins and the imposition and collection of anti-dumping duties, *see* Articles 6.10 and 9 of the ADP Agreement.

1041 WTO, *Report (2023) of the Committee on Anti-Dumping Practices*, G/L/1501, October 26, 2023, Annex C.

1042 Of the 2,000 AD measures (including definitive duties and price undertakings) reported to be in force on June 30, 2023, 24.85 percent was maintained by the United States and 5.9 percent by the EU. *Id.*

1043 As of June 2023, the number of AD measures maintained by India was 143 whereas that maintained by the EU was 118. Also, China applied 117 measures while Canada applied 115. *Id.*

1044 *Id.*

1045 WTO, *World Trade Statistical Review 2023*, *supra* note 1025, Table A6.

1046 Lee (2005), "Toward a More Open Trading System: Should Safeguards Replace Antidumping Measures?" *supra* note 1.

1047 Salvatore, *supra* note 30, p. 264.

1048 *Id.* For instance, where the fixed cost (i.e., production facilities) is covered by the domestic sale and more products can be produced without expanding existing facilities (e.g., by employing night shifts), the producers can charge less for the same product to be sold abroad since the export price does not need to cover the fixed cost.

having to reduce domestic prices.[1049] In cases of persistent dumping and sporadic dumping, the benefit to domestic consumers from low prices may actually exceed the losses of domestic producers, increasing the overall economic welfare.[1050] Therefore, economists do not tend to see any problem with these types of price discrimination.[1051]

There is yet another type of dumping that may actually harm the economic interests of both consumers and producers in the importing country. It is "predatory dumping," defined as the temporary sale of a product at a lower price abroad in order to drive foreign producers out of business, after which prices are raised to take advantage of the newly acquired monopoly power abroad.[1052] This is inherently anti-competitive behavior (or "unfair competition"), and trade restrictions to counter predatory dumping seem justified.[1053] The problem, however, is that it is difficult to ascertain the predatory intent on the part of exporters. Even where predatory intent is somehow shown, it is also doubtful that this predation attempt will be successful at all,[1054] particularly in today's world where international competition among producers is increasingly intense. Even if predatory dumping is still somehow possible, it should be much less of a concern today since safeguard measures can protect domestic industries from any predation attempt, as this sort of attempt, if successful, will inevitably cause serious injury or its threat to the domestic industry. Therefore, the availability of safeguards should discourage foreign exporters from engaging in a predation attempt since it makes little sense for them to undercut price in order to drive all competitors out of the market, only to find that their exports are restricted by safeguards. **15.14**

It was also pointed out that producers might undercut price not necessarily to drive competitors out of business, but rather to increase their market share to improve their brand familiarity with customers in hopes of seeing demand for their brand eventually increase.[1055] In any case, if dumping leads to an increase in imports that causes or threatens to cause serious injury to the domestic industry, such imports will be subject to the safeguards. **15.15**

1049 *Id.*

1050 *Id.*

1051 *See* Richard Posner, *The Robinson-Patman Act: Federal Regulation of Price Differences* (Washington, DC: American Enterprise Institute, 1976) and Thomas W. Ross, "Winners and Losers under the Robinson-Patman Act" (1984) 27 *Journal of Law and Economics* 243–279.

1052 Salvatore, *supra* note 30, p. 264.

1053 *Id.*

1054 Jacob Viner, *Dumping: A Problem in International Trade* (New York: Kelly, 1966), p. 120.

1055 *See* Jackson, *supra* note 78, p. 254.

15.16 In addition, as safeguards should be applied to all imports on the MFN basis, safeguards will also affect all other exporters as well as those who dumped. This may not be fair to the innocent exporters, and the adverse effect on their trade should be minimized. Article 5.2(b) of the Agreement on Safeguards allows the importing country to assign a lesser amount of quota to the exporting country whose export has disproportionately increased, and therefore a safeguard can be targeted at those who have increased exports by dumping and can minimize the impact of the measure on those who have not, by applying the differential quota assignment as provided under Article 5.2(b).[1056]

15.17 The economic justification for anti-dumping measures seems weak in the first two categories of dumping, and it has been shown that safeguard measures may also replace anti-dumping measures in the case of predatory dumping. In addition, the significant arbitrariness inherent in the current AD rules, as well as the prevalent abuse of AD measures, raises doubt as to the necessity of AD practices.[1057] The inherent arbitrariness lies in the core concept of AD measures: that is, the determination of dumping.

15.18 While the underlying concept of dumping (sale below normal value) seems straightforward enough, the actual determination of dumping is not.[1058] That is because of the inherent arbitrariness and complication in the determination of "normal value" (home market price). For instance, there may not be a single home market price to compare, and the complex adjusted average may have to be calculated. Perhaps the home country is not completely a market economy ("transitional economy") and the home price may not represent the true market price. The product in question may not be sold in the home market or too little of it be sold to be the basis of a valid home price. In these cases, the price needs to be "constructed" by an evaluation of cost ("constructed cost") plus reasonable profit.[1059] Finding the "export price" that is necessary to determine the exist-

1056 Another possibility is to apply safeguards to the products under certain price in order to target only the dumping exporters. However, this price measure may be considered a *de facto* violation of the MFN application of safeguards under Article 2.2 of the Agreement on Safeguards. *See* Chapter 4.4 *supra* for the relevant discussion. Another study proposed country-specific safeguard measures to replace AD measures. Wentong Zheng, "Reforming Trade Remedies" (2012) 34(1) *Michigan Journal of International Law* 151–208. Such a selective application would not be consistent with the current requirement of non-discrimination under SA Article 2.2, but the rule adjustment that allows country-specific safeguards and replaces AD measures could be considered in cases where the imports from the particular country or countries alone prove to be sufficient to cause serious injury.

1057 Lee, *supra* note 1046.

1058 For the determination of dumping, *see* Article 2 of the ADP Agreement.

1059 *Id.* The complexity is also compounded by extraneous factors such as different foreign accounting practices that may affect cost calculations, the difficulty of understanding the foreign system, and different business practices. *See* Jackson, *supra* note 78, p. 251.

ence of dumping can be equally complex, since a number of adjustments to the transaction price may be necessary to keep comparisons with home prices fair.[1060]

This complexity and arbitrariness has been a breeding ground for the abuse of AD actions.[1061] Depending upon the methodology of calculating costs and of averaging prices, the result can be vastly different; not to mention that the measure of "reasonable profit" can also vary. Therefore, national authorities that are inclined to protect domestic producers tend to adopt the methodology and calculation that will yield the least desirable result for the exporters.[1062] This perhaps explains why there are numerous AD measures taken every year.[1063] Due to this arbitrariness in the current AD rules and its adverse effect on trade, the AD rules were included in the Doha Round agenda for negotiation.[1064] However, the Doha Round was closed in 2015 without much success, and the AD rule has not been reformed.[1065] It would seem unlikely that the inherent arbitrariness in the determination of dumping could be removed by a future reform.[1066] **15.19**

All these problems with the current disciplines on AD measures suggest that there is indeed little rationale to preserve this archaic system of AD practices. AD measures are based on an inappropriate premise that somehow there is a "normal value" to be determined, and that the sale at a price lower than this normal value needs to be sanctioned as "unfair" trade practice. The price is set by the market, and as such it is not for the government to determine the normal value. As discussed above, certain anti-competitive behavior, such as predation, is cited for a justification for AD measures. Yet the likelihood of such practices is not high, and that of its success is even smaller. Safeguard measures, whose disciplines are much tighter than ADs and therefore are **15.20**

1060 Those adjustments may include consideration of warranty services, advertising costs, etc.

1061 Although the provisions of the ADP Agreement attempt to provide disciplines on the AD actions, "in common parlance, it is usual to designate all low-cost imports as dumped imports." International Trade Centre UNCTAD/WTO and Commonwealth Secretariat, *Business Guide to the Uruguay Round* (ITC/CS: Geneva, 1995), p. 181. A study also examined a case in which AD duties were applied where no dumping could have existed and concluded that a safeguard instead of AD measure should have been applied. Ben Zissimos and Jan Wouters, "US–Shrimp II (Vietnam): Dubious Application of Anti-Dumping Duties – Should Have Used Safeguards" (2017) 16(2) *World Trade Review* 183–201.

1062 Article 2 of the ADP Agreement authorizes such leeway in the determination of dumping.

1063 As of June 2023, as many as 2,000 AD measures were in force. *Supra* note 1041. In comparison, 40 safeguard measures were in force as of October 2023. WTO, *Report (2023) of the Committee on Safeguards*, *supra* note 26, Annex 3.

1064 WTO, *Ministerial Declaration*, WT/MIN(01)/DEC/1 (November 20, 2001), para. 28.

1065 For a discussion of the negotiations on anti-dumping in the Doha Round, *see* Jun Kazeki, "Anti-dumping Negotiations under the WTO and FANs" (2010) 44(5) *Journal of World Trade* 931–965.

1066 The very attempt to determine the "normal value" is inherently normative and arbitrary, and the development of more precise standards would not likely remove this inherent arbitrariness.

much less susceptible to abuse, can deal with an occurrence of predation. Therefore, AD measures should be removed from the international trading system altogether and be replaced with safeguards.

15.21 Vested political interests in AD measures[1067] would be likely to keep AD measures in place for the foreseeable future despite the lack of justification and the presence of clear problems.[1068] Some have also questioned why safeguards should be considered any better than AD measures, since both restrict trade. Although safeguard measures also restrict trade, safeguards respond *only* to *serious injury or its threat* to the domestic industry, whereas AD measures are applicable in the absence of serious injury.[1069] In addition, safeguards are applied much more sparingly than AD measures, as they are subject to higher scrutiny.[1070] The potential abuse of safeguards would, therefore, be much less than that of AD measures, causing far less damage to trade than these measures. Safeguards are unlikely to replace AD measures any time soon, but eventually they should, in the interests of open and fair trade.

15.3 CONCLUSION

15.22 *Growing Importance*. Since safeguard measures replaced trade-distorting gray-area measures with the implementation of the SA in 1995, their importance in world trade has been significant, which is demonstrated by the increased number of safeguard applications: while 150 measures were reported during the five decades of the GATT era, as many as 213 safeguard measures were imposed in less than three decades between January 1995 and December 2023.[1071] This increased resort to safeguard measures can be attributed to factors such as enhanced clarity and specificity of the new safeguard rules, suspension of retaliation, and prohibition of gray-area measures. The improved disciplines of the SA have stabilized the safeguard mechanism in world trade and contributed to the general success of the WTO system. The failure of mul-

1067 AD measures have been politically favored trade measures since these measures are relatively easier to apply than the other trade measures, such as safeguards.

1068 A study suggested that reforms of the WTO AD Agreement may increase resort to safeguards. Chad P. Bown, "Why Are Safeguards under the WTO So Unpopular?" (2002) 1 *World Trade Review* 47–62.

1069 "Material injury" is required for the application of an AD measure. Article 3 of the ADP Agreement, Article VI:1 of the GATT. The threshold for material injury is considered to be lower than that required for serious injury.

1070 As discussed, the injury standard for the authorization of safeguards is higher than that required for anti-dumping measures. The injury assessment, as required by the SA (Article 4.2), is also more stringent for safeguards.

1071 WTO, *Safeguard Measures by Reporting Member*, *supra* note 21.

tilateral control over emergency import restraints could have led to a significant disruption of world trade.

The economic rationale of import restrictions such as safeguard measures has long been debated. While economic justification for import restrictions may be controversial, a disciplined safeguard measure with well-paced liberalization plans can, at a minimum, provide Members with opportunity for economic adjustment.[1072] For political and economic reasons, it is likely that safeguards will remain a lasting part of the world trading system. The task then would be to minimize the adverse effects of import restraints with effective disciplines. Properly disciplined safeguard measures would reduce those adverse effects on international trade and, therefore, would be a much better choice in the world trading system than other alternatives without adequate disciplines, such as gray-area measures. It has been hoped that safeguard measures will replace, albeit gradually, the archaic AD measures that impose a much greater burden on world trade,[1073] but the prospect of success in this is unclear. **15.23**

Complainants have successfully challenged all but one of the disputed safeguard measures on appeal, and this has created a perception that it is difficult to apply a safeguard measure consistently with the rules.[1074] WTO panels and the Appellate Body have scrutinized disputed safeguard measures tightly against the provisions of the SA and Article XIX. A close textual interpretation of those provisions by Panels and the Appellate Body has reinforced the scrutiny. Safeguard measures need on the one hand to be properly scrutinized in order to prevent possible misuse of these measures, which could stir worldwide protectionism, as shown in the *US Steel Safeguard* case.[1075] On the other hand, the review should not become excessively stringent so as to undermine the incentives provided to Members in the SA through enhanced disciplines, so that Members may not once again be tempted to resort to undesirable remedies outside the WTO system, such as gray-area measures.[1076] In this respect, the Appellate Body decision that recognized the "unforeseen developments" clause in Article XIX as a requirement for the application of a safeguard measure may **15.24**

1072 *See* the discussion of economic adjustment in Chapter 1 *supra.*

1073 Bown, *supra* note 1068 and Lee, *supra* note 1046.

1074 To date, all of the disputed safeguard measures formally adjudicated by the WTO panels and the Appellate Body, except one on appeal, has been found to be inconsistent with the provisions of the SA and Article XIX. *See supra* note 676.

1075 *See* Chapter 14 *supra* for a discussion of the *US Steel Safeguard* case.

1076 A study observed that the interpretations and applications of the SA and Article XIX by the Appellate Body and the dispute panel in the steel case, creates nearly insurmountable obstacles to the legal use of safeguard measures. Alan O. Sykes, "The Persistent Puzzles of Safeguards: Lessons from the Steel Dispute" (2004) 37 *Journal of International Economic Law* 523–564.

reduce such incentive, since a decision such as this would subject Members to an ambiguous requirement based on a rather dubious ground.[1077]

15.25 *Proper Application*. Can a safeguard be applied consistently with the present rules? The history of disputes suggests that successful defense is challenging, as demonstrated by there having been only one successful defense (currently on appeal at the time of writing).[1078] But the dispute record does not lead to the conclusion that Members have not been able to apply the safeguard rules and adopt the measures. Members have adopted as many as 213 safeguards as of December 2023, and WTO dispute settlement panels were established for less than 10 percent of these measures,[1079] although more of them were subject to consultations under the DSU.[1080] The absence of challenges also does not mean that the measures are compliant with the rules, but there are future prospects of compliance, provided that the following conditions are met.

15.26 First, a proper application of a safeguard measure should begin with the understanding that safeguard measures are designed as *emergency* import restrictions to relieve a domestic economy of acute, short-term economic problems resulting from rapid increases in imports, such as massive unemployment. Those economic problems can cause social and political turmoil, and the purpose of the measure is to enable Members to avoid such problems and embark on the necessary adjustment by maintaining the *status quo* by adopting temporary import restrictions. Safeguards are not a device to maintain select domestic industries profitable and operational at the expense of exporters and domestic customers, without a prospect of economic adjustment, or to help governments to attribute economic problems to imports. One who contemplates applying a safeguard should not lose sight of the purpose of this measure. The US steel safeguards are an example of the trade measure applied primarily for political reasons with unclear economic and legal justifications.[1081]

15.27 Secondly, the application of a safeguard measure should be consistent with all provisions of the SA, both procedural and substantive. Panels and the Appellate Body have considered and decided on key issues in the application of a safeguard measure, and their decisions need to be carefully studied. Previous panels and the Appellate Body have emphasized, *inter alia*, the importance of

---

1077 *See* the relevant discussion on this issue in Chapter 3.2 *supra*.

1078 *See supra* note 676.

1079 *See supra* notes 70 and 71 for the cases reviewed by the WTO dispute settlement panels and the Appellate Body.

1080 DSU, Article 4.

1081 *See* the relevant discussion of the US steel safeguards in Chapter 14 *supra*.

reasoning that competent national authorities must provide to explain their determinations. All the reasoning and explanations made by the national authorities should be found in their investigation report, as required under Article 3.1 of the SA. Many of the disputed safeguard cases have exhibited apparent oversights of the rules and the lack of reasoned explanations to support the national authority's determination.

Thirdly, particular attention must be given to the procedural aspects of the SA. **15.28** The required notifications under Article 12.1 should be expeditiously made to the Committee on Safeguards. Despite possible political pressure, Members should not rush into applying a safeguard and must provide sufficient time and information about the measure prior to the consultations required under Article 12.3. Consultations should be held well before the application of the measure, so that any agreement or settlement reached during the consultations can be accommodated in the implementation of the measure.

Finally, certain ambiguities inherent in the current rules and some of rule **15.29** interpretations made by Panels and the Appellate Body have caused confusion and controversy, such as the Appellate Body decision affirming the continuing applicability of Article XIX, specifically the "unforeseen developments" clause, as discussed above.[1082] Those ambiguities need to be resolved, perhaps, by rule modifications. The author has proposed these modifications as a suggestion to improve the clarity and coherence of the current rules.[1083] Panels and the Appellate Body should also ensure that, as the interpreting authority of the safeguard rules, their decisions offer clear and coherent guidelines so that Members can apply a safeguard measure with a reasonable certainty of its compliance with the rules.[1084] When they prescribe a test or set forth a requirement, regard should be given to the technical and economic feasibility of performing such test and meeting such requirement.[1085]

Final Reminder. If a Member applies a safeguard measure as a convenient **15.30** political means to appease protectionist demands without economic and legal justifications, it would only encourage other Members to do the same, which would ultimately dismantle the multilateral framework of the trading system. The future of free trade would be endangered by such practices. Members

1082 Whereas the Appellate Body affirmed the "unforeseen developments" clause still applies as a condition for the application of a safeguard measure, the previous Panels in *Korea – Dairy Products* and *Argentina – Footwear*, as well as a number of academicians have considered that it does not. *Supra* note 182.

1083 The proposed modifications are found in Appendix 4 *infra*.

1084 There has been a critique that this has not been the case. *See supra* notes 674 and 1076.

1085 The consideration would be particularly important for developing countries with limited resources.

should also be reminded that a safeguard measure, whether or not first tempted by another safeguard measure already in place, adversely affects not only the interests of foreign exporters but also those of their own consumers, for the benefit of a select group of domestic producers.[1086]

15.31 The application of a safeguard measure will not resolve the inherent structural problems of the domestic industry that are not caused by imports, and ill-placed protection may only delay a resolution of long-term industrial problems. All of this leads to the conclusion that safeguard measures should be applied sparingly as a measure of last resort. Rampant applications of safeguards would set the stage for protectionism worldwide, which would, in the end, harm exports from every country involved, including the one that first applied the measure. Then, ironically, the subsequent difficulties in exports and the resulting economic losses may well damage domestic political interests, which should have been protected by the application of the trade measure. We have already seen some of this irony in the *US Steel Safeguard* case.

15.32 A note should be added in relation to an interesting development in which a segment or constituent part of a domestic industry may have an interest in seeking safeguards while the others in the same industry may not, as a result of globalization of production. In *United States – Certain Tyres*, it was domestic labor, allegedly injured by the increase in imports from China, that petitioned for a safeguard, not the tire producers, who voluntarily reduced domestic production as part of their global business strategy. Some producers even denied the occurrence of injury. This means that globalization may lead to divided interests within the same industry with respect to the application of a safeguard. The case was on a special safeguard (TSM) applicable exclusively to imports from China,[1087] but the same circumstance may well be replicated in the context of a general safeguard. It remains unclear whether a safeguard measure would be a proper remedy to resolve the issues associated with the globalization of production, even if the legal requirements to invoke a safeguard measure should be met.

15.33 The WTO dispute settlement system, which had worked relatively well until 2019, is now facing a crisis due to a US block of all appointments to the Appellate Body. As a result of this block, the Appellate Body does not have a quorum to review any appeal, leaving a number of dispute cases in legal

1086 *Supra* note 20.
1087 *See* Chapter 11.4 *supra* for the relevant discussions of the TSM case.

limbo, including safeguard cases.[1088] Ironically, the last such safeguard case is one which the United States prevailed at the Panel proceedings.[1089] The complainant (China) appealed the Panel's decision supporting the US position, but the United States will not see it resolved, possibly in its favor, due to its own block. As of April 2024, it is not yet clear whether the United States will cease to block appointments to the Appellate Body and restore it to full capacity. Regardless of how it is resolved in the end, the US block will leave an undesirable precedent with negative implications for the rule-based multilateral trading system, on which proper administration of trade measures, including safeguards, will depend.

1088 *United States — Photovoltaic Products, supra* note 70 and *European Union – Steel Products, supra* note 70.
1089 *United States — Photovoltaic Products, supra* note 70.

BIBLIOGRAPHY

Adhikari, Ramesh and Yongzheng Yang, "What Will WTO Membership Mean for China and Its Trading Partners?" (2002) 39(3) *Finance and Development* 1–9.

Adlung, Rudolf, "Negotiations on Safeguards and Subsidies in Services: A Never-Ending Story?" (2007) 10(2) *Journal of International Economic Law* 235–265.

Ahn, Dukgeun, "Foe or Friend of GATT Article XXIV: Diversity in Trade Remedy Rules" (2008) 11(1) *Journal of International Economic Law* 101–133.

Ahn, Dukgeun and Hyerim Kim, "Judicial Conflicts between Panels and the Appellate Body in the WTO Safeguard Jurisprudence" (2020) 54(6) *Journal of World Trade* 961–982.

Andersen, Scott and Christian Lau, "Hedging Hopes with Fears in China's Accession to the World Trade Organization" (2005) 5(3) *The Journal of World Intellectual Property* 405–476.

Applebaum, Harvey M., "Section 201 of the Trade Act of 1974," *The New Trade Law: Omnibus Trade and Competitiveness Act of 1988* (New York: Practicing Law Institute, 1988), pp. 179, 187.

Applebaum, Harvey M. and David R. Grace, "Section 201 of the Trade Act of 1974," *the GATT, the WTO and the Uruguay Round Agreements Act* (New York: Practicing Law Institute, 1995), pp. 519–536.

Asmelash, Henok, "The Turn to Safeguard Measures in the Solar Trade War" (2022) 56(5) *Journal of World Trade* 803–830.

Barringer, William H. and Kenneth J. Pierce, *Paying the Price for Big Steel* (Washington, DC: American Institute for International Steel, 2000).

Barro, Robert J., "Big Steel Doesn't Need Any More Propping Up," *Business Week* (April 1, 2001), p. 24.

Becroft, Ross, *The Standard of Review in WTO Dispute Settlement: Critique and Development* (Cheltenham: Edward Elgar Publishing, 2012).

Berg, Andrew, "The Asia Crisis – Causes, Policy Responses and Outcomes," International Monetary Fund Working Paper, WP/99/138 (October 1, 1999).

Bhagwati, J.N., *Protectionism* (Cambridge, Mass.: MIT Press, 1988).

Bhala, Raj and Kevin Kennedy, *World Trade Law* (Charlottesville, Virginia: Lexis Law Publishing, 1998), pp. 897–938.

Borsworth, Malcolm, "GATS Emergency Safeguard Measures," *Report on the Implementation of Safeguards in the Area of Trade and Distribution Services* (Seoul: Korea Institute for Industrial Economics and Trade (KIET), 1988), p. 243.

Bourgeois, Jacques, "Article 1 SA," *in* Rüdiger Wolfrum, Peter-Tobias Stoll, and Michael Koebele (eds.), *WTO: Trade Remedies*, Max Planck Commentaries on World Trade Law (Leiden: Martinus Nijhoff, 2008), pp. 260–261.

Bown, Chad P., "Why Are Safeguards under the WTO So Unpopular?" (2002) 1 *World Trade Review* 47–62.

Bown, Chad P. and Rachel McCulloch, "Nondiscrimination and the WTO Agreement on Safeguards" (2003) 2 *World Trade Review* 333.

Bown, Chad P. and Rachel McCulloch, "The WTO Agreement on Safeguards: An Empirical Analysis of Discriminatory Impact," *in* Michael J. Plummer (ed.), *Empirical Methods in International Trade* (Cheltenham: Edward Edgar Publications, 2004), pp. 145–169.

Bown, Chad P. and Mark Wu, "Safeguards and the Perils of Preferential Trade Agreements: Dominican Republic–Safeguard Measures" (2014) 13(2) *World Trade Review* 179–227.

Bronckers, M., "Voluntary Export Restraints and the GATT 1994 Agreement on Safeguards," *in* J.H.J. Bourgeois, F. Berrod, and E. Fournier (eds.), *The Uruguay Round Results: A European Lawyers' Perspective* (Brussels: European Interuniversity Press, 1995).

Canada Border Services Agency, *Customs Notice 18-08: Surtaxes Imposed on Certain Products Originating in the United States* (June 29, 2018, revised July 11, 2018).

Chaisse, Julien, Debashis Chakraborty, and Animesh Kumar, "Mastering A Two-Edged Sword: Lessons from the Rules and Litigation on Safeguards in the World Trade Organization" (2015) 13(4) *Richmond Journal of Global Law and Business* 563–592.

Chang, Ha-Joon, *Kicking Away the Ladder: Development Strategy in Historical Perspective* (London: Anthem Press, 2002).

Charnovitz, Steve and Bernard Hoekman, "US–Tyres: Upholding a WTO Accession Contract – Imposing Pain for Little Gain" (2013) 12(2) *World Trade Review* 273–296.

Choi, Won-Mog, *"Like Products" in International Trade Law: Towards a Consistent WTO Jurisprudence* (Oxford: Oxford University Press, 2003).

Choi, Won-Mog, "FTAs and Safeguard Norms: Their Variation and Compatibility" (2011) 6 *Asian Journal of WTO and International Health Law and Policy* 81–108.

Chung, Sunghoon, Joonhyung Lee, and Thomas Osang, "Did China Tire Safeguard Save U.S. Workers?" (2016) 85 *European Economic Review* 22–38.

Clogstoun, Roy, R. Trewin, and M. Bosworth, "Would Emergency Safeguard Measures Work for Services?" (2006) 20(2) *Asian-Pacific Economic Literature* 56–69.

Cohen, Stephen D., *The Route to Japan's Voluntary Export Restraints on Automobiles* (1998), https://nsarchive2.gwu.edu/japan/scohenwp.htm [https://perma.cc/NA2B-832M].

Congressional Research Service, *Section 232 Investigations: Overview and Issues for Congress* (updated November 21, 2018), at 7.

Corden, W.M., *Trade Policy and Economic Welfare* (London: Oxford University Press, 1974).

Countryman, Amanda M. and Badri G. Narayanan, "Price Volatility, Tariff Structure and the Special Safeguard Mechanism" (2017) 64 *Economic Modeling* 399–408.

Crawford, Jo-Ann, Jo McKeagg, and Julia Tolstova, *Mapping of Safeguard Provisions in Regional Trade Agreements*, WTO Staff Working Paper ERSD-2013-10 (October 21, 2013), p. 39.

Dam, Kenneth W., *The GATT, Law and International Economic Organization* (Chicago: University of Chicago Press, 1970).

Das, Abhijit, Sachin Kumar Sharma, Raihan Akhter, and Teesta Lahiri, "Special Safeguard Mechanism for Agriculture: Implications for Developing Members at the World Trade Organization" (2021) 22 *Journal of World Investment and Trade* 835–859.

Deere-Birkbeck, Carolyn (ed.), *Making Global Trade Governance Work for Development* (Cambridge: Cambridge University Press, 2011), pp. 301–327.

Department of Foreign Affairs and International Trade of Canada, available at: http://www.treaty-accord.gc.ca/text-texte.aspx?id=105072&lang=eng [https://perma.cc/9QNL-RH3V].

Destler, I.M., *American Trade Politics* (Washington, DC: Institute for International Economics, 3rd ed., 1995), pp. 145–146.

Didier, Pierre, *Les pricipaux accords de L'OMC et leur transoposition dans law Communaute Europeene* (Brussels: Bruyland, 1998), pp. 271–272.

Dolzer, Rudolf and Christoph Schreuer, *Principles of International Investment Law* (Oxford: Oxford University Press, 2008).

Dore, Ronald, *Flexible Rigidities: Industrial Policy and Structural Adjustment in the Japanese Economy, 1970–80* (Stanford: Stanford University Press, 1986).

European Union (regulations / reports)

Commission Regulation (EC) No 560/2002 of March 27, 2002.

Report to the Council from the Commission on Steel re-balancing action (July 17, 2002 and September 24, 2002).

Commission Regulation (EC) No 1694/2002 of September 27, 2002.

Press Release, June 12, 2005, MEMO/05/201, text available at: http://europa.eu/rapid/press-release_MEMO-05-201_en.htm?locale=en (accessed April 21, 2024).

Regulation (EC) No. 182/2011, Article 1.

Regulation (EU) No. 2015/478 of the European Parliament and of the Council of 11 March 2015, G/SG/N/1/EU/2 (June 12, 2015).

Fang, Mandy Meng, "Old Wine in a New Bottle? Green Industrial Policy and the Use of Safeguards in the Solar Sector" (2021) 55(4) *Journal of World Trade* 573–596.

Finger, J. Michael, "A Special Safeguard Mechanism for Agricultural Imports: What Experience with Other WTO Safeguards Tell Us about What Might Work" (2010) 9(2) *World Trade Review* 289–318.

Franck, Thomas M., "On Proportionality of Countermeasures in International Law" (2008) 102(4) *The American Journal of International Law* 742–752.

Francois, Joseph F., Bradley McDonald, and Hakan Nordstrom, *Assessing the Uruguay Round* (WTO, Geneva, 1995).

Frank, Isaiah, "Imports Quotas, the Balance of Payments and the GATT" (1987) 10 *The World Economy* 307–317.

Freebain, J.S., "Pros and Cons of Temporary Industry Assistance" (1978) 22(3) *Australian Journal of Agricultural Economics* 194.

GATT, *Report on Withdrawal by the United States of a Tariff Concession under Article XIX of the General Agreement*, GATT/CP/106 (adopted by the Contracting Parties on October 22, 1951).

GATT, BISD 20S/47–49; 26S/205; 18S/50–51 (1972).

GATT, *The Tokyo Round of Multilateral Trade Negotiations: Report by the Director-General of GATT*, April 1979, pp. 90–95 and *Supplementary Report of January 1980*, pp. 14–17.

GATT, BISD 27S/119 (1981), Report of the Panel, *Norway – Restrictions on Imports of Certain Textile Products*.

GATT, *Ministerial Decision on Dispute Settlement*, L/5424, 29S/9, 12 (November 29, 1982).

GATT, *Trade Policies for a Better Future: Proposals for Action* (1985), pp. 38, 42, 43.

GATT, *Ministerial Declaration on the Uruguay Round*, GATT/MIN.DEC 86–1572, section 1.D, 33S/19, 24–25 (September 6, 1986).

GATT, *Work Already Undertaken in the GATT on Safeguards*, MTN.GNG/NG9/W/1 (April 8, 1987).

GATT, BISD 35S/116, Report of the Panel (adopted May 4, 1988), *Japan – Trade in Semi-Conductors*.

GATT, *GATT Activities 1988* (1989), p. 45.

GATT, *The Results of the Uruguay Round of Multilateral Trade Negotiations* (Geneva, 1994).

GATT negotiation/meeting documents

Pre-Uruguay Round: GATT/CP.6/SR.19, Sales No. GATT/1951–3 (adopted by the Contracting Parties on October 22, 1951); GATT/CP/106, report adopted on October 22, 1951; L/332/Rev.1 and Addenda, adopted in March 1955, 3S/170, 182, para. 39; MTN/SG/W/21 (February 14, 1977), *United States Comments on Developing Country Safeguard Proposals*; MTN/SG/W/45 (December 11 1978), *Draft Integrated Text on Safeguards*; MTN/SG/W/46 (December 14, 1978), *Statement Made by the Spokesman for Finland, Iceland, Norway and Sweden at the Meeting of Group "Safeguards" on December 13, 1978*; L/4884/Add.1/Annex VI, adopted on November 28, 1979, 26S/219, 220; MTN.GNG/NG9/W/4 (May 25, 1987), *Communication from Australia, Hong Kong, Korea, New Zealand, and Singapore*; MTN.GNG./NG9/W/12 (December 9, 1987), *United States Thoughts on Safeguards*; MTN.GNG/NG9/W/25 (June 27, 1989); MTN.GNS/W/120 (July 10, 1991). *Service Sectoral Classification List*.

Uruguay Round: MTN.GNG/NG9/W/6 (September 16, 1987); MTN .GNG/NG9/W/23 (June 13, 1989); MTN.GMG/NG9/13 (December 12, 1989); *Draft Final Act Embodying the Results of the Uruguay Round of Multilateral Trade Negotiations*, MTN.TNC/W/FA (December 20, 1991).

Geneva Trade Platform, *Multi-Party Interim Appeal Arbitration Arrangement (MPIA)* (2024), https://wtoplurilaterals.info/plural_initiative/the-mpia/ (accessed May 14, 2024).

Glick, Leslie Alan, *Guide to the United States Customs and Trade Laws after the Customs Modernization Act* (The Hague: Kluwer Law International, 2nd ed., 1997), pp. 141–151.

Gnutzmann-Mkrtchyan, Arevik and Simon Lester, "Does Safeguards Need Saving? Lessons from the Ukraine–Passenger Cars Dispute" (2017) 16(2) *World Trade Review* 227–251.

Gorton, Gary B., *Misunderstanding Financial Crises: Why We Don't See Them Coming* (Oxford: Oxford University Press, 2012).

Grant J. and K. Meilke, *Triggers, Remedies and Tariff Cuts: Assessing the Impact of a Special Safeguard Mechanism for Developing Countries*, Canadian Agricultural Trade Policy Research Network Working Paper 2008-09 (2008).

Griffith-Jones, Stephany, José Antonio Ocampo, and Joseph E. Stiglitz (eds.), *Time for a Visible Hand: Lessons from the 2008 World Financial Crisis* (Oxford: Oxford University Press, 2010).

Grossman, Gene M., "Imports as a Cause of Injury: The Case of the U.S. Steel Industry" (1986) 20 *Journal of International Economics* 201–222.

Grossman, Gene M. and Alan Sykes, "United States – Definitive Safeguard Measures on Imports of Certain Steel Products" (2007) 6(1) *World Trade Review* 89–122.

Grynberg, Roman, *et al.*, "Bilateral Commodity Agreements – New Generation Grey Area Measures?: A Scoping Study," *in* Veniana Qalo (ed.), *Bilateralism and Development: Emerging Trade Patterns* (London: Cameron May, 2008).

Guzman, Andrew T., "Determining the Appropriate Standard of Review in WTO Dispute Resolution" (2009) 42 *Cornell Journal of International Law* 45–76.

Hahn, Michael J., "Balancing or Bending? Unilateral Reactions to Safeguards Measures" (2005) 39(2) *Journal of World Trade* 301–326.

Harris, David, *Special Safeguards and Agricultural Trade Liberalization*, Rural Industries Research and Development Corporation, 08/125 (2008).

Hart, Nina M. and Brandon J. Murrill, *Section 301 Tariffs on Goods from China: International and Domestic Legal Challenges*, Congressional Research Service, LSB10553 3–4 (July 22, 2021).

Hertel, Thomas M., Will Martin, and Amanda M. Leister, "Potential Implications of a Special Safeguard Mechanism in the World Trade Organization: the Case of Wheat" (2010) 24(2) *The World Bank Economic Review* 330–359.

Hoekman, Bernard, Aaditya Mattoo, and Philip English (eds.), *Development, Trade and the WTO* (World Bank: Washington, DC, 2002).

Hoelscher, Christoph, "A Comment on Commission Regulation (EC) No. 560/2002, Imposing Provisional Safeguard Measures Against Certain Steel Products" (2002) 36(6) *Journal of World Trade* 1081–1087.

Horn, Henry K. and Petros C. Mavroidis, "United States – Safeguard Measures on Imports of Fresh, Chilled or Frozen Lamb Meat from New Zealand and Australia: What Should Be Required of a Safeguard Investigation?" (2003) 2 *World Trade Review* 395–430.

Hou, Xingzhend and Rongming Ren, "Cooperate or Antagonize: The EU's Dilemma on Anti-dumping and Safeguard Measures against China" (2006) 14(6) *China and World Economy* 76–78.

Hufbauer, G.H., D.T. Berliner, and K.A. Elliott, *Trade Protection in the United States: 31 Cases* (Washington, DC: Institute for International Economics, 1986).

Hufbauer, G.H., Gary Clyde, and Erika Wada, *Steel Quotas: A Rigged Lottery* (Washington, DC: Institute for International Economics, June 1999).

Ikenson, Dan, *Steel Trap: How Subsidies and Protectionism Weaken the U.S. Steel Industry*, Trade Briefing Paper, Center for Trade Policy Studies (March 1, 2002), text available at: http://www.cato.org/sites/cato.org/files/pubs/pdf/tbp-014.pdf [https://perma.cc/CY9D-YGEE].

International Trade Centre UNCTAD/WTO and Commonwealth Secretariat, *Business Guide to the Uruguay Round* (ITC/CS: Geneva, 1995), p. 181.

Irwin, Douglas A., "Causing Problems? The WTO Review of Causation and Injury Attribution in US Section 201 Cases" (2003) 2(3) *World Trade Review* 297–325.

Ivashina, Victoria and David Scharfstein, "Bank Lending during the Financial Crisis of 2008" (2010) 97(3) *Journal of Financial Economics* 319–338.

Jackson, John H., *World Trade and the Law of GATT* (Indianapolis: Bobbs-Merrill, 1969), p. 555.

Jackson, John H., *The World Trading System* (Cambridge, Mass.: The MIT Press, 1997), pp. 175–211.

Jain, Tarun, "Special Safeguard Measures under the Agreement of Agriculture: A Jurisprudential Analysis" (2008) VII(3) *The Icfai University Journal of International Business Law* 7–26.

Janow M., V. Donaldson, and A. Yanovich (eds.), The *WTO: Governance, Dispute Settlement and Developing Countries* (Huntington, NY: Juris Publishing Inc., 2008).

Japan Chemical Industry Association, News Release, August 28, 2003.

Johan, Eva, "Safeguard Measures in the Framework of ASEAN–Korea Free Trade Agreement (AKFTA) on Trade in Goods Compared to GATT/WTO" (2015) 12(2) *Indonesian Journal of International Law* 208–221.

Jones, Kent, "The Safeguards Mess Revisited: The Fundamental Problem" (2004) 3 *World Trade Review* 83–91.

Jung, Youngjin and Ellen Jooyeon Kang, "Toward an Ideal WTO Safeguards Regime – Lessons from *U.S.-Steel*" (2004) 38(4) *The International Lawyer* 919–944.

Kagitani, Koichi and Kozo Harimaya, "Safeguards and Voluntary Export Restraints under the World Trade Organization: The Case of Japan's Vegetable Trade" (2015) 36 *Japan and the World Economy* 29–41.

Kazeki, Jun, "Anti-dumping Negotiations under the WTO and FANs" (2010) 44(5) *Journal of World Trade* 931–965.

Kelly, Kenneth, "The Analysis of Causality in Escape Clause Cases" (1988) 37 *Journal of Industrial Economics* 187–207.

Kennedy, Kevin C., "Voluntary Restraint Agreements: A Threat to Representative Democracy" (1987) 11 *Hastings International and Comparative Law Review* 34–35.

Khan, Haider A., *Global Markets and Financial Crises in Asia* (Basingstoke; New York: Palgrave Macmillan, 2004).

Kim, Nayung, "Trade Remedy Rules for Digital Services: Inapplicability of GATT-type Safeguard Rules" (2020) 54(5) *Journal of World Trade* 813–829.

Korean Trade Commission Office of Administration and Investigation, *Investigation Report on Industrial Injury Related to the Increase of Certain Dairy Products Imports* (October 23, 1996), pp. 38–45.

Kostecki, Michel M., "Marketing Strategies and Voluntary Export Restraints" (1991) 25 *Journal of World Trade* 87–99.

Kotera, Akira and Tomofumi Kitamura, *On the Comparison of Safeguard Measures of Free Trade Agreements*, RIETI Discussion Paper Series 07-E-017 (March 2007).

Kurland, Joshua E., "Dusting-Off Section 201: Re-Examining a Previously Dormant Trade Remedy" (2018) 49(2) *Georgetown Journal of International Law* 609–674.

Lee, Chang B., "The Results of the Fifth WTO Committee on Agriculture" *International Agricultural Reporter*, No. 57 (1998), pp. 6–7.

Lee, Yong-Shik, "Emergency Safeguard Measures under Article X in GATS – Applicability of the Concepts in the WTO Agreement on Safeguards" (1999) 33(4) *Journal of World Trade* 47–59.

Lee, Yong-Shik, "Review of the First WTO Panel Case on the Agreement on Safeguards: Korea – Definitive Safeguard Measure on Imports of Certain Dairy Products and Its Implications for the Application of the Agreement" (1999) 33(6) *Journal of World Trade* 27–46.

Lee, Yong-Shik, "Critical Issues in the Application of the WTO Rules on Safeguards – In the Light of the Recent Panel Reports and the Appellate Body Decisions" (2000) 34 *Journal of World Trade* 131–147.

Lee, Yong-Shik, "Destabilization of the Discipline on Safeguards? Inherent Problems with the Continuing Application of Article XIX after the settlement of the Agreement on Safeguards" (2001) 35 *Journal of World Trade* 1235–1246.

Lee, Yong-Shik, "Revival of Gray-Area Measures? The US–Canada Softwood Lumber Agreement: Conflict with the WTO Agreement on Safeguards" (2002) 36 *Journal of World Trade* 155–166.

Lee, Yong-Shik, "Specific Safeguard Mechanism in the Protocol on China's Accession to the WTO – A Serious Step Backward from the Achievement of the Uruguay Round" (2002) 5 *Journal of World Intellectual Property* 219–231.

Lee, Yong-Shik, "Safeguard Measures: Why Are They Not Applied Consistently with the Rules? Lessons for Competent National Authorities and Proposal for the Modification of the Rules on Safeguards" (2002) 36 *Journal of World Trade* 641–673.

Lee, Yong-Shik, *Safeguard Measures in World Trade: The Legal Analysis* (The Hague: Kluwer Law International, 1st ed., 2003).

Lee, Yong-Shik, "Continuing Controversy on 'Unforeseen Developments' – Reviewer's Note" (2003) 37 *Journal of World Trade* 1153–1157.

Lee, Yong-Shik, "Reflections on U.S. International Trade Law and Practice – Compatibility with the WTO Rules and Call for Modification" (2003) 13(2) *Currents: International Trade Law Journal* 31–43.

Lee, Yong-Shik, "Test of Multilateralism in International Trade: U.S. Steel Safeguards" (2004) 25 *Northwestern Journal of International Law and Business* 69–98.

Lee, Yong-Shik, "The Agreement on Safeguards," *in* Patrick McRory and Arthur Appleton (eds.), *The World Trade Organization: Legal, Economic and Political Analysis* (Boston: Springer, 2005), pp. 749–798.

Lee, Yong-Shik, "Toward a More Open Trading System: Should Safeguards Replace Antidumping Measures?" (2005) 1(2) *21st Century Law Review* 3–14.

Lee, Yong-Shik, "Not Without a Clue: Commentary on 'The Persistent Puzzles of Safeguards'" (2006) 40 *Journal of World Trade* 385–404.

Lee, Yong-Shik, "Bilateralism under the World Trade Organization" (2006) 26 *Northwestern Journal of International Law and Business* 357–372.

Lee, Yong-Shik, "Reconciling RTAs with the WTO Multilateral Trading System: Case for a New Sunset Requirement on RTAs and Development Facilitation" (2011) 45 *Journal of World Trade* 625–647.

Lee, Yong-Shik, "First WTO Case on Transitional Product-Safeguard Measure under Section 16 of the Protocol of China's Accession to the WTO: Affirming Discriminatory Safeguard Measure by WTO?" (2012) 44 *Journal of World Trade* 913–936.

Lee, Yong-Shik, *Reclaiming Development in the World Trading System* (Cambridge: Cambridge University Press, 2nd ed., 2016).

Lee, Yong-Shik, "The Long and Winding Road – Path Towards Facilitation of Development in the WTO: Reflections on the Doha Round and Beyond" (2016) 9(2) *Law and Development Review* 437–465.

Lee, Yong-Shik, "Safeguards," *in* Krista Nadakavukaren Schefer and Thomas Cottier (eds.), *Encyclopedia of International Economic Law* (Cheltenham: Edward Elgar Publishing, December 2017), pp. 263–266.

Lee, Yong-Shik, "Three Wrongs Do Not Make a Right: The Conundrum of the U.S. Steel and Aluminum Tariffs" (2019) 18(3) *World Trade Review* 481–501.

Lee, Yong-Shik, "The Steel and Aluminum Quota Agreements: A Question of Compatibility with WTO Disciplines and Their Impact on the World Trading System" (2019) 53(5) *Journal of World Trade* 811–832.

Lee, Yong-Shik, "Are Retaliatory Trade Measures Justified under the Agreement on Safeguards?" (2019) 22(3) *Journal of International Economic Law* 439–458.

Lee, Yong-Shik, "International Trade Law Post Neoliberalism" (2020) 68(2) *Buffalo Law Review* 413–478.

Lee, Yong-Shik, "Safeguards," "Identifying WTO Safeguards," and "Safeguards in Developing Countries," *in* Krista Nadakavukaren Schefer and Thomas Cottier (eds.), *Encyclopedia of International Economic Law* (Edward Elgar Publishing, 2024).

Lee, Yong-Shik and Jai S. Mah, "Reflections on the Agreement on Safeguards in the WTO" (1999) 21(6) *World Competition* 25–31.

Leys, David, "Does a Theory of Causation Exist under the WTO Safeguards Agreement?" (2014) 9(1) *Global Trade and Customs Journal* 10–19.

List, Friedrich, *The National System of Political Economy* (1841), trans. Sampson S. Lloyd, with an Introduction by J. Shield Nicholson (London: Longmans, Green and Co., 1909).

Liu, Huan and Laixiang Sun, "Beyond the Phaseout of Quotas in the Textile and Clothing Trade: WTO-Plus Rules and the Case of US Safeguards Against Chinese Exports in 2003" (2004) 11(1) *Asia-Pacific Development Journal* 49–71.

Low, Patrick, *Trading Free: The GATT and U.S. Trading Policy* (New York: Twentieth Century Fund Press, 1993), p. 57.

Ma, Jing, "Product-Specific Safeguard in China's WTO Accession Agreement: An Analysis of Its Terms and Its Initial Application in Section 421 Investigations" (2004) 22 *Boston University International Law Journal* 189–217.

Mah, Jai S., "Reflections on the Balance-of-Payment Provisions in the WTO" (1998) 21(5) *World Competition* 139–148.

Mah, Jai S., "Reflections on the Special Safeguard Provision in the Agreement on Agriculture of the WTO" (1999) 33(5) *Journal of World Trade* 197–204.

Mah, Jai S., "Injury and Causation in the Agreement on Safeguards" (2001) 4 *Journal of World Intellectual Property* 373–382.

Marconini, M., *Emergency Safeguard Measures in the GATS: Beyond Feasible and Desirable*, UNCTAD Working Paper (2005), UNCTAD/DITC/TNCD/2005/4.

Matsushita, M. and Y.S. Lee, "Proliferation of Free Trade Agreements and Some Systemic Issues – In Relation to the WTO Disciplines and Development Perspectives" (2008) 1(1) *The Law and Development Review* 23–50.

McMahon, J., *The WTO Agreement on Agriculture, A Commentary: Oxford Commentaries on WTO Agreements* (Oxford: Oxford University Press, 2006).

Media reports

"Tariff Exemptions Expanded," *Washington Post*, August 23, 2002, at E02.

"A tricky business," *Economist*, June 28, 2001, available at: https://www.economist.com/business/2001/06/28/a-tricky-business [https://perma.cc/FE29-LTF5].

"Farmers Bring a Lawsuit to Invalidate the Decision by the Korean Trade Commission," *Hankook Ilbo* (newspaper, US version distributed in Chicago), September 7, 2002, p. 9.

"Bush Scales Back Tariffs on Steel" *New York Times*, August 23, 2002, p. A1.

"The Americas: U.S. Findings on Canada Lumber Are Rejected," *Wall Street Journal,* April 30, 2004, at A12.

"US and China Sign Textiles Deal," *BBC News*, November 8, 2005, text available at: http://news.bbc.co.uk/1/hi/business/4416858.stm [https://perma.cc/QH44-9EAF].

Messerlin, Patrick A., "Economic Effects of China's Accession to the World Trade Organization" (2004) 18(1) *The World Bank Economic Review* 127–128.

Mexico, *Decree Modifying the Tariff Schedule of the Law of General Import and Export Taxes, the Decree establishing the General Import Tax Rate applicable during 2003 for goods originating in North America, and the Decree establishing Various Sectoral Promotion Programs* (enacted June 5, 2018; effective June 5, 2018).

Miranda, Jorge, "Should Antidumping Laws Be Dumped?" (1996) 28 *Law and Policy in International Business* 255–288.

Montemayer, Raul, *Implications of the Proposed Modalities for the Special Safeguard Mechanism: A Simulation Exercise*, ICTSD Issue Paper No. 10 (November 2007).

Moore, Michael, "Rules or Politics? An Empirical Analysis of ITC Anti-Dumping Decisions" (2007) 30 *Economic Inquiry* 449–466.

Mueller, Felix, "Is the General Agreement on Tariffs and Trade Article XIX 'Unforeseen Developments Clause' Still Effective under the Agreement on Safeguards?" (2003) 37(6) *Journal of World Trade* 1119–1151.

Nelson, D., "Making Sense of the 1981 Automobile VER: Economics, Politics, and the Political Economy of Protection," *in* A. Krueger (ed.), *The Political Economy of Trade Protection* (Chicago: University of Chicago Press, 1996), pp. 35–42.

Nordås, Hildegunn K., *The Global Textile and Clothing Industry post the Agreement on Textiles and Clothing* (WTO Discussion Papers No. 5, 2004), p. 15.

Oesch, M., *Standards of Review in WTO Dispute Resolution* (Oxford: Oxford University Press, 2003).

Pauwelyn, Joost, "The Puzzle of WTO Safeguards and Regional Trade Agreements" (2004) 7 *Journal of International Economic Law* 109–142.

Peng, Shin-Yi, "Emergency Safeguard Measures for Trade in Services: A Case Study of Intradisciplinary Fragmentation," *in* C.L. Lim and Brian Mercurio (eds.), *International Economic Law After The Global Crisis: A Tale of Fragmented Disciplines* (Cambridge: Cambridge University Press, 2015), pp. 237–261.

Petersmann, Ernst-Ulrich, "Grey Area Trade Policy and the Rule of Law" (1988) 22 *Journal of World Trade* 23–44.

Pickard, Daniel B. and Tina Potuto Kimble, "Can U.S. Safeguard Actions Survive WTO Review? Section 201 Investigations in International Trade Law" (2007) 29 *Loyola L.A. International Law and Comparative Law Review* 43–59.

Piérola, Fernando, *The Challenge of Safeguards in the WTO* (Cambridge: Cambridge University Press, 2014), pp. 83–97.

Piérola-Castro, Fernando, *WTO Agreement on Safeguards and Article XIX of GATT: A Detailed Commentary* (New York: Cambridge University Press, 2022), p. 22.

Posner, Richard, *The Robinson-Patman Act: Federal Regulation of Price Differences* (Washington, DC: American Enterprise Institute, 1976).

Prusa, Thomas, "On the Spread and Impact of Anti-Dumping" (2001) 34 *Canadian Journal of Economics/Revue Canadienne D'économique* 591–611.

Prusa, Thomas J. and Edwin A. Vermulst, "Indonesia – Safeguard on Certain Iron or Steel Products: If It Looks Like a Duck, Swims Like a Duck, and Quacks Like a Duck, Then It Is Not a Duck" (2020) 19 *World Trade Review* 152–163.

Rai, Sheela, *Recognition and Regulation of Safeguard Measures under WTO* (Abingdon, Oxon; New York: Routledge, 2011).

Raina, Akhil, "What Is a Safeguard Measure under WTO Law?" (2019) 10(2) *Trade, Law and Development* 463–481.

Raychaudhuri, Tilottama, "The Unforeseen Developments Clause in Safeguards under the WTO: Confusions in Compliance" (2010) 11(1) *The Estey Centre Journal of International Law and Trade Policy* 302–320.

Reinert, Kenneth A., "Steel, Security and the WTO Dispute Settlement Mechanism: A Trade Catastrophe in the Making," *The World Economy* (February 28, 2024), available at: https://onlinelibrary.wiley.com/doi/abs/10.1111/twec.13556 (accessed April 21, 2024).

Ricardo, David, *Principles of Political Economy and Taxation* (1817), Introduction by F.W. Kolthhammer (Cambridge; London: Empiricus, 2002).

Ross, Thomas W., "Winners and Losers under the Robinson-Patman Act" (1984) 27 *Journal of Law and Economics* 243–279.

Ryan, David, "The Effects of Section 201 Safeguards on U.S. Industries" (2012) 44(1) *Georgetown Journal of International Law* 249–310.

Salvatore, Dominick, *International Economics* (London: Prentice Hall, 5th ed., 1995), p. 261, table 9-1.

Salvatore, Dominick, *International Economics* (Hoboken, NJ: John Wiley and Sons, Inc., 11th ed., 2013), pp. 221–228, 257–260.

Schott, Jeffrey J., *The Uruguay Round, An Assessment* (Washington, DC: Institute for International Economics, 1994), p.114.

Steel Manufacturers Association, *Recommended Action to Solve the Steel Import Crisis* (May 9, 2001).

Stevens, Christopher, *The Need for Special Products and Special Safeguard Mechanisms for Agriculture in the WTO: A Situational Analysis*, IDS Working Paper (September 30, 2004), text available at: http://ictsd.org/downloads/2008/08/stevens_paper1.pdf (accessed September 23, 2013).

Stevenson, Cliff, "Are World Trade Organization Members Correctly Applying World Trade Organization Rules in Safeguard Determinations?" (2004) 38 *Journal of World Trade* 307–329.

Stewart, Terence P. (ed.), *The GATT Uruguay Round: A Negotiating History (1986–1992)* (Kluwer Law and Taxation, The Hague, 1993), pp. 1717–1820.

Sykes, Alan O., "The Safeguards Mess: A Critique of WTO Jurisprudence" (2003) 2 *World Trade Review* 261–295.

Sykes, Alan O., "The Persistent Puzzles of Safeguards: Lessons from the Steel Dispute" (2004) 37 *Journal of International Economic Law* 523–564.

Sykes, Alan O., *The WTO Agreement on Safeguards* (Oxford: Oxford University Press, 2006).

Tayal, Pratik, "A New World of Causation in Safeguards: Application of the 'But for' Test" (2015) 10(10) *Global Trade and Customs Journal* 355–363.

Thennakoon, Jayanthi and Kym Anderson, "Could the Proposed WTO Special Safeguard Mechanism Protect Farmers from Low International Prices?" (2015) 50 *Food Policy* 106–113.

Trachtman, J. and C. Thomas (eds.), *Developing Countries in the WTO Legal System* (Oxford University Press, 2009).

Trebilcock, M. and R. Howse, *The Regulation of International Trade* (Routledge, 2nd ed., 1999), p. 228.

UNCTAD, *International Investment Agreements Navigator*, available at: https://investmentpolicy.unctad.org/international-investment-agreements [https://perma.cc/LM3G-HKPA].

United States, Agreement on Reciprocal Trade, December 23, 1942, US–Mexico, Article XI, 57 Stat. 833, 845–866.

United States, *United States Suggested Charter*, Department of State Publication No. 2598 (1946), Article 29, p. 22.

United States, Sections 201–204 of the Trade Act of 1974, as amended (19 U.S.C. §§ 2251–2254).

United States, *Statement of Administrative Action for the Uruguay Round Agreement on Safeguards, Message from the President of the United States Transmitting the Uruguay Round Trade Agreements, Texts of Agreements Implementing Bill, Statement of Administrative Action on Required Supporting Statements*, H.R. Doc. No. 316 vol. 1, 103rd Cong., 2nd Sess. 956–957 (September 27, 1994).

US Census Bureau, US Imports for Consumption of Steel Products, Exhibit 1: All Steel Products (released February 21, 2002).

US Department of Commerce, "Department of Commerce and USTR Announce Final Set of Products to Be Excluded From Safeguard on Steel Products," *Commerce News* (August 22, 2002).

US Department of Commerce, *The Effect of Imports of Steel on the National Security*, An Investigation Conducted under Section 232 of the Trade Expansion Act of 1962, as amended January 11, 2018.

US Department of Commerce, *The Effect of Imports of Aluminum on the National Security*, An Investigation Conducted under Section 232 of the Trade Expansion Act of 1962, as amended January 17, 2018.

US Department of Commerce, Bureau of Industry and Security, "Requirements for Submissions Requesting Exclusions From the Remedies Instituted in Presidential Proclamations Adjusting Imports of Steel Into the United States and Adjusting Imports of Aluminum into the United States," 83 *Federal Register* 12106 (March 19, 2018).

US House of Representatives Committee on Ways and Means, *Overview and Compilation of U.S. Trade Statutes* (1997), pp. 98–104, 561–578.

US International Trade Administration, *Antidumping and Countervailing Duty Statistics, Antidumping and Countervailing Duty Orders in effect as of July 26, 2002* (2002).

US International Trade Administration, "Steel Imports Report: United States," *Global Steel Trade Monitor* (September 2018).

US judicial reports: *State* v. *Harenza*, 213 Kan. 201, 515 P.2d 1217, 1222 (November 3, 1973); *Godesky* v. *Provo City Corp.*, Utah, 690 P.2d 541, 547 (September 12, 1984); *Mitsui Petrochemicals (America)* v. *US*, 21 C.I.T. 882, 885, 1997 WL 438840, 3 (July 3, 1997).

US Proclamations: "Proclamation 7529 of March 5, 2002 – To Facilitate Positive Adjustment to Competition from Imports of Certain Steel Products" and "Memorandum of March 5, 2002 – Action Under Section 203 of the Trade Act of 1974 Concerning Certain Steel Products by the President of the United States of America," *Federal Register* Vol. 67, No. 45 (March 7, 2002); "Proclamation 9705 of March 8, 2018 – Adjusting Imports of Steel Into the United States," 83 *Federal Register* 11625 (March 15, 2018); "Proclamation 9704 of March 8, 2018 – Adjusting Imports of Aluminum Into the United States," 83 *Federal Register* 11619 (March 15, 2018); Proclamation 9740 of April 30, 2018, 83 *Federal Register* 20683 (May 7, 2018); Proclamation 9758 of May 31, 2018, 83 *Federal Register* 25849 (June 5, 2018); Proclamation 9759 of May 31, 2018, 83 *Federal Register* 25857 (June 5, 2018).

USITC investigation reports: *Certain Motor Vehicles and Certain Chassis and Bodies Therefore*, Publication 1110, Investigation No. TA-201-44 (1980); *Certain Canned Tuna Fish*, 6 I.T.R.D. (B.N.A) 2464, 2466 (1984); *Electric Shavers and Parts Thereof*, 8 I.T.R.D. (B.N.A.) 1827, 1830 (1986); *Lamb Meat*, Publication 3176 (April 1999); *Wheat Gluten*, Publication 3423 (May 2001); *Steel*, Publication 3479 (December 2001); *Fresh, Chilled, or Frozen Blueberries*, Publication 5164, Investigation No. TA-201-77 (March 2021).

Valdés, Alberto and William Foster, "Special Safeguards for Developing Country Agriculture: A Proposal for WTO Negotiations" (2003) 2 *World Trade Review* 5–31.

Vermulst, Edwin, *The WTO Anti-Dumping Agreement: A Commentary* (Oxford: Oxford University Press, 2011).

Vermulst, Edwin and Folkert Graafsma, "EU Safeguard Law and Practice: 1995–2018" (2018) 13(9) *Global Trade and Customs Journal* 355–375.

Viner, Jacob, *Dumping: A Problem in International Trade* (New York: Kelly, 1966), p. 120.

World Bank, *Poverty*, available at: http://www.worldbank.org/en/topic/poverty/overview%20[https://perma.cc/WC7U-4X5N].

WTO, *Analytical Index: Guide to GATT Law and Practice* (Geneva: WTO, 6th ed., 1995), pp. 515–559.

WTO, *Formats for Certain Notifications under the Agreement on Safeguards*, G/SG/1 (July 1, 1996).

WTO, *Technical Cooperation Handbook on Notification Requirements*, WT/TC/NOTIF/TRIP/1(October 15, 1996), available at: http://www.wto.org/english/tratop_e/trips_e/tc_notif_trips1_e.pdf [https://perma.cc/KM48-7GVF].

WTO, *Comprehensive Report of the Textiles Monitoring Body to the Council for Trade in Goods on the Implementation of the Agreement on Textiles and Clothing during the Fist Stage of the Integration Process*, G/L/179 (July 31, 1997).

WTO, *Major Review of the Implementation of the Agreement on Textiles and Clothing in the First Stage of the Integration Process*, G/L/224 (February 19, 1998).

WTO, *2001 Press Releases*, Press/243 (September 17, 2001).

WTO, *Ministerial Declaration*, WT/MIN(01)/DEC/1 (November 14, 2001).

WTO, *Protocol on the Accession of the People's Republic of China*, WT/L/432, pp. 8–9 (November 23, 2001).

WTO, *Accession of the People's Republic of China*, General Council Decision, WT/L/432 (November 23, 2001).

WTO, *Notifications Pursuant to Article 12.1 (c) and Article 9, Footnote 2, of the Agreement on Safeguards on Taking a Decision to Apply a Safeguard Measure*, G/SG/N/11/USA/5 (March 14, 2002).

WTO, *Fourth Decision on Negotiations on Emergency Safeguard Measure*, S/L/102 (March 27, 2002).

WTO, *European Communities – Provisional Safeguard Measures on Imports of Certain Steel Products*, WT/DS260/4 (August 19, 2002).

WTO, *Fifth Decision on Negotiations on Emergency Safeguard Measure*, S/L/159 (March 15, 2004).

WTO, Chairperson's Working Documents November 2007 to January 2008, No. 14, *Special Agricultural Safeguard (SSG)*, http://www.wto.org/english/tratop_e/agric_e/workdoc_14sag_e.pdf [https://perma.cc/A8G5-BFKS].

WTO, *Revised Draft Modalities for Agriculture Special Safeguard Mechanism*, TN/AG/W/7 (December 6, 2008).

WTO, *World Trade Report 2009: Trade Policy Commitments and Contingency Measures* (Geneva, 2009), pp. 47–48.

WTO, *Negotiation Group on Agriculture*, TN/AG/25 (March 22, 2010), paras. 31–36.

WTO, *Analytical Index: Guide to WTO Law and Practice* (Geneva: WTO, 3rd ed., 2012), pp. 252–254, 292–294.

WTO, *International Trade Statistics 2012*, available at: http://www.wto.org/english/res_e/statis_e/its2012_e/its2012_e.pdf [https://perma.cc/2XP8-5RSB].

WTO, Report (2012) of the Committee on Anti-Dumping Practices, G/L/1006, October 25, 2012, Annex C.

WTO, *The Result of the Uruguay Round of Multilateral Trade Negotiations: The Legal Texts* (Cambridge: Cambridge University Press, reprint 2012).

WTO, *Nairobi Ministerial Declaration*, WT/MIN(15)/DEC (December 19, 2015).

WTO, *Ministerial Decision of 19 December 2015*, *Special Safeguard Mechanism for Developing Country Members*, WT/MIN(15)/43 (December 21, 2015).

WTO, *Members and Observers* (2016), available at: http://www.wto.org/english/thewto_e/whatis_e/tif_e/org6_e.htm%20[https://perma.cc/F9WV-QBY3].

WTO, *Annual Report of the Working Party on GATS Rules to the Counsel for Trade in Services (2016)*, S/WTGR/27 (November 23, 2016).

WTO, *Annual Report of the Working Party on GATS Rules to the Counsel for Trade in Services (2017)*, S/WTGR/28 (November 16, 2017).

WTO, *Anti-dumping Measures by Reporting Member 01/01/1995 – 30/06/2023*, available at: https://www.wto.org/english/tratop_e/adp_e/AD_MeasuresByRepMem.pdf%20[https://perma.cc/ECL3-6SD3].

WTO, *World Trade Statistical Review 2023*, p. 108. available at:
https://www.wto.org/english/res_e/booksp_e/wtsr_2023_e.pdf%20[https://perma.cc/YC96-X8BM].

WTO, *Draft Text on Agriculture*, WT/MIN(24)/W/13 (February 16, 2024).

WTO, *An Unofficial Guide to Agricultural Safeguards: GATT, Old Agricultural (SSG) and New Mechanism (SSM)*, available at: http://www.wto.org/english/tratop_e/agric_e/guide_agric_safeg_e.htm#problem [https://perma.cc/99WJ-JB37].

WTO, *Disputes by agreement*, available at:
https://www.wto.org/english/tratop_e/dispu_e/dispu_agreements_index_e.htm%20[https://perma.cc/44R4-2M2P].

WTO, *Legal Texts*, available at:
http://www.wto.org/english/docs._e/legal_e/legal_e.htm%20[https://perma.cc/HDN6-L49M].

WTO, *Market Access: Special Agricultural Safeguards (SSGs)*, available at: https://www.wto.org/english/tratop_e/agric_e/negs_bkgrnd11_ssg_e.htm [https://perma.cc/B4PM-XG32].

WTO, *Safeguard Initiations by Reporting Member*, text available at: https://www.wto.org/english/tratop_e/safeg_e/SG_InitiationsByRepMember.pdf [https://perma.cc/PCM7-R3HJ].

WTO, *Safeguard Measures by Reporting Member*, text available at: https://www.wto.org/english/tratop_e/safeg_e/sg_measuresbyrepmember.pdf [https://perma.cc/4AF5-QVDR].

WTO, *Safeguard Measures by Sector*, text available at: https://www.wto.org/english/tratop_e/safeg_e/SG_MeasuresBySector.pdf%20 [https://perma.cc/6YEK-TJ3M].

WTO Committee on Safeguards, *Notification under Article 12.5 of The Agreement on Safeguards to the Council for Trade in Goods of the Means of Compensation Referred to in Article 8.1 of The Agreement on Safeguards*, G/L/1400 (September 13, 2001).

WTO Committee on Safeguards, *Statement by Head of the Chinese Delegation on the Transitional Review of China to the Committee on Safeguards*, G/SG/W/192 (November 4, 2002).

WTO Committee on Safeguards, *Chairman's Report to the Council for Trade in Goods on Transitional Review of China*, G/SG/66 (November 17, 2003).

WTO Committee on Safeguards, *Annex 2 of the Report (2012) of the Committee on Safeguards to the Council for Trade in Goods*, G/L/651 (Nov. 6, 2012).

WTO Committee on Safeguards, *Minutes of the Regular Meeting Held on 23 April 2018*, G/SG/M/53 (July 25, 2018), at 11; *Formats for Certain Notifications under the Agreement on Safeguards,* G/SG/1/Rev.3 (May 4, 2021).

WTO Committee on Safeguards Annual Reports: G/L/409 (November 23, 2000); G/L/494 (October 31, 2001); G/L/583 (Nov. 4, 2002); G/L/651 (October 24, 2003); G/L/1009 (November 6, 2012); G/L/1503 (October 26, 2023).

WTO dispute settlement cases

Panel Report, WT/DS24/R (November 8, 1996), *United States – Restrictions on Imports of Cotton and Man Made Fibre Underwear.*

Panel Report, WT/DS33/R (January 6, 1997), *United States – Measure Affecting Imports of Woven Wool Shirts and Blouses from India.*

Appellate Body Report, WT/DS26/AB/R (January 16, 1998), *European Communities – Measures Concerning Meat and Meat Products.*

Panel Report, WT/DS44/R (March 20, 1998), *Japan – Measures Affecting Consumer Photographic Film and Paper.*

Appellate Body Report, WT/DS56/AB/R (March 27, 1998), *Argentina – Measures Affecting Imports of Footwear, Textiles, Apparel and Other Items.*

Panel Report, WT/DS98/R (June 21, 1999), *Korea – Definitive Safeguard Measure on Imports of Certain Dairy Products.*

Appellate Body Report, WT/DS98/AB/R (December 14, 1999), *Korea – Definitive Safeguard Measure on Imports of Certain Dairy Products.*

Panel Report, WT/DS121/R (June 25, 1999), *Argentina – Safeguard Measures on Imports of Footwear.*

Appellate Body Report, WT/DS121/R (December 14, 1999), *Argentina – Safeguard Measures on Imports of Footwear.*

Panel Report, WT/DS166/R (July 31, 2000), *United States – Definitive Safeguard Measures on Imports of Wheat Gluten From the European Communities.*

Appellate Body Report, WT/DS166/AB/R (December 22, 2000) *United States – Definitive Safeguard Measures on Imports of Wheat Gluten From the European Communities.*

Panel Report, WT/DS177/R, WT/DS178/R (December 21, 2000), *United States – Safeguard Measures on Imports of Fresh, Chilled or Frozen Lamb Meat from New Zealand and Australia.*

Appellate Body Report, WT/DS177/AB/R, WT/DS178/AB/R (May 1, 2001), *United States – Safeguard Measures on Imports of Fresh, Chilled or Frozen Lamb Meat from New Zealand and Australia.*

Panel Report, WT/DS179/R (December 22, 2000) *United States – Anti-dumping Measures on Stainless Steel Plate in Coils and Stainless Steel Sheet and Strip from Korea.*

Appellate Body Report, WT/DS184/AB/R (July 24, 2001), para. 228, *United States – Hotrolled Steel Products from Japan.*

Panel Report, WT/202/R (October 29, 2001), *United States – Definitive Safeguard Measures on Imports of Steel Wire Rod and Circular Welded Carbon Quality Line Pipe.*

WTO dispute settlement cases (continued)

Appellate Body Report, WT/202/AB/R (February 15, 2002), *United States – Definitive Safeguard Measures on Imports of Steel Wire Rod and Circular Welded Carbon Quality Line Pipe.*

Panel Report, WT/DS207/R (May 3, 2002), *Chile – Price Band System and Safeguard Measures relating to Certain Agricultural Products.*

Panel Report, WT/DS238/R (February 14, 2003), *Argentina – Definitive Safeguard Measure on Imports of Preserved Peaches.*

Panel Report, WT/DS248~DS259/R (July 11, 2003), *United States – Definitive Safeguard Measures on Imports of Certain Steel Products.*

Appellate Body Report, WT/DS248~DS259/AB/R (November 10, 2003), *United States – Definitive Safeguard Measures on Imports of Certain Steel Products.*

Report of the Panel, WT/DS399/R (December 13, 2010), *United States – Measures Affecting Imports of Certain Passenger Vehicle and Light Truck Tyres from China.*

Appellate Body Report, WT/DS399/AB/R (September 5, 2011), *United States – Measures Affecting Imports of Certain Passenger Vehicle and Light Truck Tyres from China.*

Panel Report, WT/DS415~DS418/R (January 31, 2012), *Dominican Republic — Safeguard Measures on Imports of Polypropylene Bags and Tubular Fabric.*

Panel Report, WT/DS438/R, WT/DS444/R, WT/DS445/R (August 22, 2014), *Argentina – Measures Affecting the Importation of Goods.*

Appellate Body Report, WT/DS438/R, WT/DS444/R, WT/DS445/R (January 15, 2015), *Argentina – Measures Affecting the Importation of Goods.*

Panel Report, WT/DS468/R (June 26, 2015), *Ukraine – Definitive Safeguard Measures on Certain Passenger Cars.*

Panel Report, WT/DS490/R, WT/DS496/R (August 18, 2017), *Indonesia – Safeguard on Certain Iron or Steel Products.*

Appellate Body Report, WT/DS490/AB/R, WT/DS496/AB/R (August 15, 2018), *Indonesia – Safeguard on Certain Iron or Steel Products.*

Panel Report, WT/DS518/R (November 6, 2018), *India – Certain Measures on Imports of Iron or Steel Product.*

Panel Report, WT/DS545/R, WT/DS562/R (September 20, 2021), *United States — Safeguard Measure on Imports of Crystalline Silicon Photovoltaic Product.*

Panel Report, WT/DS546/R (February 8, 2022), *United States – Safeguard Measures on Imports of Large Residential Washers.*

WTO dispute settlement cases (continued)

Panel Report, WT/DS595/R (April 28, 2022), *European Union – Safeguard Measures on Certain Steel Products.*

Panel Report, WT/DS544/R, WT/DS552/R, WT/DS556/R, WT/DS564/R (December 9, 2022), *United States – Certain Measures on Steel and Aluminum Products.*

WTO documents on the Working Party on GATS Rules: S/WPGR/M/18 (November 13 1998); S/WPGR/W/1 (July 6, 1995); S/WPGR/W/1 (July 6, 1995); S/WPGR/W/24 (September 3, 1997); S/WPGR/W/1 (Jul. 6, 1995); S/WPGR/W/27 (November 20, 1998); S/WPGR/M/19 (January 21, 1999); S/WPGR/M/20 (March 17, 1999); S/WPGR/M/19 (January 21, 1999); S/WPGR/M/20 (March 17, 1999); S/WPGR/W/37 (October 2, 2001); S/WPGR/W/38 (January 21, 2002); S/WPGR/M/47 (April 22, 2004); S/WPGR/M/49 (October 27, 2004); S/WPGR/M/54 (February 22, 2006); S/WPGR/M/55 (May 4, 2006); S/WPGR/M/56 (July 4, 2006); S/WPGR/M/57 (May 9, 2007); S/WPGR/20 (November 8, 2010); S/WPGR/21 (April 14, 2011); S/WPGR/22 (November 10, 2011); S/WPGR/M/54 (February 22, 2006); S/WPGR/M/79 (October 16, 2012); S/WPGR/23 (November 29, 2012); S/WPGR/W/64 (September 4, 2014); S/WPGR/M/86 (May 22, 2015), S/WPGR/28 (November 16, 2017), S/WPGR/29 (November 27, 2018), S/WPGR/30 (November 21, 2019), S/WPGR/31 (November 27, 2020), S/WPGR/32 (October 18, 2021), S/WTGR/22 (December 6, 2022), S/WTGR/34 (November 27, 2023).

WTO notifications on compensation (referred to in Article 8.1 of the SA): G/L/1400 (September 13, 2001), G/L/1108 (March 5, 2015), G/L/1112 (March 31, 2015).

WTO notifications on laws, regulations and administrative procedures relating to safeguard measures: G/SG/N/1/USA/1 (April 6, 1995); G/SG/N/1/EEC/2 (November 12, 2010).

WTO notifications on special safeguard provisions and SSGs: G/AG/N/USA/4 (March 28, 1996); G/AG/N/EEC/10 (April 2, 1998); G/AG/N/USA/87 (September 13, 2012); G/AG/N/EU/9 (October 31, 2012).

WTO notifications on the application of provisional safeguard measures: G/SG/N/7/EEC/1 (April 2, 2002); G/SG/N/7/CHN/1 (May 23, 2002); G/SG/N/7/HUN/1 (May 23, 2002).

WTO notifications on the extension of negotiations on compensation: G/SG/N/12/EEC/3 (April 19, 2000); G/SG/N/12/USA/6 (May 16, 2002);

G/SG/N/12/USA/7 (May 16, 2002); G/SG/N/12/USA/8 (May 17, 2002); G/SG/N/12/USA/9 (May 17, 2002); G/SG/N/12/USA/10 (June 14, 2002).

WTO notifications on proposed retaliatory measures: G/SG/43 (May 15, 2002); G/SG/44 (May 21, 2002); G/SG/45 (May 21, 2002); G/SG/46 (May 21, 2002); G/SG/47 (May 22, 2002); G/SG/N/12/EU/1 (May 18, 2018); G/SG/N/12/RUS/2 (May 22, 2018); G/SG/N/12/CHN/1 (April 3, 2018); G/SG/N/12/TUR/6 (May 22, 2018); G/SG/N/12/IND/1/Rev.1 (June 14, 2018), G/SG/N/12/RUS/2 (May 22, 2018), G/SG/N/12/CHN/1 (April 3, 2018), G/SG/N/12/TUR/6 (May 22, 2018), G/SG/N/12/IND/1/Rev.1 (June 14, 2018).

WTO notifications on proposed safeguard measures and appeals: G/SG/N/11/USA/5 (March 14, 2002); WT/DS543/10 (October 27, 2020); WT/DS544/14 (January 30, 2023).

Xu, Jia, "One Step Forward and Two Steps Back? Evolution of Bilateral Safeguard Provisions in Preferential Trade Agreements" (2021) 55(3) *Journal of World Trade* 433–452.

Yano, Hiromi, "Rebalancing the Trading Scale? Recent Trends in the Implementation of Article 8 of the Safeguards Agreement" (2024) 19(2) *Global Trade and Customs Journal* 110–113.

Yu, Yanning, "China's Adopting Emergency Safeguard Measures for Services: A Political Economy Analysis" (2011) 6 *Asian Journal of WTO and International Health Law and Policy* 429–453.

Zheng, Wentong, "Reforming Trade Remedies" (2012) 34(1) *Michigan Journal of International Law* 151–208.

Zhou, Weihuan and Mandy Meng Fang, "'Unforeseen Developments' Before and After US – Safeguard Measure on PV Products: High Standard or New Standard?" (2023) 22(5) *World Trade Review* 541–561.

Zissimos, Ben and Jan Wouters, "US–Shrimp II (Vietnam): Dubious Application of Anti-Dumping Duties – Should Have Used Safeguards" (2017) 16(2) *World Trade Review* 183–201.

APPENDIX 1: STATISTICS ON SAFEGUARD MEASURES

Table A.1 *Safeguard initiation by reporting member*

Period: 01/01/1995 to 12/31/2023

Reporting Member	95	96	97	98	99	00	01	02	03	04	05	06	07	08	09	10	11	12	13	14	15	16	17	18	19	20	21	22	23	Total
Argentina	0	0	1	1	0	1	1	0	0	1	0	1	0	0	0	0	0	0	0	0	0	0	0	0	0	0	0	0	0	**6**
Australia	0	0	0	1	0	0	0	0	0	0	0	0	1	0	0	0	0	0	2	0	0	0	0	0	0	0	0	0	0	**4**
Brazil	0	1	0	0	0	0	1	0	0	0	0	0	0	1	0	0	0	1	0	0	0	0	0	0	0	0	0	0	0	**4**
Bulgaria[1]	0	0	0	0	0	1	1	3	1	0	0	0	0	0	0	0	0	0	0	0	0	0	0	0	0	0	0	0	0	**6**
Canada	0	0	0	0	0	0	0	1	0	0	2	0	0	0	0	0	0	0	0	0	0	0	0	1	0	0	0	0	0	**4**
Chile	0	0	0	0	2	3	2	2	0	1	0	1	0	0	1	0	0	1	2	0	4	0	0	1	0	0	0	0	0	**20**
China	0	0	0	0	0	0	0	1	0	0	0	0	0	0	0	0	0	0	0	0	0	1	0	0	0	0	0	0	0	**2**
Colombia	0	0	0	0	1	0	0	0	0	2	0	0	0	0	0	0	0	0	4	0	0	0	0	0	1	0	0	0	0	**8**
Costa Rica	0	0	0	0	0	0	0	1	0	0	0	0	0	0	0	0	0	1	0	1	0	0	0	1	1	0	0	0	0	**5**
Croatia[1]	0	0	0	0	0	0	0	0	0	0	0	0	0	0	1	0	0	0	0	0	0	0	0	0	0	0	0	0	0	**1**
Czech Republic[1]	0	0	0	0	1	2	1	5	0	0	0	0	0	0	0	0	0	0	0	0	0	0	0	0	0	0	0	0	0	**9**
Dominican Republic	0	0	0	0	0	0	0	0	0	0	0	0	0	0	3	2	0	0	0	0	0	0	0	0	0	0	0	0	0	**5**
Ecuador	0	0	0	0	2	0	0	1	4	0	0	0	0	0	0	1	0	0	0	1	0	0	0	0	1	0	0	0	0	**10**
Egypt	0	0	0	1	1	1	0	0	0	0	0	0	0	1	0	0	1	4	0	2	2	0	0	0	1	1	0	0	0	**15**
El Salvador	0	0	0	0	0	3	0	0	0	0	0	0	0	0	0	0	0	0	0	0	0	0	0	0	0	0	0	0	0	**3**
Estonia[1]	0	0	0	0	0	0	0	0	1	0	0	0	0	0	0	0	0	0	0	0	0	0	0	0	0	0	0	0	0	**1**
European Union[1]	0	0	0	0	0	0	0	1	1	1	1	0	0	0	0	1	0	0	0	0	0	0	0	1	0	0	0	0	0	**6**
Guatemala	0	0	0	0	0	0	0	0	0	0	0	0	0	0	0	0	0	0	0	0	0	0	0	0	1	0	0	0	0	**1**
Hungary[1]	0	0	0	0	0	0	0	1	2	0	0	0	0	0	0	0	0	0	0	0	0	0	0	0	0	0	0	0	0	**3**
India	0	0	1	5	3	2	0	2	1	1	0	0	0	1	10	1	1	1	3	7	2	1	1	0	3	0	0	1	1	**48**
Indonesia	0	0	0	0	0	0	0	0	0	1	1	1	0	2	0	7	4	7	0	3	1	0	0	2	5	4	0	0	0	**38**
Israel	0	0	0	0	0	0	0	0	0	0	0	0	0	0	1	0	1	0	0	0	0	0	0	0	0	0	0	0	0	**2**
Jamaica	0	0	0	0	0	0	0	0	1	0	0	0	0	0	0	0	0	0	0	0	0	0	0	0	0	0	0	0	0	**1**
Japan	0	0	0	0	0	1	0	0	0	0	0	0	0	0	0	0	0	0	0	0	0	0	0	0	0	0	0	0	0	**1**

Period: 01/01/1995 to 12/31/2023

Reporting Member	95	96	97	98	99	00	01	02	03	04	05	06	07	08	09	10	11	12	13	14	15	16	17	18	19	20	21	22	23	Total
Jordan	0	0	0	0	0	1	0	8	0	0	1	1	1	2	0	1	0	1	0	1	0	1	0	0	1	0	0	0	0	**19**
Korea, Rep. of	1	2	0	0	1	0	0	0	0	0	0	0	0	0	0	0	0	0	0	0	0	0	0	0	0	0	0	0	0	**4**
Kyrgyz Rep.[2]	0	0	0	0	0	0	0	0	0	0	0	0	0	0	2	1	0	0	1	0	0	0	0	0	0	0	0	0	0	**4**
Latvia[1]	0	0	0	0	1	0	0	1	0	0	0	0	0	0	0	0	0	0	0	0	0	0	0	0	0	0	0	0	0	**2**
Lithuania[1]	0	0	0	0	0	0	1	0	0	0	0	0	0	0	0	0	1	0	0	0	0	0	0	0	0	0	0	0	0	**1**
Madagascar	0	0	0	0	0	0	0	0	0	0	0	0	0	0	0	0	4	0	0	0	0	0	0	3	4	0	0	1	4	**12**
Malaysia	0	0	0	0	0	0	0	0	0	0	0	0	0	0	0	0	1	0	0	1	1	2	0	0	0	1	0	0	0	**6**
Mexico	0	0	0	0	0	0	0	1	0	0	0	0	0	0	0	1	0	0	0	0	0	0	0	0	0	0	0	0	0	**2**
Moldova, Rep. of	0	0	0	0	0	0	0	0	1	1	0	0	0	0	0	0	0	0	0	0	0	0	0	0	0	0	0	0	0	**2**
Morocco	0	0	0	0	0	2	0	0	0	0	1	0	0	0	1	1	0	1	0	1	1	0	0	1	2	0	1	1	0	**13**
Pakistan	0	0	0	0	0	0	0	0	0	0	1	0	0	0	0	0	0	0	0	0	0	0	0	0	0	0	0	0	0	**1**
Panama	0	0	0	0	0	0	0	0	0	0	0	1	0	0	0	0	0	0	0	0	0	0	0	0	1	0	0	0	0	**2**
Peru	0	0	0	0	0	0	0	0	0	1	0	0	0	0	1	0	0	0	0	0	0	0	0	0	0	1	1	0	0	**4**
Philippines	0	0	0	0	0	0	3	0	3	0	0	1	0	1	1	0	0	0	2	0	0	0	0	2	2	5	0	0	1	**21**
Poland[1]	0	0	0	0	0	1	0	4	0	0	0	0	0	0	0	0	0	0	0	0	0	0	0	0	0	0	0	0	0	**5**
Russian Federation[2]	0	0	0	0	0	0	0	0	0	0	0	0	0	0	0	0	1	3	0	0	0	0	0	1	2	0	0	0	0	**7**
Saudi Arabia[3]	0	0	0	0	0	0	0	0	0	0	0	0	0	0	0	0	0	0	0	0	0	2	1	0	1	0	0	0	0	**4**
Slovak Republic[1]	0	0	0	0	1	1	0	1	0	0	0	0	0	0	0	0	0	0	0	0	0	0	0	0	0	0	0	0	0	**3**
Slovenia[1]	0	0	0	1	0	0	0	0	0	0	0	0	0	0	0	0	0	0	0	0	0	0	0	0	0	0	0	0	0	**1**
South Africa[1]	0	0	0	0	0	0	0	0	0	0	0	0	1	0	0	0	0	1	1	0	0	2	0	1	1	2	0	0	0	**9**
Chinese Taipei	0	0	0	0	0	0	0	0	0	0	0	0	0	0	0	0	0	0	1	0	0	0	0	0	0	0	0	0	0	**1**
Thailand	0	0	0	0	0	0	0	0	0	0	0	0	0	0	0	1	0	2	0	1	0	1	0	0	0	1	0	0	0	**6**
Tunisia	0	0	0	0	0	0	0	0	0	0	0	2	0	0	0	0	0	0	0	2	1	0	0	0	0	0	1	1	0	**7**
Türkiye	0	0	0	0	0	0	0	0	0	5	0	5	3	1	1	0	1	0	1	3	1	0	2	2	0	2	1	0	1	**29**
Ukraine	0	0	0	0	0	0	0	0	0	0	0	0	2	1	2	3	2	0	1	0	1	0	1	0	3	4	5	0	0	**25**

Period: 01/01/1995 to 12/31/2023

Reporting Member	95	96	97	98	99	00	01	02	03	04	05	06	07	08	09	10	11	12	13	14	15	16	17	18	19	20	21	22	23	Total
United Kingdom[5]	n.a.	n.a.	n.a.	n.a.	n.a.	n.a.	n.a.	n.a.	n.a.	n.a.	n.a.	n.a.	n.a.	n.a.	n.a.	n.a.	n.a.	n.a.	n.a.	n.a.	n.a.	n.a.	n.a.	n.a.	n.a.	0	0	0	0	0
United States	1	2	1	1	2	2	1	0	0	0	0	0	0	0	0	0	0	0	0	0	2	0	0	0	0	1	0	0	0	13
Venezuela	0	0	0	0	0	4	1	1	0	0	0	0	0	0	0	0	0	0	0	0	0	0	0	0	0	0	0	0	0	6
Viet Nam	0	0	0	0	0	0	0	0	0	0	0	0	0	0	1	0	0	1	0	0	2	1	1	0	0	0	0	0	0	6
Zambia	0	0	0	0	0	0	0	0	0	0	0	0	0	0	0	0	0	0	0	0	1	0	0	0	0	0	0	0	0	1
Totals for 01/01/1995-12/31/2023	2	5	3	10	15	25	12	34	15	14	7	13	8	10	25	20	12	24	18	23	17	11	8	16	30	22	9	4	12	424

Notes: [1]The European Union enlarged its Membership on 1 May 2004, 1 January 2007, and 1 July 2013. The newly acceded countries still appear on the tables in this database as individual WTO Members as their statistics prior to joining the European Union remain valid. All figures pertaining to the European Union are counted: (a) on a 15-Member basis for the period between 1 January 1995 and 30 April 2004, (b) on a 25-Member basis for the period between 1 May 2004 and 31 December 2006, (c) on a 27-Member basis for the period between 1 January 2007 and 30 June 2013, and (d) on a 28-Member basis for the period between 1 July 2013 and 31 January 2020. The United Kingdom withdrew from the European Union as of 1 February 2020, hence the European Union is counted on a 27-Member basis from 1 February 2020.

[2] All actions taken as Eurasian Economic Union as a whole are shown under the Russian Federation. Members of the Eurasian Economic Union are: Armenia, Belarus (non-WTO Member), Kazakhstan, Kyrgyz Republic, and the Russian Federation. Individual members of the Eurasian Economic Union are not shown in this table except for Kyrgyz Republic. The row for Kyrgyz Republic indicates actions it had taken before it became a member of the Eurasian Economic Union.

[3] All actions taken as the Gulf Cooperation Council (GCC) as a whole are shown under Saudi Arabia, Kingdom of. Members of the GCC are: Kingdom of Bahrain, the State of Kuwait, Oman, Qatar, Kingdom of Saudi Arabia, and United Arab Emirates. Individual members of the GCC are not shown in this table.

[4] All actions taken as the Southern African Customs Union (SACU) as a whole are shown under South Africa. Members of the SACU are: Botswana, Eswatini, Lesotho, Namibia, and South Africa. Individual members of the SACU are not shown in this table.

Source: WTO website, https://www.wto.org/english/tratop_e/safeg_e/SG_InitiationsByRepMember.pdf [https://perma.cc/PCM7-R3HJ].

Table A.2 *Safeguard measures by reporting member*

Period: 01/01/1995 to 12/31/2023

Reporting Member	96	97	98	99	00	01	02	03	04	05	06	07	08	09	10	11	12	13	14	15	16	17	18	19	20	21	22	23	Total
Argentina	0	1	0	0	0	2	0	0	0	0	0	1	0	0	0	0	0	0	0	0	0	0	0	0	0	0	0	0	4
Brazil	0	1	0	0	0	0	1	0	0	0	0	0	0	0	0	0	0	0	0	0	0	0	0	0	0	0	0	0	2
Bulgaria[1]	0	0	0	0	0	0	2	0	0	0	0	0	0	0	0	0	0	0	0	0	0	0	0	0	0	0	0	0	2
Canada	0	0	0	0	0	0	0	0	0	0	0	0	0	0	0	0	0	0	0	0	0	0	0	1	0	0	0	0	1
Chile	0	0	0	0	2	1	2	0	0	1	1	0	0	0	0	0	1	0	0	0	1	0	0	0	0	0	0	0	9
China	0	0	0	0	0	0	1	0	0	0	0	0	0	0	0	0	0	0	0	0	0	1	0	0	0	0	0	0	2
Colombia	0	0	0	0	0	0	0	0	0	0	0	0	0	0	0	0	0	0	1	0	0	0	0	0	0	0	0	0	1
Costa Rica	0	0	0	0	0	0	0	0	0	0	0	0	0	1	0	0	0	0	0	1	0	0	0	0	1	0	0	0	2
Croatia[1]	0	0	0	0	0	0	0	0	0	0	0	0	0	0	0	0	0	0	0	0	0	0	0	0	0	0	0	0	1
Czech Republic[1]	0	0	0	1	0	1	1	0	0	0	0	0	0	0	0	0	0	0	0	0	0	0	0	0	0	0	0	0	5
Dominican Republic	0	0	0	0	0	0	0	0	0	0	0	0	0	0	2	0	0	0	0	0	0	0	0	0	0	0	0	0	2
Ecuador	0	0	0	0	0	1	0	1	1	0	0	0	0	0	1	0	0	0	0	1	0	0	0	0	0	0	0	0	5
Egypt	0	0	0	1	1	1	0	0	0	0	0	0	1	0	0	0	1	0	0	1	0	0	0	1	0	1	0	0	8
European Union[1]	0	0	0	0	0	0	1	0	1	1	0	0	0	0	0	0	0	0	0	0	0	0	0	1	0	0	0	0	4
Hungary[1]	0	0	0	0	0	0	0	3	0	0	0	0	0	0	0	0	0	0	0	0	0	0	0	0	0	0	0	0	3
India	0	0	4	0	1	0	2	0	0	1	0	0	0	3	0	1	2	0	4	0	2	0	1	0	0	0	0	2	24
Indonesia	0	0	0	0	0	0	0	0	0	0	1	0	0	2	0	7	1	1	2	3	0	0	1	1	5	4	0	0	28
Jordan	0	0	0	1	0	1	1	2	0	1	0	1	0	0	1	0	0	1	0	0	0	1	0	0	0	0	0	0	9
Korea, Rep. of	0	1	0	0	1	0	0	0	0	0	0	0	0	0	0	0	0	0	0	0	0	0	0	0	0	0	0	0	2
Kyrgyz Rep.[2]	0	0	0	0	0	0	0	0	0	0	0	0	0	1	0	0	0	1	0	0	0	0	0	0	0	0	0	0	2
Latvia[1]	0	0	0	0	0	0	0	1	0	0	0	0	0	0	0	0	0	0	0	0	0	0	0	0	0	0	0	0	2
Lithuania[1]	0	0	0	0	0	0	1	0	0	0	0	0	0	0	0	0	0	0	0	0	0	0	0	0	0	0	0	0	1

Period: 01/01/1995 to 12/31/2023

Reporting Member	96	97	98	99	00	01	02	03	04	05	06	07	08	09	10	11	12	13	14	15	16	17	18	19	20	21	22	23	Total
Madagascar	0	0	0	0	0	0	0	0	0	0	0	0	0	0	0	0	0	0	0	0	0	0	0	2	1	0	0	3	**6**
Malaysia	0	0	0	0	0	0	0	0	0	0	0	0	0	0	0	0	0	0	0	1	0	2	0	0	0	0	0	0	**3**
Moldova, Rep. of	0	0	0	0	0	0	0	0	1	0	0	0	0	0	0	0	0	0	0	0	0	0	0	0	0	0	0	0	**1**
Morocco	0	0	0	0	0	1	0	0	0	0	1	0	0	0	0	0	0	1	0	1	0	1	0	1	2	0	0	0	**8**
Panama	0	0	0	0	0	0	0	0	0	0	0	1	0	0	0	0	0	0	0	0	0	0	0	0	0	0	0	0	**1**
Philippines	0	0	0	0	0	0	1	1	3	0	0	0	0	1	0	1	0	0	0	1	0	0	0	1	0	0	1	0	**10**
Poland[1]	0	0	0	0	0	0	0	4	0	0	0	0	0	0	0	0	0	0	0	0	0	0	0	0	0	0	0	0	**4**
Russian Federation[2]	0	0	0	0	0	0	0	0	0	0	0	0	0	0	0	0	1	1	1	0	0	0	0	1	0	0	0	0	**4**
Saudi Arabia	0	0	0	0	0	0	0	0	0	0	0	0	0	0	0	0	0	0	0	0	0	0	1	1	0	0	0	0	**2**
Slovak Republic[1]	0	0	0	0	0	1	0	1	0	0	0	0	0	0	0	0	0	0	0	0	0	0	0	0	0	0	0	0	**2**
South Africa[4]	0	0	0	0	0	0	0	0	0	0	0	1	0	0	0	0	0	0	1	0	0	1	0	1	1	1	0	0	**6**
Thailand	0	0	0	0	0	0	0	0	0	0	0	0	0	0	0	1	0	1	0	1	0	1	0	0	0	0	0	0	**4**
Tunisia	0	0	0	0	0	0	0	0	0	0	0	0	0	0	0	0	0	0	0	0	0	0	0	0	0	0	0	1	**1**
Türkiye	0	0	0	0	0	0	0	0	0	2	4	1	4	1	0	1	0	0	1	1	0	1	0	1	1	1	1	0	**20**
Ukraine	0	0	0	0	0	0	0	0	0	0	0	0	1	1	0	0	0	1	1	0	1	0	1	0	1	2	0	0	**9**
United Kingdom[5]	n.a.	n.a.	n.a.	n.a.	n.a.	n.a.	n.a.	n.a.	n.a.	n.a.	n.a.	n.a.	n.a.	n.a.	n.a.	n.a.	n.a.	n.a.	n.a.	n.a.	n.a.	n.a.	n.a.	n.a.	0	0	0	0	**0**
United States	1	0	1	1	2	0	1	0	0	0	0	0	0	0	0	0	0	0	0	0	0	0	2	0	0	0	0	0	**8**
Viet Nam	0	0	0	0	0	0	0	0	0	0	0	0	0	0	0	0	0	1	0	0	2	1	1	0	0	0	0	0	**5**
Totals for 01/01/1995–12/31/2023	**1**	**3**	**5**	**5**	**7**	**9**	**14**	**15**	**6**	**6**	**7**	**5**	**6**	**10**	**4**	**11**	**6**	**8**	**11**	**11**	**6**	**9**	**7**	**12**	**12**	**9**	**2**	**6**	**213**

Notes: [1] The European Union enlarged its Membership on 1 May 2004, 1 January 2007, and 1 July 2013. The newly-acceded countries still appear on the tables in this database as individual WTO Members as their statistics prior to joining the European Union remain valid. All figures pertaining to the European Union are counted: (a) on a 15-Member basis for the period between 1 January 1995 and 30 April 2004, (b) on a 25-Member basis for the period between 1 May 2004 and 31 December 2006, (c) on a 27-Member basis for the period between 1 January 2007 and 30 June 2013, and (d) on a 28-Member basis for the period between 1 July 2013 and 31 January 2020. The United Kingdom withdrew from the European Union as of 1 February 2020, hence the European Union is counted on a 27-Member basis from 1 February 2020.

[2] All actions taken as Eurasian Economic Union as a whole are shown under the Russian Federation. Members of the Eurasian Economic Union are: Armenia, Belarus (non-WTO Member), Kazakhstan, Kyrgyz Republic, and the Russian Federation. Individual members of the Eurasian Economic Union are not shown in this table except for Kyrgyz Republic. The row for Kyrgyz Republic indicates actions it had taken before it became a member of the Eurasian Economic Union.

[3] All actions taken as the Gulf Cooperation Council (GCC) as a whole are shown under Saudi Arabia, Kingdom of. Members of the GCC are: Kingdom of Bahrain, the State of Kuwait, Oman, Qatar, Kingdom of Saudi Arabia, and United Arab Emirates. Individual members of the GCC are not shown in this table.

[4] All actions taken as the Southern African Customs Union (SACU) as a whole are shown under South Africa. Members of the SACU are: Botswana, Eswatini, Lesotho, Namibia, and South Africa. Individual members of the SACU are not shown in this table.

[5] This table takes no position regarding the timing of the imposition of the safeguard measure on certain steel products. (See, for example, notification G/SG/N/8/GBR/1/Suppl.1-G/SG/N/10/GBR/1-G/SG/N/11/GBR/1 for context.)

Source: WTO website, https://www.wto.org/english/tratop_e/safeg_e/SG_MeasuresByRepMember.pdf [https://perma.cc/V97V-2HAD].

Table A.3 *Summary of various notifications between October 24, 2022 and October 25, 2023*[1]

Reporting Member and Product		Safeguard investigations initiated[2]	Provisional safeguard measures	Definitive safeguard measures (including recommendations of imposition as well as decision to extend an existing measure)[3]	Safeguard investigations terminated without measures	Expired or terminated measures[4]
European Union	Certain steel products	26/02/2021 G/SG/N/6/EU/1/ Suppl.2 [n:26/02/2021] (Review - Extension)		G/SG/N/10/EU/1/Suppl.16[5] 01/07/2023 G/SG/N/10/EU/1/ Suppl.17[6] [n:02/06/2023]		
Costa Rica	Refined white sugar	30/06/2019 G/SG/N/6/CRI/5 [n:09/07/2019]				19/08/2023 G/SG/N/10/CRI /2/ Suppl.1 [n:04/09/2023]
India	Low Ash Metallurgical Coke	30/06/2023 G/SG/N/6/IND/49 [n:11/07/2023]				
India	Isopropyl Alcohol	04/11/2019 G/SG/N/6/IND/47 [n:15/11/2019]		01/04/2023 G/SG/N/10/IND/24/ Suppl.1 [n:05/04/2023]		
India	PVC Suspension resins with residual VCM	16/09/2022 G/SG/N/6/IND/48 [n:11/10/2022]		G/SG/N/10/IND/257 [n:14/06/2023] (Proposal)[7]		
Indonesia	Cigarette paper	23/06/2023 G/SG/N/6/IDN/37/ Suppl.1 [n:05/07/2023] (Review - Extension)		30/11/2023 G/SG/N/10/IDN/29/ Suppl.2 [n:06/09/2023] (Extension – Imposition)		
Indonesia	I and H Sections of Other Alloy Steel	02/02/2021 G/SG/N/6/IDN/25/ Suppl.4 [n:04/02/2021] (Review - Extension)		22/12/2022 G/SG/N/10/IDN/17/ Suppl.5 [n:19/12/2022] (Extension – Imposition)		
Indonesia	Curtains (Including Drapes), Interior Blinds, Bed Valances, and Other Furnishing Articles	25/04/2022 G/SG/N/6/IDN/33/ Suppl.1 [n:27/04/2022] (Review - Extension)		22/05/2023 G/SG/N/10/IDN/24/ Suppl.3 [n:19/05/2023] (Extension - Imposition)		

Reporting Member and Product		Safeguard investigations initiated[2]	Provisional safeguard measures	Definitive safeguard measures (including recommendations of imposition as well as decision to extend an existing measure)[3]	Safeguard investigations terminated without measures	Expired or terminated measures[4]
Indonesia	Carpets and other textile floor coverings	10/06/2020 G/SG/N/6/IDN/35 [n:12/06/2020] (Original investigation) 18/08/2023 G/SG/N/6/IDN/35/ Suppl.1 [n:24/08/2023] (Review - Extension)		G/SG/N/11/IDN/24/Suppl.1[8]		
Indonesia	Yarn (Other Than Sewing Thread) of Synthetic and Artificial Staple Fibre	25/04/2022 G/SG/N/6/IDN/32/ Suppl.1 [n:27/04/2022] (Review - Extension)		22/05/2023 G/SG/N/10/IDN/25/ Suppl.3 [n:19/05/2023] (Extension - Imposition)		
Indonesia	Fructose Syrup	14/04/2023 G/SG/N/6/IDN/34/ Suppl.1 [n:28/04/2023] (Review - Extension)		17/09/2023 G/SG/N/10/IDN/26/ Suppl.2 [n:26/06/2023] (Extension – Imposition) G/SG/N/11/IDN/23/ Suppl.2[9] [n:12/09/2023]		
Indonesia	Slag Wool, Rock Wool, and Similar Mineral Wools (Including Intermixtures Thereof), In Bulk, Sheets or Rolls	25/07/2023 G/SG/N/6/IDN/39 [n:27/07/2023]				
Indonesia	Evaporators	22/07/2022 G/SG/N/6/IDN/30/ Suppl.1 [n:29/07/2022] (Review - Extension)		G/SG/N/10/IDN/22/Suppl.2 [n:21/10/2022] (Proposal) 05/09/2023 G/SG/N/10/IDN/22/Suppl.3 [n:06/09/2023] (Extension – Imposition)		

Reporting Member and Product		Safeguard investigations initiated[2]	Provisional safeguard measures	Definitive safeguard measures (including recommendations of imposition as well as decision to extend an existing measure)[3]	Safeguard investigations terminated without measures	Expired or terminated measures[4]
Madagascar	Paints	01/06/2022 G/SG/N/6/MDG/8 [n:03/06/2022]	(unclear)[10] G/SG/N/7/MDG/8 [n:06/1	(unclear)[11] G/SG/N/10/MDG/8 [n:10/03/2023]		
Madagascar	Blankets and Travelling Rugs	18/02/2023 G/SG/N/6/MDG/2/ Suppl.1 [n:22/02/2023] (Review - Extension)		03/06/2023 G/SG/N/10/MDG/2/ Suppl.1 [n:02/06/2023] (Extension – Imposition)		
Madagascar	Detergent powder	18/02/2023 G/SG/N/6/MDG/3/ Suppl.1 [n:22/02/2023] (Review - Extension)		03/06/2023 G/SG/N/10/MDG/3/ Suppl.1 [n:02/06/2023] (Extension – Imposition)		
Madagascar	Pasta	18/02/2023 G/SG/N/6/MDG/4/ Suppl.1 [n:22/02/2023] (Review - Extension)		01/08/2023 G/SG/N/10/MDG/4/ Suppl.3 [n:20/07/2023] (Extension – Imposition) G/SG/N/11/MDG/4/ Suppl.5[12]		
Madagascar	Flour	18/02/2023 G/SG/N/6/MDG/10 [n:22/02/2023]	01/03/2023 G/SG/N/7/ MDG/10[13] [n:22/	24/10/2023[14] G/SG/N/10/MDG/10 [24/10/2023]		
Madagascar	Concentrated Milk	11/02/2023 G/SG/N/6/MDG/9 [n:13/02/2023]	11/02/2023 G/ SG/N/7/ MDG/9[15] [n:13/02/ 2023]	16/09/2023 G/SG/N/10/MDG/9 [n:18/09/2023] G/SG/N/11/MDG/9/ Suppl.2[16]		
Morocco	Hot-rolled sheets	26/01/2023 G/SG/N/6/ MAR/11/ Suppl.1 [n:31/01/2023] (Review - Extension)		19/06/2023 G/SG/N/10/MAR/7/ Suppl.2 [n:25/05/2023] (Extension – Imposition)		
Morocco	Welded tubes and pipes, of iron or steel	13/06/2023 G/SG/N/6/ MAR/12/ Suppl.1 [n:15/06/2023] (Review - Extension)				

Reporting Member and Product		Safeguard investigations initiated[2]	Provisional safeguard measures	Definitive safeguard measures (including recommendations of imposition as well as decision to extend an existing measure)[3]	Safeguard investigations terminated without measures	Expired or terminated measures[4]
Morocco	Inner Tubes for Bicycles, Velocipedes, Motorcycles and Scooters	03/10/2022 G/SG/N/6/MAR/14 [n:17/10/2022]			03/07/2023 G/SG/N/9/MAR/4 [n:06/07/2023]	
Peru	Clothing (1)	01/11/2020 G/SG/N/6/PER/3 [n:17/11/2020]			07/06/2021 G/SG/N/9/PER/3 [n:01/06/2023]	
Peru	Clothing (2)	24/12/2021 G/SG/N/6/PER/4 [n:30/12/2021]			01/03/2023 G/SG/N/9/PER/4 [n:02/06/2023]	
Philippines	Liquefied Petroleum Gas (LPG) Cylinders	04/04/2023 G/SG/N/6/PHL/20[17] [n:04/04/2023]				
Philippines	Cement	10/09/2018 G/SG/N/6/PHL/11 [n:24/09/2018]				G/SG/N/10/PHL /9/Suppl.318 [n:29/11/2022]
South Africa	Threaded fasteners of iron or steel	24/03/2023 G/SG/N/6/ZAF/7/Suppl.1 [n:27/03/2023] (Review - Extension)		24/07/2023 G/SG/N/10/ZAF/5/Suppl.2 [n:19/06/2023] (Extension - Proposal) 24/07/2023 G/SG/N/10/ZAF/5/Suppl.3 [n:25/07/2023] (Extension - Imposition)		
Türkiye	Polyethylene Terephthalate Chips	11/05/2023 G/SG/N/6/TUR/27/Suppl.1 [n:16/05/2023] (Review - Extension)				
Türkiye	Toothbrushes	16/07/2023 G/SG/N/6/TUR/23/Suppl.2 [n:19/07/2023] (Review - Extension)				

Reporting Member	Product	Safeguard investigations initiated[2]	Provisional safeguard measures	Definitive safeguard measures (including recommendations of imposition as well as decision to extend an existing measure)[3]	Safeguard investigations terminated without measures	Expired or terminated measures[4]
Türkiye	Yarn of nylon or other polyamides	26/01/2022 G/SG/N/6/TUR/25/ Suppl.1 [n:03/02/2022] (Review – Extension)		21/11/2022 G/SG/N/10/TUR/17/ Suppl.1 [n:24/10/2022] (Extension - Imposition)		
Ukraine	PVC profile	01/09/2021 G/SG/N/6/UKR/22 [n:08/09/2021]			G/SG/N/9/UKR/13 [n:15/11/2022]	
Ukraine	Polymeric material	25/02/2020 G/SG/N/6/UKR/17 [n:28/02/2020]				G/SG/N/10/UKR /9/Suppl.2[19] [n:15/11/2022]
United Kingdom	Certain steel products	01/10/2020 G/SG/N/6/GBR/1 [n:08/10/2020][20] 04/09/2023 G/SG/N/6/GBR/1/ Suppl.3 [n:05/09/2023] (Review - Extension)		G/SG/N/10/GBR/1/Suppl.10[21] G/SG/N/10/GBR/1/Suppl.11[22] G/SG/N/10/GBR/1/Suppl.12[23] G/SG/N/10/GBR/1/Suppl.13[24] G/SG/N/10/GBR/1/Suppl.14[25]		
United States	Crystalline Silicon Photovoltaic Cells	08/06/2023 G/SG/N/6/USA/11/ Suppl.5 [n:30/06/2023] (Review - Extension)				
United States	Large Residential Washers	05/06/2017 G/SG/N/6/USA/12 [n:12/06/2017] (Original Investigation) 15/02/2019 G/SG/N/10/USA/8/ Suppl.1 [n:25/02/2019] (Review - Extension)				07/02/2023 G/SG/N/10/USA /8/Suppl.8 [n:16/02/2023]

Reporting Member and Product		Safeguard investigations initiated[2]	Provisional safeguard measures	Definitive safeguard measures (including recommendations of imposition as well as decision to extend an existing measure)[3]	Safeguard investigations terminated without measures	Expired or terminated measures[4]
Viet Nam	Certain semifinished and finished products of alloy and nonalloy steel	04/11/2022 G/SG/N/6/VNM/5/ Suppl.2 [n:08/11/2022] (Review - Extension)		22/03/2023 G/SG/N/10/VNM/2/ Suppl.3 [n:24/03/2023] (Extension - Imposition)		
Viet Nam	Diammonium Phosphate and Monoammonium Phosphate fertilizers	28/01/2022 G/SG/N/6/VNM/6/ Suppl.2 [n: 31/01/2022]				G/SG/N/10/VNM /5/Suppl.2[26] [n:25/10/2022]

Notes: [1] Notifications indicated in bold italics are those notified during this period. Dates indicated in this table are actual dates of the initiation of the investigation and the dates of the imposition of the provisional/final measure. Dates shown between [] starting with an "n" are the dates when the notifications were submitted. For multiple-symbolled documents, only the relevant symbols are indicated in each box. Corrigenda are not indicated in this table.

[2] In order to put the information into context, this column includes notifications received before the period covered. When a measure has been extended, the initiation date of either the original investigation or the extension investigation is indicated, depending on the context. For other columns, if the notification submitted is not relevant to the timing of the measure, no date is indicated above that notification.

[3] "Proposal" in this column and in the column "provisional safeguard measures" signifies that the notification concerns a proposal/recommendation to impose a measure.

[4] This column only indicates information on expiration or termination which the relevant Member notified as such in writing.

[5] This notifications concerns adoption of the Panel Report in European Union – Safeguard Measures on Certain Steel Products (DS595).

[6] This notification concerns certain proposed adjustments to safeguard measures following a Review investigation.

[7] "The safeguard measure will be applicable from the date of issue of notification in this regard by the Department of Commerce, Ministry of Commerce and Industry, Government of India."

[8] Indonesia notified the change in the list of developing countries exempted from the safeguard measure.

[9] Indonesia notified the change in the list of developing countries exempted from the safeguard measure.

[10] "The provisional safeguard measure will enter into force on the date of publication of the related public notice following approval by the higher authorities."

[11] "The definitive safeguard measure will enter into force on the date of publication of the related public notice."

[12] This notification concerns amendments to the list of developing countries exempted from the measure.

[13] This is the same document as G/SG/N/6/MDG/10.

[14] This is the date of the notification.

[15] This is the same document as G/SG/N/6/MDG/9.

[16] This notification concerns amendments to the list of developing countries exempted from the measure.
[17] This is a notification for the initiation of a "preliminary safeguard investigation."
[18] "[The] competent authority has dismissed the application for the extension of the safeguard measure."
[19] "On 2 November 2022, the Commission suspended the safeguard measures [...] until the end of martial law in Ukraine."
[20] The United Kingdom withdrew from the European Union as of 1 February 2020. The European Union and the United Kingdom have communicated that during the transition period, which ends on 31 December 2020, European Union law, with a few limited exceptions, continues to be applicable to and in the United Kingdom. See WT/LET/1462 and WT/GC/206. The United Kingdom has separately submitted this notification to the Committee. This notification was made under the sole responsibility of the United Kingdom.
[21] This is a notification of initiation of a tariff rate quota (TRQ) review by the Trade Remedies Authority ("TRA" – the United Kingdom's competent authority) examining the exemption status of developing country Members from the measure.
[22] This is a notification of the expansion of scope of the TRQ review by TRA and issue of amended notice of initiation on 13 February 2023.
[23] This is a notification of the initial conclusion published by TRA of the TRQ review regarding the measure.
[24] This is a notification of the final recommendation of TRA in the TRQ review examining the exemption status of developing country Members from the measure.
[25] This is a notification for the acceptance of TRA's final determination and recommendation in the TRQ review by the Secretary of State for Business and Trade.
[26] "MOIT [the Ministry] has decided to not extend the safeguard measure."

Source: WTO, *Report (2023) of the Committee on Safeguards to the Council for Trade in Goods*, Annex 2, G/L/1503 (October 26, 2023).

Table A.4 *Summary of active safeguard investigations and/or existing safeguard measures as of 25 October 2023*[1]

Member & Investigation	Initiation date (first initiation date)[2]	Effective date of provisional measure, if any	Effective date of definitive measure, if any	Note[3]
Egypt				
Raw aluminium (ingots, billets & wire rod)	16/04/2020 G/SG/N/6/EGY/15		15/04/2021 G/SG/N/10/EGY/10	
European Union				
Certain steel products	26/03/2018 G/SG/N/6/EU/1		02/02/2019 G/SG/N/10/EU/1/Suppl.1	Extended 01/07/2023 G/SG/N/10/EU/1/Suppl.17
India				
Isopropyl alcohol	04/11/2019 G/SG/N/6/IND/47		01/04/2023 G/SG/N/10/IND/24/Suppl.1	
PVC suspension resins with Residual VCM above 2 PPM	16/09/2022 G/SG/N/6/IND/48		June 2023[4] G/SG/N/10/IND/25	
Low Ash Metallurgical Coke	30/06/2023 G/SG/N/6/IND/49			
Indonesia				
I and H sections of other alloy steel	12/02/2014 G/SG/N/6/IDN/25		21/01/2015 G/SG/N/10/IDN/17/Suppl.1	Extended 22/12/2022 G/SG/N/10/IDN/17/Suppl.5
Evaporators	12/06/2019 G/SG/N/6/IDN/30		11/01/2020 G/SG/N/10/IDN/22/Suppl.1	Extended 05/09/2023 SG/N/10/IDN/22/Suppl.3
Fabrics	18/09/2019 G/SG/N/6/IDN/31		27/05/2020 G/SG/N/10/IDN/23/Suppl.1	Extended 09/11/2022 G/SG/N/10/IDN/23/Suppl.2
Yarn (other than sewing thread) of synthetic and artificial staple fibres	18/09/2019 G/SG/N/6/IDN/32		27/05/2020 G/SG/N/10/IDN/25/Suppl.1	Extended 22/05/2023 G/SG/N/10/IDN/25/Suppl.3
Curtains (including drapes), interior blinds, bed valances, and other furnishing articles	18/09/2019 G/SG/N/6/IDN/33		27/05/2020 G/SG/N/10/IDN/24/Suppl.1	Extended 22/05/2023 G/SG/N/10/IDN/24/Suppl.3
Fructose Syrup	13/11/2019 G/SG/N/6/IDN/34		17/09/2020 G/SG/N/10/IDN/26/Suppl.1	Extended 17/09/2023 G/SG/N/10/IDN/26/Suppl.2

Member & Investigation	Initiation date (first initiation date)[2]	Effective date of provisional measure, if any	Effective date of definitive measure, if any	Note[3]
Carpets and other textile floor coverings	10/06/2020 G/SG/N/6/IDN/35		17/02/2021 G/SG/N/10/IDN/27/Suppl.1	(Extension investigation initiated) 18/08/2023 G/SG/N/6/IDN/35/Suppl.1
Articles of apparel and clothing accessories	01/10/2020 G/SG/N/6/IDN/36		12/11/2021 G/SG/N/10/IDN/28/Suppl.1	
Ceramic flags and paving, hearth or wall tiles	29/03/2018 G/SG/N/6/IDN/28		1/10/2018 G/SG/N/10/IDN/20/Suppl.1	Extended 18/11/2021 G/SG/N/10/IDN/20/Suppl.3
Cigarette paper	26/10/2020 G/SG/N/6/IDN/37		30/11/2021 G/SG/N/10/IDN/29/Suppl.1	Extended 30/11/2023 G/SG/N/10/IDN/29/Suppl.2
Expansible Polystyrene (EPS)	18/11/2020 G/SG/N/6/IDN/38		24/12/2021 G/SG/N/10/IDN/30/Suppl.1	
Slag Wool, Rock Wool, and Similar Mineral Wools	25/07/2023 G/SG/N/6/IDN/39			
Madagascar				
Pasta	18/07/2019 G/SG/N/6/MDG/4		February 2020[5] G/SG/N/10/MDG/4	Extended 01/08/2023 G/SG/N/10/MDG/4/Suppl.3
Blankets and Travelling Rugs	20/09/2018 G/SG/N/6/MDG/2		June 2019[6]. G/SG/N/10/MDG/2	Extended 03/06/2023 G/SG/N/10/MDG/2/Suppl.1
Detergent Powder	31/12/2018 G/SG/N/6/MDG/3		June 2019[7]. G/SG/N/10/MDG/3	Extended 03/06/2023 G/SG/N/10/MDG/3/Suppl.1
Paints	01/06/2022 G/SG/N/6/MDG/8		March 2023[8]. G/SG/N/10/MDG/8	
Flour	18/02/2023 G/SG/N/6/MDG/10	(For info:) 01/03/2023 G/SG/N/7/MDG/10	24/10/2023[9]. G/SG/N/10/MDG/10	
Concentrated Milk	11/02/2023 G/SG/N/6/MDG/9		16/09/2023. G/SG/N/10/MDG/9	
Morocco				
Wire rods and reinforcing bars	25/09/2012 G/SG/N/6/MAR/7		December 2013[10] G/SG/N/10/MAR/3	Extended 01/01/2022 G/SG/N/10/MAR/3/Suppl.5
Cold rolled sheets and plated or coated sheets	11/06/2014 G/SG/N/6/MAR/8		May 2015[11]. G/SG/N/10/MAR/4	Extended 01/01/2022 G/SG/N/10/MAR/4/Suppl.4
Coated wood and board	31/07/2018 G/SG/N/6/MAR/10		July 2019[12]. G/SG/N/10/MAR/6	Extended 20/09/2022 G/SG/N/10/MAR/6/Suppl.1

Member & Investigation	Initiation date (first initiation date)[2]	Effective date of provisional measure, if any	Effective date of definitive measure, if any	Note[3]
Hot-Rolled Sheets	29/05/2019 G/SG/N/6/MAR/11		19/06/2020. G/SG/N/10/MAR/7	19/06/2023 G/SG/N/10/MAR/7/Suppl.2
Welded tubes and pipes of iron or steel	07/10/2019 G/SG/N/6/MAR/12		September 2020[13] G/SG/N/10/MAR/8	(Extension investigation initiated) 13/06/2023 G/SG/N/6/MAR/12/Suppl.1
Philippines				
Liquefied Petroleum Gas (LPG) Cylinders	04/04/2023 G/SG/N/6/PHL/20[14]			
South Africa				
Other screws fully threaded with hexagon heads made of steel	20/04/2018 G/SG/N/6/ZAF/6		15/02/2019 G/SG/N/10/ZAF/4/Suppl.1	Extended 02/08/2021 G/SG/N/10/ZAF/4/Suppl.3
Threaded fasteners of iron or steel	01/03/2019 G/SG/N/6/ZAF/7		March – April 2020[15] G/SG/N/10/ZAF/5/Suppl.1	Extended 24/07/2023 G/SG/N/10/ZAF/5/Suppl.3
Bolts with hexagon heads of iron or steel	15/05/2020 G/SG/N/6/ZAF/8		December 2021[16] G/SG/N/10/ZAF/7	
Tunisia				
Minibuses	01/10/2021 G/SG/N/6/TUN/6			
Wire of iron or non-alloy steel	19/07/2022 G/SG/N/6/TUN/7			
Türkiye				
Toothbrushes	22/04/2017 G/SG/N/6/TUR/23		October 2017[17] G/SG/N/10/TUR/16	Extended 03/02/2021 G/SG/N/10/TUR/16/Suppl.3 (further extension investigation initiated) 16/07/2023 G/SG/N/6/TUR/23/Suppl.2
Wallpaper and similar wallcoverings	12/12/2014 G/SG/N/6/TUR/20		June 2015 G/SG/N/10/TUR/15	Extended 06/08/2021 G/SG/N/10/TUR/15/Suppl.2
Yarn of nylon or other polyamides	30/12/2018 G/SG/N/6/TUR/25		22/11/2019 G/SG/N/10/TUR/17	Extended 21/11/2022 G/SG/N/10/TUR/17/Suppl.1
Polyethylene terephthalate chips	11/06/2020 G/SG/N/6/TUR/27		13/12/2020 G/SG/N/10/TUR/18	(Extension investigation initiated) 11/05/2023 G/SG/N/6/TUR/27/Suppl.1

Member & Investigation	Initiation date (first initiation date)[2]	Effective date of provisional measure, if any	Effective date of definitive measure, if any	Note[3]
Staples fibres of polyesters	30/05/2020 G/SG/N/6/TUR/26		23/09/2021 G/SG/N/10/TUR/19	
Grinding balls and similar articles for mills	09/10/2021 G/SG/N/6/TUR/28		26/08/2022. G/SG/N/10/TUR/20	
Ukraine				
Fresh cut roses	28/05/2020 G/SG/N/6/UKR/18		21/05/2021 G/SG/N/10/UKR/10/ Suppl.1	
Sulfuric Acid and Oleum	10/08/2017 G/SG/N/6/UKR/12		01/09/2018 G/SG/N/10/UKR/6	Extended 01/09/2021 G/SG/N/10/UKR/6/Suppl.3
United Kingdom				
Certain steel products	01/10/2020 G/SG/N/6/GBR/1		01/07/2021 G/SG/N/10/GBR/1/ Suppl.1[18]	Extended 01/07/2022 G/SG/N/10/GBR/1/ Suppl.9 (Further extension investigation initiated) 04/09/2023 G/SG/N/6/GBR/1/Suppl.3
United States				
Crystalline Silicon Photovoltaic Cells	17/05/2017 G/SG/N/6/USA/11		07/02/2018 G/SG/N/10/USA/7	Extended 07/02/2022 G/SG/N/10/USA/7/ Suppl.13 (Further extension investigation initiated) 08/06/2023 G/SG/N/6/USA/11/Suppl.5
Viet Nam				
Certain semifinished and finished products of alloy and nonalloy steel	06/07/2016 G/SG/N/6/VNM/5		02/08/2016 G/SG/N/10/VNM/2	Extended 22/03/2023 G/SG/N/10/VNM/2/Suppl.3

Notes: [1] Measures the durations of which (as stipulated in the notification) have passed are deleted from this table. For provisional measures, those that are in force as of this date are shown in this table.

[2] For measures that have been extended, the original initiation dates are indicated for the purpose of this table.

[3] "Extended" in this column indicates that the measure was extended once or more. The symbol in the column indicates the notification of the most recent extension. The date is the timing when the extension took effect.

[4-13] This is the timing of the notification.

[14] This is a notification for the initiation of a "preliminary safeguard investigation."

[15] "It is expected that the definitive measure, if adopted, will come into effect between March 2020 and April 2020."

[16] This is the timing of the notification.

[17] This is the timing of the notification.

[18] The United Kingdom withdrew from the European Union as of 1 February 2020.

On 20 October 2023, the delegation of South Africa contacted the Secretariat in relation to its investigation on "Certain flat-rolled products of iron, non-alloy steel or other alloy steel." It was informed that the competent Minister rejected the Commission's recommendation regarding the extension of the measure, and the investigation was therefore terminated in December 2021. Thus, this row has been removed from the list above.

Source: WTO, *Report (2023) of the Committee on Safeguards to the Council for Trade in Goods*, Annex 3, G/L/1503 (October 26, 2023).

APPENDIX 2: TEXT OF GATT ARTICLE XIX

Emergency Action on Imports of Particular Products

1. (a) If, as a result of unforeseen developments and of the effect of the obligations incurred by a contracting party under this Agreement, including tariff concessions, any product is being imported into the territory of that contracting party in such increased quantities and under such conditions as to cause or threaten serious injury to domestic producers in that territory of like or directly competitive products, the contracting party shall be free, in respect of such product, and to the extent and for such time as may be necessary to prevent or remedy such injury, to suspend the obligation in whole or in part or to withdraw or modify the concession.
   (b) If any product, which is the subject of a concession with respect to a preference, is being imported into the territory of a contracting party in the circumstances set forth in subparagraph (a) of this paragraph, so as to cause or threaten serious injury to domestic producers of like or directly competitive products in the territory of a contracting party which receives or received such preference, the importing contracting party shall be free, if that other contracting party so requests, to suspend the relevant obligation in whole or in part or to withdraw or modify the concession in respect of the product, to the extent and for such time as may be necessary to prevent or remedy such injury.
2. Before any contracting party shall take action pursuant to the provisions of paragraph 1 of this Article, it shall give notice in writing to the CONTRACTING PARTIES as far in advance as may be practicable and shall afford the CONTRACTING PARTIES and those contracting parties having a substantial interest as exporters of the product concerned an opportunity to consult with it in respect of the proposed action. When such notice is given in relation to a concession with respect to a preference, the notice shall name the contracting party which has requested the action. In critical circumstances, where delay would cause damage which

it would be difficult to repair, action under paragraph 1 of this Article may be taken provisionally without prior consultation, on the condition that consultation shall be effected immediately after taking such action.

3. (a) If agreement among the interested contracting parties with respect to the action is not reached, the contracting party which proposes to take or continue the action shall, nevertheless, be free to do so, and if such action is taken or continued, the affected contracting parties shall then be free, not later than ninety days after such action is taken, to suspend, upon the expiration of thirty days from the day on which written notice of such suspension is received by the CONTRACTING PARTIES, the application to the trade of the contracting party taking such action, or, in the case envisaged in paragraph 1(b) of this Article, to the trade of the contracting party requesting such action, of such substantially equivalent concessions or other obligations under this Agreement the suspension of which the CONTRACTING PARTIES do not disapprove.

(b) Notwithstanding the provisions of subparagraph (a) of this paragraph, where action is taken under paragraph 2 of this Article without prior consultation and causes or threatens serious injury in the territory of a contracting party to the domestic producers of products affected by the action, that contracting party shall, where delay would cause damage difficult to repair, be free to suspend, upon the taking of the action and throughout the period of consultation, such concessions or other obligations as may be necessary to prevent or remedy the injury.

APPENDIX 3: TEXT OF THE AGREEMENT ON SAFEGUARDS[1]

Members,

Having in mind the overall objective of the Members to improve and strengthen the international trading system based on GATT 1994;

Recognizing the need to clarify and reinforce the disciplines of GATT 1994, and specifically those of its Article XIX (Emergency Action on Imports of Particular Products), to re-establish multilateral control over safeguards and eliminate measures that escape such control;

Recognizing the importance of structural adjustment and the need to enhance rather than limit competition in international markets; and

Recognizing further that, for these purposes, a comprehensive agreement, applicable to all Members and based on the basic principles of GATT 1994, is called for.

Hereby *agree* as follows:

Article 1

General Provision

This Agreement establishes rules for the application of safeguard measures which shall be understood to mean those measures provided for in Article XIX of GATT 1994.

---

1 The Agreement on Safeguards is reprinted in various sources, including WTO, *The Legal Results of the Uruguay Round of Multilateral Trade Negotiations* (Cambridge University Press, reprint 2012), pp. 275–283. The text may also be found in the WTO website, http://www.wto.org.

Article 2

Conditions

1. A Member[1] may apply a safeguard measure to a product only if that Member has determined, pursuant to the provisions set out below, that such product is being imported into its territory in such increased quantities, absolute or relative to domestic production, and under such conditions as to cause or threaten to cause serious injury to the domestic industry that produces like or directly competitive products.
2. Safeguard measures shall be applied to a product being imported irrespective of its source.

Article 3

Investigation

1. A Member may apply a safeguard measure only following an investigation by the competent authorities of that Member pursuant to procedures previously established and made public in consonance with Article X of GATT 1994. This investigation shall include reasonable public notice to all interested parties and public hearings or other appropriate means in which importers, exporters and other interested parties could present evidence and their views, including the opportunity to respond to the presentations of other parties and to submit their views, *inter alia*, as to whether or not the application of a safeguard measure would be in the public interest. The competent authorities shall publish a report setting forth their findings and reasoned conclusions reached on all pertinent issues of fact and law.
2. Any information which is by nature confidential or which is provided on a confidential basis shall, upon cause being shown, be treated as such by the competent authorities. Such information shall not be disclosed without permission of the party submitting it. Parties providing confidential information may be requested to furnish non-confidential summaries thereof

---

1 A customs union may apply a safeguard measure as a single unit or on behalf of a member State. When a customs union applies a safeguard measure as a single unit, all the requirements for the determination of serious injury or threat thereof under this Agreement shall be based on the conditions existing in the customs union as a whole. When a safeguard measure is applied on behalf of a member State, all the requirements for the determination of serious injury or threat thereof shall be based on the conditions existing in that member State and the measure shall be limited to that member State. Nothing in this Agreement prejudges the interpretation of the relationship between Article XIX and paragraph 8 of Article XXIV of GATT 1994.

or, if such parties indicate that such information cannot be summarized, the reasons why a summary cannot be provided. However, if the competent authorities find that a request for confidentiality is not warranted and if the party concerned is either unwilling to make the information public or to authorize its disclosure in generalized or summary form, the authorities may disregard such information unless it can be demonstrated to their satisfaction from appropriate sources that the information is correct.

Article 4

Determination of Serious Injury or Threat Thereof

1. For the purposes of this Agreement:

(a) "serious injury" shall be understood to mean a significant overall impairment in the position of a domestic industry;
(b) "threat of serious injury" shall be understood to mean serious injury that is clearly imminent, in accordance with the provisions of paragraph 2. A determination of the existence of a threat of serious injury shall be based on facts and not merely on allegation, conjecture or remote possibility; and
(c) in determining injury or threat thereof, a "domestic industry" shall be understood to mean the producers as a whole of the like or directly competitive products operating within the territory of a Member, or those whose collective output of the like or directly competitive products constitutes a major proportion of the total domestic production of those products.

2. (a) In the investigation to determine whether increased imports have caused or are threatening to cause serious injury to a domestic industry under the terms of this Agreement, the competent authorities shall evaluate all relevant factors of an objective and quantifiable nature having a bearing on the situation of that industry, in particular, the rate and amount of the increase in imports of the product concerned in absolute and relative terms, the share of the domestic market taken by increased imports, changes in the level of sales, production, productivity, capacity utilization, profits and losses, and employment.
(b) The determination referred to in subparagraph (a) shall not be made unless this investigation demonstrates, on the basis of objective evidence, the existence of the causal link between increased imports of the product concerned and serious injury or threat thereof. When factors other than

increased imports are causing injury to the domestic industry at the same time, such injury shall not be attributed to increased imports.
(c) The competent authorities shall publish promptly, in accordance with the provisions of Article 3, a detailed analysis of the case under investigation as well as a demonstration of the relevance of the factors examined.

Article 5

Application of Safeguard Measures

1. A Member shall apply safeguard measures only to the extent necessary to prevent or remedy serious injury and to facilitate adjustment. If a quantitative restriction is used, such a measure shall not reduce the quantity of imports below the level of a recent period which shall be the average of imports in the last three representative years for which statistics are available, unless clear justification is given that a different level is necessary to prevent or remedy serious injury. Members should choose measures most suitable for the achievement of these objectives.
2. (a) In cases in which a quota is allocated among supplying countries, the Member applying the restrictions may seek agreement with respect to the allocation of shares in the quota with all other Members having a substantial interest in supplying the product concerned. In cases in which this method is not reasonably practicable, the Member concerned shall allot to Members having a substantial interest in supplying the product shares based upon the proportions, supplied by such Members during a previous representative period, of the total quantity or value of imports of the product, due account being taken of any special factors which may have affected or may be affecting the trade in the product.
(b) A Member may depart from the provisions in subparagraph (a) provided that consultations under paragraph 3 of Article 12 are conducted under the auspices of the Committee on Safeguards provided for in paragraph 1 of Article 13 and that clear demonstration is provided to the Committee that (*i*) imports from certain Members have increased in disproportionate percentage in relation to the total increase of imports of the product concerned in the representative period, (*ii*) the reasons for the departure from the provisions in subparagraph (a) are justified, and (*iii*) the conditions of such departure are equitable to all suppliers of the product concerned. The duration of any such measure shall not be extended beyond the initial period under paragraph 1 of Article 7. The departure referred to above shall not be permitted in the case of threat of serious injury.

Article 6

Provisional Safeguard Measures

In critical circumstances where delay would cause damage which it would be difficult to repair, a Member may take a provisional safeguard measure pursuant to a preliminary determination that there is clear evidence that increased imports have caused or are threatening to cause serious injury. The duration of the provisional measure shall not exceed 200 days, during which period the pertinent requirements of Articles 2 through 7 and 12 shall be met. Such measures should take the form of tariff increases to be promptly refunded if the subsequent investigation referred to in paragraph 2 of Article 4 does not determine that increased imports have caused or threatened to cause serious injury to a domestic industry. The duration of any such provisional measure shall be counted as a part of the initial period and any extension referred to in paragraphs 1, 2 and 3 of Article 7.

Article 7

Duration and Review of Safeguard Measures

1. A Member shall apply safeguard measures only for such period of time as may be necessary to prevent or remedy serious injury and to facilitate adjustment. The period shall not exceed four years, unless it is extended under paragraph 2.
2. The period mentioned in paragraph 1 may be extended provided that the competent authorities of the importing Member have determined, in conformity with the procedures set out in Articles 2, 3, 4 and 5 that the safeguard measure continues to be necessary to prevent or remedy serious injury and that there is evidence that the industry is adjusting, and provided that the pertinent provisions of Articles 8 and 12 are observed.
3. The total period of application of a safeguard measure including the period of application of any provisional measure, the period of initial application and any extension thereof, shall not exceed eight years.
4. In order to facilitate adjustment in a situation where the expected duration of a safeguard measure as notified under the provisions of paragraph 1 of Article 12 is over one year, the Member applying the measure shall progressively liberalize it at regular intervals during the period of application. If the duration of the measure exceeds three years, the Member applying such a measure shall review the situation not later than the mid-term of the measure and, if appropriate, withdraw it or increase the pace of

liberalization. A measure extended under paragraph 2 shall not be more restrictive than it was at the end of the initial period, and should continue to be liberalized.

5. No safeguard measure shall be applied again to the import of a product which has been subject to such a measure, taken after the date of entry into force of the WTO Agreement, for a period of time equal to that during which such measure had been previously applied, provided that the period of non-application is at least two years.
6. Notwithstanding the provisions of paragraph 5, a safeguard measure with a duration of 180 days or less may be applied again to the import of a product if:
(a) at least one year has elapsed since the date of introduction of a safeguard measure on the import of that product; and
(b) such a safeguard measure has not been applied on the same product more than twice in the five-year period immediately preceding the date of introduction of the measure.

Article 8

Level of Concessions and Other Obligations

1. A Member proposing to apply a safeguard measure or seeking an extension of a safeguard measure shall endeavour to maintain a substantially equivalent level of concessions and other obligations to that existing under GATT 1994 between it and the exporting Members which would be affected by such a measure, in accordance with the provisions of paragraph 3 of Article 12. To achieve this objective, the Members concerned may agree on any adequate means of trade compensation for the adverse effects of the measure on their trade.
2. If no agreement is reached within 30 days in the consultations under paragraph 3 of Article 12, then the affected exporting Members shall be free, not later than 90 days after the measure is applied, to suspend, upon the expiration of 30 days from the day on which written notice of such suspension is received by the Council for Trade in Goods, the application of substantially equivalent concessions or other obligations under GATT 1994, to the trade of the Member applying the safeguard measure, the suspension of which the Council for Trade in Goods does not disapprove.
3. The right of suspension referred to in paragraph 2 shall not be exercised for the first three years that a safeguard measure is in effect, provided that the safeguard measure has been taken as a result of an absolute increase

in imports and that such a measure conforms to the provisions of this Agreement.

Article 9

Developing Country Members

1. Safeguard measures shall not be applied against a product originating in a developing country Member as long as its share of imports of the product concerned in the importing Member does not exceed 3 per cent, provided that developing country Members with less than 3 per cent import share collectively account for not more than 9 per cent of total imports of the product concerned.[2]
2. A developing country Member shall have the right to extend the period of application of a safeguard measure for a period of up to two years beyond the maximum period provided for in paragraph 3 of Article 7. Notwithstanding the provisions of paragraph 5 of Article 7, a developing country Member shall have the right to apply a safeguard measure again to the import of a product which has been subject to such a measure, taken after the date of entry into force of the WTO Agreement, after a period of time equal to half that during which such a measure has been previously applied, provided that the period of non-application is at least two years.

Article 10

Pre-existing Article XIX Measures

Members shall terminate all safeguard measures taken pursuant to Article XIX of GATT 1947 that were in existence on the date of entry into force of the WTO Agreement not later than eight years after the date on which they were first applied or five years after the date of entry into force of the WTO Agreement, whichever comes later.

Article 11

Prohibition and Elimination of Certain Measures

1. (a) A Member shall not take or seek any emergency action on imports of particular products as set forth in Article XIX of GATT 1994 unless such

---

2 A member shall immediately notify an action taken under paragraph 1 of Article 9 to the Committee on Safeguards.

action conforms with the provisions of that Article applied in accordance with this Agreement.

(b) Furthermore, a Member shall not seek, take, or maintain any voluntary export restraints, orderly marketing arrangements or any other similar measures on the export or the import side.[3] [4] These include actions taken by a single Member as well as actions under agreements, arrangements, and understandings entered into by two or more Members. Any such measure in effect on the date of entry into force of the WTO Agreement shall be brought into conformity with this Agreement or phased out in accordance with paragraph 2.

(c) This Agreement does not apply to measures sought, taken or maintained by a Member pursuant to provisions of GATT 1994 other than Article XIX, and Multilateral Trade Agreements in Annex 1A other than this Agreement, or pursuant to protocols and agreements or arrangements concluded within the framework of GATT 1994.

2. The phasing out of measures referred to in paragraph 1(b) shall be carried out according to timetables to be presented to the Committee on Safeguards by the Members concerned not later than 180 days after the date of entry into force of the WTO Agreement. These timetables shall provide for all measures referred to in paragraph 1 to be phased out or brought into conformity with this Agreement within a period not exceeding four years after the date of entry into force of the WTO Agreement, subject to not more than one specific measure per importing Member,[5] the duration of which shall not extend beyond 31 December 1999. Any such exception must be mutually agreed between the Members directly concerned and notified to the Committee on Safeguards for its review and acceptance within 90 days of the entry into force of the WTO Agreement. The Annex to this Agreement indicates a measure which has been agreed as falling under this exception.

3. Members shall not encourage or support the adoption or maintenance by public and private enterprises of non-governmental measures equivalent to those referred to in paragraph 1.

3 An import quota applied as a safeguard measure in conformity with the relevant provisions of GATT 1994 and this Agreement may, by mutual agreement, be administered by the exporting Member.

4 Examples of similar measures include export moderation, export-price or import-price monitoring systems, export or import surveillance, compulsory import cartels, and discretionary export or import licensing schemes, any of which afford protection.

5 The only such exception to which the European Communities is entitled is indicated in the Annex to this Agreement.

Article 12

Notification and Consultation

1. A Member shall immediately notify the Committee on Safeguards upon:
(a) initiating an investigatory process relating to serious injury or threat thereof and the reasons for it;
(b) making a finding of serious injury or threat thereof caused by increased imports; and
(c) taking a decision to apply or extend a safeguard measure.
2. In making the notifications referred to in paragraphs 1(b) and 1(c), the Member proposing to apply or extend a safeguard measure shall provide the Committee on Safeguards with all pertinent information, which shall include evidence of serious injury or threat thereof caused by increased imports, precise description of the product involved and the proposed measure, proposed date of introduction, expected duration and timetable for progressive liberalization. In the case of an extension of a measure, evidence that the industry concerned is adjusting shall also be provided. The Council for Trade in Goods or the Committee on Safeguards may request such additional information as they may consider necessary from the Member proposing to apply or extend the measure.
3. A Member proposing to apply or extend a safeguard measure shall provide adequate opportunity for prior consultations with those Members having a substantial interest as exporters of the product concerned, with a view to, *inter alia*, reviewing the information provided under paragraph 2, exchanging views on the measure and reaching an understanding on ways to achieve the objective set out in paragraph 1 of Article 8.
4. A Member shall make a notification to the Committee on Safeguards before taking a provisional safeguard measure referred to in Article 6. Consultations shall be initiated immediately after the measure is taken.
5. The results of the consultations referred to in this Article, as well as the results of mid-term reviews referred to in paragraph 4 of Article 7, any form of compensation referred to in paragraph 1 of Article 8, and proposed suspensions of concessions and other obligations referred to in paragraph 2 of Article 8, shall be notified immediately to the Council for Trade in Goods by the Members concerned.
6. Members shall notify promptly the Committee on Safeguards of their laws, regulations and administrative procedures relating to safeguard measures as well as any modifications made to them.
7. Members maintaining measures described in Article 10 and paragraph 1 of Article 11 which exist on the date of entry into force of the WTO

Agreement shall notify such measures to the Committee on Safeguards not later than 60 days after the date of entry into force of the WTO Agreement.

8. Any Member may notify the Committee on Safeguards of all laws, regulations, administrative procedures and any measures or actions dealt with in this Agreement that have not been notified by other Members that are required by this Agreement to make such notifications.
9. Any Member may notify the Committee on Safeguards of any non-governmental measures referred to in paragraph 3 of Article 11.
10. All notifications to the Council for Trade in Goods referred to in this Agreement shall normally be made through the Committee on Safeguards.
11. The provisions on notification in this Agreement shall not require any Member to disclose confidential information the disclosure of which would impede law enforcement or otherwise be contrary to the public interest or would prejudice the legitimate commercial interests of particular enterprises, public or private.

Article 13

Surveillance

1. A Committee on Safeguards is hereby established, under the authority of the Council for Trade in Goods, which shall be open to the participation of any Member indicating its wish to serve on it. The Committee will have the following functions:

(a) to monitor, and report annually to the Council for Trade in Goods on, the general implementation of this Agreement and make recommendations towards its improvement;

(b) to find, upon request of an affected Member, whether or not the procedural requirements of this Agreement have been complied with in connection with a safeguard measure, and report its findings to the Council for Trade in Goods;

(c) to assist Members, if they so request, in their consultations under the provisions of this Agreement;

(d) to examine measures covered by Article 10 and paragraph 1 of Article 11, monitor the phase-out of such measures and report as appropriate to the Council for Trade in Goods;

(e) to review, at the request of the Member taking a safeguard measure, whether proposals to suspend concessions or other obligations are "substantially equivalent," and report as appropriate to the Council for Trade in Goods;

(f) to receive and review all notifications provided for in this Agreement and report as appropriate to the Council for Trade in Goods; and
(g) to perform any other function connected with this Agreement that the Council for Trade in Goods may determine.

2. To assist the Committee in carrying out its surveillance function, the Secretariat shall prepare annually a factual report on the operation of this agreement based on notifications and other reliable information available to it.

Article 14

Dispute Settlement

The provisions of Articles XXII and XXIII of GATT 1994 as elaborated and applied by the Dispute Settlement Understanding shall apply to consultations and the settlement of disputes arising under this Agreement.

Annex: Exception referred to in paragraph 2 of Article 11

Members concerned	Product	Termination
EC/Japan	Passenger cars, off road vehicles, light commercial vehicles, light trucks (up to 5 tonnes), and the same vehicles in wholly knocked-down form (CKD sets)	December 31, 1999

APPENDIX 4: PROPOSED MODIFICATION OF THE AGREEMENT ON SAFEGUARDS

The Agreement on Safeguards is considered a successful result of the Uruguay Round as these new disciplines of safeguards provide detailed substantive and procedural rules for the application of a safeguard measure. Nevertheless, inherent ambiguities in certain provisions of the Safeguards Agreement have caused disputes and problems in the application of safeguards. The WTO panel and the Appellate Body decisions have cleared some of those ambiguities, but many still remain unresolved. Therefore, the author proposes modification of certain provisions of the SA to enhance clarity and consistency of the rules on safeguards. The suggested modifications are italicized in the relevant SA provisions as cited below. Some of those modifications have already been introduced in the author's previous work, "Safeguard Measures: Why Are They Not Applied Consistently With the Rules? Lessons for Competent National Authorities and Proposal for the Modification of the Rules on Safeguards" (2002) 36 *Journal of World Trade* 663–666.

Article 1

General Provisions

This Agreement establishes *the comprehensive rules for the application of a safeguard measure.*

Note 1 (Article 1)

The legal relationship between the GATT Article XIX and the SA should be clarified. As discussed extensively in Chapter 3.2 above, there is a clear indication that the negotiators in the Uruguay Round intended the Safeguard Agreement to be the sole authority in the disciplines of safeguards. Nevertheless, the Appellate Body decisions that gave a legal effect to the "unforeseen developments" clause in the GATT Article XIX added a requirement which does not exist in the SA, causing ambiguity and confusion to the disciplines of safeguards.[1] The current provisions of the SA do not clarify the relationship between Article XIX and the SA, and therefore, the suggested modification would clarify that the SA is the sole authority on safeguards.

Article 2

Conditions

Footnote 1: … *A member State of a customs union may exempt imports from another member State from its safeguard measure if it establishes that increased imports from the non-member States alone cause or threaten to cause serious injury to its domestic industry.*

Note 2 (Article 2)

It has been an issue whether or not a member State of a customs union may exempt imports from another member State from its safeguard measure. The Appellate Body affirmed that it may not do so where it considered imports from all sources in its injury determination. Yet the Appellate Body did not clarify whether it could do so if it considers imports only from non-member States in the injury assessment.[2] The footnote of Article 2 authorizes a customs union to apply a safeguard measure on behalf of its individual member State against non-member States, and an individual member State should also be allowed to exempt imports from another member State from its safeguard measure as discussed in Chapter 4.4 above. The current provision is not clear on this point, and the exemption should be clearly authorized in the SA.

Article 3

Investigation

2. … Such information shall not be disclosed without permission of the party submitting it. *The statistics pertaining to the injury factors provided for in paragraph 2 of Article 4 shall be made available to the public unless clear justification is made that the disclosure of such statistics is seriously prejudicial to the interest of the domestic industry ….*

---

1 *See supra* Chapter 3.2 for the relevant discussion.

2 *See supra* Chapter 4.4.

Note 3 (Article 3)

It is also necessary to limit the wide discretion allowed to national authorities under Article 3.2 with respect to confidential information. Although confidential information needs to be protected, nondisclosure of essential information would make a safeguard measure unreviewable and unverifiable. The wide discretion allowed under Article 3.2 should therefore be narrowed to ensure transparency. At a minimum, the provision of Article 3.2 should require that the statistics pertaining to the mandatory injury factors specified under Article 4.2(a) be made available to the public in order to ensure transparency and reviewability of the proposed measure.[3] In addition, a standard protocol regulating the request and treatment of confidential information during the panel proceedings should also be prepared so that a panel's future request for confidential information can be met.

Article 4

Determination of Serious Injury or Threat Thereof

2. (a) *The competent national authorities shall make a clear and discreet determination on the condition of the domestic industry whether it has sustained serious injury or is facing a threat thereof…*
(b) … When factors other than increased imports are causing injury to the domestic industry at the same time, such injury shall not be attributed to increased imports *unless this investigation demonstrates that the increased imports have clearly contributed to the injury as a major cause after having made an adequate assessment of the injurious effects of the imports separate from those of other factors.*

Note 4 (Article 4)

The determination of serious injury or its threat was also controversial in *United States – Line Pipe*. The Appellate Body, reversing the previous Panel decision, found that Members may apply a safeguard measure based on its indiscreet determination that their domestic industry has *either* sustained serious injury *or* faced threat thereof, without a clear distinction between the two. As discussed above, "serious injury" and "threat of serious injury" represent two distinctively different conditions of domestic industry, one with a significant overall impairment in its position (Article 4.1(a)) and the other without it. Therefore,

3 The statistics of individual companies need not be made available to the public. The aggregate statistics for the industry should be sufficient.

national authorities fail to establish the basis for the application of a safeguard measure if they cannot even determine whether their domestic industry has sustained serious injury or is facing a threat of injury. An application of emergency import restrictions such as safeguards is hardly justifiable without a clear identification of the condition of the domestic industry. The Appellate Body based its decision, *inter alia*, on the current wording of Article 4.2(a), in particular, the use of "or" in the phrase.[4] Therefore, it seems necessary to modify the wording of the Article to ensure the national authorities' responsibility to make a discreet determination on the condition of their domestic industry.

The non-attribution requirement in Article 4.2(b) in the presence of multiple causal factors should also be further clarified in the text. As discussed in Chapter 5.2 above, the panels and the Appellate Body differed repeatedly in their decisions on the sufficiency of the increase in imports as a causal factor.[5] This repeated disagreement indicates the ambiguous nature of the clause, and a clarification needs to be made in the text.

Article 5

Application of Safeguard Measures

A Member shall apply safeguard measures only to the extent necessary to prevent or remedy serious injury and to facilitate adjustment. *A Member shall also consider adequate adjustment plans prior to the determination of specific measures. Where it is determined that factors other than increased imports are causing injury to the domestic industry at the same time, safeguard measures shall not exceed the extent necessary to prevent or remedy the portion of injury caused by increased imports.* If a quantitative restriction is used, such a measure shall not reduce the quantity of imports below the level of a recent period which shall be the average of imports in the last three representative years *terminating two months preceding the month in which the decision for the investigation provided for in paragraph 1 of Article 3 is made. If a measure other than a quantitative restriction is used, it shall not be more restrictive than a quantitative restriction with the*

4 The relevant provision states, "In the investigation to determine whether increased imports have caused *or* are threatening to cause serious injury to a domestic industry under the terms of this Agreement ..." (emphasis added).

5 Both Panels in *United States – Wheat Gluten* and *United States – Lamb Meat* held that the increased imports need not be a sole cause for the injury but need to be significant enough to cause the injury *by and of themselves.* The Appellate Body disagreed with the panel decision in both cases and ruled that increased imports need not be capable of causing the injury *by and of themselves.* According to the Appellate Body, the causation requirement is fulfilled as long as the increased imports clearly contribute to the injury. *See* the relevant discussion in Chapter 5.2 *supra.*

minimum quota levels provided for in this paragraph unless clear justification is made that a more restrictive measure is necessary to prevent or remedy serious injury. Any tariff increase taken as a safeguard measure shall be refunded without delay (i) where, pursuant to the dispute settlement provisions provided for in Article 14, the measure is found inconsistent with the provisions of this Agreement or found not taken as a result of an absolute increase in imports by a decision of the Dispute Settlement Body and (ii) where no means of trade compensation provided for in paragraph 1 of Article 8 has been agreed and no suspension of concessions or any obligations under GATT 1994 as provided for in paragraph 2 of Article 8 has been applied. Members should choose measures most suitable for the achievement of these objectives. *A Member shall not apply a quantitative restriction unless that Member has reached agreement with all other Members having a substantial interest in supplying the product concerned, on means of trade compensation provided for in paragraph 1 of Article 8.*

Note 5 (Article 5)

The extent of a safeguard measure should be proportionate to the amount of injury that the increased imports have caused.[6] The adjustment plans should also be required to ensure that a safeguard measure is applied with a prospect of structural adjustment. The beginning and the end points of the reference period to determine minimal quota levels also need to be specified, as those points may affect the amount of imports, and henceforth, the quota levels.[7] A ceiling for non-quantitative restrictions should also be introduced. Non-quantitative restrictions are known to be less trade-restrictive than quantitative measures in general. Nevertheless, non-quantitative measures can still be made more restrictive than quantitative restrictions.

Article 6 requires that any tariff increase taken as a provisional measure is promptly refunded if a negative injury determination is made. A refund of increased tariffs should also be required where Members are entitled to apply immediate retaliation under Article 8.3 (subject to the procedural requirements under Article 8.2) but nevertheless refrained from doing so and instead resorted to the dispute settlement procedure. An additional limit should be imposed on the application of quantitative restrictions since they are the most trade-restrictive measures. Thus, Members should be authorized to apply quantitative restrictions only where they reach agreement with the exporting Members on compensation.

---

6 *See* the relevant discussions in Chapter 7 *supra*.

7 *Id.*

Article 7

Duration and Review of Safeguard Measures

2. The period mentioned in paragraph 1 may be extended provided that the competent authorities of the importing Member have determined, in conformity with the procedures set out in Articles 2, 3, 4 and 5 that the safeguard measure continues to be necessary to prevent or remedy serious injury and that there is evidence that the industry is adjusting, and provided that the pertinent provisions of Articles 8 and 12 are observed. *The period mentioned in paragraph 1 shall not be extended by a developed country Member where at least two-thirds of the imports subject to the safeguard measure are originating in developing countries.*
4. In order to facilitate adjustment in a situation where the expected duration of a safeguard measure as notified under the provisions of paragraph 1 of Article 12 is over one year, the Member applying the measure shall progressively liberalize it at regular intervals during the period of application. *The measure shall be liberalized by the minimum of six percent per annum in its restriction level.* If the duration of the measure exceeds three years, the Member applying such a measure shall review the situation not later than three years, the Member applying such a measure shall review the situation not later than the mid-term of the measure and, if appropriate, withdraw it or increase the pace of liberalization. *The mid-term review shall be conducted in accordance to the procedures set out in Articles 2, 3, 4 and 5.*

Note 6 (Article 7)

As discussed in Chapter 15, an extension of a safeguard measure should not be authorized where at least two-thirds of the imports subject to the safeguard measures are originating in developing countries. This modification seeks to achieve a balance between the interests of facilitating exports from developing countries to support their economic development and the needs to apply safeguards, by limiting an extension of a measure where a substantial majority of imports subject to safeguards is originating in developing countries. As the purpose of this provision is to facilitate the economic development of developing countries, it is imposed on developed country Members rather than developing country Members.

The current provision does not stipulate a minimum pace of liberalization. The liberalization required under Article 7.4 should be made sufficient to induce adjustment. Therefore, a minimum pace should be stipulated in the text to discourage a Member from implementing a merely nominal liberalization. In addition, Article 7.4 does not apply any procedural requirement for the mid-term review. The lack of the procedural requirement may lead to an arbitrary review by national authorities. Therefore, the procedural requirements for the extension of the measure should also be made applicable to the mid-term review.

Article 8

Level of Concessions and Other Obligations

1. A Member proposing to apply a safeguard measure or seeking an extension of a safeguard measure shall endeavour to maintain a substantially equivalent level of concessions and other obligations to that existing under GATT 1994 between it and the exporting Members which would be affected by such a measure, in accordance with the provisions of paragraph 3 of Article 12. To achieve this objective, the Members concerned may agree on any adequate means of trade compensation for the adverse effects of the measure on their trade. *A developed country Member shall not apply a safeguard measure to a product originating in a developing country Member unless due trade compensation is made to that developing country Member as agreed when the safeguard measure is being applied.*
2. If no agreement is reached within 30 days in the consultations under paragraph 3 of Article 12, then the affected exporting Members shall be free, not later than 90 days after the measure is applied, *to announce the suspension of the application of substantially equivalent concessions or any other obligations under GATT 1994, to the trade of the Member applying the safeguard measure, the suspension of which the Council for Trade in Services does not disapprove. A proposed suspension of concessions and other obligations referred to in this paragraph shall be notified to the Council for Trade in Goods in detail, including the date of the scheduled implementation, not later than 90 days after the measure is applied. A Member in no circumstance may apply a suspension of concessions and other obligations referred to in this paragraph that is retrospective and cumulative in nature.*
3. The right of suspension referred to in paragraph 2 shall not be exercised for the first three years that a safeguard measure is in effect, provided that the safeguard measure has been taken as a result of an absolute increase in imports and that such a measure conforms to the provisions of this Agreement. *The right of suspension referred to in paragraph 2 may be exercised by a developing country Member immediately if a developed country Member has failed to provide due trade compensation referred to paragraph 1 above.*

Note 7 (Article 8)

As discussed in Chapter 14, a safeguard measure may set a considerable barrier to exports from developing country Members whose economic development depends on trade. The economic injury caused to the developing country Members by safeguards needs to be compensated. A developed country Member must provide compensation for the loss of trade caused by the safeguard. When the developed country Member fails to provide trade compensation, the affected developing country Member should be authorized to apply retaliatory measures immediately.

As discussed in Chapter 8, the affected exporting Members should also be allowed to apply retaliatory measures later than the 90 days specified, as long as the specifics of the proposed retaliatory measures are announced within that time limit. Retrospective retaliations should be prohibited.

Article 9

Developing Country Members

Safeguard measures shall not be applied against a product originating in a developing country Member as long as its share of imports of the product concerned in the importing Member does not exceed *five* percent, provided that developing country Members with less than *five* percent Import share collectively account for not more than *15* percent of total imports of the product concerned. *Safeguard measures shall not be applied against a product originating in a least-developed country Member.*

Note 8 (Article 9)

As discussed in Chapter 15, a de-minimis ceiling for the non-application of safeguards to the products originating from developing country Members need to be increased. Also, safeguard measures should not be applied to a product originating in the least-developed country Members in consideration of their dire economic needs.

Article 12

Notification and Consultation

1. A Member shall immediately notify the Committee on Safeguards upon, *and under any circumstances no later than seven days from*:

...

3. A Member proposing to apply or extend a safeguard measure shall provide adequate opportunity for prior consultations with those Members having a substantial interest as exporters of the product concerned, with a view to, inter alia, reviewing the information provided under paragraph 2, exchanging views on the measure and reaching an understanding on ways to achieve the objective set out in paragraph 1 of Article 8. *A Member proposing to apply or extend a safeguard measure shall provide all pertinent information on the proposed measure provided for in paragraph 2 of this Article no later than sixty days before the implementation of the measure and shall furnish opportunity for consultations no later than thirty days before its implementation.*

Note 9 (Article 12)

The timing of notifications and consultations should also be specified in the SA as they have been a subject of repeated controversy in previous cases.[8] Neither Panels nor the Appellate Body prescribed specific time limits for notifications and consultations. Concerning the notifications, the SA requires that the notifications be made immediately upon the relevant actions of competent national authorities (Article 12.1). Nonetheless, notifications cannot be made overnight due to the administrative and logistical issues. A previous Panel determined that a five-day gap between the relevant decision and the notification was acceptable but substantially longer delays were not. To avoid further confusion, it would be necessary to stipulate the time frame for the notifications in the text. The timing for consultations should be decided on a case-by-case basis taking into account the relevant circumstances. Nevertheless, for the interest of clarity, the time limit also needs to be stipulated to ensure the right of exporting Members to have adequate consultations.

Article 14

Dispute Settlement

2. *The panel shall review (i) whether competent national authorities have examined all facts in its possession or which they should have obtained in accordance with Article 4.2 of the Agreement on Safeguards, (ii) whether adequate explanation had been provided of how the facts as a whole supported the determination made and, consequently, (iii) whether the determination made*

8 *See supra* Chapter 6.

was consistent with the international obligation of the Member applying the safeguard measure. The said authorities shall be given opportunity to justify its determination, where necessary, with explanations supplementary to those set forth in the report referred to in paragraph 1 of Article 3.

3. (a) *In its assessment of the facts of the matter, the panel shall determine whether the authorities' establishment of the facts was proper and whether their evaluation of those facts was unbiased and objective. If the establishment of the facts was proper and the evaluation was unbiased and objective, even though the panel might have reached a different conclusion, the evaluation shall not be overturned.*

(b) *The panel shall interpret the relevant provisions of the Agreement in accordance with customary rules of interpretation of public international law. Where the panel finds that a relevant provision of the Agreement admits of more than one permissible interpretation, the panel shall find the authorities' measure to be in conformity with the Agreement if it rests upon one of those permissible interpretations.*

Note 10 (Article 14)

The standard of review is another area that calls for an express clarification in the text. As discussed in Chapter 4, difficulty arises where two different conclusions can be drawn from the same set of facts through different yet adequate alternative reasoning. The Appellate Body ruled that "a panel must find that an explanation is not reasoned, or is not adequate, if some *alternative explanation* of the facts is plausible, and if the competent authorities' explanation does not seem adequate in light of that alternative explanation."[9] According to this decision, the reasoning and conclusion of national authorities will not be approved unless they are defensible against all possible alternative explanations. It would be onerous for the authorities to consider all those possible alternative explanations *beforehand*. The Appellate Body presumed that those challenging arguments would always be brought to the attention of the national authorities during the investigation, but it may not necessarily be the case. Therefore, the national authorities should be given opportunity to defend their position, with additional reasoning if necessary, should their position be challenged during the panel proceedings.

Also, as discussed in Chapter 4 above, Article 17.6 of the ADP Agreement provides substantial deference to competent national authorities with respect to factual evaluation and legal interpretation. Since the WTO dispute settle-

9 *United States – Lamb Meat*, WT/DS177/AB/R, WT/DS178/AB/R, para. 106.

ment panels have repeatedly affirmed that they would not engage in a *de novo* review, there is no reason to allow a lesser degree of deference to the national authorities in safeguard cases. Thus the addition of provisions identical to the relevant provisions in the ADP Agreement is proposed (paragraph 3).

APPENDIX 5: PROPOSED TEXT OF THE RULES ON EMERGENCY SAFEGUARD MEASURES

GENERAL COMMENT

This appendix proposes a text of the rules for emergency safeguard measures (ESM). This proposed text is modeled after the Agreement on Safeguards and adopts the general conditions for the application of a safeguard measure set forth in the SA. Many concepts and provisions in the SA, which have been developed and refined through decades of negotiations, could be adopted in the rules for emergency safeguard measures, since they provide a good regulatory structure for the ESM. The proposed text is, therefore, based on the existing structure of the SA, with the modifications necessary to accommodate the unique characteristics of service transactions. The proposed text is not necessarily put forward as the final text of the rules for the ESM. By proposing this text, the author wishes to add reference to ongoing discussions and negotiations. The italicized phrases in the main text, except those in the preamble, represent changes made to the original provisions of the SA.

Agreement on Emergency Safeguards

Members

Having in mind the overall objective of the Members to develop an effective international trade system for services based on GATS;

Recognizing the need of developing countries to facilitate improvement of services within their territories;

Recognizing the importance of structural adjustment and the need to enhance rather than limit competition in international service trade; and

Recognizing further that, for these purposes, a comprehensive agreement, applicable to all Members is called for;

Hereby *agree* as follows:

Note 1 (Preamble)

The Preamble sets forth important objectives for emergency safeguard measures: i.e., development of an effective international trade system for services, recognition of the needs of developing countries, facilitation of the structural adjustment and enhancement of the competition in the service trade, and finally, fulfillment of the need for a comprehensive agreement on emergency safeguard measures.

Article 1

General Provision

An emergency safeguard measure shall be understood to mean a temporary measure taken by a Member to the import of a service to remedy serious injury or prevent threat thereof to its domestic industry.

Note 2 (Article 1)

This Article provides a general definition of an emergency safeguard measure. This definition uses the term "import of a service" instead of "service of another Member" that has been used in the concept paper submitted by the ASEAN Members to the WTO Working Party on emergency safeguard measures (Job No. 6830, October 31, 2000). The latter term, which is used in the GATS as well as in the concept paper, is based on the notion of nationality. As safeguard measures should protect a domestic industry that may include foreign investments, a term based on nationality might not be appropriate. (Nonetheless, services supplied through presence of natural persons of another Member in the territory of the importing country may be excluded from the ambit of domestic services as shown in Article 2.) For this reason, the concept of "import" that excludes services supplied by foreign investments is adopted and used in the definition of an emergency safeguard.

Article 2

Definitions

For the purpose of this Agreement:

(a) "import of a service" shall be understood to mean the consumption of a service supplied from the territory of, or through presence of natural persons of, another Member;
(b) "imports" shall be understood to mean services imported as referred to in subparagraph (a) of this Article;

(c) "serious injury" shall be understood to mean a significant overall impairment in the position of a domestic industry;
(d) "threat of serious injury" shall mean serious injury that is clearly imminent, in accordance with the provisions of Article 5. A determination of the existence of a threat of serious injury shall be based on facts and not merely on allegation, conjecture or remote possibility; and
(e) in determining injury or threat thereof, a domestic industry shall be understood to mean the suppliers as a whole of the like or directly competitive services supplied within the territory of a Member excluding those supplied through presence of natural persons of another Member, whose collective output of the like or directly competitive services constitutes a major proportion of the total domestic supply of those services.

Note 3 (Article 2)

"Import" of a service should be distinguished from the "import" of a tangible good. While goods are imported through their physical movement into the territory of a Member from that of another, import of a service cannot be properly described in terms of physical movement due to the intangible nature of services. Services do not take place until supply meets consumption. Therefore, "import of a service" shall be understood to mean the consumption of a service supplied from the territory of another Member or supplied through presence of natural persons of another Member in the territory of the importing Member. Services provided by foreign suppliers through commercial presence are excluded from the scope of imports; many Members have economic interests to protect foreign investments, and the application of a safeguard to the supply of a service through commercial presence may lead to divestment.

Article 3
Conditions

1. A Member[1] may apply an emergency safeguard measure to a service only if that Member has determined, pursuant to the provisions set out below, that such service is being imported in such increased quantities, absolute or relative to domestic supply, and under such conditions as to cause or

1 A customs union may apply an emergency safeguard measure as a single unit or on behalf of a member State. When a customs union applies an emergency safeguard measure as a single unit, all the requirements for the determination of serious injury or threat thereof under this Agreement shall be based on the conditions existing in the customs union as a whole. When an emergency safeguard measure is applied on behalf of a member State, all the requirements for the determination of serious injury or threat thereof shall be based on the conditions existing in that member State and the measure shall be limited to that member State. *A member State of a customs union may exempt imports from another member State from its safeguard measure if it establishes that increased imports from non-member States alone cause or threaten to cause serious injury to its domestic industry.*

threaten to cause serious injury to the domestic industry that supplies like or directly competitive services.

2. Emergency safeguard measures shall be applied to a service being imported irrespective of its source.

Note 4 (Article 3)

This Article adopts the general conditions for the application of a safeguard measure set forth in the SA as follows: (i) an increase in imports; (ii) causing or threatening to cause; and (iii) serious injury to the domestic industry that produces like or directly competitive products. Article X of the GATS also requires that the most-favored-nation (MFN) principle applies to emergency safeguard measures. Therefore, the measures should apply to imported services irrespective of their sources.

Article 4

Investigation

1. A Member may apply an emergency safeguard measure only following an investigation by the competent authorities of that Member pursuant to procedures previously established and made public. *The competent authorities may initiate an investigation on its own initiative or at the request of a domestic service supplier.* This investigation shall include reasonable public notice to all interested parties and public hearings or other appropriate means in which importers, exporters and other interested parties could present evidence and their views, including the opportunity to respond to the presentations of other parties and to submit their views, *inter alia*, as to whether or not the application of an emergency safeguard measure would be in the public interest. The competent authorities shall publish a report setting forth their findings and reasoned conclusions reached on pertinent issues of fact and law.
2. Any information which is by nature confidential or which is provided on a confidential basis shall, upon cause being shown, be treated as such by the competent authorities. Such information shall not be disclosed without permission of the party submitting it. *Statistics pertaining to the injury factors provided for in paragraph 1 of Article 5 shall be made available to the public unless clear justification is provided that the disclosure of such statistics is seriously prejudicial to the interest of the domestic industry.* Parties providing confidential information may be requested to furnish non-confidential summaries thereof or, if such parties indicate that such information cannot be summarized, the reasons why a summary cannot be provided. However, if the competent authorities find that a request for confiden-

tiality is not warranted and if the party concerned is either unwilling to make the information public or to authorize its disclosure in generalized or summary form, the authorities may disregard such information unless it can be demonstrated to their satisfaction from appropriate sources that the information is correct.

Note 5 (Article 4)

An investigation for emergency safeguard measures should be allowed to begin either at the request of a domestic service supplier or on the initiative of the competent national authorities. A wide discretion of national investigation authorities in the determination of confidential information, as provided in Article 3.2 of the SA, should be narrowed in order to ensure transparency of the process.[2]

Article 5

Determination of Serious Injury or Threat Thereof

1. *The competent national authorities shall make a clear and discrete determination on the condition of the domestic industry whether it has sustained serious injury or is facing threat thereof.* In the investigation to determine whether increased imports have caused or are threatening to cause serious injury to a domestic industry under the terms of this Agreement, the competent authorities shall evaluate as many relevant factors of an objective and quantifiable nature having a bearing on the situation of that industry as possible. *For instance*, the competent authorities shall consider, as statistics are available, the rate and amount of the increase in imports of the service concerned in absolute and relative terms; the share of domestic market taken by increased imports; revenue from value-added tax; offer/sales statistics; the number of suppliers in the market; changes in prices and the price structure; capital flows; profits and losses; and employment. *The Member applying an emergency safeguard measure has the burden of proof to establish the existence of serious injury or threat thereof.*
2. The determination referred to in subparagraph (a) shall not be made unless this investigation demonstrates, on the basis of objective evidence, the existence of the causal link between increased imports of the service concerned and serious injury or threat thereof. When factors other than increased imports are causing injury to the domestic industry at the same time, such injury shall not be attributed to increased imports *unless this investigation demonstrates that the increased imports have clearly contributed*

2 See Appendix 4, *note 3 supra*.

to the injury as a major cause after having made an adequate assessment of the injurious effects of the imports separate from those of other factors.

3. The competent authorities shall publish as promptly as possible, in accordance with the provisions of Article 4, a detailed analysis of the case under investigation as well as a demonstration of the relevance of the factors examined.

Note 6 (Article 5)

The competent authorities should demonstrate the existence of a serious injury or threat thereof by examining relevant injury factors. Considering the complexity of service transactions as well as the limited availability of relevant statistics, an illustrative list of injury factors, rather than the one included in Article 4.2(a) of the SA for mandatory consideration, seems more appropriate. The competent authorities bear the burden of proof to establish the existence of serious injury or threat thereof. Where factors other than increased imports are contributing to the injury at the same time, the effects of increased imports should be assessed separately from those of other factors.

Article 6

Application of Emergency Safeguard Measures

1. A Member may apply emergency safeguard measures against the import of a service in a form that it considers appropriate to prevent or remedy serious injury and to facilitate adjustment. *Where it is determined that factors other than increased imports are causing injury to the domestic industry at the same time, emergency safeguard measures shall not exceed the extent necessary to prevent or remedy the portion of injury caused by increased imports.* In the application of an emergency safeguard measure, a Member may suspend its specific commitments provided for in PART III of GATS.
2. *Any taxes or fees imposed as an emergency safeguard measure shall be refunded without delay (i) where, pursuant to the dispute settlement provisions provided for in Article 14, the measure is found inconsistent with the provisions of this Agreement or found not taken as a result of an absolute increase in imports by a decision of the Dispute Settlement Body and (ii) where no means of trade compensation provided for in paragraph 1 of Article 9 has been agreed and no suspension of concessions or any obligations under GATT 1994 as provided for in paragraph 2 of Article 9 has been applied.* Members should choose measures most suitable for the achievement of these objectives.

Note 7 (Article 6)

Reflecting the complexity of service transactions, the form of an emergency safeguard measure is likely to be more diverse than general safeguards.

Considering this diversity, rules governing the assignment of a quota and the limit on quota levels provided in the SA are not adopted as they are predicated on the physical quantity of imported goods. Some necessary limitations on the extent of an emergency safeguard measure could later be identified when the prevalent forms of restrictions become clearer. However, whatever the form an ESM may take, the measure should not exceed the extent of injury or threat thereof that is attributed to increased imports. Any taxes or fees imposed as an ESM must be refunded if the measure is found inconsistent by a decision of the DSB where no compensation has been made and no retaliatory measure has been applied.

Article 7

Provisional Safeguard Measures

In critical circumstances where delay would cause damage which it would be difficult to repair, a Member may take a provisional safeguard measure pursuant to a preliminary determination that there is clear evidence that increased imports have caused or are threatening to cause serious injury. The duration of the provisional measure shall not exceed 200 days, during which period the pertinent requirements of Articles 3 through 8 and 12 shall be met. The duration of any such provisional measure shall be counted as a part of the total period of the emergency safeguard measure.

Note 8 (Article 7)

A provisional safeguard measure should be adopted for critical circumstances in which there is no time to complete the regular procedure under this Agreement and where the injury is not reparable. A limit on the form of provisional measure is not adopted in consideration of the diverse nature of services and the need for more diverse measures.

Article 8

Duration and Review of Emergency Safeguard Measures

1. A Member shall apply emergency safeguard measures only for such period of time as may be necessary to prevent or remedy serious injury and to facilitate adjustment. The period shall not exceed four years, unless it is extended under paragraph 2.
2. The period mentioned in paragraph 1 may be extended provided that the competent authorities of the importing Member have determined, in conformity with the procedures set out in Articles 3, 4, 5 and 6 that the safeguard measure continues to be necessary to prevent or remedy serious

injury and that there is evidence that the industry is adjusting, and provided that the pertinent provisions of Articles 9 and 12 are observed.

3. The total period of application of an emergency safeguard measure including the period of application of any provisional measure, the period of initial application and any extension thereof, shall not exceed eight years.
4. In order to facilitate adjustment in a situation where the expected duration of a safeguard measure as notified under the provisions of paragraph 1 of Article 12 is over one year, the Member applying the measure shall progressively liberalize it at regular intervals during the period of application. *The measure shall be liberalized by the minimum of six percent per annum in its restriction level.* If the duration of the measure exceeds three years, the Member applying such a measure shall review the situation not later than the mid-term of the measure. The measure shall continue to be applied after the mid-term review only if the competent authorities of the importing Member have determined, *in conformity with the procedures set out in Articles 3, 4, 5, and 6*, that the emergency safeguard measure continues to be necessary to prevent or remedy serious injury or that there is evidence that the industry is adjusting. The Member shall withdraw it or increase the pace of liberalization. A measure extended under paragraph 2 shall not be more restrictive than it was at the end of the initial period, and should continue to be liberalized.
5. No emergency safeguard measure shall be applied again to the import of a service which has been subject to such a measure for a period of time equal to that during which such measure had been previously applied, provided that the period of non-application is at least two years.
6. Notwithstanding the provisions of paragraph 5, a safeguard measure with a duration of 180 days or less may be applied again to the import of a service if:
   (a) at least one year has elapsed since the date of introduction of an emergency safeguard measure on the import of that service; and
   (b) such an emergency safeguard measure has not been applied on the same service more than twice in the five-year period immediately preceding the date of introduction of the measure.

Note 9 (Article 8)

The concepts of extension, liberalization of a measure for over one year, and mid-term review are also adopted from the SA. A minimal pace of liberalization is added, and the procedure for a mid-term review is also provided.

Article 9

Level of Concessions and Other Obligations

1. A Member proposing to apply an emergency safeguard measure or seeking an extension of an emergency safeguard measure shall endeavor to maintain a substantially equivalent level of concessions and other obligations to that existing under GATS between it and the exporting Members which would be affected by such a measure, in accordance with the provisions of paragraph 3 of Article 12. To achieve this objective, the Members concerned may agree on any adequate means of trade compensation for the adverse effects of the measure on their trade. *A developed country Member shall not apply a safeguard measure to a product originating in a developing country Member unless due trade compensation is made to that developing country Member as agreed when the safeguard measure is being applied.*
2. If no agreement is reached within 30 days in the consultations under paragraph 3 of Article 12, then the affected exporting Members shall be free, not later than 90 days after the measure is applied, *to announce the suspension of the application of substantially equivalent concessions or other obligations under GATS, to the trade of the Member applying the emergency safeguard measure, the suspension of which the Council for Trade in Services does not disapprove. The proposed suspension of concessions and other obligations referred to in this paragraph shall be notified to the Council for Trade in Services with the pertinent information including the date of the scheduled implementation, not later than 90 days after the measure is applied. In no circumstance may a Member apply the suspension of concessions and other obligations referred to in this paragraph that is retrospective and cumulative in nature.*
3. The right of suspension referred to in paragraph 2 shall not be exercised for the first three years that an emergency safeguard measure is in effect, provided that the emergency safeguard measure has been taken as a result of an absolute increase in imports in terms of either quantity or value and that such a measure conforms to the provisions of this Agreement. *The right of suspension referred to in paragraph 2 may be exercised by a developing country Member immediately if a developed country Member has failed to provide due trade compensation referred to paragraph 1 above.*

Note 10 (Article 9)

A Member applying an emergency safeguard measure should endeavor to maintain the balance of concessions with affected exporting Members. Members affected by the measure should be entitled to compensation. If no agreement on compensation is made, these Members should also be authorized to suspend substantially equivalent concessions or other obligations under GATS to maintain the balance of concessions. A developed country must not apply an ESM to the imports from a developing country without compensation in consideration of its economic needs. Members planning to suspend concessions or other obligations in response to an emergency safeguard measure should be allowed to suspend the implementation of retaliatory actions beyond 90 days after the application of the original safeguard so long as notification of the proposed suspension is made within the 90 days. The application of a retrospective retaliatory measure should not be allowed. The SA suspends retaliatory actions for the first three years when the safeguard measure is in effect, provided that the measure conforms to the provisions of the SA and it is applied as a result of an absolute increase in imports. It is an incentive for Members to comply with the SA and to apply a measure for a shorter duration. This incentive is also valid for the ESM and, therefore, should be adopted. A preferential treatment for a developing country Member with respect to compensation is also included.[3]

Article 10

Developing Country Members

1. Emergency safeguard measures shall not be applied against a service originating in a developing country Member as long as its share of imports of the service concerned in the importing Member does not exceed *five* percent, provided that developing country Members with less than *five* percent import share collectively account for not more than *15* percent of total imports of the service concerned. *Safeguard measures shall not be applied against a product originating in a least-developed country Member.*[4]
2. A developing country Member shall have the right to extend the period of application of an emergency safeguard measure for a period up to two years beyond the maximum period provided for in paragraph 3 of Article 8. Notwithstanding the provisions of paragraph 5 of Article 8, a developing country Member shall have the right to apply an emergency safeguard measure again to the import of a service which has been subject to such a measure after a period of time equal to half that during which such a measure has been previously applied, provided that the period of non-application is at least two years.

---

3 *See* Appendix 4, *note 7 supra.*

4 A Member shall immediately notify an action taken under paragraph 1 of Article 10 to the Committee on Emergency Safeguards.

Note 11 (Article 10)

The preferential treatment for developing countries provided in Article 9 of the SA could also be adopted in the ESM. Ceilings for the exemption in relevant SA provisions are raised. Imports from a least-developed country Member are exempted from emergency safeguards.[5]

Article 11

Prohibition of Certain Measures

1. (a) A Member shall not take or seek any emergency action on imports of particular services unless such action conforms with the provi sions of this Agreement.
   (b) Furthermore, a Member shall not seek, take or maintain any voluntary restraints on the consumption or supply of imports or any other agreement of the similar effect. These include actions taken by a single Member as well as actions under agreements, arrangements and understandings entered into by two or more Members.
2. Members shall not encourage or support the adoption or maintenance by public and private enterprises of non-governmental measures equivalent to those referred to in paragraph 1.

Note 12 (Article 11)

The SA prohibits all gray-area measures. Trade distorting "gray-area" measures should also be prohibited in the service trade.

Article 12

Notification and Consultation

1. A Member shall notify the Committee on Emergency Safeguards upon, *and under any circumstances no later than seven days from*:
   (a) initiating an investigatory process relating to serious injury or threat thereof and the reasons for it;
   (b) making a finding of serious injury or threat thereof caused by increased imports; and
   (c) taking a decision to apply an emergency safeguard measure.
2. In making the notifications referred to in paragraphs 1(b) and 1(c), the Member proposing to apply or extend an emergency safeguard measure

5 *See* Appendix 4, *note 8 supra.*

shall provide the Committee on Emergency Safeguards with all pertinent information, which shall include evidence of serious injury or threat thereof caused by increased imports, precise description of the service involved and the proposed measure, proposed date of introduction, expected duration and timetable for progressive liberalization. In the case of an extension of a measure, evidence that the industry concerned is adjusting shall also be provided. The Council for Trade in Services or the Committee on Emergency Safeguards may request such additional information as they may consider necessary from the Member proposing to apply or extend the measure.

3. A Member proposing to apply or extend an emergency safeguard measure shall provide adequate opportunity for prior consultations with those Members having a substantial interest as exporters of the service concerned, with a view to, *inter alia*, reviewing the information provided under paragraph 2, exchanging views on the measure and reaching an understanding on ways to achieve the objective set out in paragraph 1 of Article 9. *A Member proposing to apply or extend an emergency safeguard measure shall provide all pertinent information on the proposed measure provided for in paragraph 2 of this Article no later than sixty days before the implementation of the measure and shall furnish an opportunity for consultations no later than thirty days before its implementation.*
4. A Member shall make a notification to the Committee on Emergency Safeguards before taking a provisional safeguard measure referred to in Article 7. Consultations shall be initiated immediately after the measure is taken.
5. The results of the consultations referred to in this Article, as well as the results of mid-term reviews referred to in paragraph 4 of Article 8, any form of compensation referred to in paragraph 1 of Article 9, and proposed suspensions of concessions and other obligations referred to in paragraph 2 of Article 9, shall be notified immediately to the Council for Trade in Services by the Members concerned.
6. Members shall notify promptly the Committee on Emergency Safeguards of their laws, regulations and administrative procedures relating to emergency safeguard measures as well as any modifications made to them.
7. Any Member may notify the Committee on Emergency Safeguards of all laws, regulations, administrative procedures and any measures or actions dealt with in this Agreement that have not been notified by other Members that are required by this Agreement to make such notifications.
8. Any Member may notify the Committee on Emergency Safeguards of any non-governmental measures referred to in paragraph 2 of Article 11.

9. All notifications to the Council for Trade in Services referred to in this Agreement shall normally be made through the Committee on Emergency Safeguards.
10. The provisions on notification in this Agreement shall not require any Member to disclose confidential information the disclosure of which would impede law enforcement or otherwise be contrary to the public interest or would prejudice the legitimate commercial interests of particular enterprises, public or private.

Note 13 (Article 12)

Adequate notifications and consultations would enhance transparency of the application process for emergency safeguards. Relevant provisions in the SA are closely followed. The timing of notifications has repeatedly been controversial in SG cases. The proposed provisions set forth the maximum time limits on notifications as well as consultations.

Article 13

Surveillance

1. A Committee on Emergency Safeguards is hereby established, under the authority of the Council for Trade in Services, which shall be open to the participation of any Member indicating its wish to serve on it. The Committee will have the following functions:
   (a) to monitor, and report annually to the Council for Trade in Services on, the general implementation of this Agreement and make recommendations towards its improvement;
   (b) to find, upon request of an affected Member, whether or not the procedural requirements of this Agreement have been complied with in connection with an emergency safeguard measure, and report its findings to the Council for Trade in Services;
   (c) to assist Members, if they so request, in their consultations under the provisions of this Agreement;
   (d) to review, at the request of the Member taking an emergency safeguard measure, whether proposals to suspend concessions or other obligations are "substantially equivalent," and report as appropriate to the Council for Trade in Services;
   (e) to receive and review all notifications provided for in this Agreement and report as appropriate to the Council for Trade in Services; and
   (f) to perform any other function connected with this Agreement that the Council for Trade in Services may determine.

2. To assist the Committee in carrying out its surveillance function, the Secretariat shall prepare annually a factual report on the operation of this agreement based on notifications and other reliable information available to it.

Article 14

Dispute Settlement

1. The provisions of the Dispute Settlement Understanding shall apply to consultations and the settlement of disputes arising under this Agreement.
2. *A panel, established pursuant to the provisions of Article 6 of the Dispute Settlement Understanding, shall review (i) whether competent national authorities have examined all facts in their possession or which they should have obtained, (ii) whether adequate explanations had been provided of how the facts as a whole supported the determination made and, consequently, (iii) whether the determination made was consistent with the international obligation of the Member applying a safeguard measure. The authorities shall be given opportunity to justify their determinations, where necessary, with explanations supplementary to those set forth in the report referred to in paragraph 1 of Article 4.*
3. *(a) In its assessment of the facts of the matter, the panel shall determine whether the authorities' establishment of the facts was proper and whether their evaluation of those facts was unbiased and objective. If the establishment of the facts was proper and the evaluation was unbiased and objective, even though the panel might have reached a different conclusion, the evaluation shall not be overturned.*

   (b) The panel shall interpret the relevant provisions of the Agreement in accordance with customary rules of interpretation of public international law. Where the panel finds that a relevant provision of the Agreement admits of more than one permissible interpretation, the panel shall find the authorities' measure to be in conformity with the Agreement if it rests upon one of those permissible interpretations.

Note 14 (Articles 13 and 14)

Article 13 establishes the Committee on Emergency Safeguards. The Committee conducts all necessary surveillance. Article 14 provides that the Dispute Settlement Understanding is applicable. The standard of review, adopted by previous Panels and approved by the Appellate Body, is stipulated under Article 14. For the same reason noted in Appendix 4, Note 10, above, sufficient deference should be given to competent national authorities with respect to factual evaluation and legal interpretation.

APPENDIX 6: APPLICATION OF SAFEGUARDS – THE CHECKLIST

No other trade measure has been more disputed than safeguard measures since the beginning of the WTO.[1] No disputed safeguard measure, with the exception of one case on appeal (as of April 2025), has been found consistent with the WTO safeguard rules by the Panel or the Appellate Body. This failure has created an impression that safeguard measures are difficult to defend against the strengthened scrutiny provided under the rules of the SA. While it is true that the SA imposes a number of substantive and procedural requirements on Members applying a safeguard measure, the author believes that safeguard measures can be applied in compliance with the rules and can be made defensible *provided that* the competent national authorities understand and apply substantive as well as procedural rules for the application of a safeguard measure correctly, with a reasoned explanation for their determinations.[2]

The following checklist provides brief guidelines for the application of safeguards. This checklist is not a replacement for professional legal analysis, but it provides an essential inventory list, serving as a road map. Many safeguard measures in the past, including those applied by the most advanced nations, were found inconsistent with the provisions of the SA and Article XIX since their national authorities missed some of the apparent requirements on the following list. The Checklist provides internal references as well as the relevant provisions of the SA and Article XIX.

The Checklist

I. General conditions for the application of a safeguard measure

A. Increase in imports

a. *Either* absolute or relative increase in imports – SA Art. 2.1; Chapters 2.2, 4.2

1 *Supra* note 674.

2 See Chapter 4.1 *supra* for a discussion of the applicable standard of review.

b. Requisite increase in imports – SA Art. 2.1, 4.2(a); Chapters 2.2, 4.2

B. Causing or threatening to cause

a. Measure of cause – SA Art. 4.2(b); Chapter 5.2

b. Issue of multiple causes – SA Art. 4.2(b); Chapter 5.2

C. Serious injury to the domestic industry

a Injury assessment – mandatory consideration of injury factors – SA Art. 4.2(a); Chapter 5.1

b. Definition of domestic industry – SA Art. 4.1(c); Chapter 4.3

c. Provisional safeguard measure – SA Art. 6; Chapter 9.2

D. Unforeseen developments

a. Developments reasonably unforeseen – GATT Art. XIX:1(a); Chapters 2.2, 3.2

b. Unforeseen developments leading to the increase in imports – GATT Art. XIX:1(a); Chapters 2.2, 3.2

II. Application of a safeguard measure

A. Requirement of parallelism

a. General prohibition of a discriminatory application – SA Art. 2.2; Chapter 4.4

b. Exemption of imports from FTA members – SA Art. 2.1, n. 1; Chapter 4.4

B. The proper extent of the measure

a. Form of safeguards – SA Art. 5.1; Chapters 7.1, 7.2

b. Requirements on quota – SA Art 5.2; Chapters 7.1, 7.2

c. Non-quota measures – SA Art. 5.1; Chapters 7.1, 7.2

C. Exemption of imports from developing country Members – SA Art. 9; Chapter 9.2

D. Duration, re-application, liberalization

a. Duration – SA Arts 7.1, 7.2; Chapter 7.1

b. Re-application – SA Arts 7.5,7.6; Chapter 7.1

c. Liberalization – SA Art. 7.4; Chapters 7.1, 7.3

E. Mid-term review, extension

a. Mid-term review – SA Art. 7.4; Chapter 7.1

b. Extension – SA Art. 7.4; Chapter 7.1

Procedural requirements

III. Investigation

A. Conduct of investigation – SA Art. 3.1; Chapter 6.1

B. Investigation report – SA Art. 3.1; Chapter 6.1

C. Treatment of confidential information – SA Art. 3.2; Chapter 6.1

IV. Notification and consultation
  A. Notification
    a. Immediacy requirement – SA Art. 12.1; Chapter 6.2
    b. Required contents – SA Art. 12.2; Chapter 6.2
  B. Consultation
    a. Required timing – SA Art. 12.3; Chapter 6.3
    b. Information necessary for consultations – SA Arts 12.2, 12.3; Chapter 6.3
V. Compensation and retaliation
  A. Compensation
    a. Agreement on compensation – SA Art. 8.1; Chapters 8.1, 8.2
    b. Measure of compensation – SA Art. 8.1; Chapters 8.1, 8.2
  B. Retaliation
    a. Suspension of retaliation – SA Art. 8.3; Chapters 8.1, 8.3
    b. Application of retaliation – SA Art. 8.2; Chapters 8.1, 8.3

INDEX